S0-BEB-043

PRACTICAL PASSIVE SOLAR DESIGN

A Guide to Homebuilding and Land Development

JOHN S. CROWLEY
and
L. ZAURIE ZIMMERMAN

An Energy Learning Systems Book
McGRAW-HILL BOOK COMPANY

New York, St. Louis, San Francisco, Auckland, Bogotá, Hamburg, Johannesburg, London, Madrid,
Mexico, Montreal, New Delhi, Panama, Paris, Saõ Paulo, Singapore, Sydney, Tokyo, Toronto

FIGURE CREDITS

Figures 1.1, 1.2, 1.3, 2.1, 2.2 Aladar Olgyay and Victor Olgyay, *Solar Control and Shading Devices.* Copyright © 1957 by Princeton University Press. Figs. 52, 78, 79, 109, and 110 reprinted by permission of Princeton University Press.
Figures 1.4, 1.10a–f, 1.14, 2.7 and the description of the time zones and the example of conversion to sun time.
Charles George Ramsey and Harold Reese Sleeper, *Architectural Graphic Standards* sixth edition, John Wiley & Sons, Inc. NY, 1970 pages 67, 71, 70, and 78.
Figures 1.5, 3.1, 3.4, 3.5 through 3.15, 4.2a & b, 4.9, 4.10, 4.12, 4.14, 4.16 through 4.27 and 4.29 Martin Jaffe and Duncan Erley, *Site Planning for Solar Access: A Guidebook for Residential Developers and Site Planners.* The American Planning Association for the U.S. Department of Housing and Urban Development and the U.S. Department of Energy, May 1980 HUD-PDT-481(2).
Figures 1.6, 1.8, 4.15 Donald W. Abrams and Richard E. Seedorf, *Building with Passive Solar*, Atlanta, GA: Southern Solar Energy Center, 1981, p. 21 and 40.
Figure 1.7 Environmental Design and Research.
Figures 1.9, 2.4, 2.5 Small Homes Council-Buildings Research Council, University of Illinois at Urban-Champaign, Council Notes, C3.2 *Solar Orientation*, fall 1977, pp. 4, 2, 5.
Figures 1.11, 1.12 (redrawn by Mazria from Govt. Doc.), 1.13 (redrawn), 2.6, 3.16 Edward Mazria, *The Passive Solar Energy Book*. Rodale Press: Emmaus, PA, 1979, pp. 318, 313, 312, 103, 327.
Figures 3.2a & b J. Zanetto, J. Hammond, and C. Adams, prepared for the California Energy Commission, Sacramento, CA *Planning Solar Neighborhoods*, consultant report, April 1981, pp. 129, 118
Figures 3.18, 4.30, 4.33 Gary O. Robinette, editor, *Landscape Planning for Energy Conservation*, Environmental Design Press, 1977, Reston, Virginia American Society of Landscape Architects Foundation pp. 188, 22, 15.
Figure 4.5 Land Design/Research, Inc., *Energy—Conscious Development: Options for Land Use and Site Planning Regulations*, Fairfax County Virginia, September 1981, prepared for the U.S. Dept. Energy, p. 19.
Figure 4.6 D. Bainbridge, J. Corbett, J. Hofacre, *Village Homes' Solar House Designs*, Rodale Press, Emmaus, PA, 1979, p. 15.
Figures 4.8, 4.13, 4.28 (adapted) California Energy Commission, *Solar Access: A Local Responsibility*, Sacramento, CA, 1978, pp. 15, 17, 14.
Figures 4.31, 4.32 Gary O. Robinette, *Plants, People and Environmental Quality*, published by the U.S Dept. of the Interior, National Park Service, Wash. D.C. in collaboration with the American Society of Landscape Architects Foundation 1972, pp. 77, 99.
Figure 5.1 Prepared for Peterson Construction Co. by Robert Dawson, AIA, Hemphill Vierk and Dawson Architects, Lincoln, NB.
Figures 6.1–6.16 credit is given at the end of each case study
Figures 9.1, 9.2, 9.3, 9.4, 9.5, 9.6, 9.7, 9.8, 9.9, 9.11, 9.13a, 9.14, 9.16, 9.18, 9.23, 9.24 Housing and Urban Development Association of Canada and Ontario Ministry of Energy, *Builders Guide to Energy Efficiency in New Housing*. Copyright © October 1980 by Her Majesty the Queen Right of Ontario, as represented by the Ministry of Energy, figures from Chapters 3, 4 and 6.
Fig. 9.10, Oak Ridge National Laboratory-Drawing number 74–11866R. Oak Ridge National Laboratory, Aigonne Ill.
Fig. 9.12, 9.15, 9.17, 12.1, 12.2, 12.3, 12.4 U.S Department of Housing and Urban Development, Office of Policy Research and Development. *Energy Efficient Residence Research Results.* September 1980. Figures 1, 3, 4, 8, 9 Table 1, 2, 3, 4
Fig.9.19, 9.20, Table 9A American Society of Heating, Refrigeration and Air Conditioning Engineers (ASHRAE) Handbook of Fundamentals 1981
Fig. 9.21 Capitol Products, Inc. Harrisburg, Pa.
Fig. 9.22 Kool-o-Matic Corporation Niles, Michigan. From Bulletin 3600-REV.-1979
Fig. 10.4 Selkowitz, JStephen, Rubin, Michael, and Creswick, Richard, *Average Transmittance Factors for Multiple Glazed Window Systems* (1979) Energy and Environment Division. Lawrence Berkeley Laboratory, University of California. Berkeley Ca 94720
Fig 10.14a & b Place, Wayne, Kammerud, Ronald, Andersson, Brandt et al. *Human Comfort and Auxiliary Control Considerations in Passive Solar Structures*, LBL Report 10034 (1980) Proceedings, AS/ISES Solar Jubilee, 2–6 June 1980.
Fig 11.4, Fig 11.19, Fig 11.20, 11.30 Abrams, Donald and Seedorf, Richard *Building with Passive Solar, an Application Guide for the Southern Builder. 1981* U.S. Department of Energy Southern Solar Energy Center. Sp-41191 pg. 84, 86, 95
Fig. 11.5, 11.11 Hastings, Robert and Crenshaw, Richard *Window Design Strategies to Conserve Energy*. June 1977, National Bureau of Standards, U.S. Department of Commerce. pg. 2–24, 2–33.
Fig. 11.8 Koolshade Corporation 1976 product literature.
Fig. 11.12, 11.13 1981 Passive and Hybrid Cooling Conference Proceedings.
Fig. 11.14 Watson, Donald and Glover, Raymond *Solar Control Workbook, Teaching Passive Design in Architecture.* 1981 Published by Association of Collegiate Schools of Architecture, 1735 New York Ave. NW. Washington D.C. 20006 p. 18, 19.
Fig. 11.15 University of Illinois at Urbana-Champaign Small Homes Council-Building Research Council. Council Notes: C3.2 *Solar Orientation* Volume 2, Number 2 Fall 1977. p. 4
Fig. 9.13b, 11.16 Johnson, Ralph J. and Johnson Arthur. *Insulation Manual for Homes and Apartments.* 1979 NAHB Research Foundation, Inc. P.O. Box 1627 Rockville, MD. 20850 37, 54
Fig. 11.17, 11.18 Schwolsky, Richard "Building it Right—Detailing Overhangs." Solar Age Magazine. December 1981 pg. 57, Fig. 1; pg. 58, Fig. 2.
Figure 11.21 Builders and Remodelers 80' Conference proceedings, a collection of Articles, Facts and Figures on Energy Efficient Home Design, 1980.
Fig. 11.22, 11.23, 11.24, 11.25, 11.26, 11.27, 11.28 Passive and Hybrid Cooling Conference Proceeding, 1982 AS/15ES
Fig. 11.32 Balcomb, Douglas et al. Passive Solar Design Handbook, Volume 2. January 1980. U.S. Department of Energy. DOE/cs-0127/2 pg. 54.
Fig. 11.6 U.S. Department of Housing and Urban Development, Office of Policy Development and Research. In Cooperation with U.S. Department of Energy. *Regional Guidelines for Building Passive Energy Conserving Homes*. July 1980. HUD-PDR—355(2) p. 154.
Fig. 11.29 Appropriate Technology Corp., Window Quilt product literature.

Library of Congress Cataloging in Publication Data

Crowley, John S.
Practical passive solar design.

Includes index.
1. Solar energy -- Passive systems. 2. Solar houses -- Design and construction. 3. Real estate development.
I. Zimmerman, L. Zaurie. II. Title.
TH7413.C76 1983 690'.869 83-12039
ISBN 0-07-014769-8

1234567890 KGP/KGP 89876543

ISBN 0-07-014769-8

Contents

Contents

Preface

This book provides a comprehensive set of principles, guidelines, rules-of-thumb and specific nuts-and-bolts information to assist developers, homebuilders, land planners and architects in both solar land development and direct gain passive solar home design.

The housing market of the 1980s will belong to designers and builders who meet the challenge of our energy dilemma. Today's homebuyers demand energy efficiency, and they are willing to pay for it. Seventy-eight percent of the buyers recently surveyed by *Professional Builder* magazine said they would spend an additional $1,000 to reduce heating and cooling bills by $100 per year. The challenge of the building industry for the coming decade is to offer energy-conserving homes that are affordable and attractive. Leading homebuilders are responding to market demands by insulating to the maximum R-values recommended for their regions as well as installing higher performance glazing and door systems. A good energy conservation package as outlined in this book can reduce a home's annual energy consumption by up to 50 percent over a typical home constructed in the late 1970s. If a home also incorporates the passive solar features and window management techniques presented, the need for purchased fuel can be reduced by an additional 25 to 30 percent.

Passive solar design takes advantage of the sun and the home's natural environment to reduce the need for increasingly expensive nonrenewable fuel supplies. The passive solar design and land development techniques presented in this guide may be integrated easily into a wide range of architectural styles and topographic conditions. Passive solar homes include features that have buyer appeal as well as an energy-saving function; bright sunny living spaces; open spaces such as great rooms; masonry and tile floors; and exterior architectural features which enhance curb appeal including extended overhangs, increased south glazing, trellises, porticos and awnings.

Passive solar design and land development techniques will not only improve a home's marketability but also are affordable. The sample passive solar home designs in this book generally cost $1,000 to $3,000 or more than their nonsolar counterpart.

The solar field is rapidly changing—new materials and products quickly become available and the economic frame of reference is not constant. The principles, guidelines and techniques detailed within the pages of this book provide a solid framework for incorporating new materials and products as they become available and feasible for local market areas.

The book is organized so that each of the three parts stands alone to facilitate its easy use depending on the specific interest of the reader. This necessarily involves some duplication, although an effort has been made to keep this to a minimum. Cross-references are noted as appropriate. This enables readers to turn to the specific section which contains the particular information in which they are most interested.

Part One: Solar Fundamentals is a brief summary of essential solar concepts that will give the reader some background knowledge and understanding of the relationship between sun, season and building site.

Part Two: Solar Land Planning and Development takes the reader from site evaluation through planning and regulatory issues, to actual construction of necessary shadow patterns to ensure adequate solar access.

ACKNOWLEDGMENTS

The authors wish to express their appreciation and thanks for the continued support, assistance and contributions of the many dozens of people who have so kindly participated in this two-year-long project.

We owe special appreciation to the following organizations, advisory groups and individuals: to The National Fenestration Council for funding the early work that has made this book possible; to Ralph J. Johnson, President of the NAHB Research Foundation, Inc. for his valuable guidance, recommendations and support throughout the long process; to our consultants Herman H. York and Raymond E. Schenke of York and Schenke Architects, P.C., whose years of experience in designing homes have been invaluable in preparing Chapter 8, Suntempered Home Design; to Frederick D. Jarvis and Constance Dimond of Land Design/Research, Inc. for contributions to Chapter 5, Land Use Regulations; and to Duncan Erley and Martin Jaffe, whose earlier work *Site Planning for Solar Access* provided the foundation for Part Two: Solar Land Planning and Development.

We also wish to thank the following individuals who participated on our two Advisory Panels for their helpful comments, criticisms and time spent reviewing our outlines and draft materials:

R. Patrick Bowe, Century 21/Virginia Homes Unlimited, Inc.

James C. Cashman, the Cashman Group and Chairman of the NAHB Land Development Committee

James W. Leach, Downing·Leach and Associates

John C. Odegaard, Mayhill Homes Corporation

Michael F. Shibley, Director NAHB Land Use and Development Department

David C. Smith, David C. Smith and Sons and Chairman of the NAHB Energy Committee.

We would like to acknowledge Stephanie J. Gibson and William A. Wright of the Cambridge Energy Corporation for their invaluable assistance in analyzing and evaluating the voluminous computer simulations and field data used to prepare many of the recommendations throughout this book. We would also like to credit those members of the Southern Solar Energy Center, Lawrence Berkeley Laboratories and Los Alamos National Laboratories who reviewed this work in its early stages.

Finally, we would like to express our sincerest gratitude to Judith Bean who has so generously given time and undaunted support while assisting in the preparation of the manuscript and graphic material.

John S. Crowley
L. Zaurie Zimmerman
May, 1983

PART ONE

SOLAR FUNDAMENTALS

CHAPTER ONE

Solar Geometry

To understand solar access and principles of passive solar design, it is necessary to review some basic information about the sun's path in the sky. The movement of the earth revolving around the sun annually and rotating on its axis once a day, combined with the effects of latitude, topography and local climate, determine how much sun falls onto a particular building site.

THE PATH OF THE EARTH

The earth travels around the sun annually in an almost circular orbit. It also rotates once a day on an axis that runs from the North Pole to the South Pole. This axis is tilted approximately 23.5° away from a line perpendicular to its orbit (Fig. 1.1). The earth's tilt causes the seasons to change. On December 21, the North Pole is tilted away from the sun the full 23.5° and the Northern Hemisphere receives the least number of hours of sunshine and experiences winter. On June 21, the North Pole is inclined 23.5° toward the sun and thus the Northern Hemisphere receives the greatest amount of sunshine at the most perpendicular angle to the earth's surface and experiences summer.

From the earth's surface, the sun appears to move in an arc through the sky, but for our purposes it is convenient to assume that the earth is stationary and flat at a given site and that the sun moves over it. Figure 1.2 depicts with parallel one-half circles the paths of the sun through the sky for the summer solstice (June 21), the equinox (September 21 and March 21) and the winter solstice (December 21). The hours of the day when the sun is at a given position are indicated in tiny circles with noon at the highest point. In order to

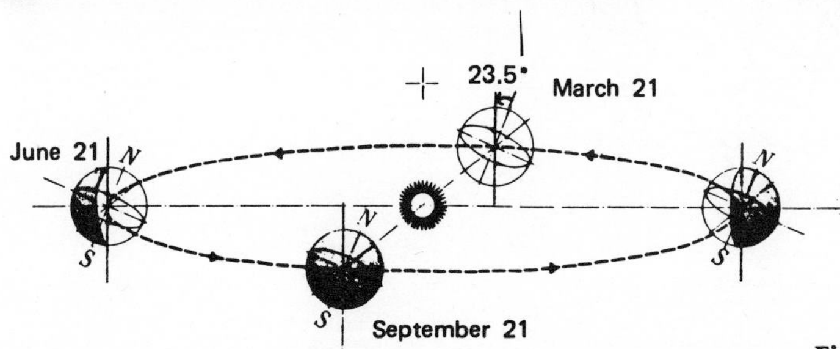

Fig. 1.1 The path of the earth around the sun.

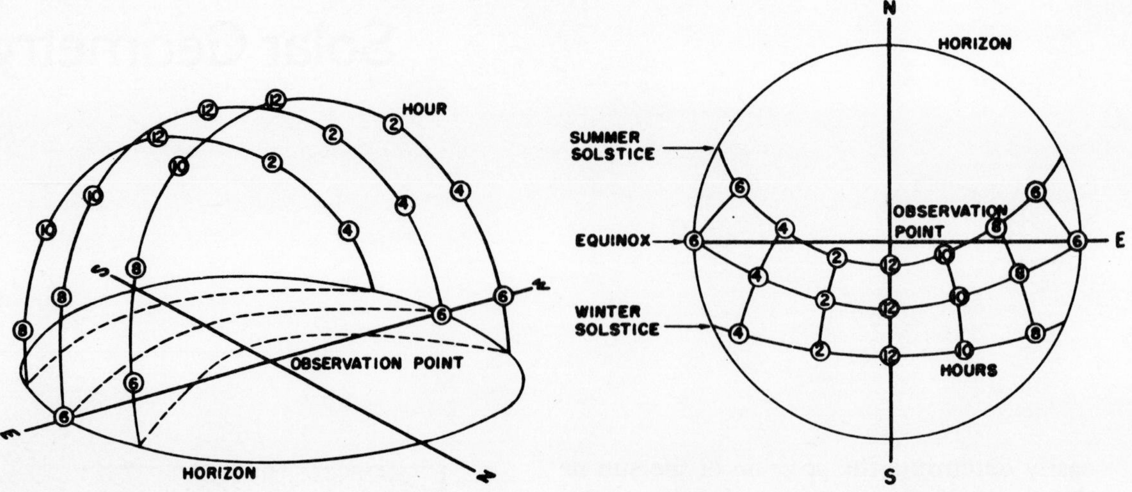

Fig. 1.2 The projections of the sun paths are shown in dashed lines on the horizon plane.

Fig. 1.3 Projected diagram of the sky-vault, called a sun path diagram.

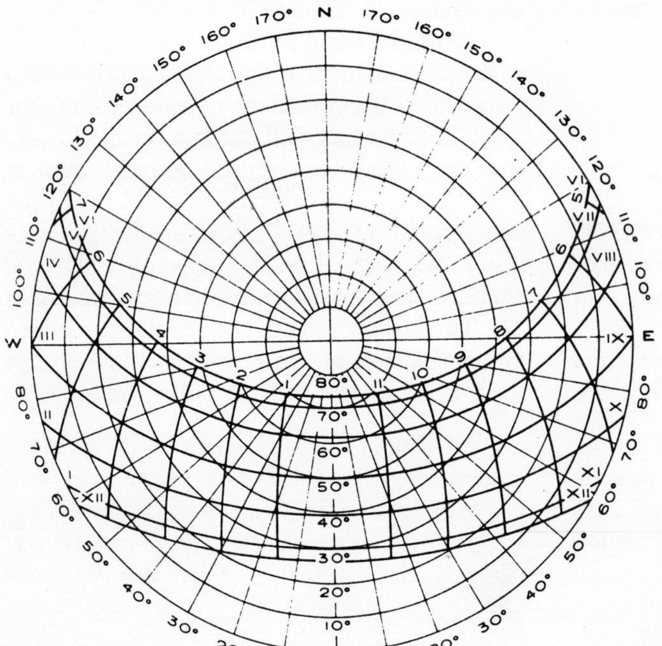

Fig. 1.4 Sun path diagram.

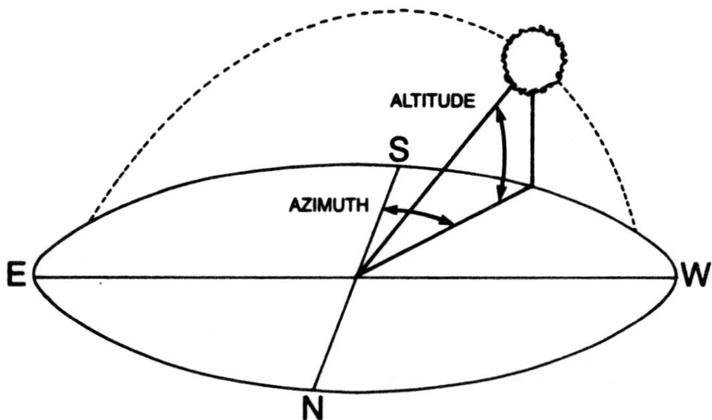

Fig. 1.5 Azimuth and altitude

easily determine the position of the sun in the sky, it is necessary to project the three-dimensional sun paths onto a two-dimensional plane (Fig. 1.3).

Figure 1.4 illustrates a more complete sun path diagram, the next step in development from the diagram in Figure 1.3. It includes lines representing altitude and azimuth angles. This complete sun path diagram is a simple graphic tool that can be used to determine the sun's location for any month at any hour at a specific latitude.

ALTITUDE AND AZIMUTH ANGLES

The sun's position in the sky at any time of the day for any day of the year is defined by its altitude and azimuth angles (Fig. 1.5). It is valuable to know the sun's position for building siting, site shading analysis, shading device design and sunlight penetration purposes. The *altitude angle* is the sun's height above the horizon (Fig. 1.6). At sunrise the altitude of the sun is zero. During the day the sun's altitude increases until it reaches a maximum at solar noon (the time at which the sun is true south) and then decreases to zero again at sunset. Low morning and afternoon altitude angles make east and west windows difficult to shade. The sun's position with respect to its azimuth and altitude

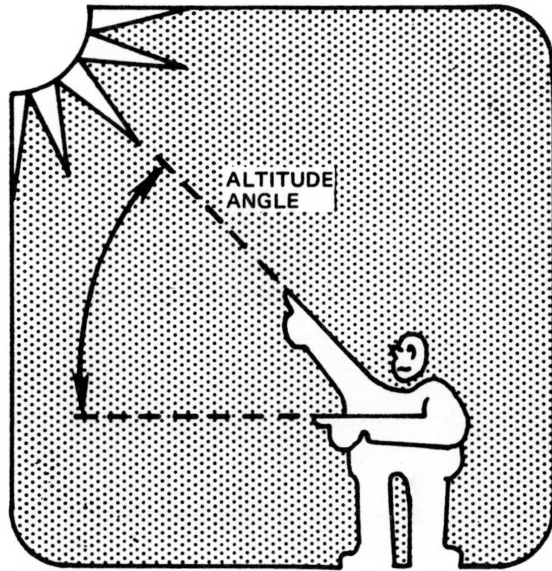

Figure 1.6

angle changes throughout the year because, as previously described, the earth is tilted 23.5° on its axis in relation to the sun. The sun's altitude is lower during the winter months and higher during the summer months in all latitudes in the Northern Hemisphere. As the year progresses from winter to summer, the maximum daily altitude of the sun (at solar noon) increases until

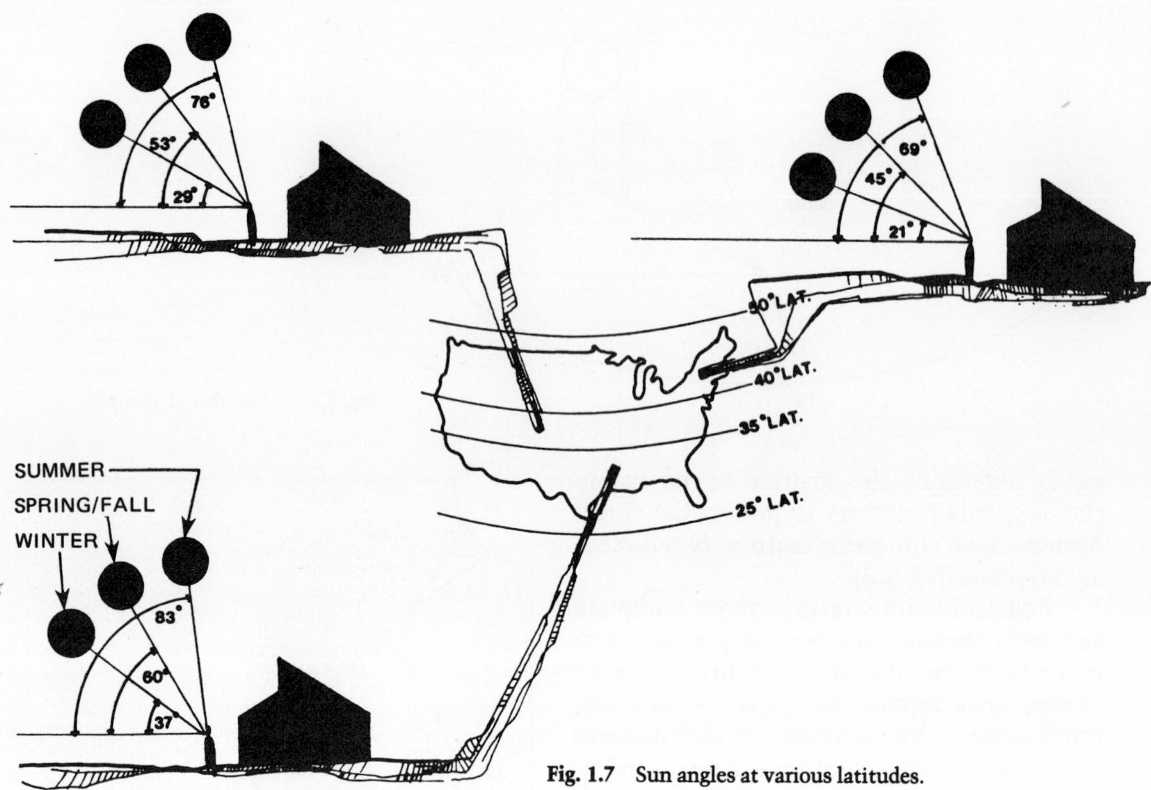

Fig. 1.7 Sun angles at various latitudes.

it reaches its highest point on June 21, the summer solstice. After June 21, the maximum daily altitude angle decreases until it reaches its lowest point on December 21, the winter solstice. This fact makes shading of south facing windows in summer a relatively easy task.

Altitude angles vary with latitude (Fig. 1.7). A rule-of-thumb for determining the noon altitude angle of the sun on the equinox (March 21 is the spring equinox and September 21 is the fall equinox) is 90° minus site latitude. For example, in Philadelphia, Pennsylvania (40° North latitude) the sun's altitude at solar noon is 90° minus 40° equals 50°. Knowing the altitude of the sun on March 21 and September 21 is helpful, for example, in determining whether window shading devices are causing unwanted shade on south facing windows on these dates. To determine the sun's noon altitude on June 21, add 23.5° to the noon altitude angle on March 21. (23.5° is the tilt of the earth's axis). For Philadelphia it would be 50° plus 23.5° equals 73.5°. On December 21, the altitude angle is the September 21 angle minus the earth's tilt or 50° minus 23.5° equals 26.5°. The sun's altitude is smallest when the earth's axis is tilted furthest from the sun, which occurs at noon on December 21.

The *azimuth angle* is the position of the sun east or west of south (Fig. 1.8). It is measured in degrees from south from 0° to 180° such that an azimuth angle of S 90° E is due east and S 90° W is due west. Azimuth angle is sometimes referred to as *bearing angle.*

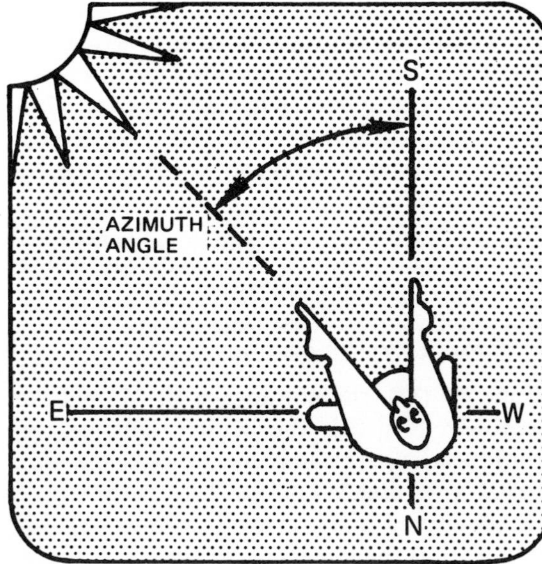

Figure 1.8

TABLE 1.1 Altitude Angle of the Sun at Solar Noon for the Winter and Summer Solstices (Azimuth Angle = 0° at Solar Noon)

Degrees North Latitude	December 21 Altitude Angle at Solar Noon	June 21 Altitude Angle at Solar Noon
28°	38.5°	85.4°
32°	34.5°	81.5°
36°	30.5°	77.5°
40°	26.5°	73.5°
44°	22.5°	69.5°
48°	18.5°	65.5°

TABLE 1.2 Azimuth Angle of the Sun at Sunrise and Sunset for the Winter and Summer Solstices

Degrees North Latitude	December 21 Azimuth Angle	June 21 Azimuth Angle
28°	S 63° E/W	S 117.5° E/W
32°	S 62° E/W	S 118° E/W
36°	S 60° E/W	S 118.5° E/W
40°	S 59° E/W	S 121° E/W
44°	S 56.5° E/W	S 125° E/W
48°	S 53.5° E/W	S 127° E/W

At sunrise the azimuth angle might be 59° east of south (S 59° E) (Fig. 1.9). As the day progresses, the azimuth angle decreases to zero at solar noon and afterwards increases to 59° west of south (S 59° W). Azimuth angles change with the seasons, too, because the sun rises and sets farther north in summer than it does in winter. The greater amount of sunlight from the east and west in summer make it especially important to assess carefully the impact of east and west windows on annual energy consumption.

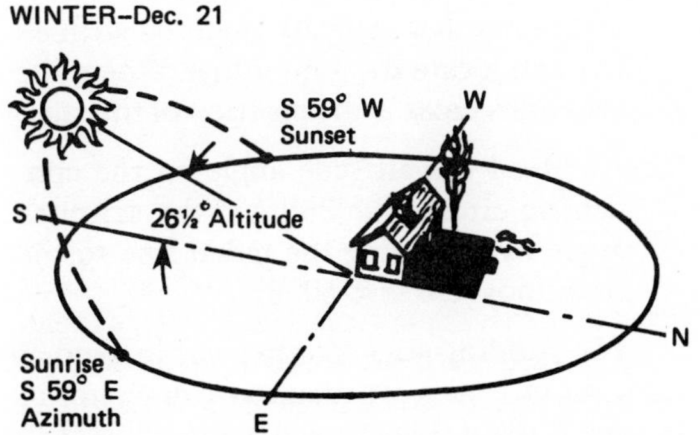

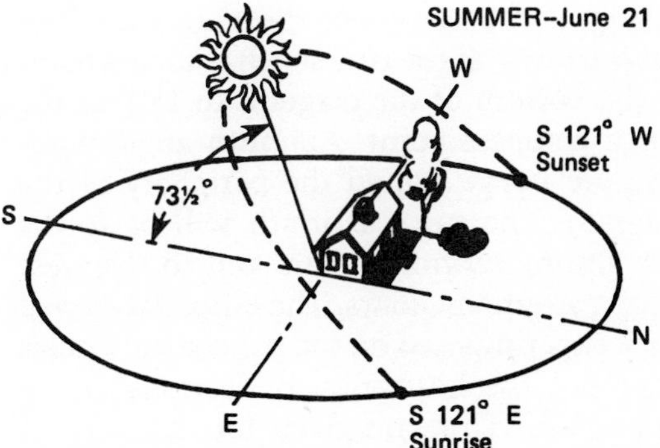

Fig. 1.9 Position of sun at noon for latitude 40°N.

Table 1.1 lists altitude angles for solar noon and Table 1.2 lists azimuth angles at sunrise and sunset on the winter and summer solstices. Note that at higher latitudes the altitude angle of the sun is consistently lower than at lower latitudes, throughout the year.

While solar noon is an important time, it is often helpful to know the sun's position at other times of the day. The sun path diagram is the most practical method for determining the position of the sun at *any* hour of *any* day.

THE SUN PATH DIAGRAM

As mentioned earlier (see Fig. 1.2), the sun path diagram graphically projects the arc of the sun through the sky onto a horizontal plane. Figure 1.10a is the sun path diagram for 28° North latitude. The horizon is represented as a circle with the observation point in the center. The diagram is constructed in equidistant projection. The altitude angles are represented at 10° intervals by equally spaced concentric circles, ranging from 0° at the outer circle (the horizon) to 90° at the center point (the sun directly overhead). The altitude angle is denoted by the numbers (10° to 80°) listed in a vertical line from the south compass point at the bottom of the diagram up to the center of the diagram.

Azimuth angles are represented at 10° intervals by equally spaced radial lines originating at the center of the diagram. They range from 0° at the true south compass point at the bottom of the diagram to 180° at the north compass point. Azimuth angle numbers are listed around the periphery of the diagram. The sun's azimuth will be to the east during morning hours and to the west during afternoon hours. The elliptical curved lines superimposed on the concentric circles represent the horizontal projections of the sun's path. They are given for the twenty-first day of each month. Roman numerals designate the months.

As the sun's path is composed of two identical halves (from summer to winter solstice and back again), it follows the same path on two corresponding dates each year. Thus, each sun path line is marked with two Roman numerals, one at each end. For reference, the corresponding dates are:

January 21 (I)	&	November 21 (XI)
February 21 (II)	&	October 21 (X)
March 21 (III)	&	September 21 (IX)
April 21 (IV)	&	August 21 (VIII)
May 21 (V)	&	July 21 (VII)

June 21 (VI), the summer solstice, and December 21 (XII), the winter solstice, are unique sun paths and have no corresponding date. The June 21 (VI) sun path is the uppermost curved line and the December 21 (XII) sun path is the lowest curved line.

A cross-grid of curves running vertically divide the sun path lines into the hours of the day. The hours are listed along the uppermost sun path, with noon at the center, the morning hours to the right (east) and afternoon hours to the left (west).

Six sun path diagrams at 4° intervals from 28°N to 48° north latitude are illustrated in Figures 1.10a–f. For example, to find the sun's position in Nashville, Tennessee on September 21 at 9:00 AM:

Step 1. Locate Nashville on a map (Fig. 1.12). The latitude is 36°N.

Step 2. On the 36° sun path diagram, select the September sun path (marked with an IX), and locate the 9-hour line. Where the two lines cross is the position of the sun.

Step 3. Read the altitude angle on the concentric circle line (35°) and the azimuth angle by following the radial line to the outermost circle (S 60° E).

For building sites in cities not located at the same latitudes as the sun path diagrams in Figures 1.10a–f, select the diagram closest to the site latitude or interpolate (average the numbers) between the two nearest latitudes.

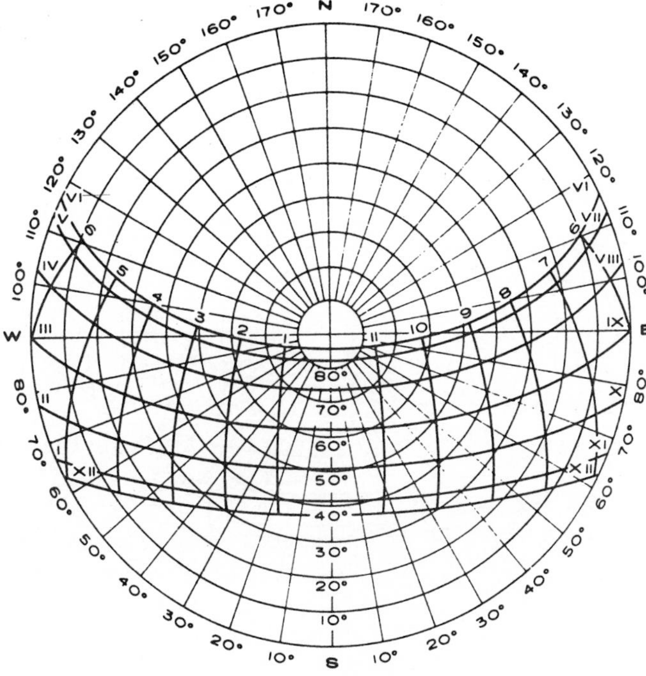

(a) 28°N Latitude

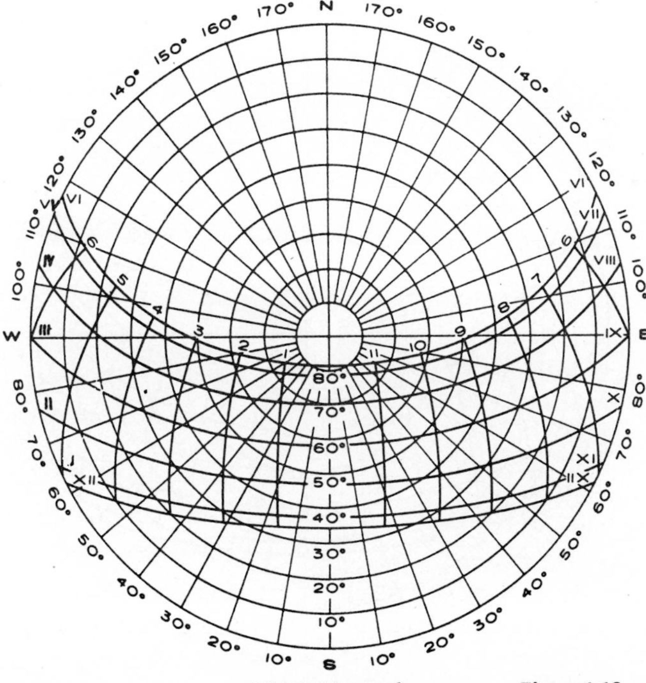

(b) 32°N Latitude

Figure 1.10

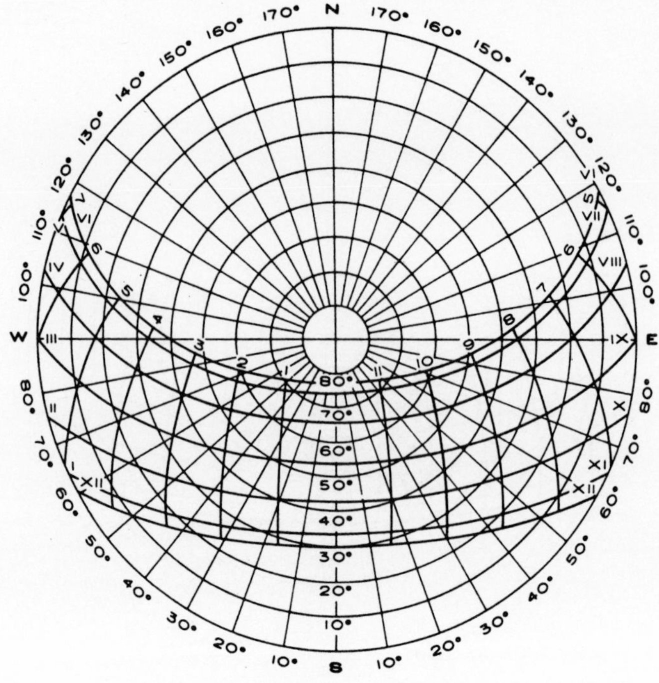

(c) 36°N Latitude

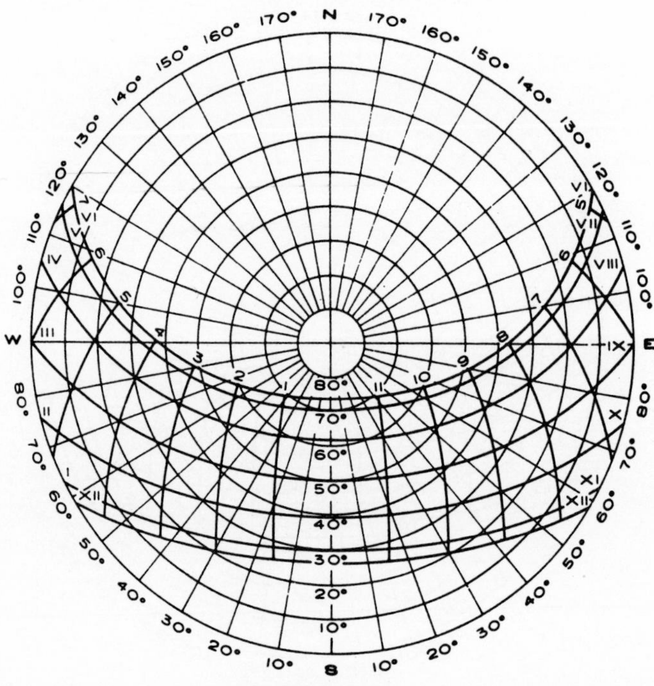

Figure 1.10 (continued)

(d) 40° Latitude

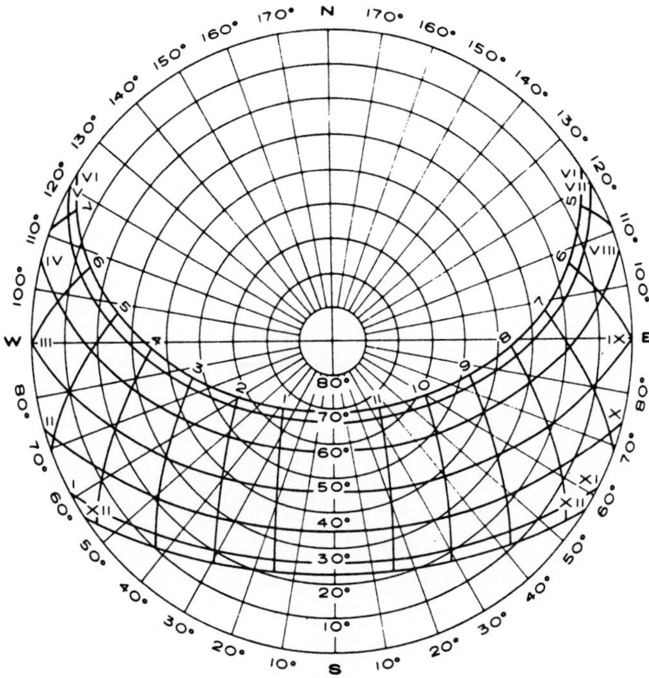

(e) 44°N Latitude

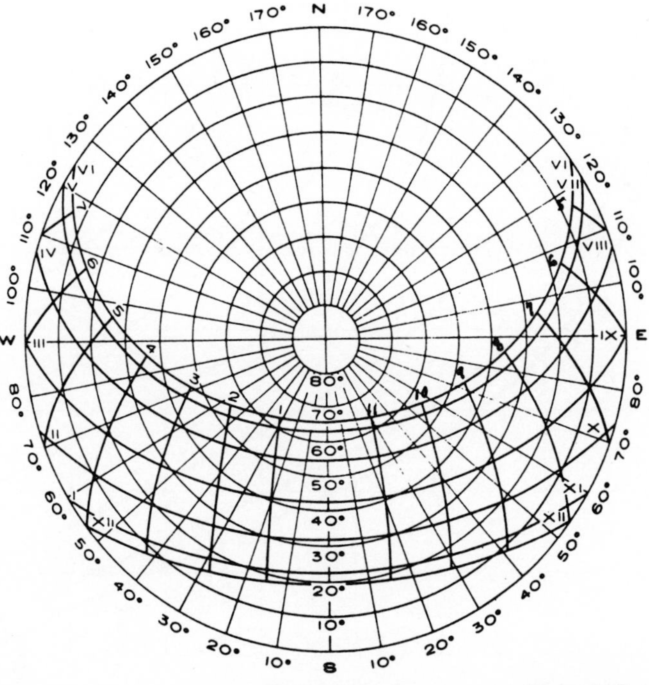

(f) 48° Latitude

Figure 1.10

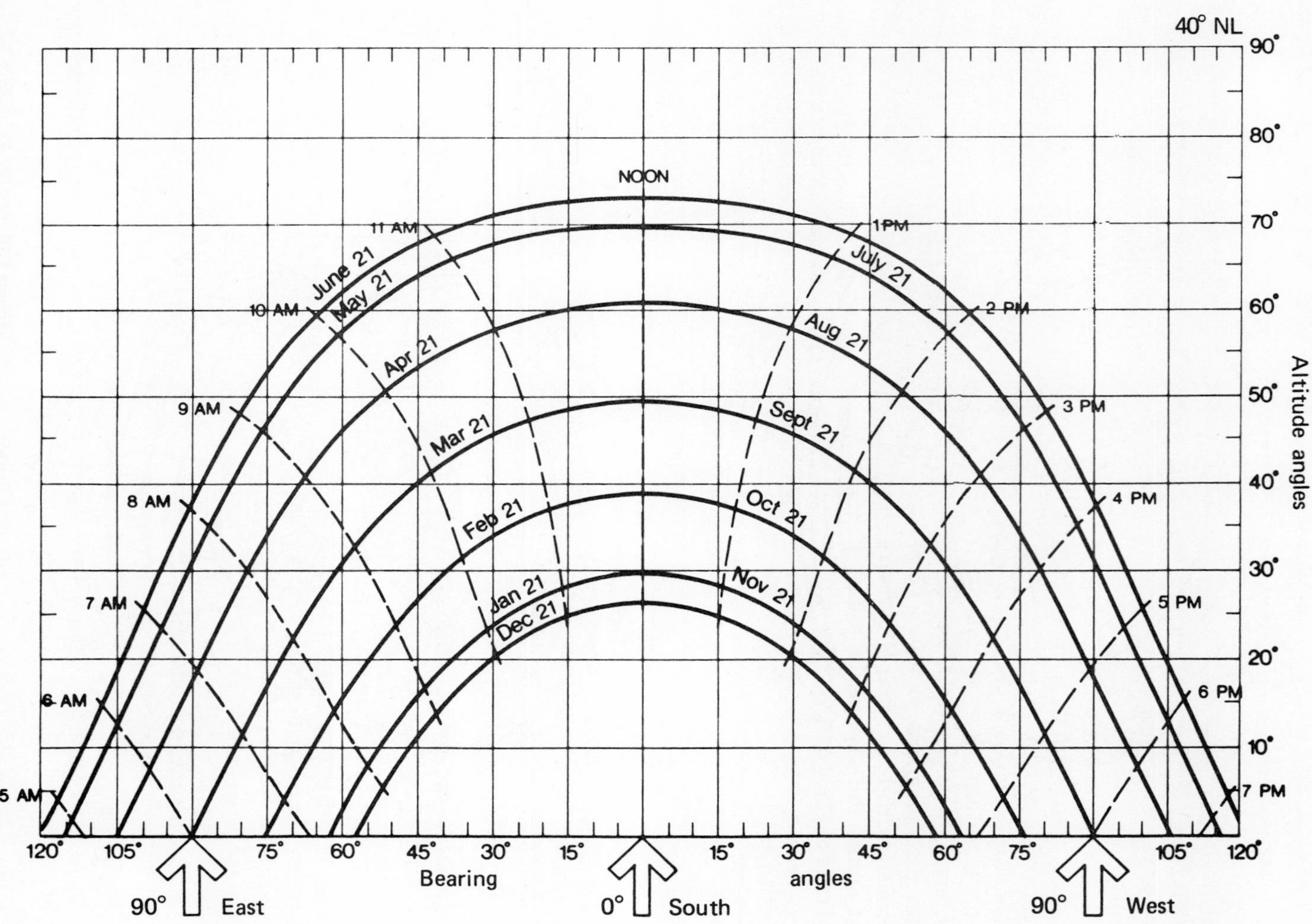

40° NL
Altitude angles
90°
80°
70°
60°
50°
40°
30°
20°
10°
NOON
5 AM
6 AM
7 AM
8 AM
9 AM
10 AM
11 AM
1PM
2 PM
3 PM
4 PM
5 PM
6 PM
7 PM
June 21
May 21
Apr 21
Mar 21
Feb 21
Jan 21
Dec 21
July 21
Aug 21
Sept 21
Oct 21
Nov 21
120°
105°
75°
60°
45°
30°
15°
15°
30°
45°
60°
75°
105°
120°
Bearing
angles
90° East
0° South
90° West

Figure 1.11

The sun path diagrams reproduced here are from *Architectural Graphic Standards** (Ramsey and Sleeper). A graphical solar radiation calculator in an overlay size can also be found in that book. The Libbey-Owens-Ford Glass Company's "Sun Angle Calculator" is a useful tool which takes sun path diagrams a few steps further. Sun charts for eight latitudes 24° to 52° come with transparent overlays which can be used to determine profile angles of shading devices and daylight availability. The LOF Sun Angle Calculator is available from LOF (Toledo, Ohio) for a small charge. Sun path diagrams projected vertically to form an earth-based view of the sun's movement across the sky can be found in Edward Mazria's *The Passive Solar Energy Book*† (Fig. 1.11). Transparent radiation and shading calculator overlays are included with the professional edition of the book.

LATITUDE

Latitude is the angular distance north or south of the equator, measured in degrees along a meridian. The equator is at zero degrees and the poles are at 90° latitude. Sun angles and the amount of solar radiation received increase as latitude decreases because the sun's rays strike the surface of the earth at progressively more perpendicular angles near the equator. For example, on December 21 in northern Minnesota (48° north latitude) the altitude angle of the sun at noon is 18.6°. A thousand miles south in northern Georgia (35° north latitude) the altitude angle at noon on this day is 30°. The lower solar altitudes in the northern latitudes mean that a given quantity of the sun's rays fall on a larger area as the north latitude increases. So, the concentration of the sun's energy per square foot decreases as north latitude increases.

A very important implication of latitude is its effect on shading. At northern latitudes the sun is lower in the sky, causing trees and buildings to cast longer shadows than in the south and making it more difficult to protect south facing windows from shadows.

TRUE SOUTH

A magnetic compass needle points to magnetic north, which differs from "true" or "solar" north at any locality by an amount known as the *magnetic deviation*. The wavy lines from top to bottom in the isogonic chart in Figure 1.12 show compass deviations across the United States. A line of zero deviation (where true and magnetic north are the same) runs from the eastern end of Lake Michigan to the Atlantic coast in northern Georgia. In locations on the east side of the line, a compass needle will point to the west of true north. This is called a "westerly variation." For example, the map shows a deviation of 14.5° west for Boston. This means that a compass will point 14.5° to the west of true north, or true north is 14.5° to the east of compass-indicated north. True south, then, is 14.5° west of compass south (Fig. 1.13). For locations to the west of the zero deviation line, the conditions are reversed.

True south should always be used in solar design. The exact figure for every town can be obtained from a local land surveyor. This figure should be used for determining building orientations, calculation of the sun's position, assessing shading on a site, and so forth.

SUN TIME

Standard time is the conventional time for the zone containing a particular site. It is measured uniformly in hours, minutes and

* Ramsey and Sleeper, *Architectural Graphic Standards*, 6th ed. (New York: John Wiley & Sons, Inc., 1970), pp. 70–71.

† Mazria, *The Passive Solar Energy Book* (Emmaus, PA: Rodale Press, 1979).

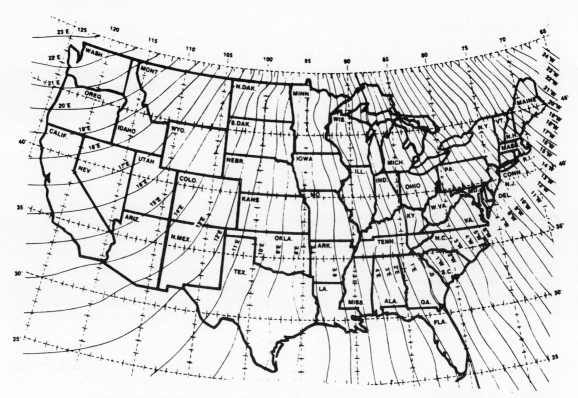

Fig. 1.12 Isogonic chart showing magnetic deviation from true south. (Source: Redrawn by Mazria from the Isogonic Chart of the United States, U.S. Department of Commerce, Coast and Geodetic Survey, 1965.)

seconds throughout the day and year. Sun time is measured by the position of the sun above the horizon, with solar noon corresponding to the sun at its highest point and true south. The intervals of time vary such that the length of the solar day can grow as much as 30 minutes. This is because the varying speed of the earth orbiting the sun (depending on its distance from the sun) causes variations between earth and sun time. Sun path diagrams always use sun time.

The map in Figure 1.14 depicts the four standard time zones of the United States.

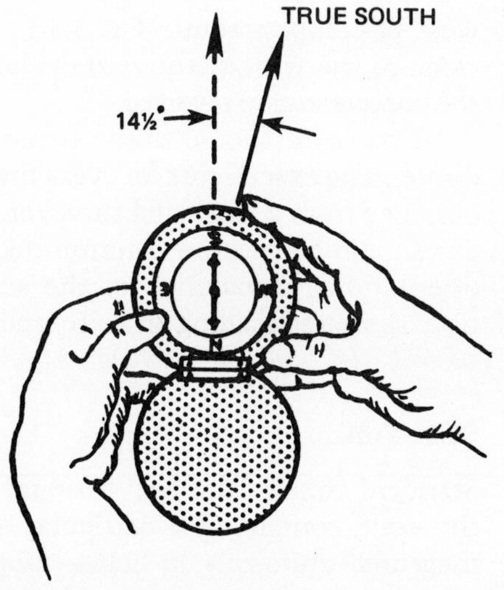

Fig. 1.13 A westerly variation.

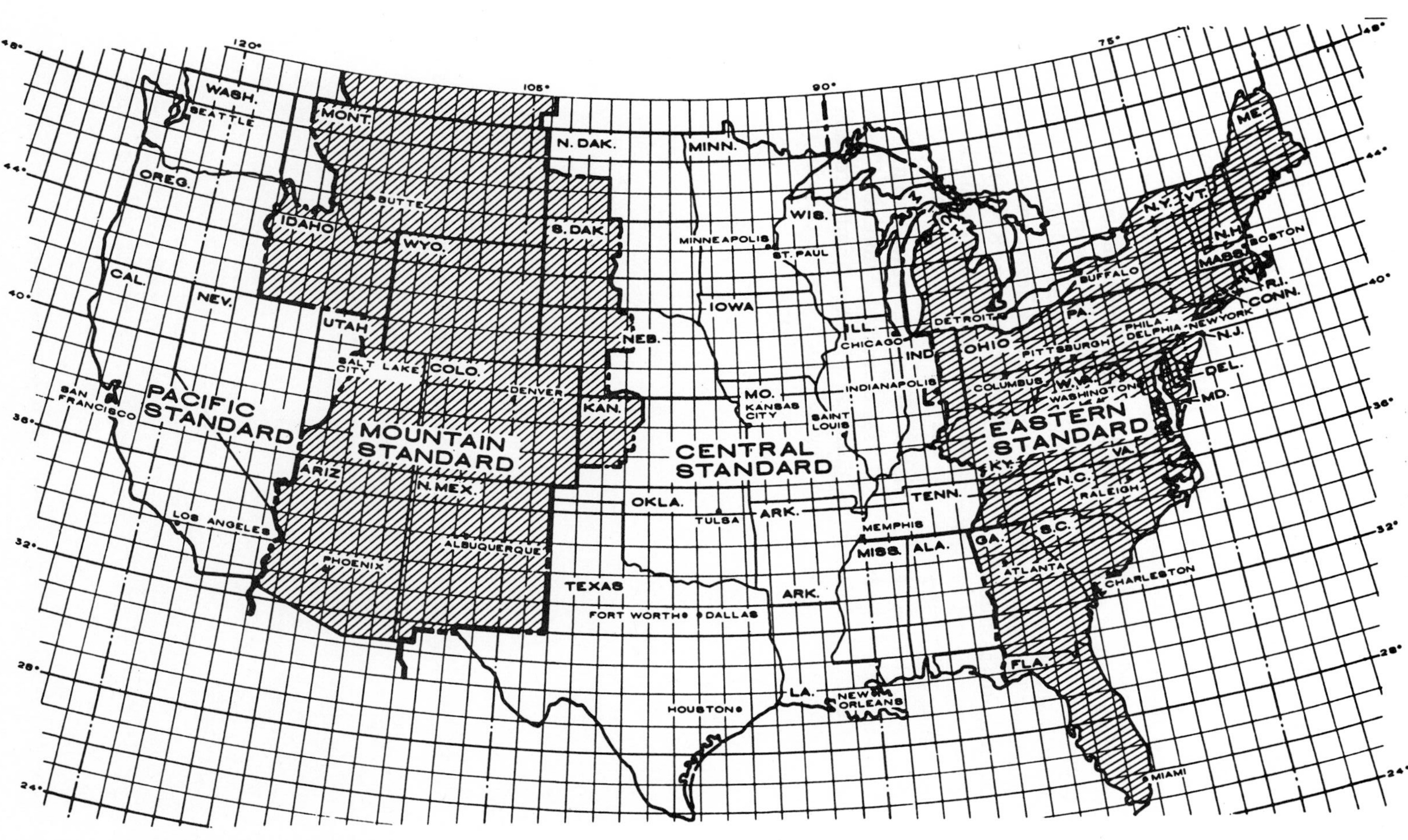

Fig. 1.14 Standard time zones of the United States.

Time Zones: Central longitudes of time zones are: Eastern Standard Time at 75°; Central S. T. at 90°; Mountain S. T. at 105°; Pacific S. T. at 120°. If conversion to SUN TIME is desired for site location then: 1) If Daylight Savings Time is in effect subtract one hour from local time. 2) Subtract 4 minutes for every degree of longitude if site is west of central longitude or add 4 mins. for every degree of longitude if site is east of it. 3) Correct time variations for day and months; add or subtract minutes as follows:

Jan. 21	−11.4	July 21	−6.2
Feb. 21	−13.8	Aug. 21	−3.1
Mar. 21	−7.4	Sept. 21	+6.8
Apr. 21	+1.2	Oct. 21	+15.3
May 21	+3.6	Nov. 21	−14.1
June 21	−1.5	Dec. 21	+2.0

An example of conversion to sun time: Calculate sun time at site for Columbus, Ohio at 12 noon local time on June 21st.

Step 1. As in June, Daylight Savings Time is in effect, subtract one hour from local time to 11:00 o'clock.

Step 2. Locate Columbus on map. The longitude is 83°. This is in the Eastern time Zone with the central longitude of 75°. As Columbus is 8 degrees west of the central longitude: subtract 8 × 4 minutes or 32 minutes from 11:00 o'clock, changing the time to 10:28 o'clock.

Step 3. To correct time variation for June 21st, subtract 1.5 minutes. The result indicates 10 hours, 26 minutes and 30 seconds; which will be the sun time at 12 noon, local time.

CHAPTER TWO

Solar Radiation

Solar radiation or "insolation," the energy source that powers all life on our planet, is made up of three components: direct radiation from the sun; diffuse radiation from the sky (caused by atmospheric scattering of direct sunlight); and reflected radiation from the ground and adjacent buildings. Of the three, direct radiation is by far the most important source of heat for the earth.

The intensity of direct solar radiation reaching the earth's surface from space is largely determined by the thickness and density of the earth's atmosphere through which it must pass. When the sun is directly overhead, solar radiation travels through the least amount of atmosphere on its way to the earth's surface. As the sun moves closer to the horizon (i.e., towards sunset) its radiant beam must pass through an increasingly greater quantity of atmosphere, thus reducing its intensity considerably (Fig. 2.1). This is the reason we can look directly at the sun as it rises or sets, but not at noon. Figure 2.2 shows the relationship between solar altitude and radiation received in BTUs per hour, perpendicular to the surface it is striking.

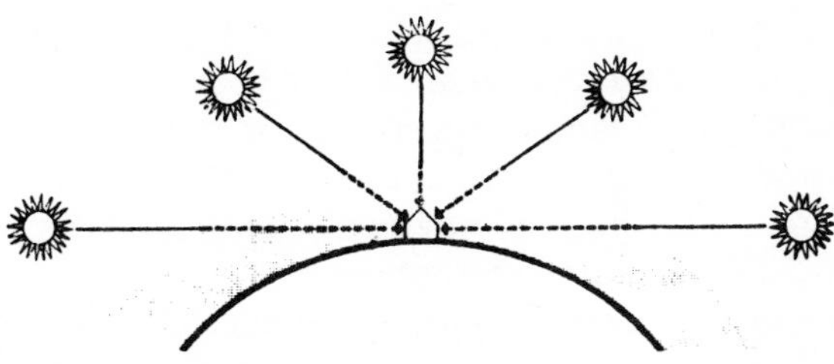

Fig. 2.1 The path of sunbeams through the atmosphere.

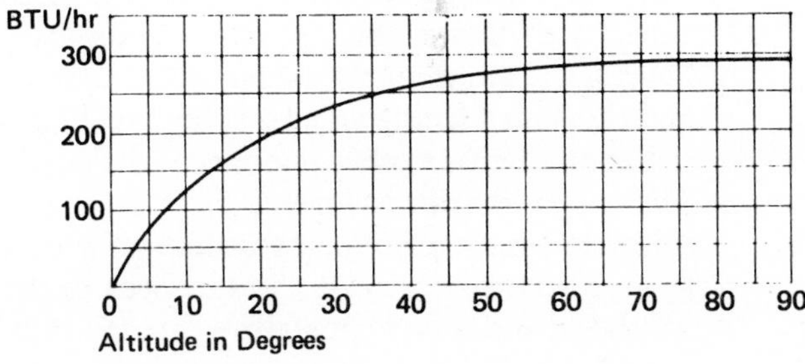

Fig. 2.2 Solar energy in relation to the sun's altitude.

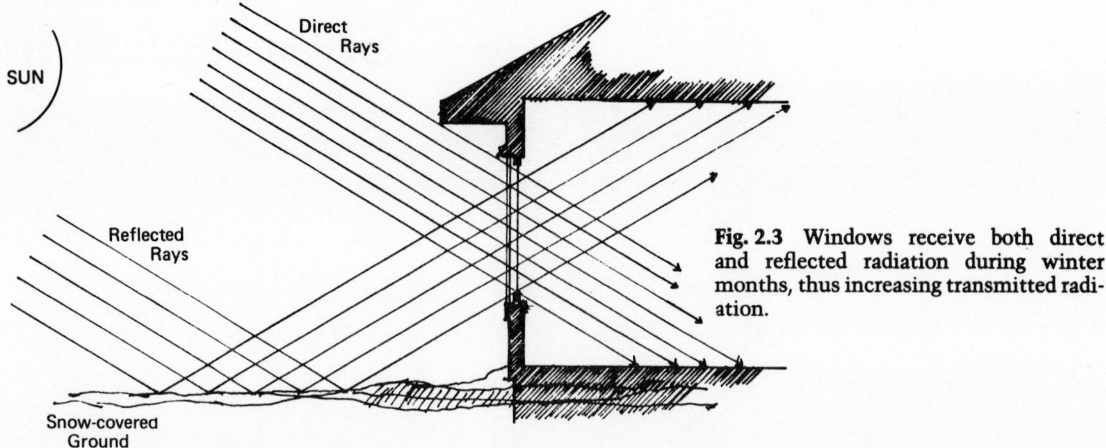

Fig. 2.3 Windows receive both direct and reflected radiation during winter months, thus increasing transmitted radiation.

Reflected as well as direct radiation can contribute to passive solar heating. The reflectance or albedo of the ground surface in front of a window can greatly enhance the amount of radiation received by the window and, hence, into a home. Snow on the ground, a common winter occurrence in northern latitudes, results in greater amounts of solar radiation being transferred into homes when it is most needed. This tends to lessen the difference in the quantity of wintertime solar gain between northern and southern latitudes (Fig. 2.3). Fine white gravel or sand spread directly in front of south facing windows is an easy way to augment solar radiation. Table 2.1 lists the reflectance values for a number of typical ground surface materials.

TABLE 2.1 Reflectance of Solar Radiation by Various Surfaces

Surface	Percent Reflectance
Fresh snow cover	75–95
White gravel	85–90
Old snow cover	60–90
Dry grass	32
Green leaves	25–32
Sandy soil	15–40
Bare ground	10–20
Asphalt	15

AMOUNT OF SOLAR RADIATION

The map in Figure 2.4 shows the average hours of sunshine available per day in December, January and February in the United States. Even though much of the northern part of the country appears to receive only four to five hours of sun a day, the heating load in those areas is high enough to benefit significantly from the radiation that is available (800 to 1000 BTU/sq. ft./day on south facing glass). Conversely, many areas showing a higher number of hours of sun daily have small heating requirements and higher cooling needs and cannot always utilize the available radiation effectively. Thus, a relatively low daily number of hours of sunshine during the winter should not be viewed as a deterrent to solar building projects.

In the northern latitudes 32° to 56°, the south facing side of buildings receive three times more solar radiation in winter than sides with other than south orientations. During the summer the situation is reversed and the south facing side receives much less radiation than any other side except the north. There are two reasons for this. First, the south side receives more hours of sunshine in winter than in summer because the sun rises in the southeast and sets in the southwest in winter,

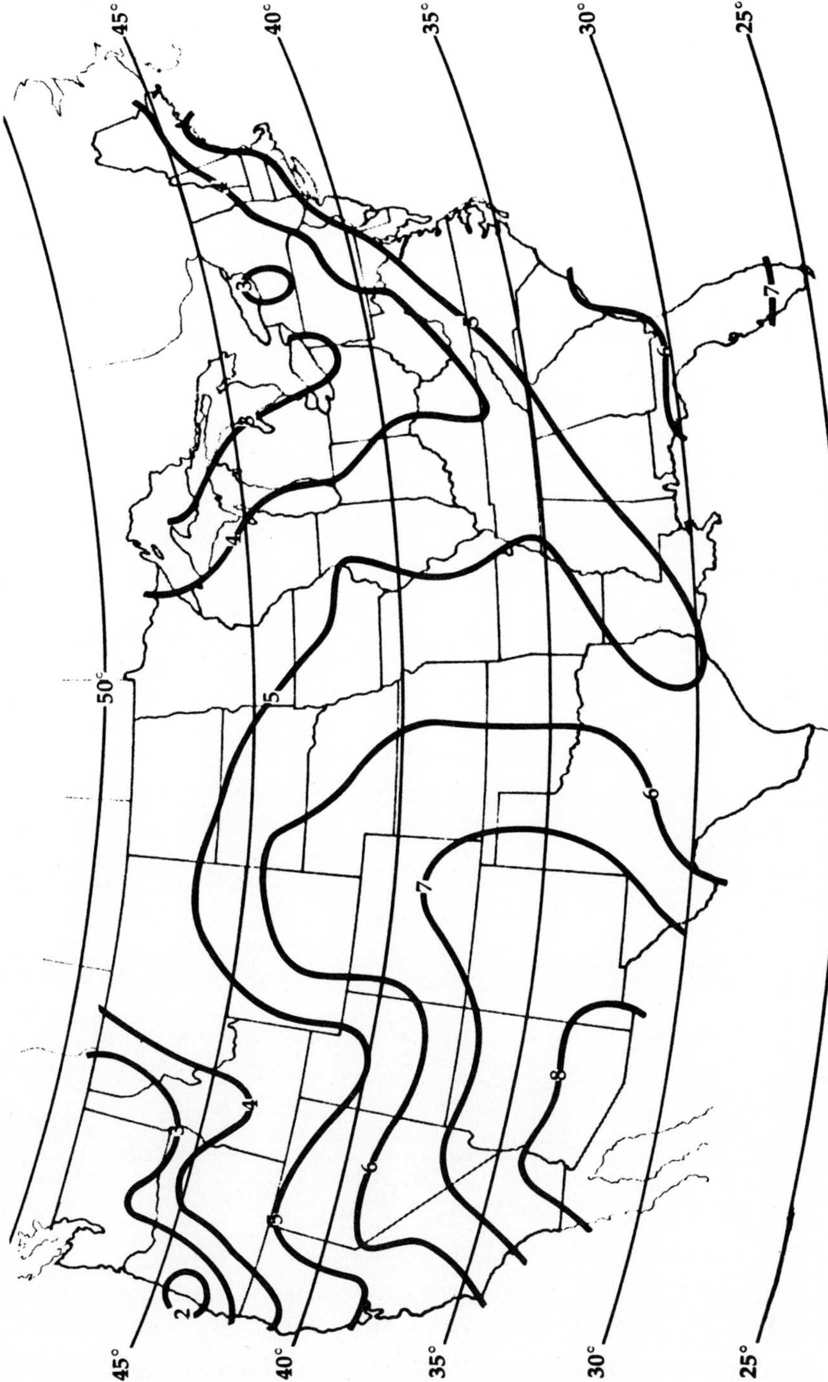

Fig. 2.4 Average hours of sunshine per day (December, January, February). Adapted from USDA Yearbook of Agriculture.

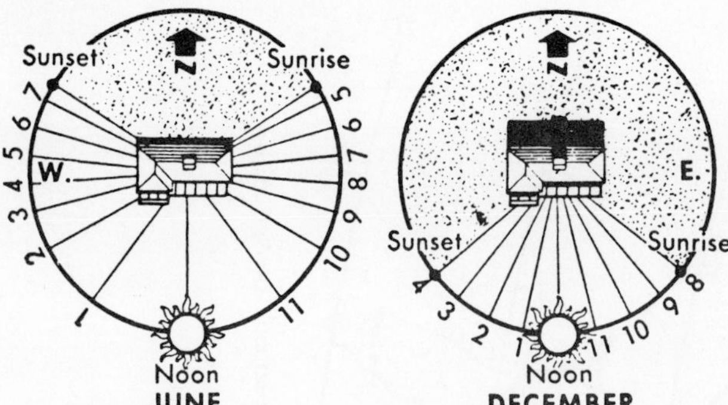

Fig. 2.5 Hourly direction of sunlight.

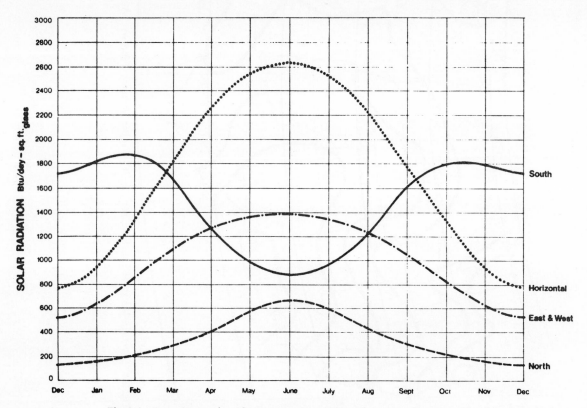

Fig. 2.6 Comparison of window orientations. (Note: This graph represents clear day solar radiation values, on the surfaces indicated, for 40°NL.)

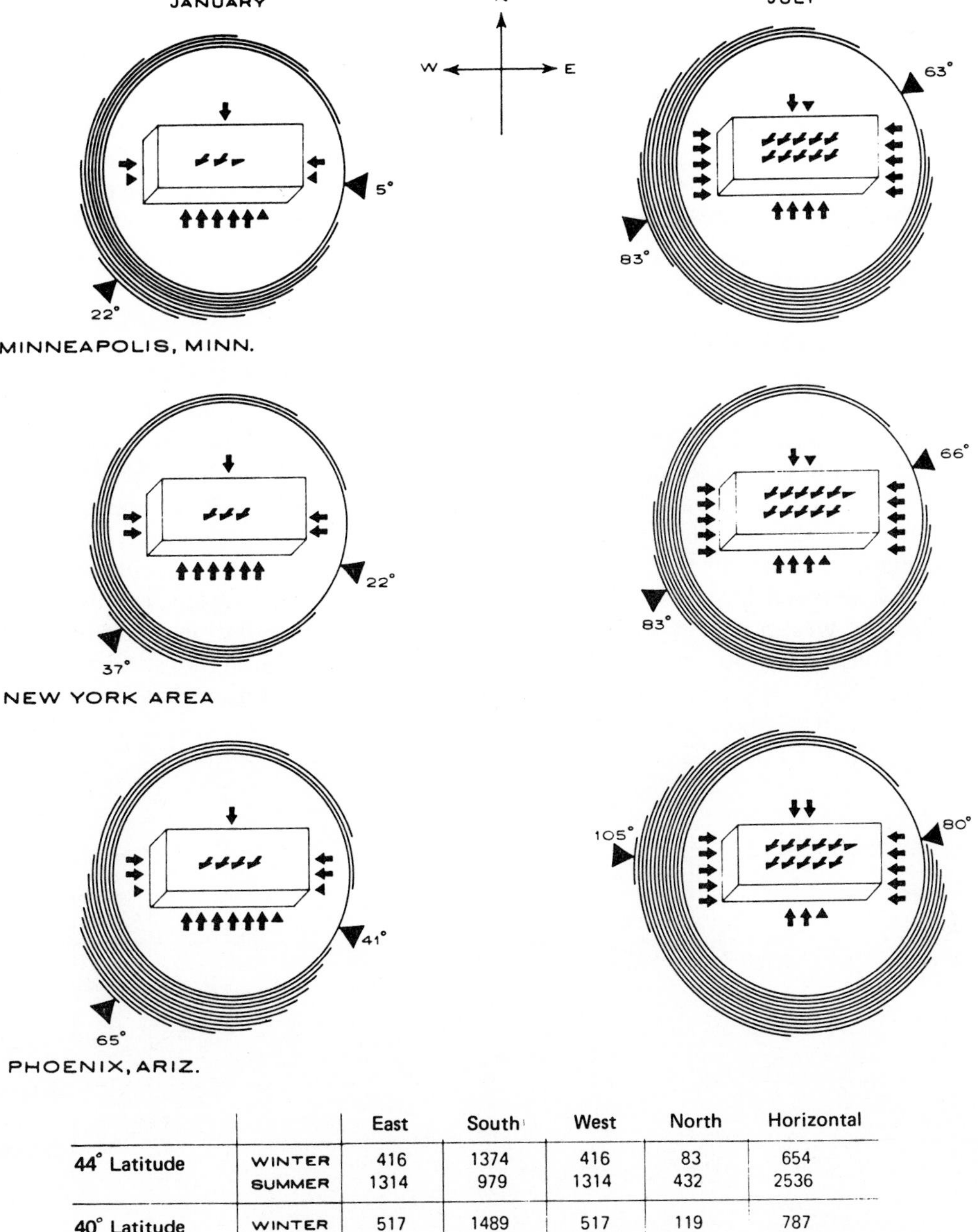

		East	South	West	North	Horizontal
44° Latitude	WINTER	416	1374	416	83	654
	SUMMER	1314	979	1314	432	2536
40° Latitude	WINTER	517	1489	517	119	787
	SUMMER	1277	839	1277	430	2619
32° Latitude	WINTER	620	1606	620	140	954
	SUMMER	1207	563	1207	452	2596

Fig. 2.7 Impact of orientation.

thus concentrating all the hours of sunshine on south facing surfaces. In summer, the sun rises to the north of east and sets to the north of west at all latitudes in the continental United States, and though the hours of sunshine are greater than in winter, the sunlight is distributed over the east, west *and* south sides of a building (Fig. 2.5). Second, the lower altitude of the winter sun means that its rays strike south facing surfaces more perpendicularly than in summer, thus transferring a greater amount of radiation through them.

Figure 2.6 compares the solar radiation received on vertical north, south, east and west facing windows and a horizontal surface for every month of the year at 40° north latitude. Note how much more radiation the south facing window receives in winter than in summer. Figure 2.7 depicts the thermal impacts on five exposed surfaces (vertical north, south, east, west and horizontal) for three north latitudes, 32°, 40° and 44°. The impact of solar radiation on the various sides of the building is indicated with arrows. Each arrow represents 250 BTU/sq. ft./day radiation. The box at the bottom of the figure summarizes the arrows numerically.

The air temperature variation is indicated by the concentric circles around the buildings. Each line represents 2°F difference from the lowest daily temperature. The direction of the impact is shown according to the sun's direction as the temperatures occur. Note the low temperatures on the east sides and high ones on the west.

In all latitudes the south facing side of a building receives considerably more radiation in winter than in summer, and the reverse is true for east and west facing sides. In summer, the west exposure is more troublesome thermally than the east exposure, because the high afternoon temperatures combine with the effects of radiation and can cause serious overheating problems. In all latitudes the north facing side receives only a small amount of radiation, mainly in the summer. The horizontal roof surface receives more radiation in summer than do any of the sides.

PART TWO

SOLAR LAND PLANNING AND DEVELOPMENT

Planning for solar access introduces important new considerations into the conventional development process. Solar land planning takes into account factors affecting energy conservation and the availability of sunlight for displacing annual energy demands, and includes the laying out of streets, buildings, landscaping and open space so that unobstructed solar energy can be received by existing and future south facing windows, glass doors or solar collectors. However, solar access is but one consideration in a land planning and development process where tradeoffs prevail. Terrain usually dictates principal development decisions where costs are a concern.

Solar access should be considered along with other land planning techniques in the lot designation process to increase the potential for future solar energy use in a development. While acknowledging that solar access is not the most important concern in land planning, providing for it is the focus of this part of the book. Land for solar homes is being developed *now* at little or no extra cost over conventional developments. Reports from builders of these developments indicate that enhancing the beneficial use of the sun's energy adds to the marketability of their homes and suggest that resale values of homes and lots with good solar orientation may be greater than those of conventional homes and lots. In addition, banks are currently considering utility costs (along with insurance and taxes) in qualifying buyers for mortgage loans. See the Case Studies in Chapter 6 for details.

The general principles for providing for solar access are simple and straightforward. The objective is to lay out streets and lots in such a way that as many homes as possible have proper orientation to the sun and to avoid shading south facing glazing during the heating season while providing shade during the cooling season. The authors realize that most proposed development sites are not of a textbook variety, however, and that many builders must use lots that have been laid out with little or no reference to solar access. Chapters 3 through 5 will illustrate steps which can be taken to maximize solar access for homes built on sites that do not conform to the general principles as well as for those which do.

Comments of various builders and developers are:

- "In most cases, the land plan for a solar access subdivision is not that much different from the plan for a conventional subdivision layout."
- "Solar access planning must be integrated with other land planning techniques."
- "Even with increased densities, solar access *can* be provided."
- "Solar access projects give the builder room for negotiation with local approval agencies."
- "We work only with true south orientation and we have not lost a single lot for solar access."

Part Two is comprised of four chapters which are intended to provide, as succinctly as possible, sufficient information to allow architects, land planners, builders, and developers to immediately begin practicing to plan for solar access. For more extensive information on land planning, consult the list of references at the end of the book.

Chapter 3, *Site Evaluation*, discusses topography, shadow pattern construction for vegetation and structures, and microclimatic considerations as they relate to the availability of sunlight and opportunities for energy conservation.

Chapter 4, *Planning Guidelines*, introduces the concept of climate regions used to target planning and development recommendations given in this book and presents many design options for achieving solar access in both large and small developments.

Chapter 5, *Land Use Regulations*, presents methods for overcoming potential regulatory barriers to solar development and information on legal protection of solar access.

Chapter 6 is a series of documented *Case Studies* from all over the United States.

The authors assume that builders, developers and related professionals who read this book are already familiar with conventional land development practices, and that readers have a basic understanding of passive solar design principles.

CHAPTER THREE

Site Evaluation

Planning a development for solar access begins with the choice and analysis of a site. While it involves many of the same procedures used in designing conventional developments, planning for solar access also demands the consideration of both the availability of sunlight and the extent of shading on the site. Solar access can be affected by the natural elements of the site, such as topography or atmospheric conditions, or by obstructions (man-made or natural, such as buildings or trees).

Additionally, the energy saving features of the site must be considered. Features that moderate the local climate (such as trees or large bodies of water) can have a great effect on the efficiency of a solar energy system.

Finally, site data pertaining to these considerations should be gathered and compile˙ on base maps of the site.

TOPOGRAPHY AND AVAILABILITY OF SUNLIGHT

The latitude and topography of a site affects both the availability of sunlight and the length of shadows cast by objects on the site. Likewise, changes in topography affect the angle at which the sun hits the ground. During the winter on south slopes, as at lower latitudes, sunlight is more nearly perpendicular, so shadows are shorter than on flat land or on a north facing slope (Fig. 3.1). The slope and orientation of the land largely determine the amount of radiation received. South facing slopes receive the greatest amount of sunlight in the winter. General guidelines for positioning residential developments in all regions of the continental United States are:

South Slope—Preferred (warm winters, early spring, late fall)
East Slope—Acceptable (warm winter mornings, cool summer evenings)
West Slope—Undesirable (hottest in summer)
North Slope—Least desirable (coldest in winter)

It is useful to keep in mind that shade can be provided if the sun is a nuisance, but adequate solar exposure can be difficult to achieve once a dwelling is located on a shady north facing slope. Solar energy availability and shadow length also vary with slope gradient. The basic concept here is that the steeper the slope, the more the microclimatic conditions associated with the slope direction are accentuated.

For instance, a site which slopes 10 percent to the south will receive as much solar

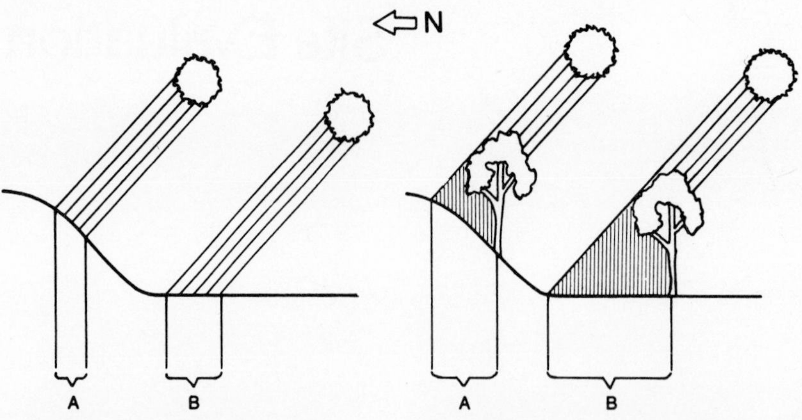
N
A
B
A
B
Area of ground receiving the ray on flat ground (B) is larger than area on south slope (A). Thus more energy is received per unit area on the slope.
Shadow cast by tree on flat ground (B) is longer than the one cast by same tree on south slope (A).

Fig. 3.1 Radiation and shadow length on a south slope.

radiation and will thus have the same climate as a flat site six degrees closer to the equator, or the difference in latitude between Boston, Massachusetts and Nashville, Tennessee. Since the sun's altitude (which determines the amount of radiation received) increases about one degree for every 70 miles distance to the south, the amount of solar radiation received on a south facing slope increases proportionately to each degree it slopes. Therefore, south slopes are preferable for solar energy use, because they absorb more winter solar radiation than other slopes and tend to be warmer. Shorter shadows cast on south slopes enable buildings to be built taller and closer together without obstructing solar access, thus making higher density developments easier.

Flat land has better solar access than east, west or north slopes, but is less desirable than a south slope. Streets may be laid out in an east/west orientation more easily on flat land than on contoured land.

As east and west facing glazing is difficult to shade, homes built on east or west slopes should be oriented toward south with the major glass area located on the south wall.

North slopes are the least desirable for solar energy use, but with careful planning they can also provide homes with solar access. (See Chapter 6, Case Study 2 in Richmond, VA, with solar homes laid out on a steep north facing slope.) On north slopes shadow lengths tend to be extremely long (especially in higher latitudes), less radiation is received on the ground and sites are often exposed to dominant north winter winds.

ATMOSPHERIC CONDITIONS

The effects of fog, cloudiness and temperature inversions on solar radiation, intensity and availability warrant consideration. Affected zones can have sharp boundaries; sites within a few hundred feet of each other may have very different levels of available solar radiation. Fog prone areas should be avoided because fog can severely reduce the amount of solar radiation received by homes. Sites with occasional morning fogginess can be improved by orienting the major glass area slightly west of due south. Low-lying areas should be avoided as building sites, since cold

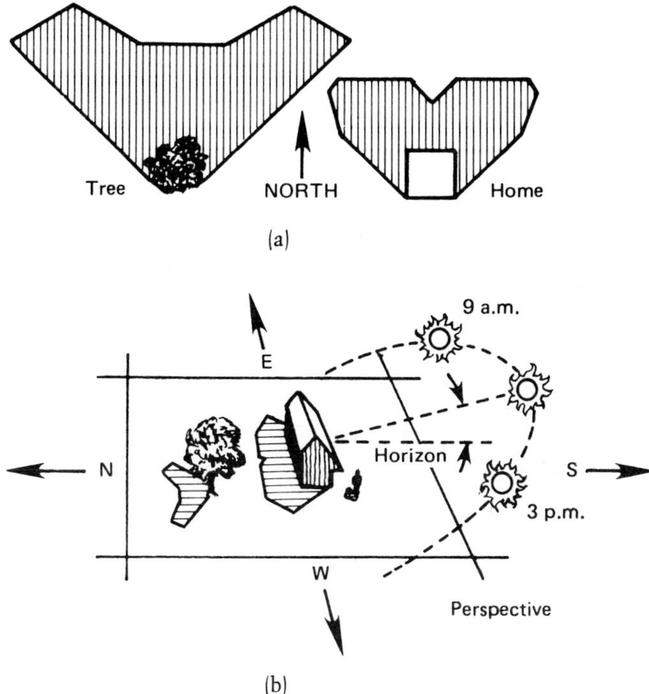

Figure 3.2

air flows into them and settles, thus increasing the heating load of structures located there.

SHADING

It is extremely important that existing features on a site be assessed for potential shading in winter and summer. Trees, buildings and hills can potentially cause shading problems for south facing glass during winter months. However, in summer or in hot climates such shading is desirable, and the location of tall trees and buildings can become an asset that helps to reduce a home's cooling energy requirement.

Shadows cast on the south facing windows of buildings during winter months are detrimental to solar heating performance, so it is necessary to determine the *shadow patterns* of trees, buildings and hills near the south facing windows. Shadow patterns enable the land planner to determine areas where shading may or may not be a problem for each season.

A shadow pattern is the composite shape of a shadow cast by an object over a given period of time (Fig. 3.2). Winter shadow patterns should be used in planning for solar access, since the longest shadows of the year are cast on December 21.

CONSTRUCTING AND USING SHADOW PATTERNS

For the sake of convenience, the boundaries of the shadow pattern are defined by the sun's December 21 azimuth—two shadows, one falling 45° northwest and the other 45° northeast of a north/south line running through the center of the object. This in effect creates a right angle whose sides are aimed northeast and northwest.

TABLE 3.1a–e. Shadow length tables for a one-foot high pole on December 21

a. 30° North Latitude

Orientation		N			NE			E			SE			S			SW			W			NW		
Time		AM	NOON	PM	AM	NOON	PM	AM	NOON	PM	AM	NOON	PM	AM	NOON	PM	AM	NOON	PM	AM	NOON	PM	AM	NOON	PM
Slope	0%	2.7	1.3	2.7	2.7	1.3	2.7	2.7	1.3	2.7	2.7	1.3	2.7	2.7	1.3	2.7	2.7	1.3	2.7	2.7	1.3	2.7	2.7	1.3	2.7
	5%	2.9	1.4	2.9	2.7	1.4	3.1	2.4	1.4	2.9	2.4	1.3	2.7	2.4	1.3	2.4	2.7	1.3	2.4	2.9	1.4	2.4	3.1	1.4	2.7
	10%	3.3	1.6	3.3	2.7	1.5	3.6	2.2	1.4	3.3	2.1	1.2	2.7	2.2	1.2	2.2	2.7	1.2	2.1	3.3	1.4	2.2	3.6	1.5	2.7
	15%	3.7	1.7	3.7	2.7	1.6	4.4	2.1	1.4	3.7	1.9	1.2	2.7	2.1	1.1	2.1	2.7	1.2	1.9	3.7	1.4	2.1	4.4	1.6	2.7
	20%	4.3	1.9	4.3	2.7	1.7	5.7	1.9	1.4	4.3	1.7	1.2	2.7	1.9	1.1	1.9	2.7	1.2	1.7	4.3	1.4	1.9	5.7	1.7	2.7

b. 35° North Latitude

Orientation		N			NE			E			SE			S			SW			W			NW		
Time		AM	NOON	PM	AM	NOON	PM	AM	NOON	PM	AM	NOON	PM	AM	NOON	PM	AM	NOON	PM	AM	NOON	PM	AM	NOON	PM
Slope	0%	3.5	1.6	3.5	3.5	1.6	3.5	3.5	1.6	3.5	3.5	1.6	3.5	3.5	1.6	3.5	3.5	1.6	3.5	3.5	1.6	3.5	3.5	1.6	3.5
	5%	4.0	1.8	4.0	3.5	1.7	4.2	3.1	1.6	4.0	3.0	1.5	3.5	3.1	1.5	3.1	3.5	1.5	3.0	4.0	1.6	3.1	4.2	1.7	3.5
	10%	4.6	2.0	4.6	3.5	1.8	5.3	2.8	1.6	4.6	2.6	1.5	3.5	2.8	1.4	2.8	3.5	1.5	2.6	4.6	1.6	2.8	5.3	1.8	3.5
	15%	5.5	2.2	5.5	3.5	2.0	7.2	2.5	1.6	5.5	2.3	1.4	3.5	2.5	1.3	2.5	3.5	1.4	2.3	5.5	1.6	2.5	7.2	2.0	3.5
	20%	6.8	2.5	6.8	3.5	2.2	11.4	2.3	1.7	6.8	2.0	1.3	3.5	2.3	1.3	2.3	3.5	1.3	2.0	6.8	1.7	2.3	11.4	2.2	3.5

c. 40° North Latitude

Orientation		N			NE			E			SE			S			SW			W			NW		
Time		AM	NOON	PM	AM	NOON	PM	AM	NOON	PM	AM	NOON	PM	AM	NOON	PM	AM	NOON	PM	AM	NOON	PM	AM	NOON	PM
Slope	0%	4.8	2.0	4.8	4.8	2.0	4.8	4.8	2.0	4.8	4.8	2.0	4.8	4.8	2.0	4.8	4.8	2.0	4.8	4.8	2.0	4.8	4.8	2.0	4.8
	5%	5.7	2.2	5.7	4.8	2.2	6.2	4.1	2.0	5.7	3.8	1.9	4.8	4.1	1.8	4.1	4.8	1.9	3.8	5.7	2.0	4.1	6.2	2.2	4.8
	10%	7.2	2.5	7.2	4.8	2.3	9.1	3.6	2.0	7.2	3.2	1.8	4.8	3.6	1.7	3.6	4.8	1.8	3.2	7.2	2.0	3.6	9.1	2.3	4.8
	15%	9.6	2.9	9.6	4.8	2.6	16.6	3.2	2.0	9.1	2.8	1.7	4.8	3.2	1.6	3.2	4.8	1.7	2.8	9.6	2.0	3.2	16.6	2.6	4.8
	20%	14.5	3.4	14.5	4.8	2.8	97.5	2.8	2.0	14.5	2.4	1.6	4.8	2.8	1.5	2.8	4.8	1.6	2.4	14.5	2.0	2.8	97.5	2.8	4.8

d. 45° North Latitude

Orientation		N			NE			E			SE			S			SW			W			NW		
Time		AM	NOON	PM	AM	NOON	PM	AM	NOON	PM	AM	NOON	PM	AM	NOON	PM	AM	NOON	PM	AM	NOON	PM	AM	NOON	PM
Slope	0%	7.2	2.5	7.2	7.2	2.5	7.2	7.2	2.5	7.2	7.2	2.5	7.2	7.2	2.5	7.2	7.2	2.5	7.2	7.2	2.5	7.2	7.2	2.5	7.2
	5%	9.6	2.9	9.6	7.2	2.8	11.2	5.7	2.5	9.6	5.3	2.3	7.2	5.7	2.2	5.7	7.2	2.3	5.3	9.6	2.5	5.7	11.2	2.8	7.2
	10%	14.6	3.4	14.6	7.2	3.1	25.6	4.8	2.5	14.6	4.2	2.2	7.2	4.8	2.0	4.8	7.2	2.2	4.2	14.6	2.5	4.8	25.6	3.1	7.2
	15%	30.3	4.1	30.3	7.2	3.5	—	4.1	2.6	30.3	3.5	2.0	7.2	4.1	1.9	4.1	7.2	2.0	3.5	30.3	2.6	4.1	—	3.5	7.2
	20%	—	5.2	—	7.2	4.0	—	3.6	2.6	—	2.9	1.9	7.2	3.6	1.7	3.6	7.2	1.9	2.9	—	2.6	3.6	—	4.0	7.2

e. 48° North Latitude

Orientation		N			NE			E			SE			S			SW			W			NW		
Time		AM	NOON	PM	AM	NOON	PM	AM	NOON	PM	AM	NOON	PM	AM	NOON	PM	AM	NOON	PM	AM	NOON	PM	AM	NOON	PM
Slope	0%	10.1	3.0	10.1	10.1	3.3	10.1	10.1	3.0	10.1	10.1	3.0	10.1	10.1	3.0	10.1	10.1	3.0	10.1	10.1	3.0	10.1	10.1	3.0	10.1
	5%	15.8	3.5	15.8	10.1	3.3	20.5	7.5	3.0	15.8	6.7	2.7	10.1	7.5	2.6	7.5	10.1	2.7	6.7	15.8	3.0	7.5	20.5	3.3	10.1
	10%	35.7	4.3	35.7	10.1	3.8	—	5.9	3.0	35.7	5.0	2.5	10.1	5.9	2.3	5.9	10.1	2.5	5.0	35.7	3.0	5.9	—	3.8	10.1
	15%	—	5.4	—	10.1	4.4	—	4.9	3.0	—	4.0	2.3	10.1	4.9	2.1	4.9	10.1	2.3	4.0	—	3.0	4.9	—	4.4	10.1
	20%	—	7.5	—	10.1	5.2	—	4.2	3.0	—	3.3	2.1	10.1	4.2	1.9	4.2	10.1	2.1	3.3	—	3.0	4.2	—	5.2	10.1

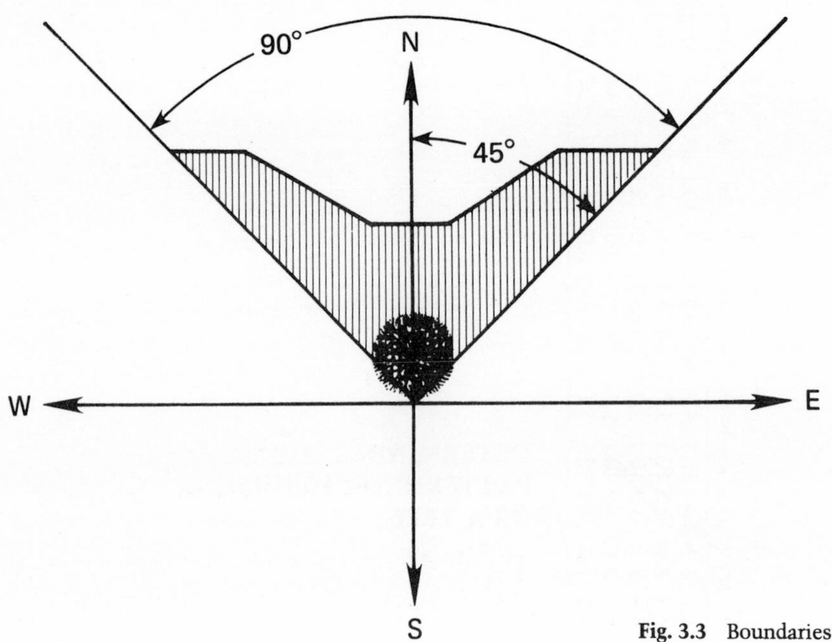

Fig. 3.3 Boundaries of the shadow pattern.

For most northern latitudes in mid-winter, significant shadows will be cast roughly between the hours of 9:00 AM and 3:00 PM. A shadow pattern represents every spot shaded by an object during these hours (the time period needed to form the right angle), although only a portion of the shadow pattern would actually be in shade at any given time. (Figure 3.3).

Shadow patterns can be constructed graphically by using shadow length tables (Tables 3.1a–e). Various shadow lengths for three times of day are laid out on paper and connected to form the final pattern. The example below shows how the shadow pattern of a pole is constructed. The pole is used because it is the simplest ground-anchored object that can cast a shadow. More complex objects such as trees or houses can be drawn by abstracting their forms into a series of poles and then drawing shadows for each pole.

Example: Constructing the Shadow Pattern of a Pole. Pole is 30 feet high. The pole is located at 40° north latitude. Pole is on land that slopes to the southeast at 10 percent grade.

Step 1: From the appropriate table (in this case Table 3.1c for 40° north latitude) find the shadow length values for AM, PM, and noon.

Read the intersection of the columns labeled "SE" and "10%".

Step 2: The values given in the table are for a one-foot pole, so they must be multiplied by the height of the pole—in this case 30 feet.

AM value	× pole height=	AM shadow length
3.2	30	96 feet
noon value	× pole height=	noon length
1.8	30	54 feet
PM value	× pole height=	PM length
4.8	30	144 feet

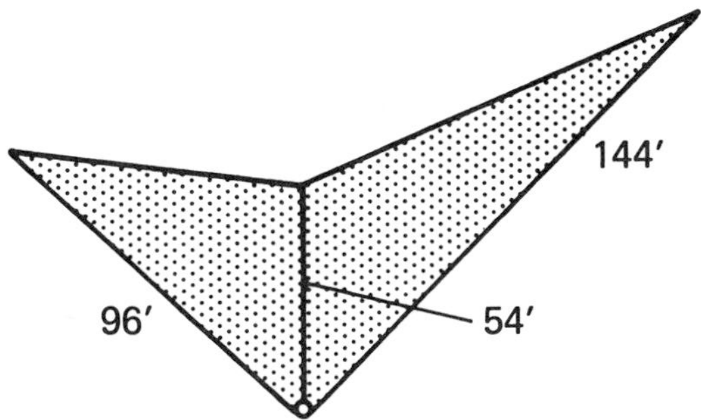

Figure 3.4

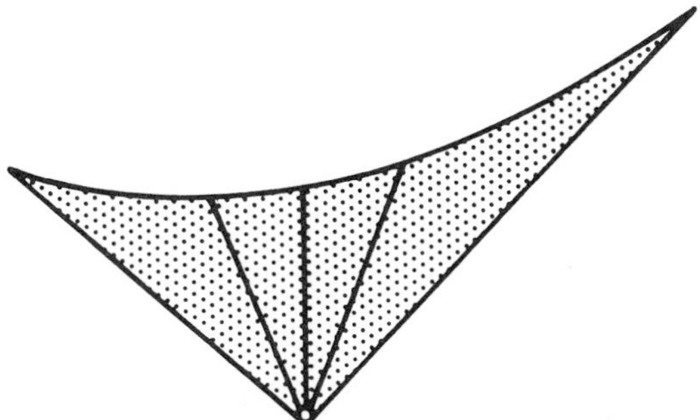

Figure 3.5

Step 3: Scale the shadow lengths out on paper as viewed from overhead and connect the end points (Fig. 3.4). The resulting figure approximates the complete shadow pattern. (The shadow pattern is not symmetrical because the pole is on sloping land.) If this figure were plotted with more points it would result in a curve opposite the right angle (Fig. 3.5). However, shadow patterns constructed with three shadow lengths are quite adequate for site planning purposes.

DETERMINING THE SHADOW PATTERN FOR A BUILDING OR A TREE

The shadow pattern for a building or a tree can be determined in much the same way used to determine the pattern for a single pole, by treating a building or tree as a number of poles (Fig. 3.6). Keep in mind that trees have depth, just like buildings. For maximum accuracy, therefore, additional poles should be located to the north of the tree crown

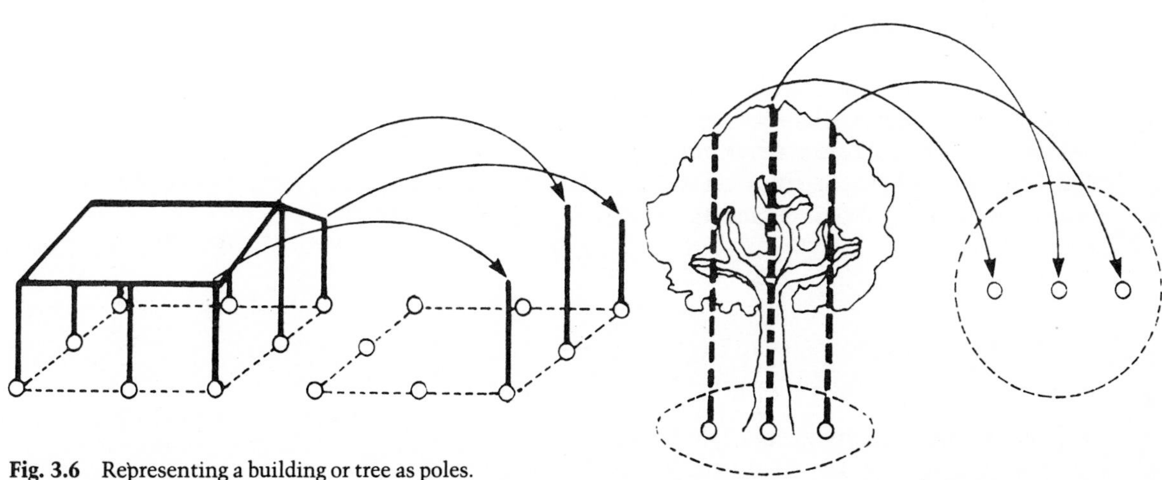

Fig. 3.6 Representing a building or tree as poles.

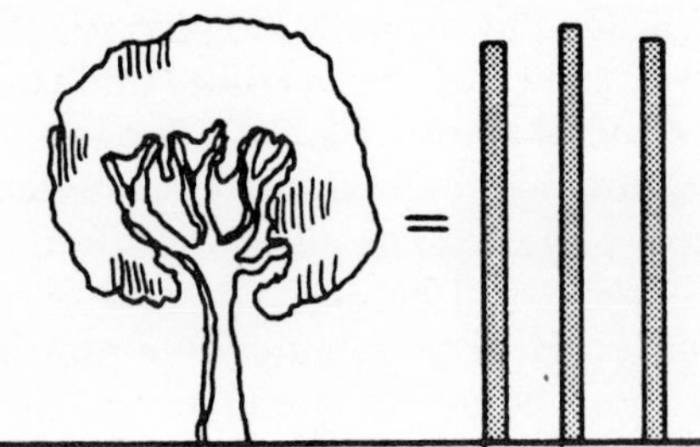

Fig. 3.7 Representing common tree shapes as poles.

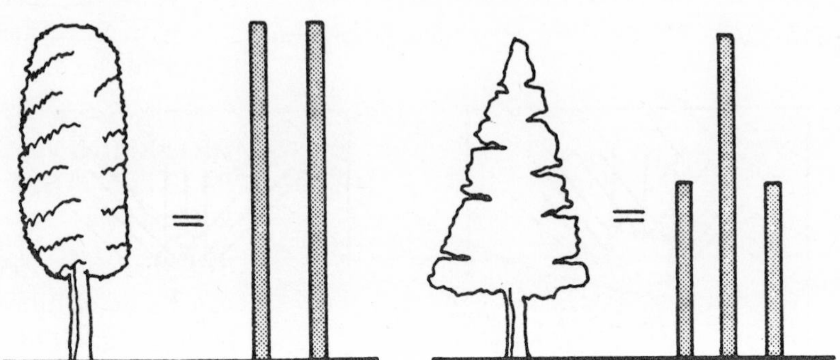

"centerline." Trees with various common shapes also can be represented by poles of varying heights (Fig. 3.7).

STEP-BY-STEP EXAMPLE OF SHADOW PATTERN CONSTRUCTION

When shadow lengths for each pole at the critical times of day are laid out, the composite yields the pattern for the building or tree. The following example shows how this is done for a building and tree simultaneously:

> Building is 9′ high at eaves and 12′ high at peak. (Fig. 3.8)
> Tree is 40′ high and 30′ wide. (Fig. 3.9)
> Latitude of location is 35° north.
> Land slopes to southwest at 15% grade.

Step 1: From the appropriate table, in this case Table 3.1b for 35° north latitude, find the shadow length values for AM,

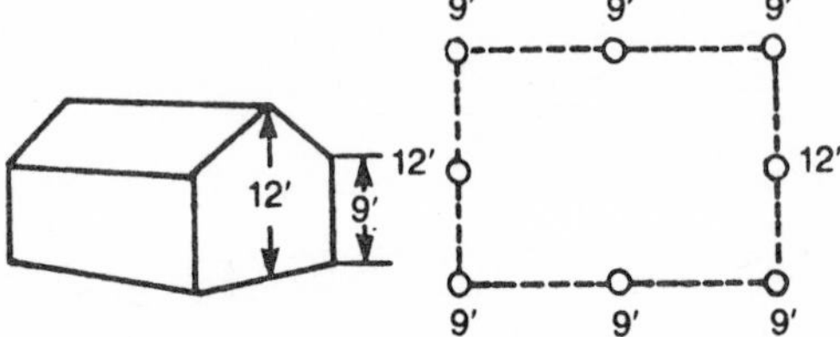

Figure 3.8

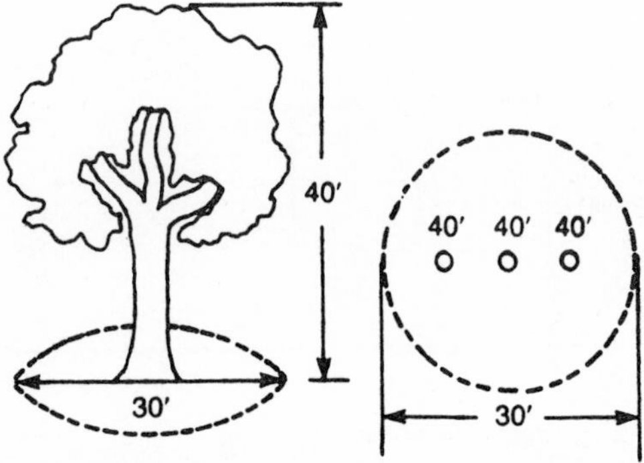

Figure 3.9

noon, and PM. They are:

AM = 2.3 noon = 1.4 PM = 3.5

Step 2: Multiply the ratios times the height of the poles used in the building and tree examples (Table 3.2).

Step 3: Scale the shadow lengths out on the overhead views of the building and tree (Figs. 3.10a and d). The boundaries of the pattern are 45° east and west of north. Finally, connect the end points of the shadow lines for the shadow pattern (Figs. 3.10c and f).

TABLE 3.2

	Height of Pole	Shadow Length AM	NOON	PM
Building	9′	21′	13′	32′
	12′	28′	17′	42′
Tree	40′	92′	56′	140′

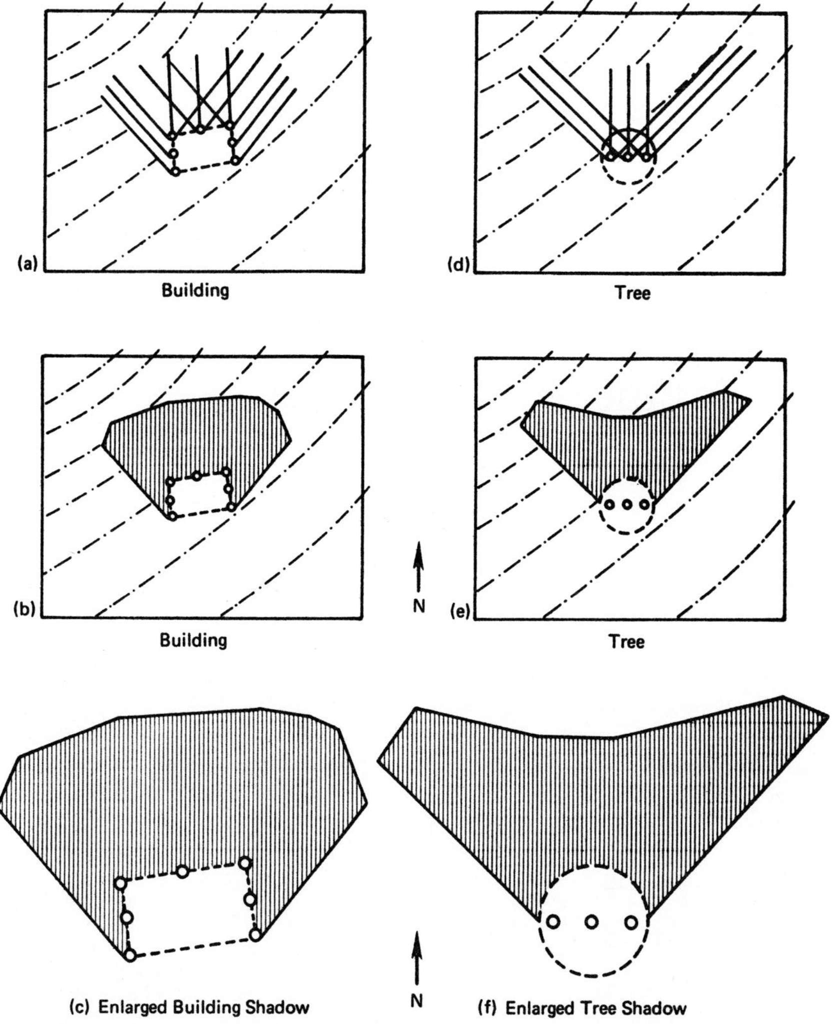

Fig. 3.10 Shadow pattern construction for a building and a tree.

SHADOW PATTERN TEMPLATES FOR DEVELOPMENT SITES WITH SPECIFIED HOUSE DESIGNS

Shadow patterns can be standardized for buildings and vegetation, provided that the terrain is relatively uniform and the buildings themselves are similar. Once the developer or site planner develops several shadow patterns to accomodate the anticipated structures in the development, templates of these patterns can be moved about the base map which was developed in preliminary site planning and a rough estimate of anticipated shading can be assessed. This procedure can be used where the terrain is uniform, and the building dimensions known (Figs. 3.11 to 3.15).

The procedure is different on sites where the slope changes radically. Instead of using shadow templates for the various building types, the site planner or developer must construct individual shadow patterns for each structure based on the terrain. Slope direction and gradient change the shadow lengths and shadow patterns. The shadow length tables must be consulted for each change in terrain and building dimensions (Tables 3.1a–e).

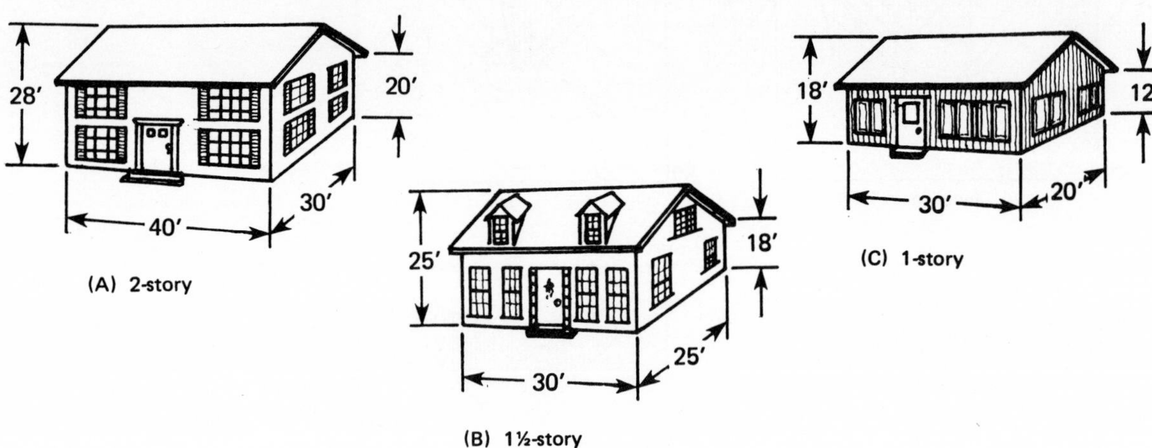

Fig. 3.11 Step one: Identify major building types and dimensions in the development.

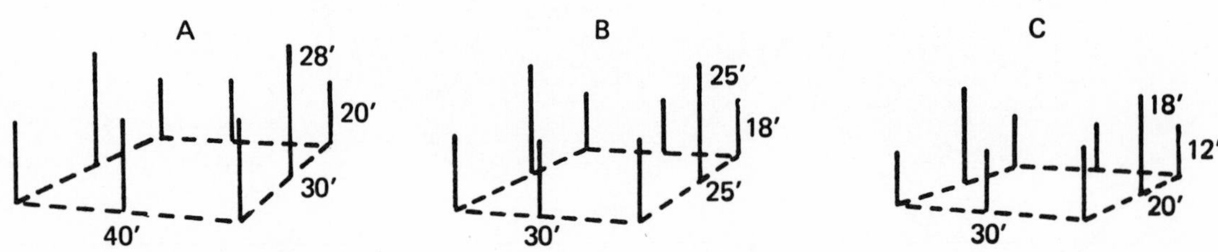

Fig. 3.12 Step two: Abstract the buildings into a number of poles.

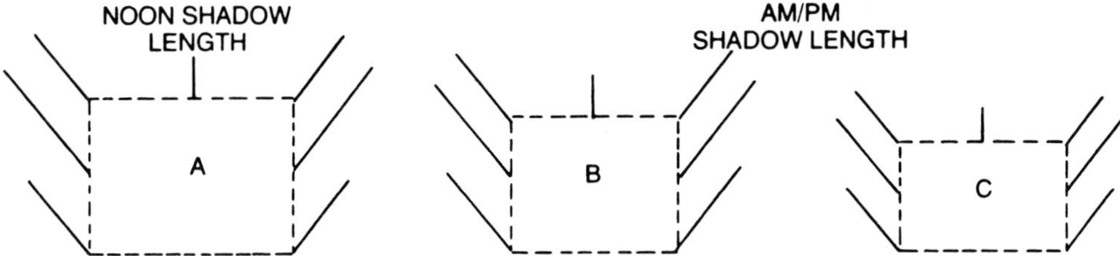

Fig. 3.13 Step three: Develop shadow lengths for each pole.

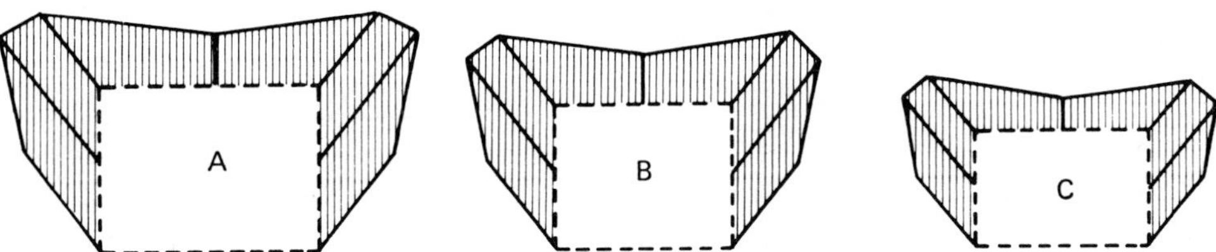

Fig. 3.14 Step four: Connect the shadow length lines from the poles to derive the shadow pattern of the building.

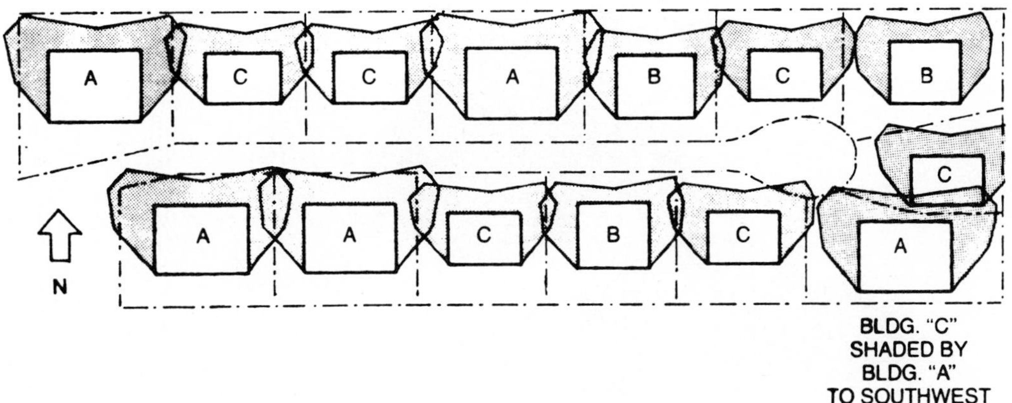

Fig. 3.15 Step five: Make a template of the building shadow patterns and arrange the shadow patterns on the site so that shading is minimized.

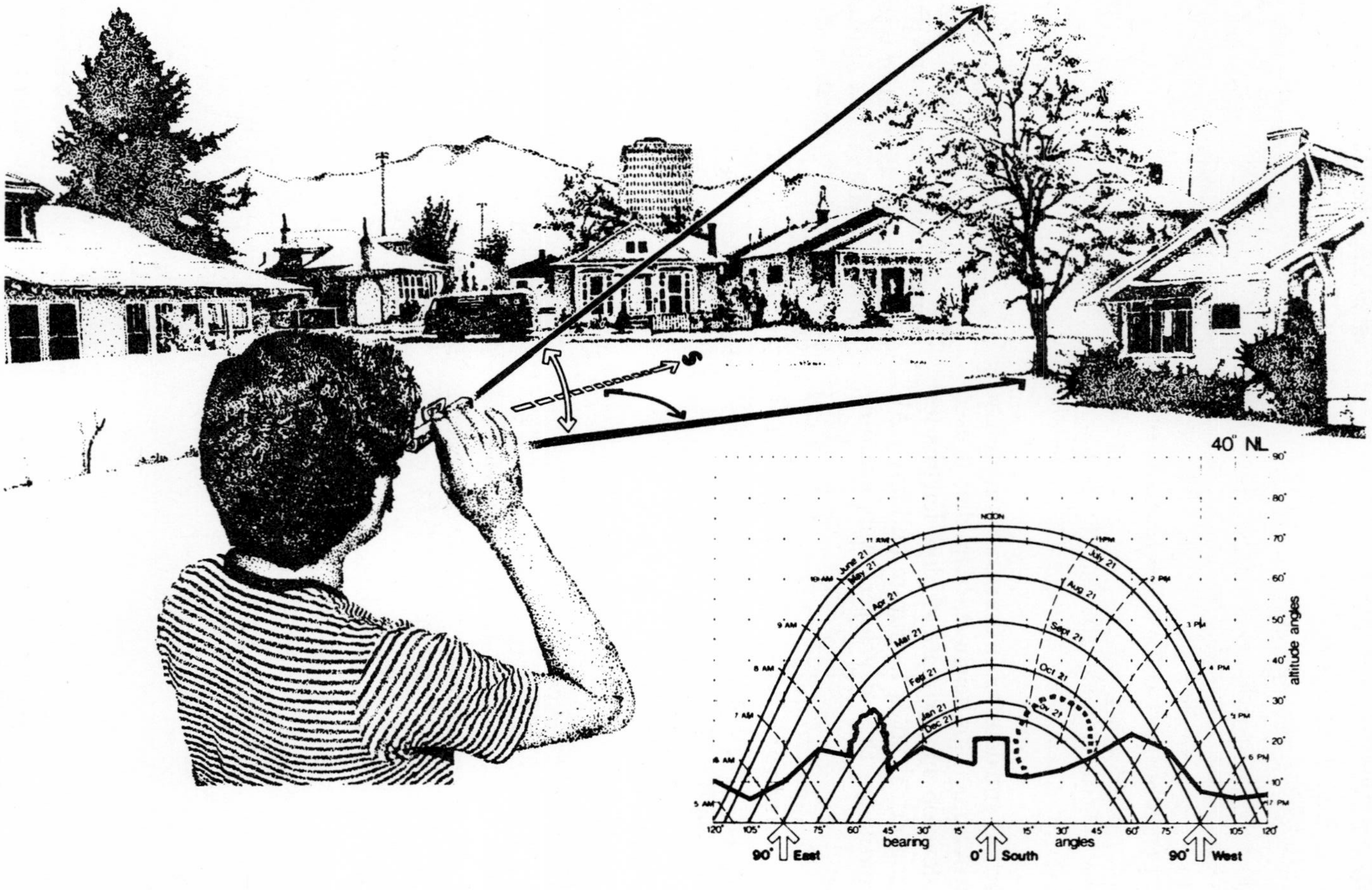

Fig. 3.16 Plotting the skyline.

SHADOW PATTTERN TEMPLATES FOR DEVELOPMENT SITES WITHOUT SPECIFIED HOUSE DESIGNS

A similar approach can be used when the developer does not intend to build the project but merely intends to subdivide and improve the land for others to develop. In this case, the developer or site planner first approximates the dimensions and locations of the buildings on the lots. The easiest way to do this is to examine the zoning ordinance and other regulations and determine the maximum height restrictions. This height standard then is used to develop approximate shadow lengths for hypothetical poles for future buildings. Alternatively the developer can examine nearby completed developments whose buyers represent the target group for marketing. The site planner or developer, assuming that similar buildings of similar dimensions will be built in his or her subdivision, can base shadow pattern templates on these existing structures.

OTHER METHODS

Several additional methods for assessing existing shading and determining shadow lengths are available. To determine the extent of shading on a given site, the "skyline" of hills, trees, and houses can be plotted using a transit or compass, a hand level and a copy of the sun chart for the site. Find true south with the transit or compass, determine the altitude of objects on the skyline 120° to the east and west of south in 15° azimuth increments, plot the points on the sun chart and connect them with a line. The open areas above the line on the sun chart are the times when the sunlight will reach those points on the site. See Mazria's *The Passive Solar Energy Book* for more information on this method (Fig. 3.16).

To quickly determine the winter shadow length (not the whole pattern) for an object true south of a home, you can use the angle of the sun's altitude at noon on December 21 to draw a line in section from the peak of the home's roof to the ground (Fig. 3.17). For an object within 45° east or west of south, use the 9:00 AM/3:00 PM altitude angle. Table 3.4 lists hourly altitude and azimuth angles for December 21 for six north latitudes. Percentages of available radiation are also indicated to give an idea of how much energy a south facing wall will lose if shaded during a certain hour of the day.

MICROCLIMATE

In addition to evaluating solar availability and shading, the developer should also consider the site's microclimate characteristics, important determinants of the amount of energy that will be needed to heat and cool a building on a site. In warm, humid climates, hill tops, ridge lines, the shores of

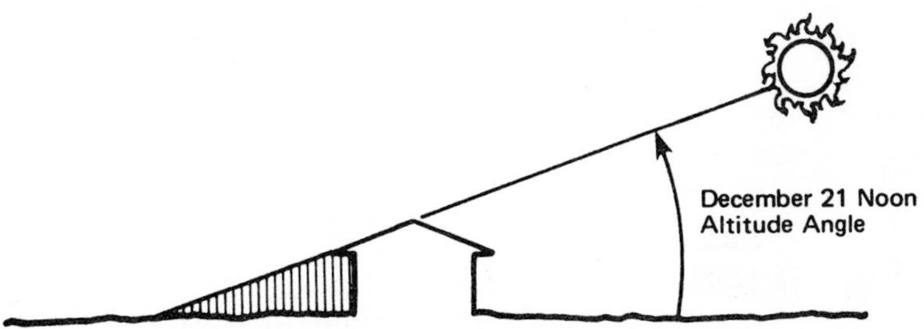

Fig. 3.17 Noon shadow length on the winter solstice.

TABLE 3.3 Table of Hourly Altitude, Azimuth, and Percent of Available Radiation on December 21

North Latitude		8 am	9 am	10 am	11 am	12	1 pm	2 pm	3 pm	4 pm
24°	Alt	14.3°	28.8°	33.5°	39.4°	41.6°	39.4°	33.5°	24.8°	14.3°
	Az	55.1°	45.6°	33.4°	17.9°	0.0°	17.9°	33.4°	45.6°	55.1°
	%Rad	8.7	11.0	11.9	12.3	12.4	12.3	11.9	11.0	8.7
30°	Alt	11.4°	21.3°	29.3°	34.6°	36.6°	34.6°	29.3°	21.3°	11.4°
	Az	54.2°	44.1°	31.7°	16.8°	0.0°	16.8°	31.7°	44.1°	54.2°
	%Rad	7.9	11.0	12.1	12.6	12.8	12.6	12.1	11.0	7.9
35°	Alt	8.5°	17.7°	25.0°	29.9°	31.6°	29.9°	25.0°	17.7°	8.5°
	Az	53.5°	42.9°	30.4°	15.9°	0.0°	15.9°	30.4°	42.9°	53.5°
	%Rad	6.7	11.0	12.5	13.2	13.3	13.2	12.5	11.0	6.7
40°	Alt	5.5°	14.0°	20.7°	25.0°	26.6°	25.0°	20.7°	14.0°	5.5°
	Az	53.0°	42.0°	29.4°	15.2°	0.0°	15.2°	29.4°	42.0°	53.0°
	%Rad	4.5	11.0	13.2	14.1	14.4	14.1	13.2	11.0	4.5
45°	Alt	2.5°	10.2°	16.3°	20.2°	21.6°	20.2°	16.3°	10.2°	2.5°
	Az	52.7°	41.2°	28.5°	14.7°	0.0°	14.7°	28.5°	41.2°	52.7°
	%Rad	1.0	10.7	14.4	15.8	16.2	15.8	14.4	10.7	1.0
48°	Alt	0.6°	8.0°	13.7°	17.3°	18.6°	17.3°	13.7°	8.0°	0.6°
	Az	52.6°	40.9°	28.2°	14.4°	0.0°	14.4°	28.2°	20.9°	52.6°
	%Rad	0.0	9.7	14.8	16.8	17.3	16.8	14.8	9.7	0.0

Notes: On azimuth designations: 0° = due south, up to 90° from 8 am to 11 am are to the east; and up to 90° from 1 pm to 4 pm are to the west.

The percent radiation value is the portion of daily solar radiation falling in the hour-long time period one-half hour before and after the time given on the table. For example, for the 2:00 column, it is the percent radiation falling from 1:30 until 2:30.

lakes and water bodies and other open locations are preferred building sites because of their ventilative potential.

Wind flow can be affected by strategically located trees, which can block cold winter winds and hot dusty summer winds. Trees also provide shade for homes and paved areas, and can channel cooling breezes to places where they are needed . Large bodies of water have a moderating effect on the microclimate of a site as they produce cooling breezes in summer. Water bodies, both small and large, moderate the microclimates of adjacent land; their cooling effect is attributable to the addition of moisture caused by evaporation of air moving across them. The higher vapor pressure over the body of water enhances air movement toward the adjacent land mass. Olgyay cites the effect of the Great Lakes on their adjacent region, "The average July temperature is decreased by about 3°F and the average January temperature is raised by about 5°F." Mountains and hills also can act as windbreaks.

SITE EVALUATION MAPPING

Site evaluation and preliminary land planning usually proceed simultaneously on a base map (either aerial or topographical). The following checklist outlines one process for analyzing the solar access and energy conserving features of a site (Fig. 3.18).

On the base map:

A. *Map topographic and major site features.*

- Indicate slopes and flat areas.

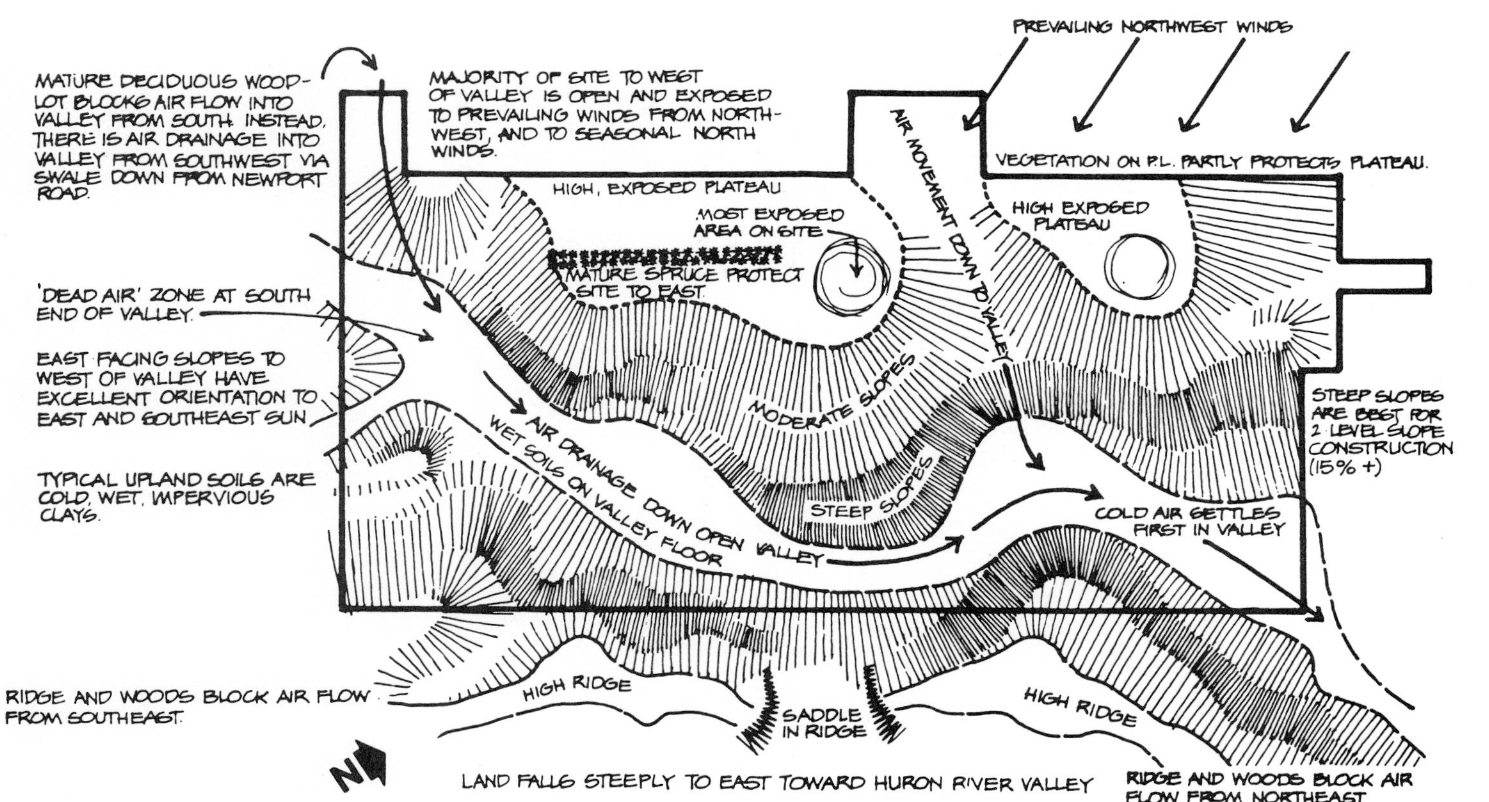
PREVAILING NORTHWEST WINDS
MATURE DECIDUOUS WOOD-LOT BLOCKS AIR FLOW INTO VALLEY FROM SOUTH. INSTEAD, THERE IS AIR DRAINAGE INTO VALLEY FROM SOUTHWEST VIA SWALE DOWN FROM NEWPORT ROAD.
MAJORITY OF SITE TO WEST OF VALLEY IS OPEN AND EXPOSED TO PREVAILING WINDS FROM NORTH-WEST, AND TO SEASONAL NORTH WINDS.
AIR MOVEMENT DOWN TO VALLEY
VEGETATION ON P.L. PARTLY PROTECTS PLATEAU.
HIGH, EXPOSED PLATEAU
MOST EXPOSED AREA ON SITE
MATURE SPRUCE PROTECT SITE TO EAST
HIGH EXPOSED PLATEAU
'DEAD AIR' ZONE AT SOUTH END OF VALLEY.
EAST FACING SLOPES TO WEST OF VALLEY HAVE EXCELLENT ORIENTATION TO EAST AND SOUTHEAST SUN
MODERATE SLOPES
STEEP SLOPES ARE BEST FOR 2 LEVEL SLOPE CONSTRUCTION (15% +)
TYPICAL UPLAND SOILS ARE COLD, WET, IMPERVIOUS CLAYS.
AIR DRAINAGE DOWN OPEN VALLEY
WET SOILS ON VALLEY FLOOR
STEEP SLOPES
COLD AIR SETTLES FIRST IN VALLEY
RIDGE AND WOODS BLOCK AIR FLOW FROM SOUTHEAST.
HIGH RIDGE
SADDLE IN RIDGE
HIGH RIDGE
N
LAND FALLS STEEPLY TO EAST TOWARD HURON RIVER VALLEY
RIDGE AND WOODS BLOCK AIR FLOW FROM NORTHEAST

Fig. 3.18 Site evaluation map.

- Mark site elevations and contours.
- Mark all significant natural features, such as water courses or historic sites.

B. *Map all potential solar access obstructions.*

- Indicate individual trees, noting species, height, and whether coniferous (evergreen) or deciduous.
- Indicate all tall objects on the site or on adjoining property that can cast shadows on the site; estimate location and height.
- Indicate all north slopes or other areas with poor solar access, such as fog pockets.
- Sketch shadow patterns of potential obstructions on the plan.

C. *Map all energy-conserving factors of the site.*

- Indicate seasonal wind directions and features which can influence wind flows.
- Mark all possible frost or fog pockets.
- Note bodies of water.
- Indicate ground surfaces such as bare soil, pavement and grass. Note reflective surfaces such as sand, water and concrete.

D. *Discuss the terrain and site limitations* with neighbors and other people familiar with the area.

E. *Obtain local weather data.*

The site map will now have both good development potential and good solar access characteristics marked on it. This buildable area should be analyzed and housing allocations derived for the site.

At this point preliminary site planning is finished. Housing and land uses can be allocated broadly on the site according to environmental constraints and solar access requirements. The next step is to examine specific strategies for developing the site according to the development objectives and the site plan, so that solar access is maintained in those areas with good solar energy potential.

CHAPTER FOUR

Planning Guidelines

This chapter offers a number of solar access design strategies for common aspects of site planning. In some cases, the choice of strategy may be confined by local regulations or the peculiar characteristics of the site to a few alternatives, whereas other development situations may permit several alternatives to be considered concurrently. Strategies to conserve energy and achieve solar access include proper orientation of streets, lots and homes; lot design and building siting techniques; and landscape design techniques for winter and summer.

CLIMATE REGIONS

Specific planning guidelines vary depending on site location and climate. Four broad regional climate zones for the continental United States illustrate recommendations in this book (Fig. 4.1):

- Climate Region A is characterized by cold to severe winters (greater than 5000 heating degree-days) and relatively mild to hot summers (less than 900 cooling hours).
- Climate Region B is characterized by relatively mild to cold winter temperatures (between 3000 and 5000 heating degree-days) and a hot summer (between 900 and 1300 cooling hours).
- Climate Region C is characterized by relatively mild winter temperatures (less than 3000 heating degree-days) and long, very hot summers (greater than 1300 cooling hours).
- Climate Region D is characterized by conditions that have not been studied in preparing this book. To obtain the latest design information for these areas, contact either the Florida Solar Energy Center for the eastern section of the United States or the California Energy Commission for the western section. (See Chapter 10 for information on the derivation of these climate regions.)

ORIENTATION

Proper orientation of streets, lots and homes is the single most important design strategy in energy-conserving solar access planning. Proper home orientation controls heat loss and gain, allowing the maximum amount of solar radiation to be received during the heating season and the minimum during the cooling season (Figs. 4.2a and b). As discussed in Chapter 2, a south facing surface receives two

two to three times more radiation in winter than in summer and the summer heat gain is easily controlled. Therefore, proper orientation for a home is achieved when it is sited with the longest wall facing south. A home sited in this way usually requires a lot oriented towards south.

Lot orientation usually depends on street orientation. However, most regulations require the exterior walls of a home to be parallel to the lot lines and the lot lines to be perpendicular or radial to the street, so the orientation of a home generally must follow the orientation of the street on which it is built. Therefore, street orientation is likely to be the critical factor in siting homes to meet suggested orientation guidelines. Proper solar orientation for homes is much easier to achieve along streets aligned in an east/west direction because all lots either face or back-up to south (Fig. 4.3). Topography and other factors often will predetermine street orientation, but try to lay out the majority of streets to run as close to true east/west as possible.

The preferred orientation for streets is true east/west. When this is not possible, the following ranges of degrees north and south

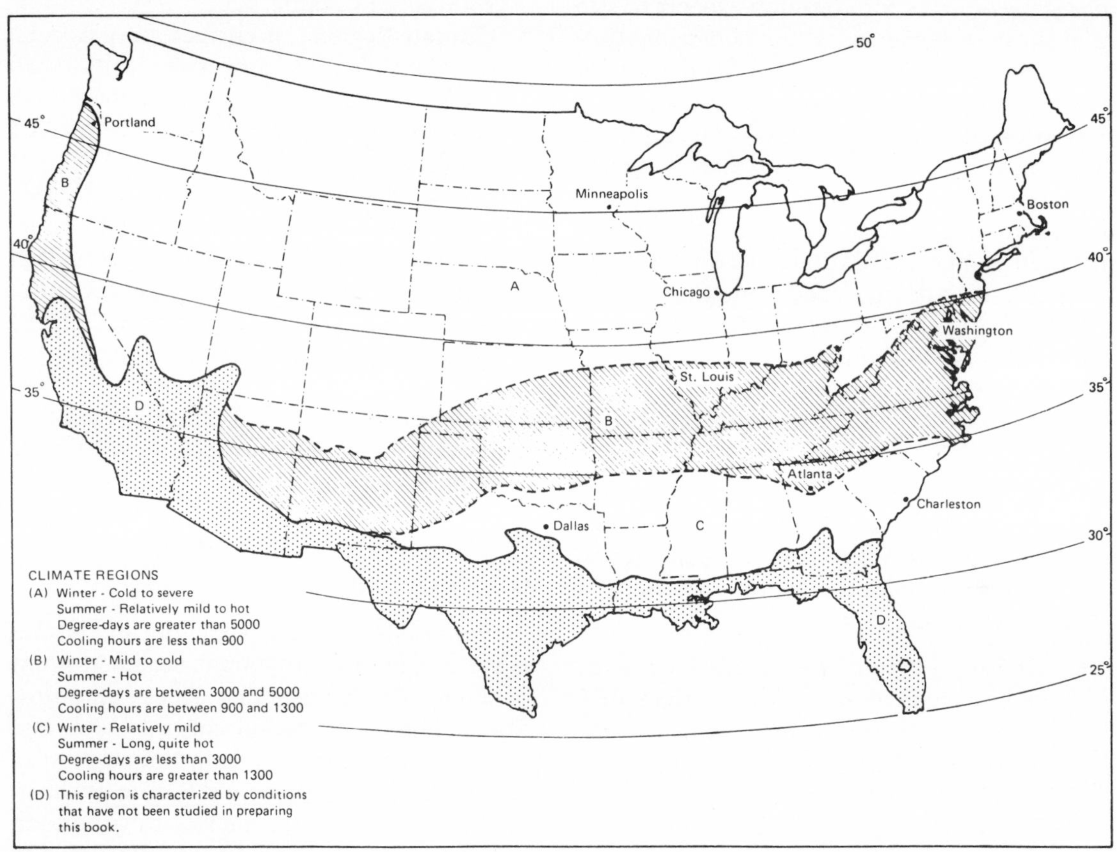

Fig. 4.1 Climate regions.

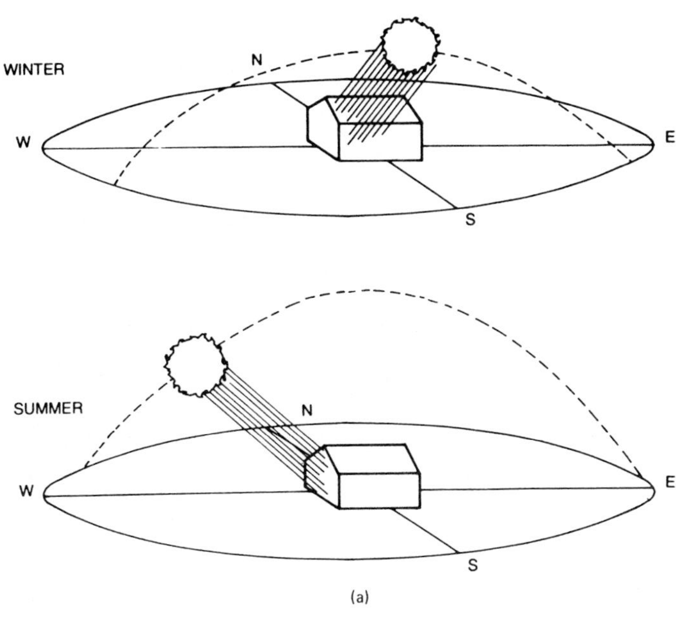

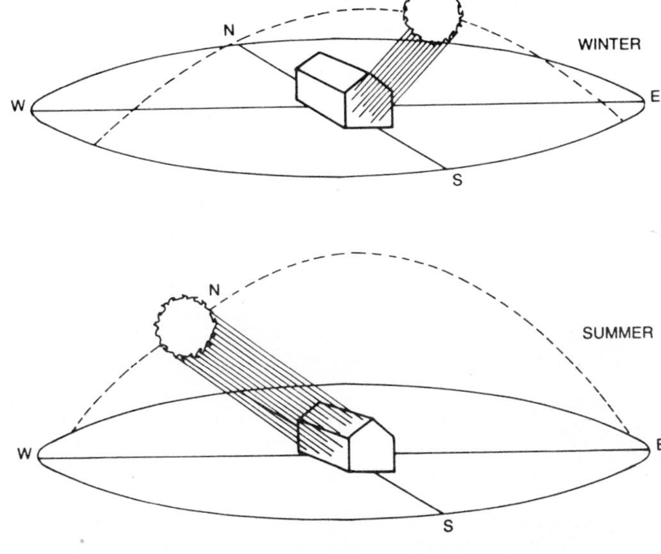

Fig. 4.2 (a) Proper orientation on east/west axis—good winter access for heating and small area of building vulnerable to summer overheating versus (b) orientation on north/south axis—poor winter heat gain and large area of building vulnerable to overheating.

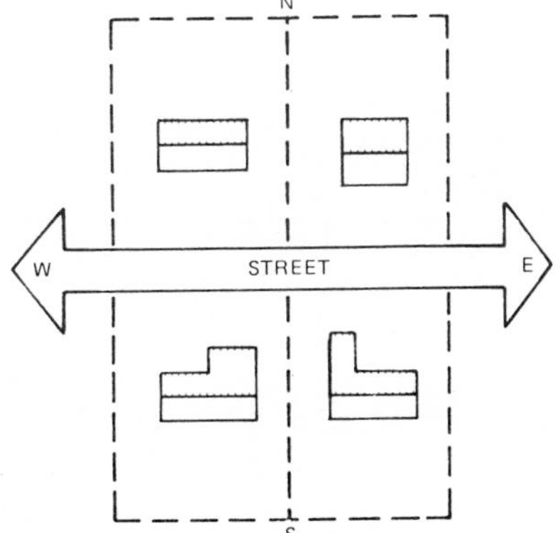

Fig.4.3 Orientation on east/west streets.

of east/west are recommended:

> In Climate Region A locations, lay out streets to run within 25° of east/west (Fig. 4.4a).
> In Climate Region B locations, lay out streets to run within 20° of east/west (Fig. 4.4b).
> In Climate Region C locations, lay out streets to run within 10° of east/west (Fig. 4.4c).

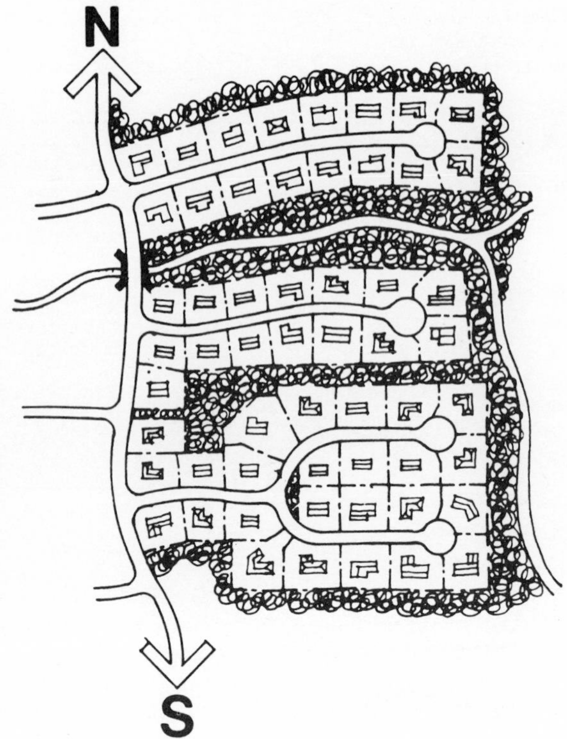

These guidelines can be even more flexible in situations where land use regulations do not require lot lines and buildings to follow the alignment of the street. (See Chapter 5, Land Use Regulations.)

The need for proper site orientation does not mean all the homes in a passive solar community must be placed side-by-side in south facing rows along straight east/west streets. Patterns of gently curvilinear streets and cul-de-sacs can provide just as easily for solar access. (See Chapter 6, Case Studies, for

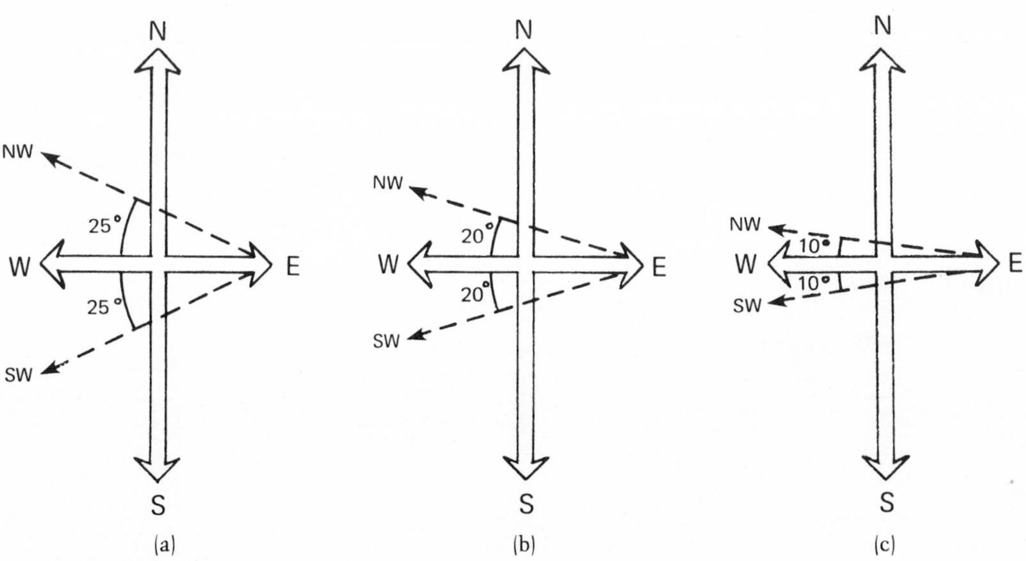

Fig. 4.4 (a) Street orientation guidelines for Climate Region A. (b) Street orientation guidelines for Climate Region B. (c) Street orientation guidelines for Climate Region C.

Fig. 4.5 East/west cul-de-sacs tied into north/south collector streets.

examples of predominantly east/west street patterns.) One of the most practical street patterns for providing solar access short east/west cul-de-sacs tied into long consists of north/south collector streets (Fig. 4.5). Figures 4.6 and 4.7 illustrate a subdivision which uses this street pattern (Village Homes in Davis, California). Note the network of pedestrian/bicycle paths running north/ south and the way in which garages and parking areas on the south side of the cul-de-sacs have been handled.

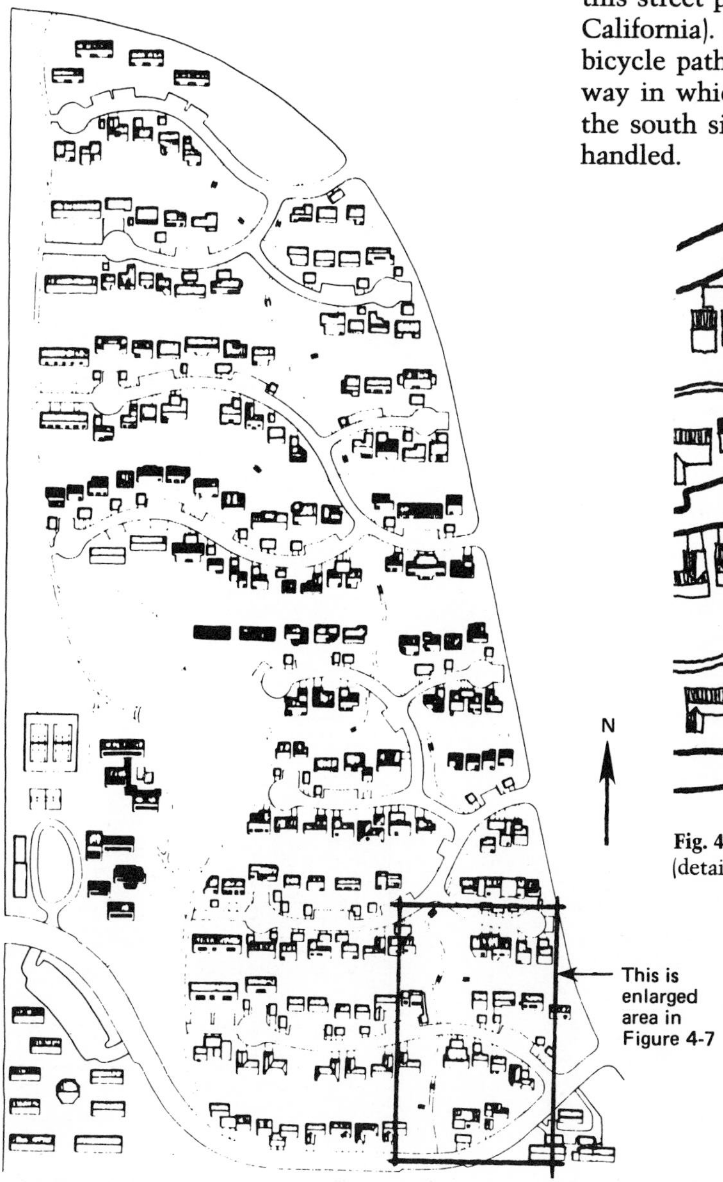

N

This is enlarged area in Figure 4-7

Figure 4.6

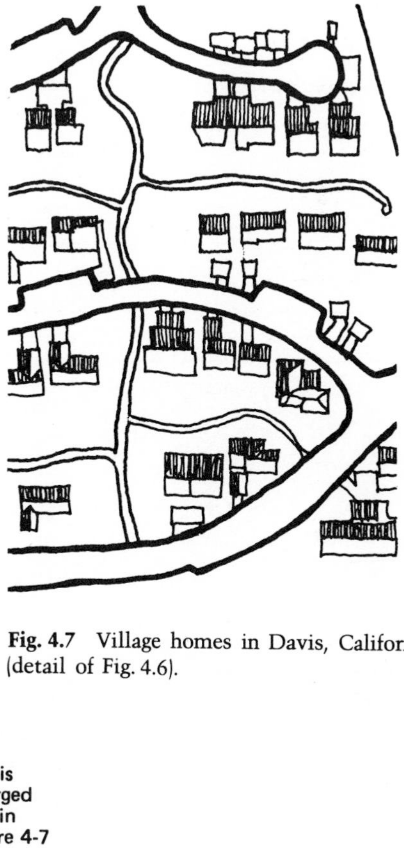

Fig. 4.7 Village homes in Davis, California (detail of Fig. 4.6).

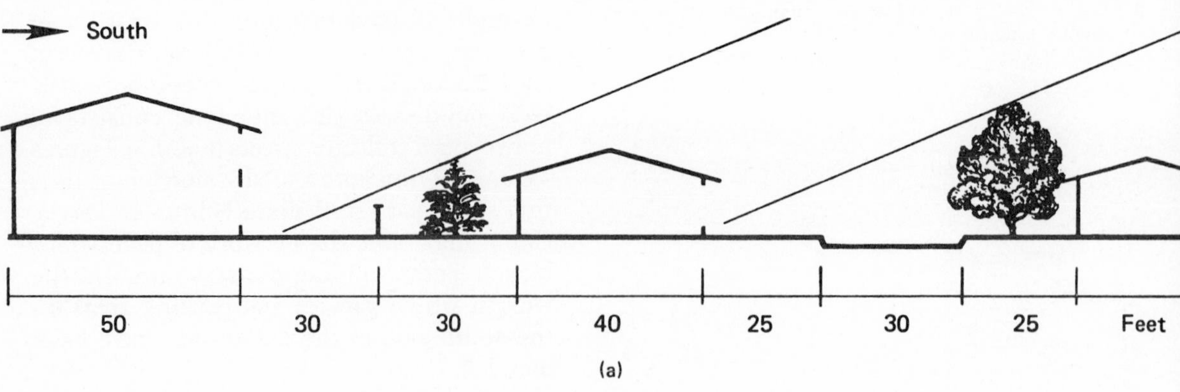

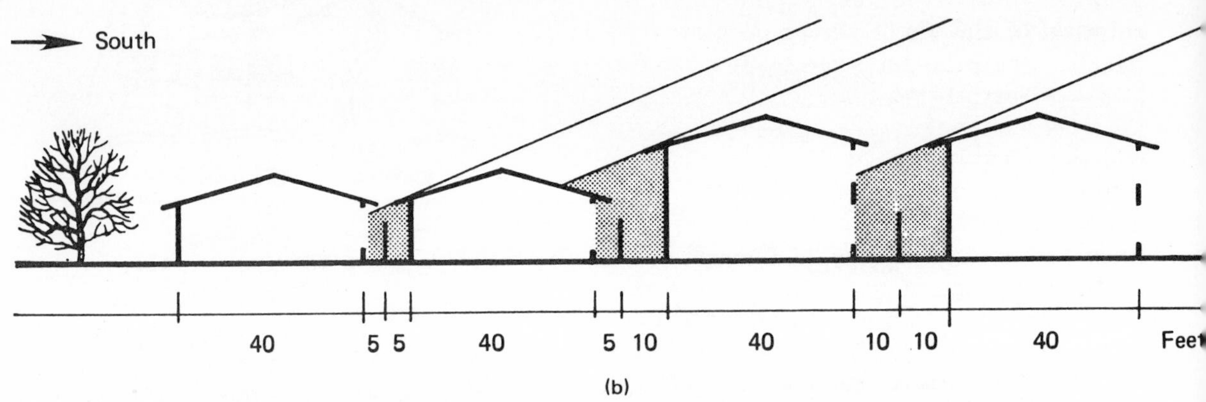

Fig. 4.8 (a) Front and backyard setbacks on east/west streets are usually adequate for solar access. (b) Sideyard setbacks on north/south streets are usually not adequate for solar access.

North/south streets are less desirable from a solar access standpoint because the sideyard setbacks required along them usually are not adequate to prevent homes from shading each other's south facing walls (Fig. 4.8). In most cases where streets run north/south because of topography, views or other economic or site design conditions, proper solar orientation still can be provided by taking any of the following steps:

1. *Create short east/west cul-de-sacs* that tie into north/south collector streets as frequently as possible.

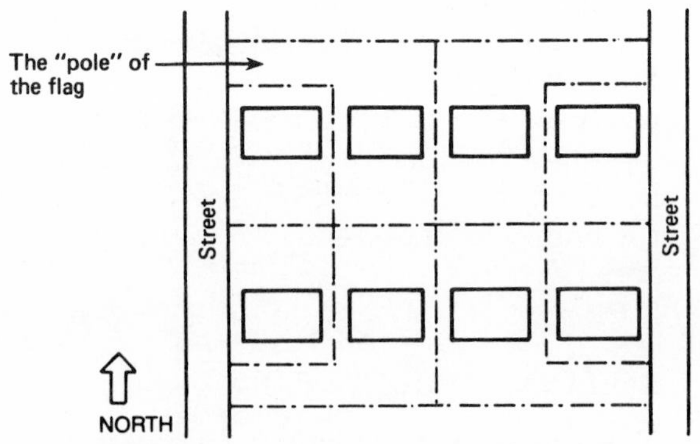

Fig. 4.9 Using flag lots for proper orientation on north/south streets.

2. *Create lots wide enough for sideyard solar access* (modifying house type from a rectangle to an L-shape and reducing height would minimize lot width increases).

3. *Use flag lots* when streets are spaced so far apart that four lots can be run in an east/west direction, with the "pole" of the flag connecting the inner lots to the street (Fig. 4.9).

LOT ORIENTATION

Ideally, lot orientation should be determined by orientation to the sun and not by the orientation of the street except on east/west streets, where proper solar orientation for lots is easy to achieve. When it is not possible for streets to run east/west, lots still can be laid out for proper solar home orientation. Where regulations permit lot lines which are not perpendicular to the street, lay out the lot lines to conform to the following recommended orientation guidelines for each climate region, regardless of street orientation.

In all locations, the preferred orientation for the long axis of a lot is true north/south. When this is not possible, lots should conform to the building orientation guidelines which follow. If streets run from northwest to southeast, for example, lot lines can be laid out at oblique angles to the street (Fig. 4.10). The diagram shows the long axis of the lots running north and south, making it relatively easy to site the homes for proper solar orientation. (Note: Angle A in Fig. 4.10 must be 45° or greater to prevent the south walls of the homes from being shaded by their neighbors.)

BUILDING ORIENTATION

The orientation guidelines for streets and lots set the stage for the most critical step in passive solar design: building orientation.

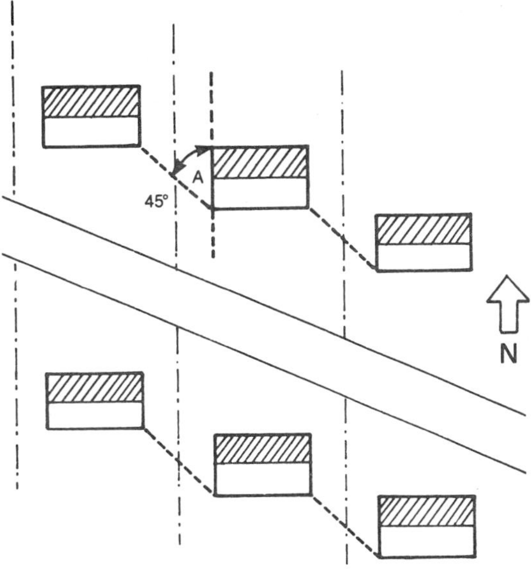

Fig. 4.10 Lot orientation on diagonal streets. Maintaining south orientation of housing where streets are shifted from the east/west axis. Angle A is formed by the intersection of north/south with a line connecting the southwest corner of one house to the southeast corner of its western neighbor.

Orientation alone can produce significant energy savings for even a moderately well-insulated home in any United States climate, according to a Lawrence Berkeley Laboratory computer study of a reference home (see Appendix II). True south is the preferred orientation for homes in all climate regions. As orientation varies toward east or west of south, the amount of solar radiation received on south facing surfaces decreases in winter and the amount of radiation received on east and west surfaces increases in summer. Thus, as orientation deviates from true south, less sun is available to offset heating costs in winter and more sun is available to increase cooling costs in summer.

For warmer climates, where cooling loads are higher and annual energy consumption becomes increasingly sensitive to building

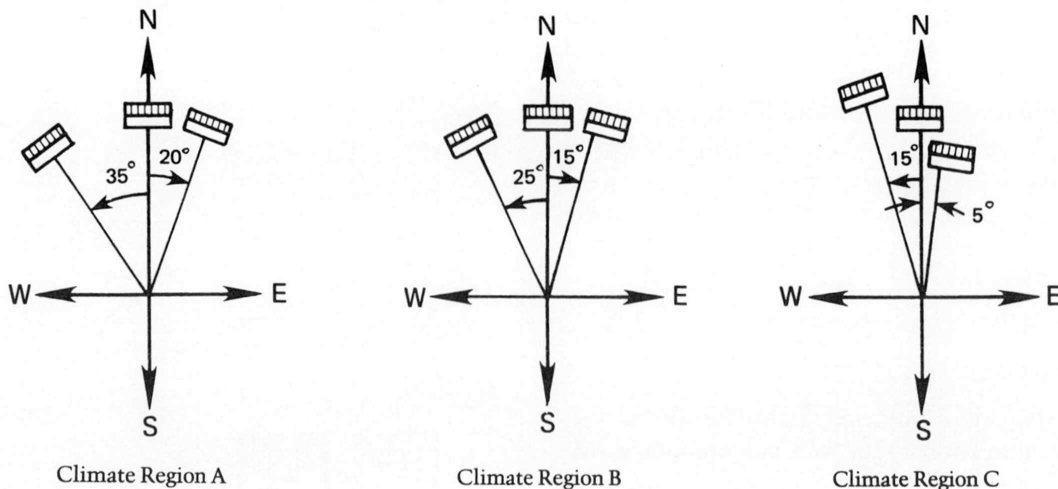

Fig. 4.11 Building orientation guidelines.

orientations off true south, the orientation recommendations are narrowed with respect to true south. An east-of-south variation is always preferable to one west of south, because morning air and home temperatures generally are cooler than afternoon temperatures. Thus, solar radiation received from the east can be accommodated more easily without causing overheating. In colder climates where summer cooling is not as great a concern, the orientation recommendations off true south are more liberal, though still with a preference for east over west variations. Whereas true south is the preferred orientation for the long wall of a home, variations on the order of 20° from true south, depending on climate region, are possible without significant energy consumption penalties.

Figure 4.11 illustrates a rule-of-thumb for proper solar orientation in each climate region. For the purposes of this study, proper solar orientation is defined as the placement of a home on a site within a given range of degrees east or west of true south.

True south is the ideal orientation for the long wall of a home for the lowest annual energy consumption. Orientation up to 35° east of south or 20° west of south are acceptable for homes in Climate Region A, as are variations up to 25° east of south or 15° west of south in Climate Region B, and up to 15° east of south and 5° west of south in Climate Region C. (See Chapter 10 for a detailed discussion of orientation and annual energy consumption.)

LOT DESIGN AND BUILDING SITING TECHNIQUES

In addition to proper orientation, topography, lot shape, setback requirements and building siting are key determinants of solar access.

Topography

In site development, topography affects the location of streets, buildings and utilities. As discussed in Chapter 3, the slope and orientation of the land largely determine the amount of solar radiation received on a site. Since south slopes receive the greatest amount of sunlight in the winter and shadow lengths are

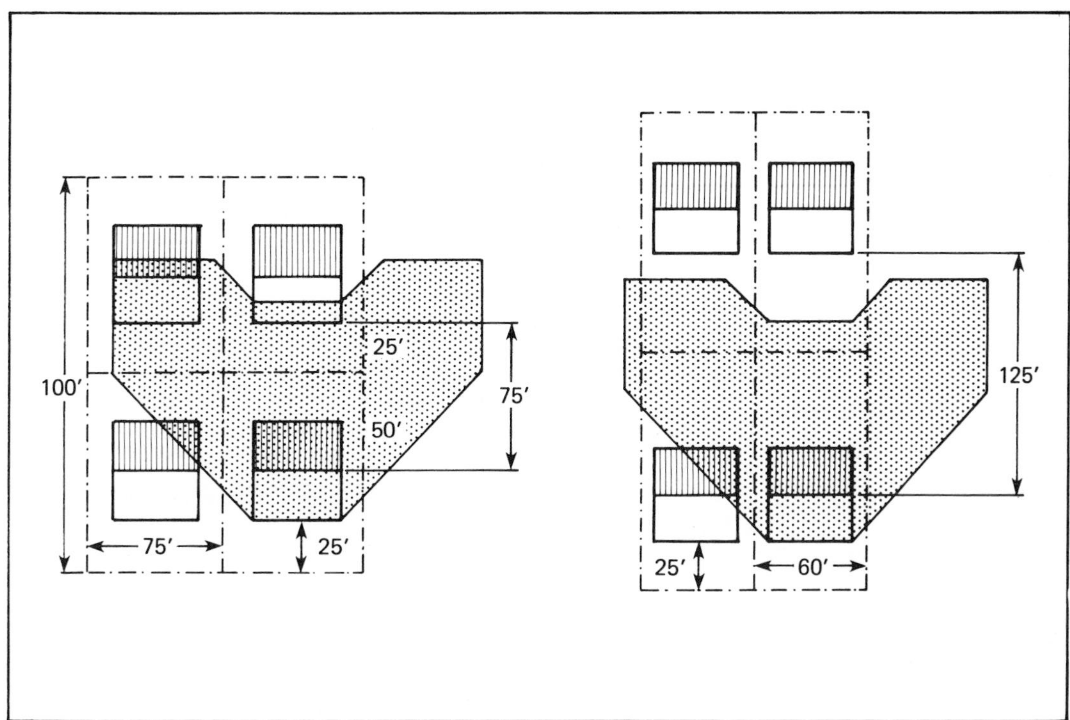

Fig. 4.12 By reducing frontage from 75 feet to 60 feet, plan can accommodate 112 foot north shadow projection cast by 28 foot-high buildings.

shorter, dense development should be concentrated there. Southeast and southwest facing slopes and flat land are the next most preferable topographic conditions for dense developments. Shaded areas should be used for open space, recreational purposes, streets and storage areas.

Lot Shape

Regardless of street orientation, the most appropriate lot shape for solar access is one elongated in the north/south direction. The ideal is to develop lots with adequate space between buildings from north to south to avoid south lot buildings from shading north lot buildings, thus ensuring better solar access.

On an east/west street, a long lot with narrow street frontage provides better solar access than a square-shaped lot of the same area. The greater distance north to south of the elongated lot can accommodate longer north shadows, and thus minimize shading from adjacent structures (Fig. 4.12).

A reduced street frontage approach to planning also can result in a development plan having more lots per street and thus a higher density. This can reduce land, street and utility costs and result in more affordable energy efficient homes for buyers.

On a north/south street, a lot elongated in the north/south direction would be short and wide with a large street frontage. Fewer lots of this shape would fit on a street, so the cost per lot would increase. An alternative for north/south streets would be the use of flag

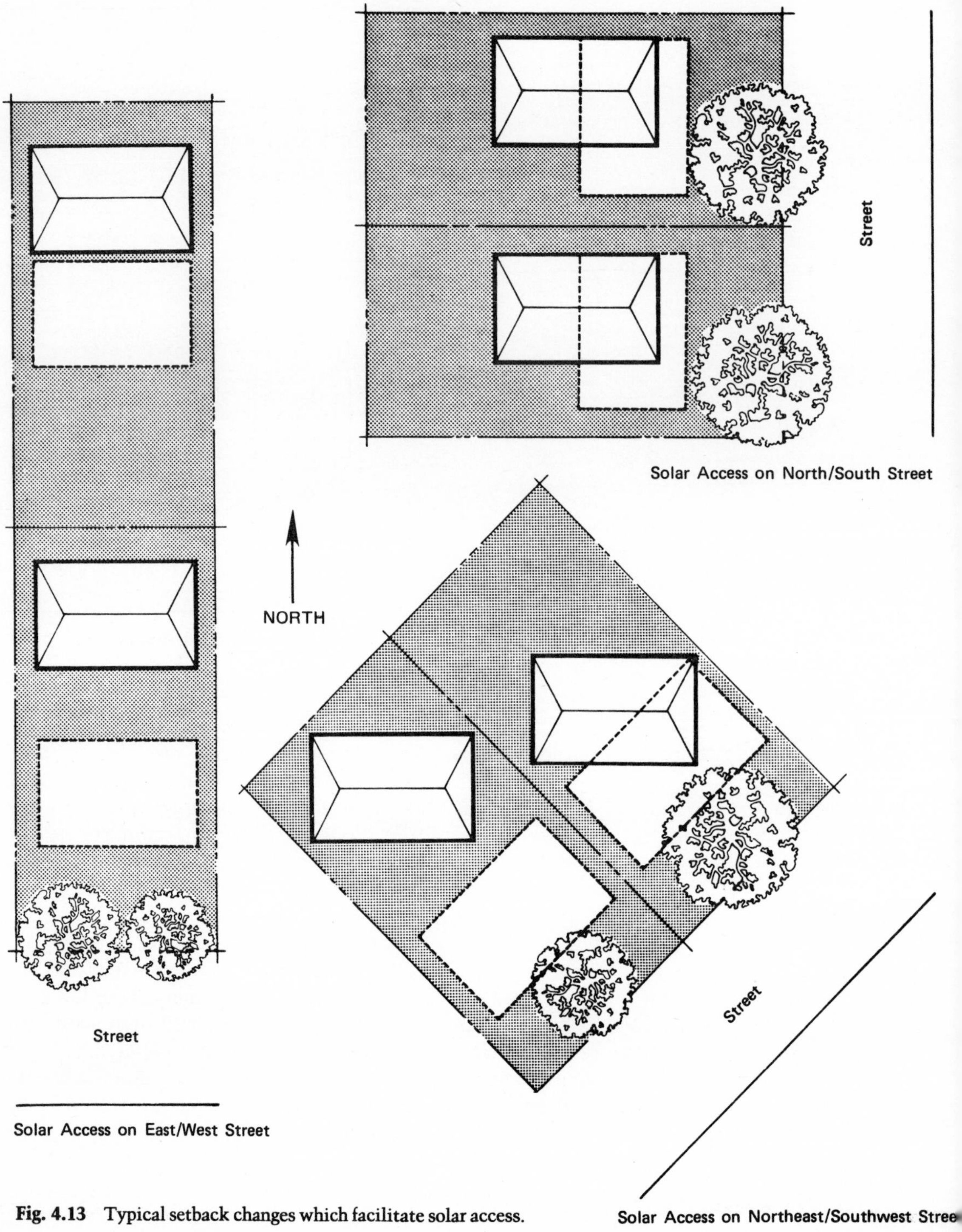

Street

Solar Access on North/South Street

NORTH

Street

Solar Access on East/West Street

Street

Fig. 4.13 Typical setback changes which facilitate solar access.

Solar Access on Northeast/Southwest Stree

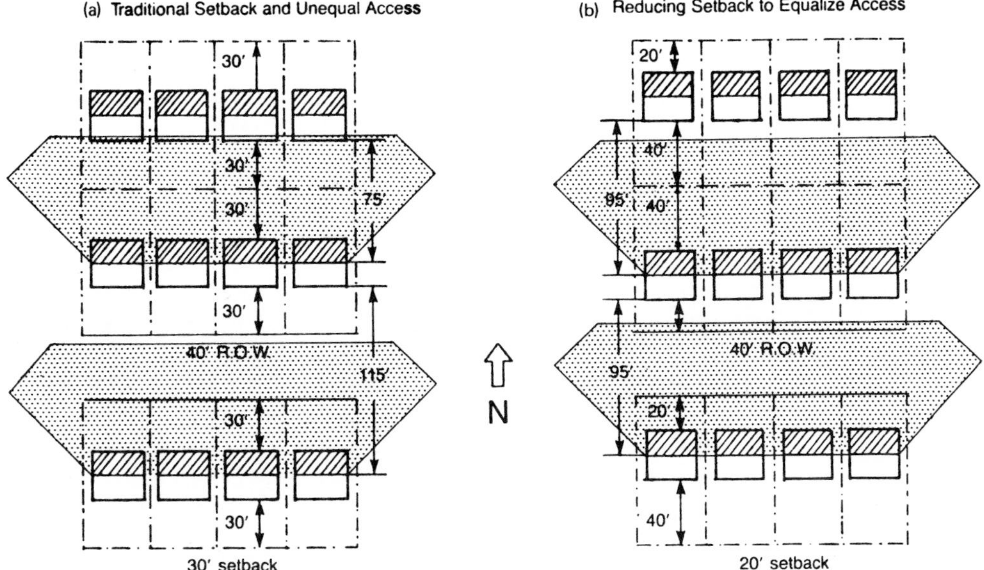

Fig. 4.14 In (a) only buildings to the north of road right-of-way have south-wall access. By reducing setback by 10 feet (from 30 feet to 20 feet), all structures have south-wall access in (b). This affects shading only by buildings; street trees must be regulated to prevent shading problems.

lots internal to a block and connected to the street by only a narrow strip of land (the "pole" of the flag (Fig. 4.9). This unconventional technique may not be allowed under local regulations, and though it may result in higher utility connection costs for the inner lots, it does have the benefit of creating conventional spacing between the sides of buildings. On angular or diagonal streets (off east/west orientations) solar access can be either improved or impeded by increased or decreased lot frontage. Preparation of shadow diagrams for homes on these streets is recommended; morning and afternoon shading is the major problem.

Setback Requirements

Uniform setback requirements for all lots cannot take into account the varying solar access needs of buildings located on streets with different orientations. Figure 4.13 depicts typical setback changes which facilitate solar access. For sites on each of three different street orientations, dotted lines surround the buildable area defined by typical setback standards. The solid outlines of homes represent favorable site locations for solar access. The significant differences between the two sets of buildable area outlines demonstrate why uniform setback requirements for all lots can be a barrier to solar access.

On east/west streets, reducing front yard setbacks and increasing rear yard set- backs protects the solar access of homes on the south side of the street because of the greater distance between homes from north to south (Fig. 4.14). This makes generally little-used front yards smaller, rear yards larger, reduces the length and cost of utilities and driveways and utilizes the street as a buffer against shading. The precise change in yard space depends on latitude, topography, and orientation of the homes. In general, this strategy is most effective on east/west streets, although it may also work on diagonal streets. A shadow pattern analysis should be done for final setback determinations. Lots on north/south streets would not gain from these setback modifications as their shading problems come from the side.

On north/south streets, larger sideyard setbacks are needed to protect the solar access of neighboring homes, therefore wider and shallower lots are recommended. The exact width of north-to-south lots necessary to prevent shading by adjacent structures must be determined by a shadow pattern analysis. Zero or north lot line siting can help to minimize lot width increases for this street alignment, as can the use of flag lots.

The setback strategies recommended here do not take into account possible shading by trees. Along east/west streets, homes sited closer to the street could have shading problems caused by street trees. In the case of homes on north/south streets with sideyard solar access, trees on adjacent parcels could have a detrimental effect on solar access. Therefore, consider setback changes only when the location of trees and shrubs can be controlled.

Building Siting Techniques

For solar access protection, the optimum placement of a home on a lot is toward the north end. This will maximize the space to the south both for control of shading problems and for enjoyable use (Fig. 4.15).

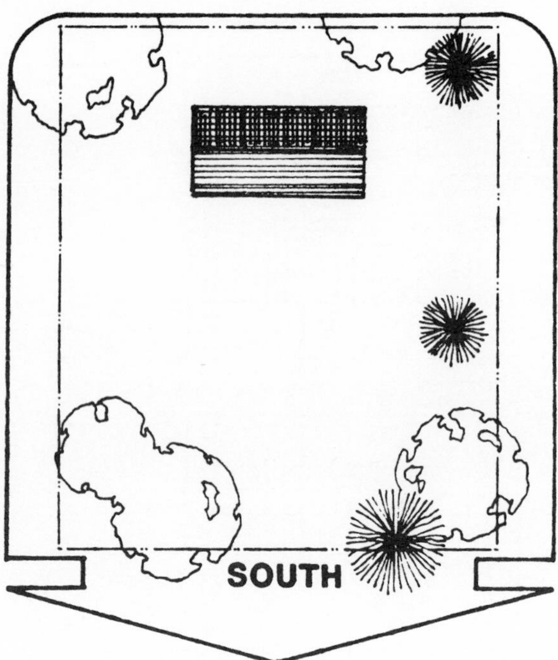

Fig. 4.15 The optimum home placement is toward the north end of the lot so that there is more control over potential shading problems.

North Lot Line Siting

One design option particularly useful for protecting solar access in a development is a variation of zero lot line siting, an innovative technique in which buildings are sited so that they abut property lines. For solar access, allowing buildings to abut the *north* lot lines provides the greatest possible yard area to the south of each building (Fig. 4.16). This technique is equally applicable to homes and lots on east/west or north/south streets. The north lot line technique may also be useful for lots and buildings on diagonal streets.

Skewed Building Placement

Often, buildings can face south even if lots do not. If topographical or other conditions prevent east/west street orientation and local regulations prohibit the use of slanted lot lines (ones not perpendicular to the street), consider skewed building placement as a siting technique (Fig. 4.17). This generally requires wider lots, unless setback variances can be obtained (i.e., to permit *average* side-

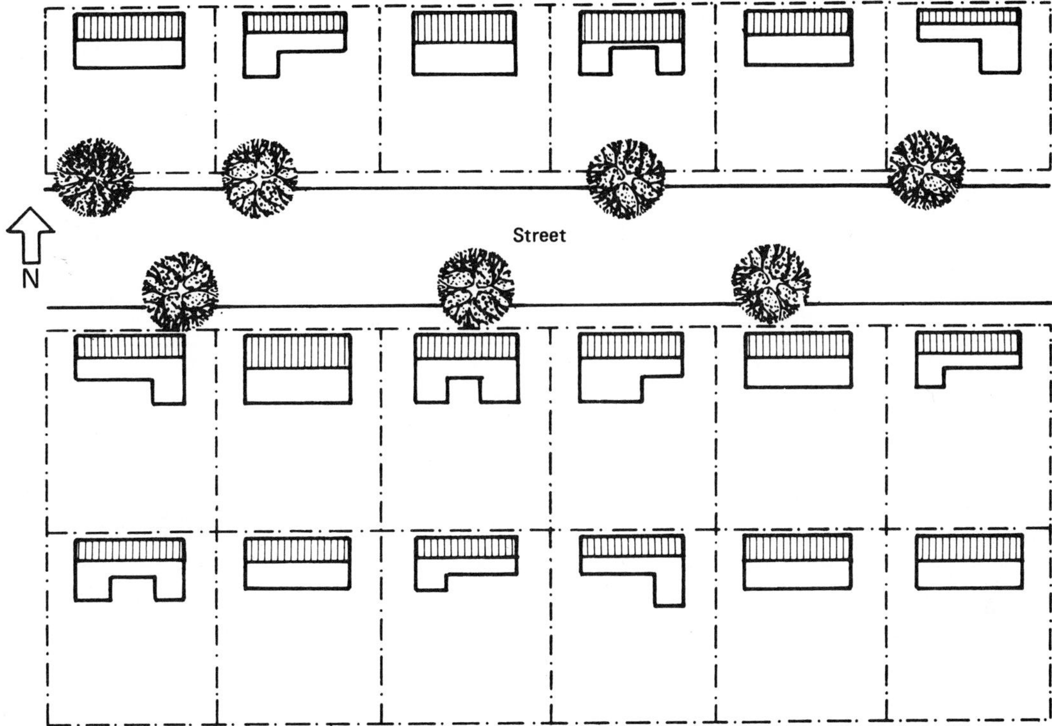

Fig. 4.16 North lot line siting.

yard setbacks). In one community built with skewed building placement, buyers appreciated the more interesting streetscape of homes built without uniform setbacks (See Chapter 6, Case Study 1.)

Reducing Building Height

An obvious, although often not feasible, way to reduce shadow lengths caused by buildings is to lower their height (Fig. 4.18). At higher latitudes, on north slopes, or in higher density developments, reducing building heights is a viable option to provide better south wall solar access. The amount of the height reduction to protect solar access depends on the shadow lengths created by latitude, topography, and the sun's position in the sky. The necessary reduction in building height can be

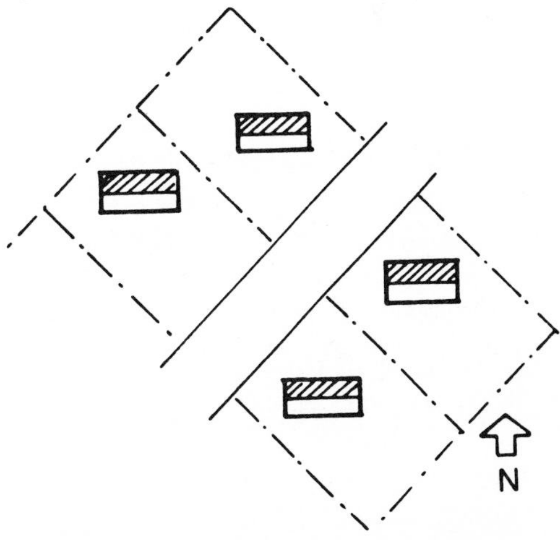

Fig. 4.17 Buildings face south even though lots do not.

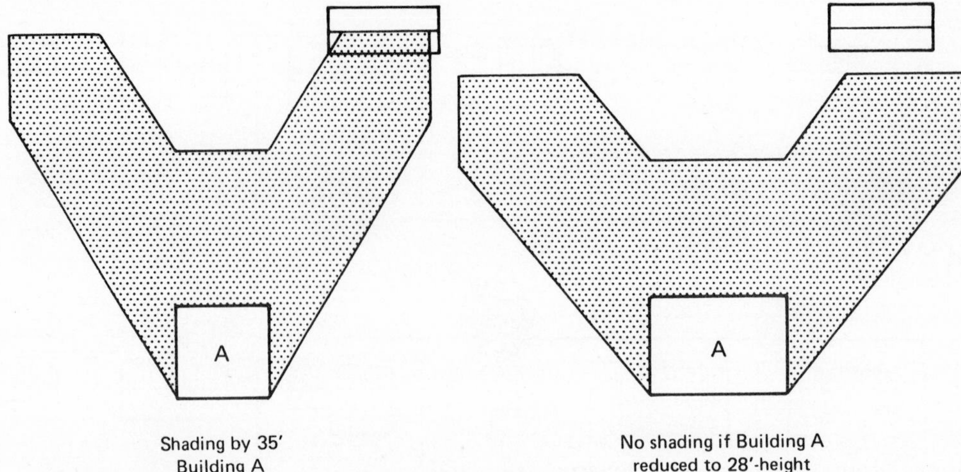

Fig. 4.18 Reducing building height to improve solar access.

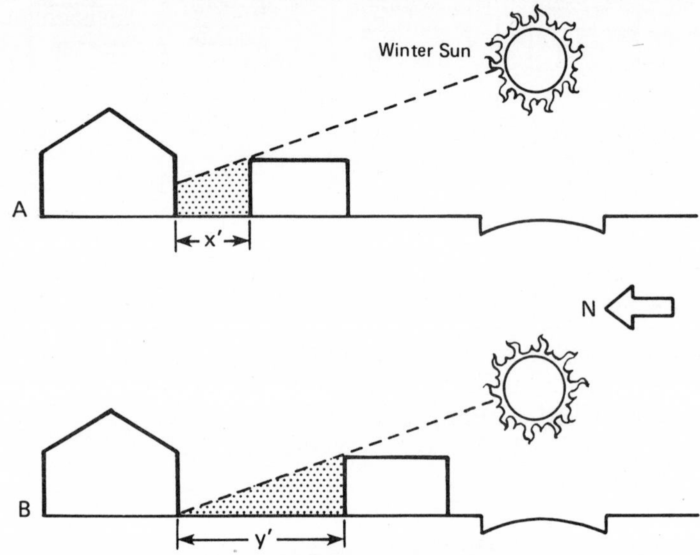

Fig. 4.19 Placement of garages.

mined by using the shadow pattern technique described in Chapter 3.

Placement of Garages Carports, and Fences

Garages, fences and other accessory structures must be planned so that they do not shade the south walls of buildings requiring solar access. The principle is simple: accessory structures should be sited to the north of the main building whenever possible. When garages or fences are sited to the south, they must be set far enough back from the main building that their shadows do not encroach on the south wall during the months that heating is required. For this reason, siting them as close as possible to the southern property line is desirable (Fig. 4.19).

LANDSCAPE DESIGN TECHNIQUES FOR ENERGY CONSERVATION AND SOLAR ACCESS

In land planning for energy conservation and solar access, give as much attention to landscape elements as to the other components of a development. Properly located trees, shrubs and vines provide shade during the cooling season, control wind and allow solar radiation to reach south facing windows during the heating season, thus reducing annual home energy costs.

As recommended in Chapter 3, the species, height and location of existing trees and their shadow patterns should be sketched on a site evaluation map. The developer must decide which is the stronger selling point, solar access or a nice canopy of trees for those parts of the site where there is a conflict. Usually a compromise can be reached, so that some buildings can be given solar access while the most valuable or beautiful stands of trees are preserved.

LOCATING VEGETATION USING THE SOLAR SKYSPACE CONCEPT

Ideally, the south wall of a home should be kept completely free of shadows between 9:00 AM and 3:00 PM on December 21, the day the sun is at its lowest altitude and casts the longest shadows. If you protect solar access on this date, you will automatically protect it for the entire heating season. Shadow patterns in plan and section should be drawn to determine which trees shade a south wall during the important times of the day. Only trees in the 90° southwest-to-southeast wedge to the south of a home will interfere with solar access. This is the home's solar skyspace.

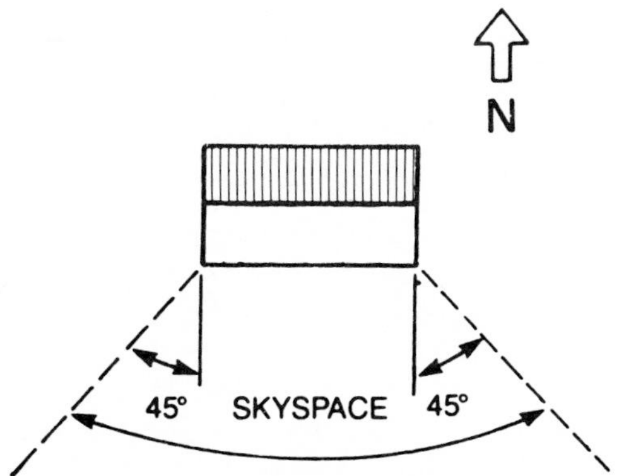

Fig. 4.20 Solar skyspace (plan view).

THE SOLAR SKYSPACE CONCEPT

The solar skyspace or individual unit of solar access defines that portion of the sky which must remain unobstructed for solar access to be protected. The solar skyspace is defined as the area above the December 21 sun path between approximately 9:00 AM solar time (or an azimuth of 45° east of south) and 3:00 PM solar time (or azimuth of 45° west of south) (Fig. 4.20). All trees, fences, garages and accessory structures should be kept below the altitude of the December 21 sun path. Altitude angles defining this path are given in Table 4.1.

The skyspace azimuth lines should be drawn in plan from the corners of the nearest-to-south-facing wall of a home, out 45° to the east and west of true south, regardless of the exact orientation of the "south facing" wall (Fig. 4.21). In the vertical direction, the lower skyspace boundary for south wall solar access

TABLE 4.1 December 21 Altitude Angles

North Latitude	AM/PM Altitude of the Sun*	Altitude of the Sun at Noon**
30°	20°	37°
35°	16°	32°
40°	14°	27°
45°	10°	22°

Note: Choose latitude closest to your location or interpolate between latitudes.

* Azimuth is 45° east or west of south.

** Azimuth is 0° (true south).

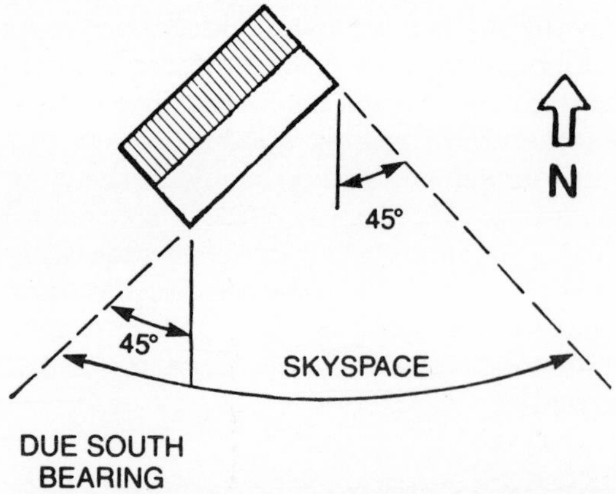

Fig. 4.21 Skyspace for buildings not facing true south.

is the bottom of the south wall. The upper boundary is formed by the December 21 sun path from 9:00 AM to 3:00 PM (Fig. 4.22).

While the shadow pattern technique described in Chapter 3 is a more thorough method for assessing shading, it only results in a plan view of a shadow. The altitude angles given for the solar skyspace can also be used to quickly determine, in section, the winter north shadow length caused by homes, garages and trees. For an object due south of a home, simply draw a line in section from the top of the object to the ground using the noon altitude angle given (Fig. 4.23). For objects within 45° east or west of south, draw a line in section using the 9:00 AM/3:00 PM altitude angle given. This method can give the developer or land planner a quick indication of whether or not proposed structures or trees will shade a home (See Fig. 4.27).

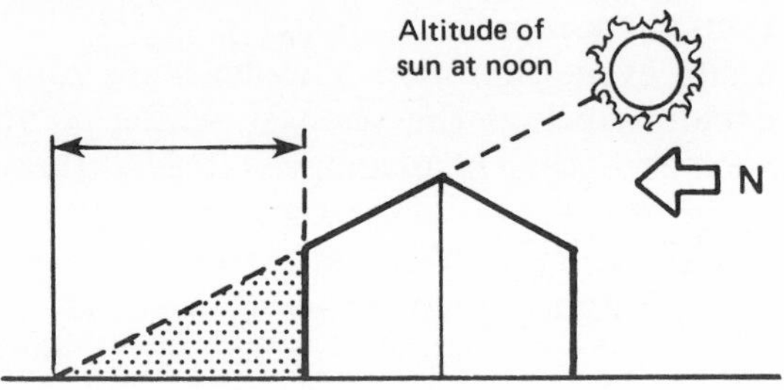

Fig. 4.23 Winter north shadow length method.

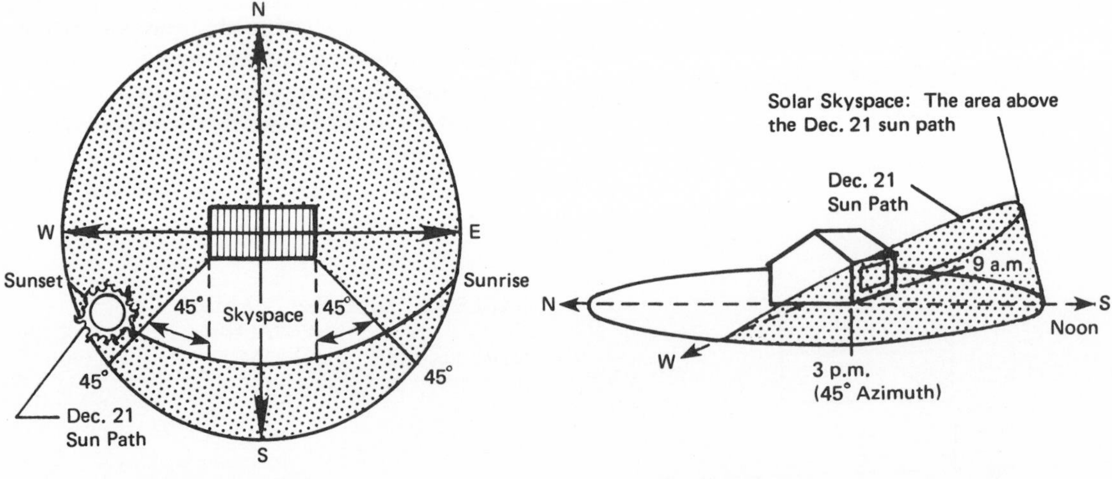

Fig. 4.22 Solar skyspace (plan and isometric views).

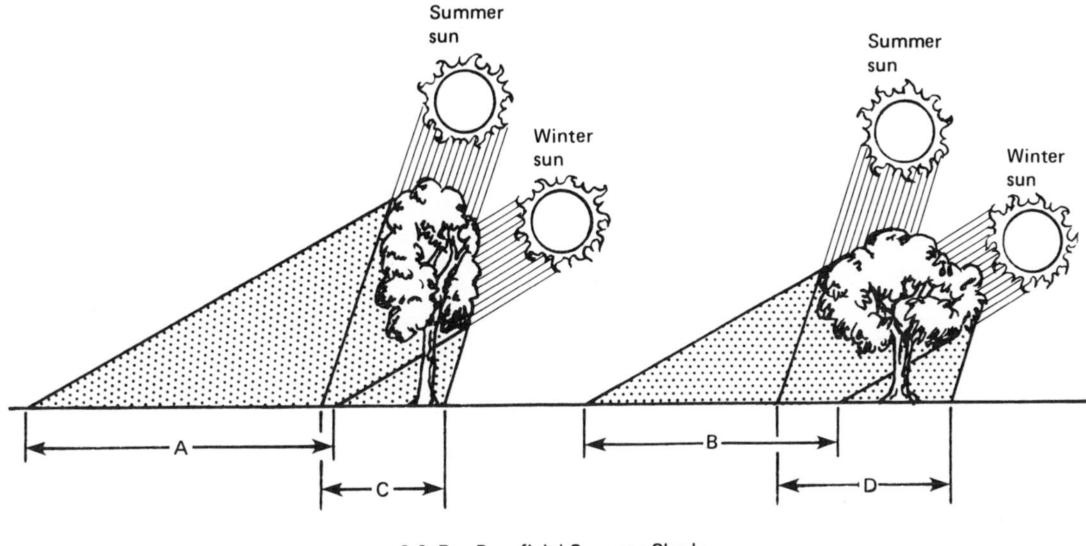

Fig. 4.24 Comparison of tree forms: B < A and D > C so, wide, short trees give better shade patterns both summer and winter.

TREE SELECTION CRITERIA

The key criteria for selecting tree species to minimize winter shading and maximize summer shading are:

Form: Short, wide trees give better shade patterns than do tall, narrow trees (i.e., shorter winter shadows and wider summer shadows) (Fig. 4.24).

Type: Use mainly deciduous trees because they shade fully in summer and lose their leaves in winter. Coniferous trees and shrubs are best for winter wind control.

Fig. 4.25 Variations in bare twig density give variations in penetration of winter sunlight.

TABLE 4.2 Percent Solar Radiation Blockage for Various Deciduous Tree Species

Tree Species	% Sunlight Blockage	
	Winter	Summer
White Alder	65	89
European Ash	45	89
European White Birch	54	89
Red Horse Chestnut	47	92
Siberian Elm	76	91
Little Leaf Linden	58	98
Black Locust	45	95
Honey Locust	54	70
Big Leaf Maple	60	85
Norway Maple	39	89
Silver Maple	37	86
London Plane Tree	40	87
White Poplar	70	72

Source: *Planning Solar Neighborhoods*, California Energy Commission.

Growth Rates: Choose trees which grow fast initially but grow slowly after reaching optimum form.

Bare Branch Density: The bare winter branches of deciduous trees can cause a substantial amount of winter shading (blocking 30 to 80 percent of the available solar radiation) depending on the type of tree, and thus should not be used near south facing glazing (Fig. 4.25). Table 4.2 lists the percent of solar radiation blockage for a number of species of trees.

These are the primary factors that should be considered when selecting species for landscaping a solar project. The site planner or developer is advised to consult a local nurseryman, United States Forestry Service Extension Agent, or other expert familiar with local species.

WINTER LANDSCAPE DESIGN TECHNIQUES

The most important concern relevant to landscape design during the heating season is the prevention of shading of south facing walls of homes.

Existing Vegetation

The species, height and location of existing trees and their shadow patterns should be sketched on the site map so that both beneficial summer and detrimental winter shading can be evaluated. Existing vegetation too near a home's south facing wall may require pruning or thinning, while trees farther away may require regular top trimming. Very tall trees or those with most branches higher than a home are acceptable close to a home's south side. Tree removal should be considered only when a future building's placement cannot be changed to avoid winter shading of the south wall by existing vegetation (Fig. 4.26).

New Vegetation

The key criteria for locating plantings are:

1. Plant trees with a tall mature height outside the solar skyspace of a home (the arc 45° to the southeast and southwest of true south) to avoid detrimental winter shading. Plant only shrubs or trees with a short mature height near the south wall of a home. The closer to the home, the shorter they must be so as not to cast shadows on south facing collector areas. The developer should imagine a light plane running from the sun to the bottom of the south wall of the home under which trees must fit (Fig. 4.27).

2. Plant trees to shade east and west windows, outdoor use areas and paved areas such as streets, driveways and parking lots.

3. Plant taller street trees on the south side of streets and shorter trees on the north side. This allows the width of the street and front yard setback to act as a shadow buffer to prevent shadows from the taller trees from reaching the south walls of homes across the street. This arrangement not only protects solar access but also shades the street pavement during the summer (Fig. 4.28).

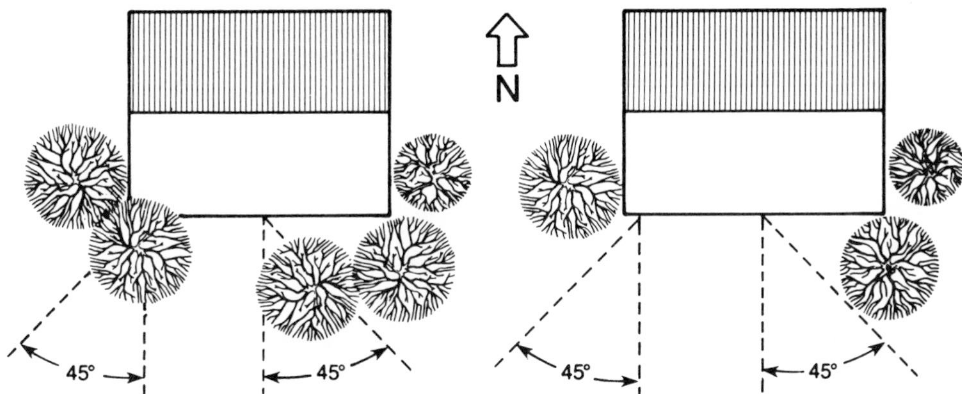

Fig. 4.26 Selective tree removal from skyspace.

4. Plant trees in groups, because they cast a smaller total shadow on a site than do the same number of separate trees, thus making solar access easier to plan (Fig. 4.29).

Shadow patterns of proposed trees (using mature heights) should be diagrammed in plan view on the site map before planting to aid in determining building placement on individual lots.

Another major concern during the winter is how to block the wind to reduce infiltration and conduction losses in homes. The

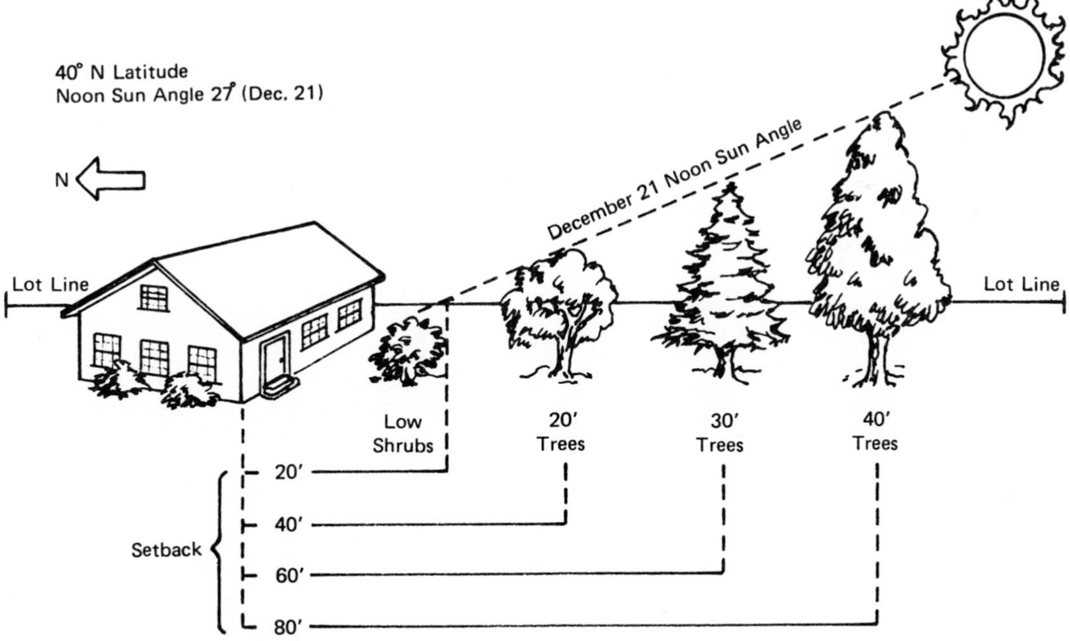

Fig. 4.27 Imagine a light plane running from the sun to the south wall of the home under which trees must fit.

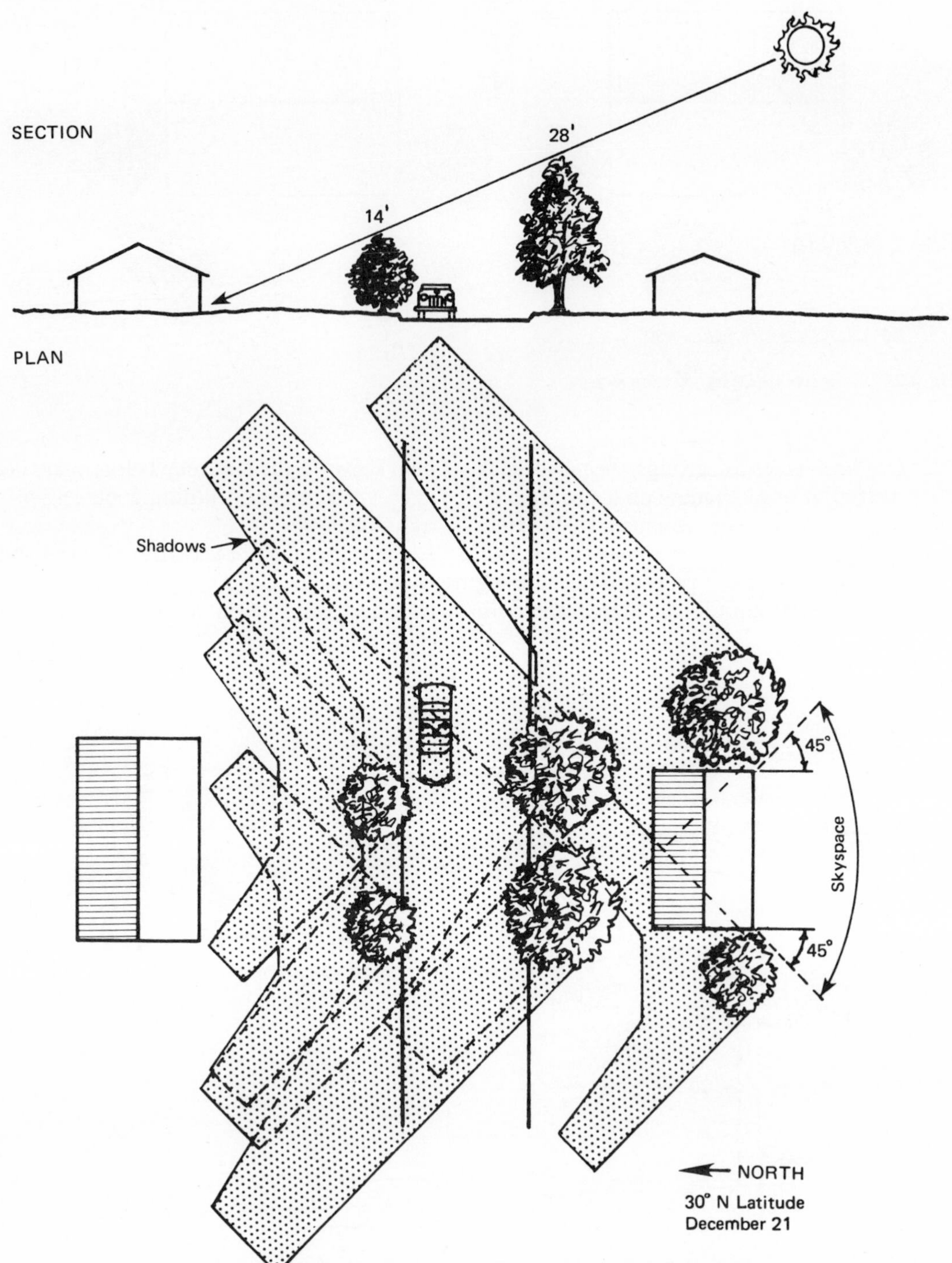

Fig. 4.28 Shorter street trees on the north side of a street increase solar access.

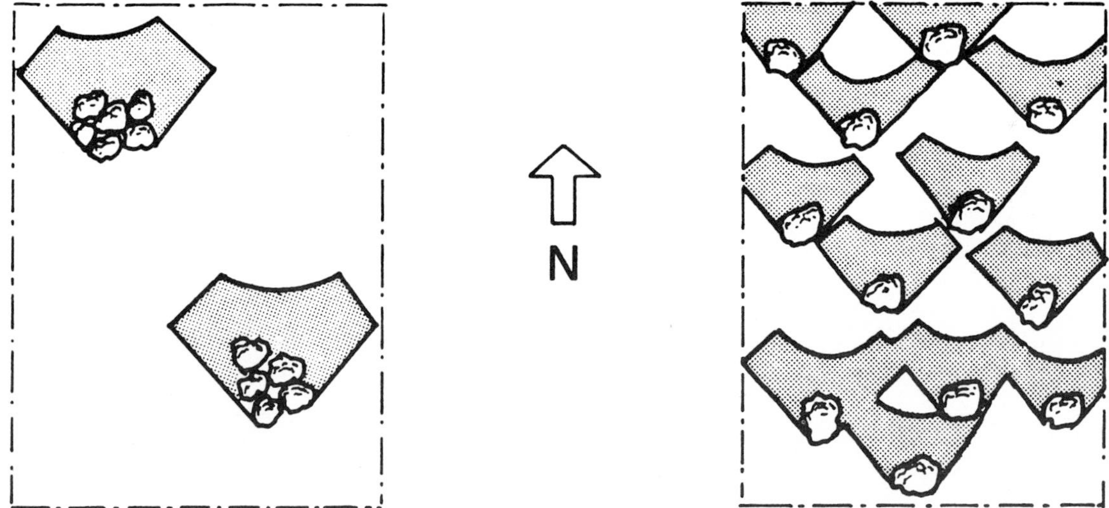

Fig. 4.29 Stands of trees. A dozen trees in two clumps leave large expanses with good solar access. Dispersed, they shade out most of the site.

value of trees in reducing wind speed and the resulting heat loss from buildings is well documented. The two basic locations for blocking the wind are at the edge of a development and on individual lots adjacent to homes. If north winter winds are a problem, shelterbelts (linear strips of trees and shrubs used as wind barriers) placed at the edge of a development can reduce wind speed significantly. Gary O. Robinette, in *Plants, People, and Environmental Quality*, states that studies have shown that shelterbelts are most effective when placed perpendicular to the prevailing winds and that wind velocity may be reduced by 50 percent for a distance 10 to 20 times the tree height downwind of a shelterbelt. The degree of protection and wind reduction depend upon the height, width and

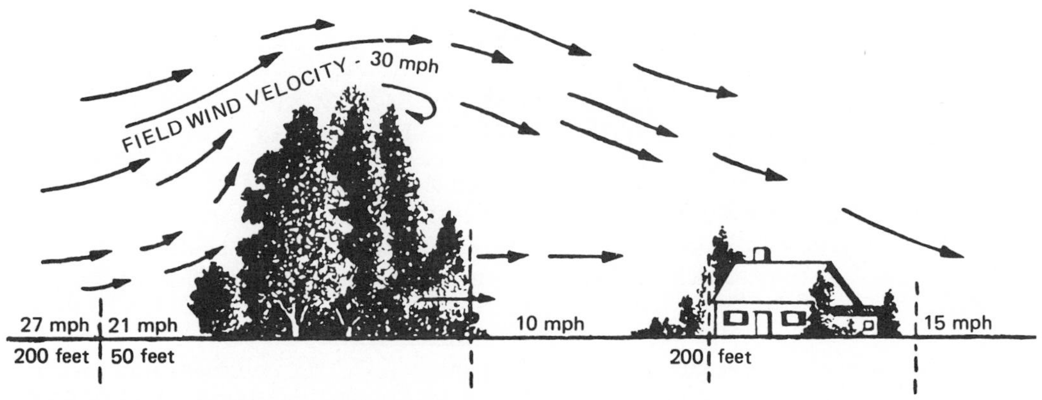

Fig. 4.30 The effectiveness of a windbreak protecting a home.

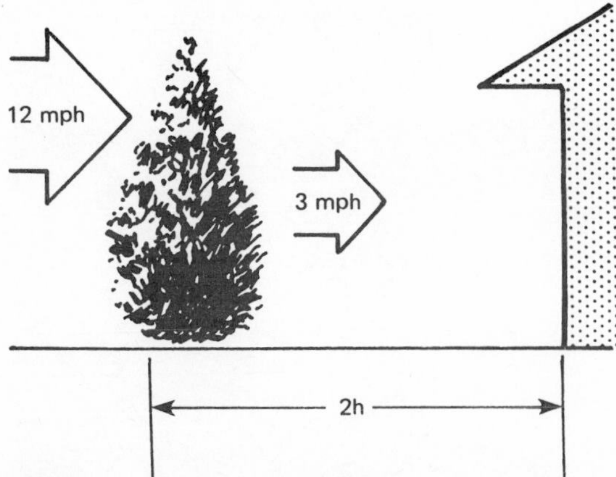

Fig. 4.31 A barrier will reduce wind velocities next to buildings.

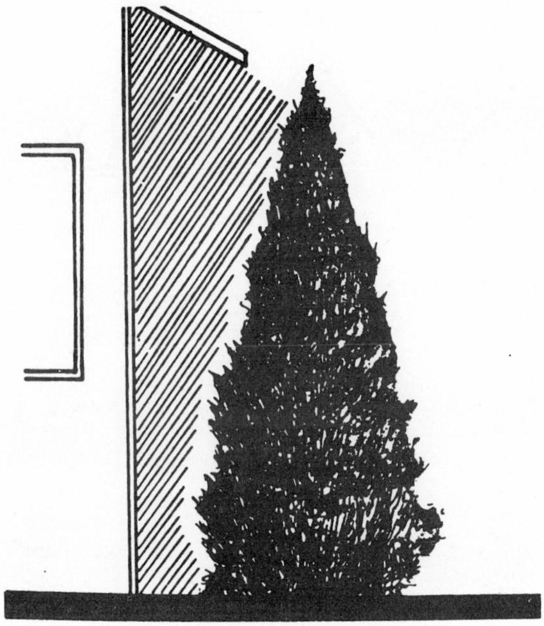

penetrability of the plants used. Arthur E. Ferber, regional forester for the Soil Conservation Service, in "Windbreaks for Conservation" states that: "A dense windbreak reduces a 30-mile-per-hour wind to 10 to 15 miles per hour"[1] (Fig. 4.30).

Coniferous trees and shrubs that keep their foliage all winter and branch to the ground are generally the most effective year-round plants for wind control. Deciduous trees and shrubs, when in leaf, are most effective in summer. Flank trees with high branches with coniferous shrubs to fill in the gaps under the leaf canopies; the shrubs will deflect the wind upward and increase the effectiveness of the wind barrier.

Benefits of Vegetation Adjacent to Homes

Vegetative barriers can significantly reduce wind velocities and create still-air spaces next to homes. Conifers that branch to the ground are especially effective. Wind velocity leeward of a dense planting of spruce or fir can be reduced 75 to 89 percent, while a loose planting of lombardy poplar reduces leeward wind velocity 40 percent[2] (Fig. 4.31). A row of dense conifers planted close together next to a wall creates a still-air space with insulating properties and reduces the heat loss from a building (Fig. 4.32).

Fig. 4.32 Still air space.

SUMMER LANDSCAPE DESIGN TECHNIQUES

The most beneficial use of landscape elements during the cooling season is for temperature control through shading (Fig. 4.33). Shading of east and west walls and windows,

[1] United States Department of Agriculture, Soil Conservation Service, Agriculture Information Bulletin 339, October 1969, p. 3.

[2] Robinette, G. O., *Plants, People and Environmental Quality*, United States Government Printing Office, 1972, p. 77.

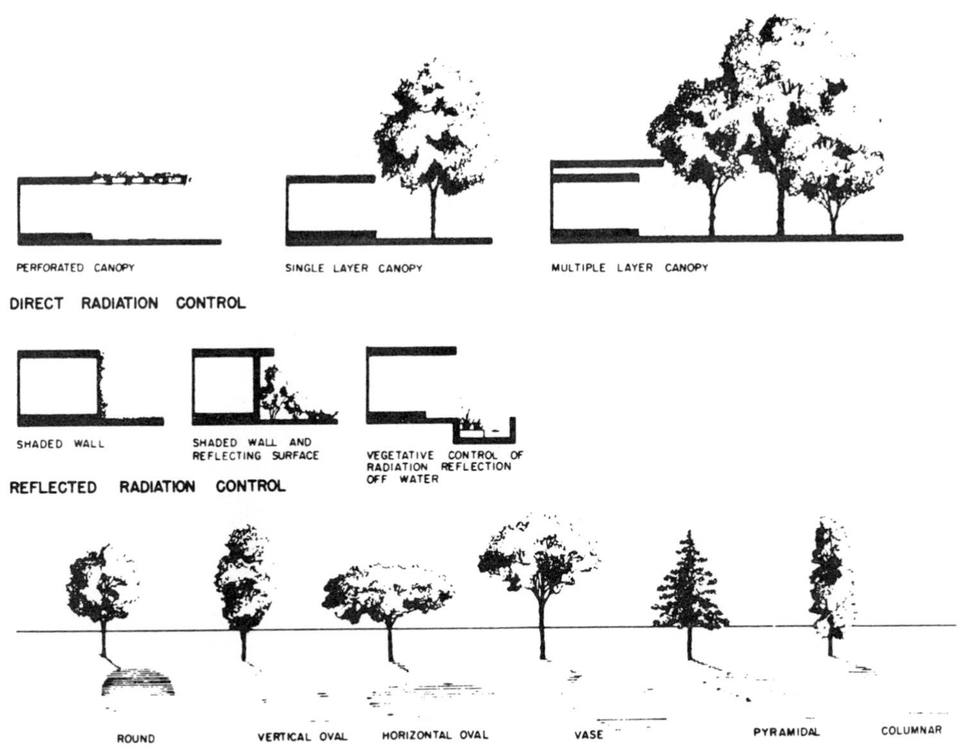

Fig. 4.33 Use of trees during the cooling season.

paved areas such as streets, driveways and parking lots and outdoor use areas by trees, can significantly reduce the amount of cooling energy needed to maintain comfort in nearby homes. Remember though, that domestic hot water heating collectors, swimming pools and gardens need sunlight during the summer at the same times that homes, streets and other paved areas need shade.

Deciduous tree and vine leaves correspond very closely with shading needs. Dr. Geoffrey Standford of Greenhills Research Center in Cedar Hill, Texas, reports that homes using grape vines on a roof trellis could be 21°F cooler. Select vine and tree species with a leaf out and leaf drop date to match overheated periods. Robert Ticknor reported in *Weeds, Trees and Turf* (February 1981) on an Alabama study which shows 104°F temperatures inside house trailers in full sun, and 80°F in the shade of trees. Ground temperatures of 136°F to 152°F in California's Imperial Valley were reportedly reduced by an average of 36°F in five minutes from shading by overhead foliage.

Vegetation should be located within about 20 feet of a home to maximize shading and cooling of the structure and the immediate adjacent ground. Vegetation placed farther away will have only a minor effect on reducing cooling requirements, except in the case of very large trees.

Existing Vegetation

Use existing, properly located vegetation to reduce summer cooling loads. Shadow patterns for July 21 should be constructed to analyze the potential benefits of summer shading from existing vegetation. Consider changing the siting of future homes on the site map if the locations do not take advantage of existing trees for cooling, especially in warmer climate regions.

New Vegetation

Use July 21 sun angles for shade planning since this is the height of the cooling season. Use morning/evening shadows to plan for shading of east and west windows. Use the noon sun angle of July 21 to plan for shading of paved areas, since this is the most critical time for shading outdoor surfaces. Plant trees close to roadways to provide "tunnels of shade" with continuous closed canopies.[3]

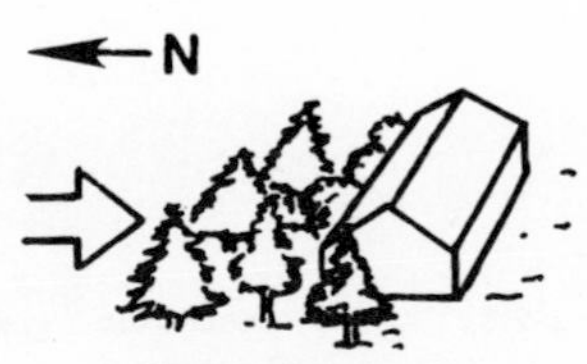

Figure 4.34 Climate Region A

Figure 4.35 Climate Region B

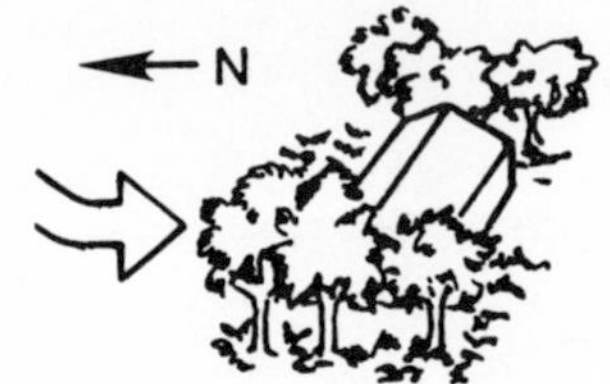

Figure 4.36 Climate Region C

PLANTING RECOMMENDATIONS BY CLIMATE REGION

(See Figure 4.1 for map)

Climate Region A

Winter: Cold to severe

Summer: Relatively mild to hot

Avoid all shading of south walls by any type of tree (use moveable exterior shading devices). Only plant trees outside of 45° arcs to the east and west of south walls. Use dense plantings of coniferous trees and shrubs along north and northwest walls to break prevailing winter winds. Shade west walls and paved areas with deciduous trees if summer heat gain is excessive (Fig. 4.34).

Climate Region B

Winter: Relatively mild to cold

Summer: Hot

Avoid all shading of south walls by any type of tree (use moveable exterior shading devices). Only plant trees outside of 45° arcs to the east and west of south walls. Use coniferous trees and shrubs along north and north west walls to break winter winds, if they are a problem. Shade west walls, east walls and paved areas with deciduous trees and vines so that summer radiation will be blocked out but some winter radiation will be admitted (Fig. 4.35).

Climate Region C

Winter: Relatively mild

Summer: Long and quite hot

Avoid all shading of south walls by any type of tree (use moveable exterior shading devices). Only plant trees outside of 45° arcs to the east and west of south walls. Shade west walls, east walls and paved areas with deciduous trees, shrubs and vines planted as densely as possible to reduce summer cooling loads and minimize overheating during the other seasons. Use trees with high, thin branches to allow breeze penetration (Fig. 4.36).

[3] Zanetto, *Landscape Architecture*, Volume 68, No. 6 (November 1978), p. 516.

CHAPTER FIVE

Land Use Regulations

Subdivision and zoning regulations may present obstacles or incentives to solar land development. This chapter describes potential regulatory barriers to solar land development and recommendations for overcoming them; the benefits of using ordinances which promote large-scale development; and vehicles for legally protecting solar access.

The key to better energy planning and development is greater flexibility in local land use regulations. Within this framework of existing controls, flexible street orientation, setbacks and lot lines which are non-perpendicular to the street are the most desirable modifications. Submitting solar developments as cluster or planned unit developments may be the best strategy for obtaining approvals as cluster and PUD ordinances often provide the necessary flexibility to permit adequate solar access. Planning for solar utilization and energy conservation will also add favorable connotations of "working with nature" to development proposals, thus increasing the likelihood of approval.

OVERCOMING REGULATORY BARRIERS TO SOLAR DEVELOPMENT

Modifying Regulations

Many communities throughout the United States have modified their subdivision and zoning ordinances to incorporate solar siting considerations. Regulations governing the layout of streets and lots, setbacks, the height and location of vegetation and the design of buildings have been affected. Listed below are potential regulatory barriers, followed by recommended modifications and examples of localities which have adopted versions of them.

Potential Barrier: Street Alignment Requirements

Regulations which require new streets to continue the direction of existing streets into adjacent areas may not always be favorable to solar orientation guidelines.

Proper solar orientation is much easier to achieve when streets are located within 15° to 25° of a true east/west alignment. Even at higher development densities, most homes located on east/west streets can be provided with excellent solar orientation. Where existing streets do not run in a predominantly east/west direction and are required to be continued, proper solar orientation still can be provided for most lots by bending the streets toward east/west in as short a distance as allowable and/or by designating the non-east/west (either north/south or diagonal) streets as collector streets and creating east/west cul-de-sacs of concentrated development that tie into them (Fig. 4.5).

Recommendation
Street planning standards should be revised to encourage the development of east/west streets to the greatest extent possible . Flexible street orientation regulations should be advocated on the basis of their encouragement of solar development.

Example: Naugatuck, Connecticut
Street planning provisions have been revised to promote "to the greatest extent possible" street alignments within a 15° range of a due east/west direction.

Potential Barrier: Lot Line Location Restrictions
Where lot lines must be located at right angles to the street, proper solar orientation may be difficult to establish for each lot. Subdivision regulations commonly require that lot lines be established perpendicular to the street or radial to curved streets. This requirement will pose no problems on east/west or north/south streets, but can make proper solar orientations for lots located on diagonal streets (i.e., northeast to southwest) difficult (Fig. 4.10).

Example: Naugatuck, Connecticut
When alternative lot configurations can secure greater solar access than conventional ones, Naugatuck waives the requirement that lot lines be perpendicular or radial to streets.

Potential Barrier: Minimum Lot Frontage Requirements
Strict, uniform requirements for minimum frontage on streets may limit the number of lots which can be provided with proper solar orientation. Flexible requirements should be advocated. Lots fronting on east/west streets require less total street frontage to provide solar access than do lots fronting on north/south streets. Therefore, by reducing lot frontage on east/west streets the number of lots with solar access can be increased.

"Flag" lots with very narrow street frontage can also be prohibited under these minimum lot frontage requirements. This lot configuration can be advantageous in providing the greatest number of developable lots with proper solar orientation (Fig. 4.9).

Zoning Regulations

Potential Barrier: Setback Requirements
Inflexible setback requirements may establish a buildable zone which precludes taking advantage of a lot's solar potential or other energy conserving characteristics.

Setback requirements often impose lot-centered building siting which may have little relationship to a site's natural characteristics. For example, a well oriented slope may be outside the buildable zone, or existing trees that can provide winter windbreaks or summer shade may have to be cleared.

Uniform setback requirements cannot take into account the varying solar access needs of buildings located on streets with different alignments. On east/west streets, reduced front yard setbacks and longer minimum rear yard setbacks are appropriate to ensure solar access. On north/south streets wider minimum sideyard setbacks are needed. On diagonal streets uniform front yard setbacks may cause buildings to cast shadows which limit solar access for neighboring structures.

Recommendation

Setback regulations should be made more flexible to encourage the provision of solar access for the maximum number of lots. They should permit variable setbacks, zero lot line siting and waivers of minimum setbacks when this is beneficial to solar access.

Example: Port Arthur, Texas

Local ordinances state that building setback lines shall be designed so that at least 80 percent of the buildings in a subdivision can be oriented with their long axes within a specified number of degrees of parallel to east/west.

Potential Barrier: Building Placement Regulations

Regulations that require the long axis of buildings to be located parallel to streets and perpendicular to lot lines can unnecessarily restrict solar access.

"Skewed" building locations can often achieve good solar access even when the building lot does not have an optimum north/south orientation. Not all zoning ordinances prohibit this, though most discourage it.

Recommendation

Building placement regulations should be flexible enough to permit a house to be sited "skewed" on its lot to ensure the best possible solar orientation. In addition, allowances for variable setbacks, provisions for slanted lot lines, or large enough lots on which to skew the buildings within the setbacks are needed.

Example: Chesterfield County, Virginia

Since local subdivision regulations prohibited slanted (or nonperpendicular) lot lines, the developers of the Solar I Subdivision (See Chapter 6, Case Study 1) skewed homes on their lots (which was not prohibited) to achieve solar access.

Potential Barrier: Architectural Projection Regulations

Regulations that limit the extent to which architectural shading devices can project into sideyards can limit the effectiveness of these important energy conservation devices. Strict limitations on the extent to which roof overhangs, awnings, vertical fins and other architectural shading devices can project into required sideyards can make it difficult to block unwanted summer sun effectively. Thus, cooling loads may be higher than necessary.

Recommendation

For new construction and remodeling, regulations should allow architectural shading devices to be excluded from the building width limit.

Potential Barrier: Landscape Requirements

Local planting or tree preservation requirements for new development may not always be consistent with solar access needs. Street tree planting and/or requirements for the preservation of existing vegetation may cause unwanted shade on south facing windows in winter. Even deciduous trees can reduce solar gain in winter by 30 to 80 percent.

Recommendation

Local jurisdictions should review their landscaping standards in order to avoid the potential impairment of solar access.

Example: Sacramento, California

Here, the selection and planting of street trees must consider solar access impacts on residential development.

Using Ordinances Which Promote Large-Scale Development To Provide Maximum Solar Access

Submitting sizeable solar developments as cluster developments or PUDs may be the best strategy for obtaining approvals. Because greater flexibility is allowed in establishing street layouts, lot configurations, setbacks and densities under cluster and PUD ordinances, developers are likely to have more success in obtaining approvals for solar site plans submitted under them than under more conventional development categories.

Under cluster and PUD ordinances, increased development densities can be established more easily in the site areas where solar orientation is best (on south facing slopes and along east/west streets) and offset by larger common open space areas which can be located in shaded areas, sited to protect solar access or to take advantage of the energy conserving potential of existing vegetation.

Solar access can be protected easily and effectively in these developments by the establishment of covenants and other enforceable private agreements which prohibit solar obstructions.

Solar access design is one of the means by which developers can qualify for density bonuses under cluster development and PUD ordinances in some communities. In Lincoln, Nebraska a 20 percent density increase can be obtained by assuring present and future solar access and energy conservation through proper layout of streets, lots and landscaping. Building and tree shadow plans must be indicated on site plans to demonstrate solar access compliance (Fig. 5.1). Multnomah County, Oregon provides a 25 percent density increase to developers who satisfy the energy policies of the county's Comprehensive Plan.

In communities where growth management policies limit development, such as Aspen and Boulder, Colorado, the solar and energy conservation aspects of development proposals are carefully evaluated and weigh heavily in the favor of the developers.

Some communities now require that solar orientation be provided to the maximum extent feasible in all new subdivisions. In Port Arthur, Texas at least 80 percent of all buildings in new subdivisions must be "solar oriented." In Cheshire, Connecticut a special solar planned development ordinance (based on more conventional PUD procedures) requires that 90 percent of all new units be oriented within 20° of true south and be designed to make use of solar space heating. Several local jurisdictions in California (Sacramento County, Santa Clara County and the city of Davis) now require that solar orientation and natural cooling be provided "to the extent feasible" in all new subdivisions. Ferrisburgh, Vermont requires that new subdivisions be oriented for solar use to the maximum extent feasible.

These examples show what communities can do to promote solar development, but states also play a critical role. The influence of state legislation is outlined below.

THE ROLE OF THE STATES IN PROMOTING SOLAR DEVELOPMENT AND PROTECTING SOLAR ACCESS

State Enabling Legislation

Enabling legislation at the state level is desirable and often necessary. At least 13 states[1] now give local governments the specific right to regulate the protection of solar access through compehensive planning, subdivision regulations and/or zoning ordinances. Where state enabling legislation is not required, state action may still be needed to spur local authorities to react positively to the special needs of solar development.

State Statute

State governments may directly regulate the protection of solar access. California has

[1] Arizona, California, Colorado, Connecticut, Maine, Minnesota, Nebraska, New York, Oregon, Tennessee, Vermont, Washington, Wyoming.

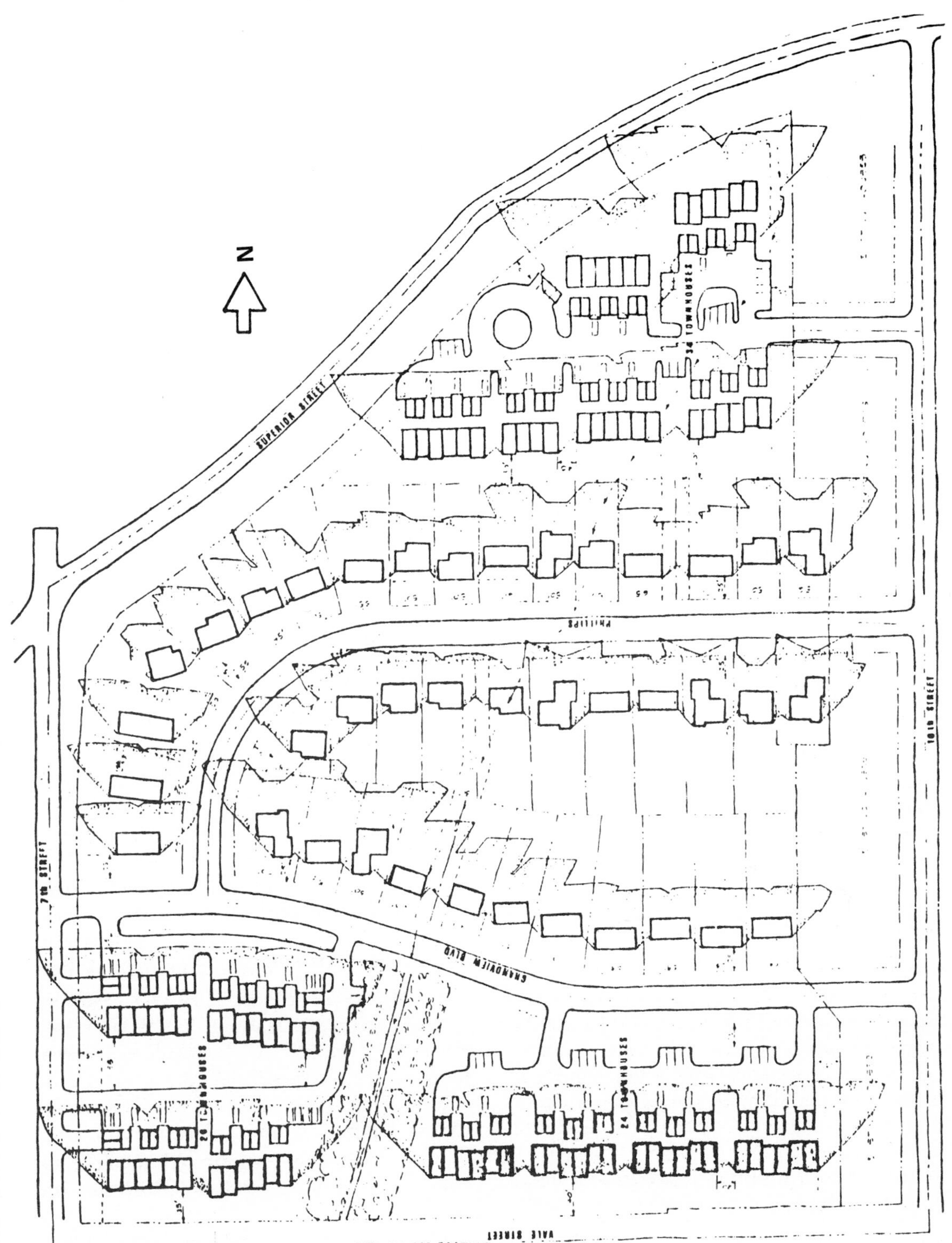

Fig. 5.1 Example of a final plan submitted in Lincoln, Nebraska to seize the 20% density bonus for protected solar access. Note the required shadow patterns which demonstrate compliance.

taken the strongest position of any state in this respect, by prohibiting plantings that cast shadows on south facing windows. California's local jurisdictions also are empowered to require the granting of solar easements before approving new subdivisions. Wyoming and New Mexico have declared existing solar access to be a "property right" similar to other rights inherent in the ownership of land.

Protection of Solar Access

Any investment in solar features will be less attractive if there is no guarantee of solar access (the ability to receive unobstructed sunlight). Legal guarantees as well as proper site planning are necessary to ensure this access. These guarantees can be provided by state statute, solar access easements or through restrictive covenants.

Nearly half of the fifty states[2] have established that private easements and covenants guaranteeing solar access are equal under the law to other covenants and enforceable through civil actions. Information on easements and covenants for the protection of solar access is given later in this chapter.

Tax Credits, Exemptions and Reductions

Tax exemptions, reductions or credits help ease the cost of solar systems. They also provide economic incentives for energy conservation by insuring that increased property tax bills do not cancel the dollar savings of substituting solar for oil, gas or electricity.

Connecticut, Virginia, Arizona, Tennessee, Texas, Massachusetts, Maryland, New Hampshire, North Dakota, Iowa and Oregon are the states in which solar systems currently are eligible for short term or permanent local property tax exemptions. In Colorado, solar heating and cooling devices are assessed at five percent of their value; many other states offer reduced tax rates.

Covenants and Easements to Protect Solar Access

Solar access also must be protected after lots or buildings are sold and occupied. A carelessly planted tree, for example, can undo careful site planning and development design, and an addition to a house or a new garage can cast shadows across wall areas planned for solar collection. For these reasons developers must consider the use of private agreements to protect future access as well as to ensure existing solar access in new developments.

Private agreements are common techniques used to preserve desirable characteristics of new developments, such as common open space, large front yards and architectural design. Private agreements suitable for solar access protection include restrictive covenants and easements.

Restrictive Covenants

A restrictive covenant, the most common private agreement, is a contract between two or more persons which involves mutual promises of reciprocal benefits and burdens among consenting landowners. This means that all persons involved in a covenant benefit from it and that all are burdened by restricting an activity, such as construction of an otherwise allowable structure that could cast a shadow on the south wall of a neighbor.

Restrictive convenants often are created by a developer at the time a subdivision or

---

[2] As of 1980, states with such protection included Arizona, California, Colorado, Florida, Georgia, Idaho, Indiana, Kansas, Maryland, Minnesota, Missouri, Montana, Nebraska, Nevada, New Jersey, New York, North Dakota, Ohio, Oregon, Tennessee, Utah, Virginia and Washington.

development is approved by local government. The restrictions apply to lots within the development and usually are inserted into the deeds of all parcels to be developed. The covenants may be enforced by the developer, by a lot owner within the development or, frequently, by a homeowners' association created to manage certain aspects of the development. Because these covenants often appear in the deeds, they are also called "deed restrictions."

An example covenant provision to protect solar access is printed below. In using this type of provision, remember that the laws affecting restrictive covenants vary from state to state. This example is not meant as a model but may provide guidance to developers considering similar provisions in their own developments.

Restrictive Covenants of
[Name of Development]
In [Municipality or County]

The following restrictive covenants are incorporated in this deed and in all other deeds to parcels within the [name of development], which is located in [complete legal description of the development], as recorded in [legal records of named county]. These covenants are binding upon all present and future owners of land within this development with the same effect as if they were incorporated in each subsequent deed.

(1) No vegetation, structure, fixture, or other object shall be so sited that it casts a shadow at a distance greater than 20 feet (6.1 meters) across any property line on December 21 between the hours of 9:00 AM and 3:00 PM Standard time), provided that this restriction does not apply to utility wires and similar objects which obstruct little light and which are needed and situated for reasonable use of the property in a manner consistent with other covenants in this deed. By adopting this covenant, the landowners within this development recognize the desirability of creating and maintaining a common plan to ensure access to direct sunlight on all parcels within the development for public health, aesthetic, and other purposes, specifically including access to sunlight for south facing walls and solar energy collectors.

The two introductory sentences would preface the list of restrictive covenants, which in some developments might number 20 or more. Of course, provision (1) alone would be valid if it were one in a list of other covenants, if the list was validly incorporated into a plat or deed and the covenant was consistent with others in the list.

The restriction on shadows is designed to allow the use of active as well as passive solar energy collectors. The sample distance of 20 feet in the covenant example should be adjusted, of course, to fit specific circumstances. The distance selected will depend on such factors as latitude, topography, lot size and density of structures. Developers considering covenant provisions similar to this example also may wish to restrict shading only across the northern lot line, instead of across *any* lot line. Whether a proposed object will violate the covenant can be determined with knowledge of the latitude of the development and the proposed height and distance from the lot line of the object. The shadow length tables in Chapter 3 can be used to calculate the appropriate distances across any lot line.

Three hours before and three hours after solar noon normally is adequate for the effective operation of both active and passive solar collectors. These times generally correspond to the 45° azimuths used to define solar skyspace in most latitudes.

Easements

Easements are another type of private agreement that can be used to protect solar access. Easements are interest in real property that can be transferred, like the property itself. One of the most common examples is a utility easement, a right purchased or otherwise obtained by a utility company to run utility lines across property. Easements for solar access would be negotiated by individual lot owners, or by a developer, with the owner of adjacent property. Essentially, the owner of the burdened property agrees to keep areas of his property free of objects that could shade a neighboring south wall or solar collector. Easements are recorded with a public agency, usually the city clerk or registrar of deeds.

Easements for solar access protection may be drafted under exisiting property law in all states. A number of states, however, have adopted specific legislation which sets forth the technical requirements for solar access easements. A landowner considering solar access easements should check the state law to make sure that the easements are both recordable and enforceable.

Below is an example of a solar access easement.[3] Its content and format are only illustrative.

Solar Skyspace Easement

Section 1: Estates Burdened and Benefited by the Solar Skyspace Easement

[Grantor(s)] hereby conveys, grants, and warrants to [Grantee(s)] for the sum of[$__________] a negative easement to restrict in accordance with the following terms the future use and development of the real property of Grantor(s) recorded as follows with the [registrar of deeds] of [County]:

The boundaries of the solar skyspace for the active and passive solar collector(s) of Grantee(s) are as follows:

[Alternative (A)] All space over the above-described property of the Grantor(s) at a height greater than [30 feet].

[Alternative (B)] All space at a height greater than [30 feet] over the above-described property of the Grantor(s), extending from a line parallel to and [25 feet] from the [front] property along [name of street] to a line parallel to and [55 feet] from the [rear] property line at the [least] edge of the [name of subdivision].

[Alternative (C)] All space over the above-described property of the Grantor(s) at a height above the burdened property that is described by a plane that intersects the property line between the burdened and benefited estates and that extends [southward] over the burdened property at an angle.

Section 2: Conditions of the Easement

[Alternative (A)] No structure, vegetation, or activity of land use other than the ones which exist on the effective date of this easement and which are not required to be removed herein or excepted herein shall cast a shadow on the south facing wall or solar energy collector of Grantee(s) described above during the time specified in this section. Exceptions are utility lines, antennas, wires and poles that in the aggregate do not obstruct more than one percent of the light that otherwise would be received at the south facing wall or solar energy collector(s) and [other exceptions].

[Optional] A shadow shall not be cast from [3 hours] before noon to [3 hours] after noon from [September 22 through March 21] and from [4 hours] before noon to [4 hours] after noon from [March 22 through September 21], when all times refer to mean solar time.

[Alternative (B)] No structure, vegetation, or activity or land use other than the ones which exist on the effective date of this easement and which are not required to be removed herein or excepted herein shall penetrate the airspace at a height greater than [__________] over the [above-described real property of Grantor(s)] following areas of the above-described real property of the Grantor(s) [__________] with the exception of [__________].

Section 3: Effect and Termination

Burdens and benefits of this easement are transferable and run with the land to subsequent grantees of the Grantor(s) and of the Grantee(s). This solar skyspace easement shall remain in effect until use of the south facing wall or solar energy collector described above is abandoned but not sooner than [10 years] after creation of this easement, or until the Grantee(s) and Grantor(s) or their successors in interest terminate it.

Section 4: Definitions

Define south facing wall collector, solar energy collectors, solar skyspace and structure.

Section 5: (Optional)

The attached map showing the affected properties and the protected areas of the solar skyspace is incorporated as part of this instrument.

---

[3] Thomas Miller, and Robbins, *Overcoming Legal Uncertainties About Use of Solar Energy Systems*, p. 45.

Section 6
[Other matters depending upon state laws: notary clause, signatures, attestation and recordation.]

Several alternatives are presented for Sections 1 and 2 of the example easement. In Section 1, three different alternative clauses are used to define the boundary of the easement established by the instrument. Alternative (A) uses an approach analogous to the height restriction of a conventional prescriptive zoning ordinance. Alternative (B) uses a similar approach but limits the development restriction to only a portion of the burdened lot. Alternative (C) uses an approach similar to the bulk plane provisions in some zoning ordinances.

Section 2 also considers alternative conditions. Two alternative sections of the easement are provided, but they accomplish nearly identical objectives. The restriction can be defined as an Alternative (A), where a three-dimensional space is defined within which development is allowed, similar to the bulk plane and building envelope techniques found in public zoning. Alternative (B) is similar to a performance standard limiting the times of day during which a collector must remain unshaded.

In both easement provisions, the numbers and phrases inserted in the brackets depend on a number of factors: the latitude and topography of the site; the type (active or passive), use and location of the proposed collector system; the solar access objectives of the parties creating the easement; and the degree of development restriction both parties are willing to tolerate to achieve solar access. Thus the numbers and descriptive terms must be created on a case-by-case basis and no uniform suggestions can be made.

The information on covenants and easements in this chapter was adapted from *Site Planning for Solar Access* by D. Erley and M. Jaffe, United States Government Document Number HUD-PDR-481 (2).

CHAPTER SIX

Case Studies

Evidence of the sound logic behind the practice of solar land planning and development can be easily shown through case studies of solar developments which have been planned and/or built throughout the United States.

Written and graphic descriptions of seven solar developments of varying size and type, covering all climate regions and terrain conditions, are presented. Topics discussed in each case study include economics, marketing techniques, barriers encountered, and how solar access is protected in each development. The developments are located and named as follows:

1. Richmond, Virginia: Solar I
2. Richmond, Virginia: Solar II
3. Barling, Arkansas: Sundance Village
4. Overland Park, Kansas: Bridge Creek
5. Boulder, Colorado: Winding Trail Village
6. Boulder, Colorado: Wonderland Hill VI, Quail Court
7. Sacramento, California: Larchmont Summerfield

There are a great many other solar developments in the United States and abroad. These case studies were chosen because of the variety in approaches to solar development they represent.

CASE STUDY 1
Solar I

Solar I near Richmond, Virginia is a 213-unit passive solar development of single-family detached homes. Prices for the ten available passive solar plans are in the $60,000+ range. Figure 6.1 shows the first phase of development. Forty-three homes were laid out on the rolling terrain in such a way that none of them will shade another. Shadow patterns for December 21, the day shadows are the longest, were drawn on the site plan by the developer to determine the layout of the homes. Figure 6.2 is a photo of one of the Solar I home models.

When the tentative development plan was first designed, the developers were not thinking of solar homes. Consequently, the best use of the existing terrain was the consideration, not east/west streets. It is interesting to observe that not a single lot was lost due to the building of solar homes. (Every home is solar and none are adversely affected by shadows.) As the national economy started to decline, the developers added more passive solar house plans that could be sold in the $60,000 range. Adding the new plans generated 26 sales in four months.

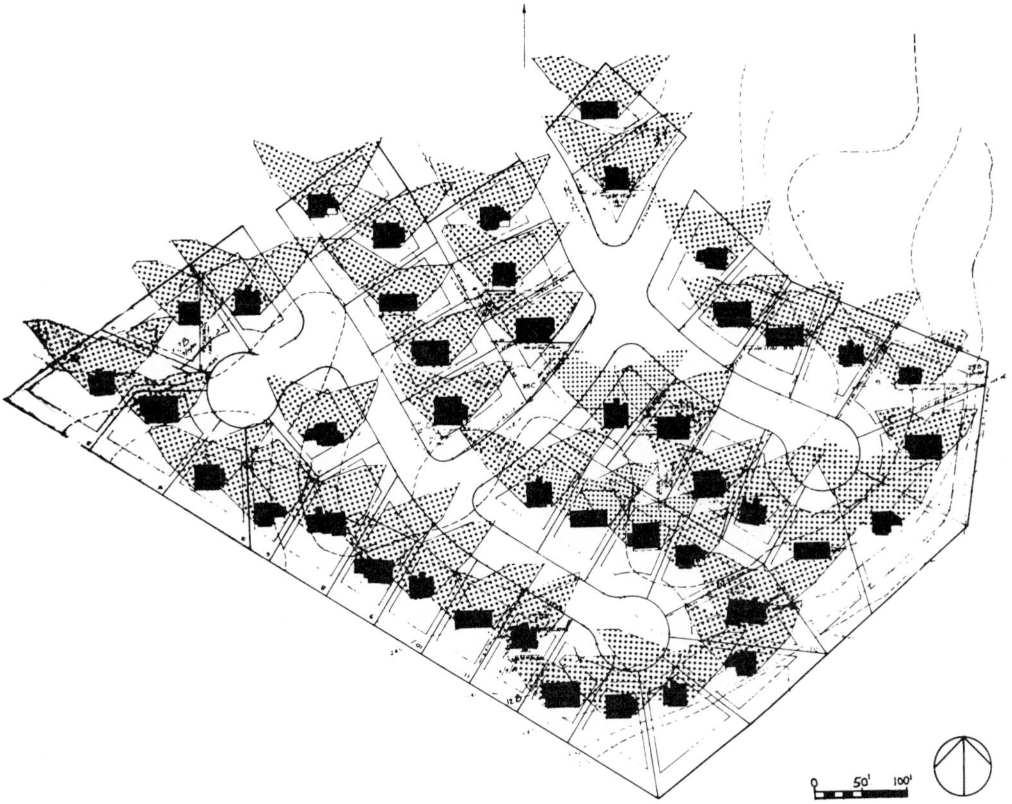

Fig. 6.1 *Solar I* near Richmond, Virginia.

Fig. 6.2 A *Solar I* home.

General Background
Name: Solar I
Location: Chesterfield County, Virginia (near Richmond)
Climate: 4,100 heating degree-days with hot, humid summers; Region B
Credits: Developers: R. Patrick Bowe, David J. Sowers; Builder: David J. Sowers, T. N. Ingram, and D. N. Cole; Architects: The Design Co-Operative
Status: Started building in June of 1980, currently 64 houses built and sold. Price range: $60,000+
Size: 12.7 acres: 43 lots: Section 1; 18.7 acres: 61 lots: Section 2
Type: Passive solar homes using Trombe walls, with sunspaces, water walls and greenhouses. (Section 2 uses traditional windows for glazing and internal thermal storage distributed throughout the house.)
Density: 3.4 units/acre
Solar access: 100 percent of units have solar access guaranteed through precalculated shadow plans and restrictive covenants.

Economics
Interest rates: Market
Additional costs: The only additional cost for solar access was having the house corners staked from the shadow plan by their engineer at approximately $100 per house.
Savings from solar access: The developers were able to move at a more rapid pace than their competitors, resulting in less interest expense at a time when rates were at an all-time high.
Density bonus consideration: Unheard of in this area for any reason.
Time lag: No difference that they were able to detect.
Added value to lots: The cost of their lots did not increase because of solar access. As the market becomes more sophisticated and people understand what the benefits really are, the developers believe that buyers will indeed pay more, but it is still too early now.

Marketing
Broker open-houses accounted for most of the sales, but people were brought to the development through advertising; TV news coverage, newspaper stories, and general curiosity. They built their model home on a main street and funneled interested buyers into the subdivision from this home. Sales in this particular subdivision, which the developers classify as a third-home market, have been severely hurt by the high interest rates. They noted that it is hard for a family to trade a very low energy bill ($100 or less per year) for a ridiculously high mortage payment every month. Once interest rates drop they feel that sales will again boom.

Barriers
Terrain: The terrain must always dictate the development where dollars are a concern. Once the lot is designated through the normal development process, the developers look at solar access. They do not work with + or − 30°, only with true south.
Zoning: The developers follow the conventional subdivision development procedures; however, they "skew" the houses on the lots to face south because nonperpendicular lot lines are prohibited.
Planning boards: An uneducated planning board can ruin any development. Homework is required as with any zoning.
Land planners: The developers have used land planners with no solar access planning experience and have educated them.

Solar Access Protection
In the state of Virginia there are no legislative rights to the sun. The developers have protected their subdivisions with restrictive covenants that guarantee solar access.

Comparative Data
The developers feel that the beauty of solar access is that once the commitment to it has been made, any subdivision can have 100

percent solar access. While it may require taking a chance by abandoning the standard practice of orienting homes parallel to the street, once the development is built with everything oriented to the sun, the aesthetics are actually just as pleasing. About the only change they actually made was the direction of a few minor cul-de-sacs for better solar access.

CASE STUDY 2
Solar II

Solar II near Richmond, Virginia is an outgrowth of the Solar I project by the same developers. They believe very strongly in the benefits offered by solar housing. A great many people were attracted to their Solar I development but could not afford the $60,000+ homes when the economy started declining. The developers decided to do a first-time home buyer's subdivision modeled on the successful Solar I project, but with drastically reduced square footage (850–1100 sq. ft.) in the homes. The sales prices dropped to $40,000–$52,000.

The moderately to heavily rolling terrain, much of it sloping to the northwest, and a wide utility easement posed no problems for these solar developers. Figure 6.3 shows the site plan and Fig. 6.4 one view of Solar II.

The Solar II development amazes everyone in its area. It has sold as well as any development within the area has ever sold, but during its short life it has seen only bad economic times. This seems to indicate that people think more about utility costs during depressed times, or that more people are becoming concerned with excessively high energy costs.

General Background

Name: Solar II
Location: Chesterfield County, Virginia (near Richmond)
Climate: 4,100 heating degree-days with hot, humid summers; 1010 cooling hours; Region B
Credits: Developers: R. Patrick Bowe, David J. Sowers; Builder: T. N. Ingram and D. N. Cole; Architects: The Design Co-Operative.
Status: Started building Section 1 in October 1980. First house staked December 31, 1980. The last house (65th) in Section 1 was sold on October 30, 1981 (10 months later). Section 2 completed December 1982.
Size: 18.3 acres: 62 lots: Section 1
Type: 850–1100 square feet, one-bedroom and three-bedroom passive solar homes: sales prices ranged from $40,000 to $52,000 (including land).
Density: 3.4 units/acre
Solar access: 100 percent units have solar access guaranteed through pre-calculated shadow plans and restrictive covenants.

Economics

Interest rates: Market-mortage rates were 17½ to 18 percent in November, 1981; the best they have seen during the life of the project is about 14 percent.
Additional costs: With high interest rates prevailing, a quick sellout more than compensates for the small amount of extra work involved in calculating shadow plans.

Marketing Techniques

They built two models to start with and let the market dictate from there. They tried three-bedroom homes with no frills, and one-bedroom homes loaded with amenities. It appeared that the buyers were more willing to pay the price of $600 per month for the one-bedroom, which has less square footage, but more amenities. They added another one-bedroom model and an earth-sheltered home for a Parade of Homes. They sold both homes during the Parade as well as twelve of the one-bedroom homes.

Barriers

The greatest barrier is the lack of solar access guarantees within the State of Virginia. The

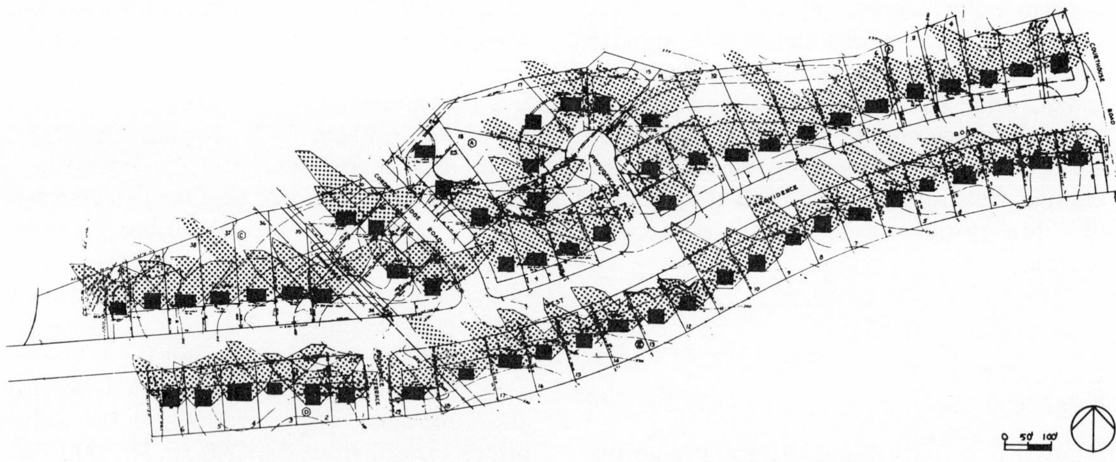

Fig. 6.3 *Solar II* near Richmond, Virginia.

Fig. 6.4 View of homes in the *Solar II* development.

terrain, moderately to heavily rolling contours, or a 225′ to 195′ or 60′ difference in elevations, presented no problems for them. (See site plan in Fig. 6.3).

Solar Access Protection

The restrictive covenant is the only way for them to guarantee solar access to their home buyers.

Comparative Data

In their opinion, there is no such thing as "before" and "after" (solar access considerations) site plans. The normal considerations for development must dictate streets, drainage, sewers, etc. They do not attempt to force solar lots with east/west streets. They develop a subdivision first and then look at solar access. To date they have developed 187 lots and have not lost a single one for solar use. The setbacks are normally 40-feet front, 30-feet rear with 7½-foot sidelines. They draw their own shadow patterns and work within the established boundaries. A normal size lot is 70-feet × 140-feet.

Information, figures, and photographs for Case Studies 1 and 2 were provided by R. Patrick Bowe, President of Century 21/Virginia Homes Unlimited, Inc., 11011 Trade Road, Richmond, Virginia 23235.

CASE STUDY 3
Sundance Village

Sundance Village is a thirty-unit active and passive solar home development in Barling, Arkansas. It is part of a 150 home Whole Energy Subdivision begun in 1974 which consists of a series of homes built in four phases. The homes in each successive phase incorporated more energy-saving features than the previous phase. Units in the first phase had standard 2-inch × 4-inch walls with blackboard, R-24 attic insulation, single glazed windows, and wood exterior doors. Second Phase units had standard 2-inch × 4-inch walls with foil foam sheathing, R-28 attic insulation, and double glazed windows. Third Phase units were built using techniques developed by Owens Corning Fiberglass as part of the Arkansas Story program, with 2-inch × 6-inch walls, R-38 attic insulation, double glazed windows, and steel insulated exterior doors.

The Sundance Village Phase consists of homes with 2-inch × 6-inch walls, R-38 attic insulation, triple glazed windows for passive solar gain, steel insulated exterior doors, sill sealers, caulk and weatherstripping used to insure a tightly sealed building, a vapor barrier on inside surfaces of all exterior walls and ceilings, and active solar hot water and space heating systems. An evaluation of the comparative performance of these homes after a few years of monitoring will provide invaluable data on the relative cost effectiveness of the various energy saving features included in the homes of each phase.

Figure 6.5 shows the site plan of the Sundance Village portion of the Whole Energy Subdivision. Figure 6.6 depicts several of the units.

General Background

Name: Sundance Village

Location: Barling, Arkansas, a suburb of Ft. Smith on the Arkansas River

Climate: 3,300 heating degree-days; 1300 cooling hours, on the borderline of regions B and C

Credits: The project was conceived and developed by Ernest R. Coleman, President of ERC Properties, Inc. Acknowledgements also go to Jennings Orr of the Farmers Home Administration, Kal Turkia of the Southern Solar Energy Center and Joel Bucker of Worthen Bank and Trust in Little Rock, Arkansas. Architect: Tim Risely of Risely-Childers Association, Architects

Status: Construction began in March, 1981, with completion date set for May 1982.

Size: 11.3 acres: 35 lots, 30 of which are being utilized for the solar development.

Type: 30 solar units; 27 have active solar space and water heating, 3 are passive solar with active solar water heating only. There are three different three-bedroom plans.

Density: 3.25 units/acre

Solar access: 100 percent of units have solar access.

Economics

Interest rates: Units are financed by the Farmers Home Administration under their FmHA 502 low income financing program. Effective interest rate is 13.24 percent, but can go as low as 1 percent with subsidies.

Savings from solar access: The savings were far greater than the cost because of energy savings to the homeowner, a higher density

Fig. 6.5 *Sundance Village* in Barling, Arkansas.

Fig. 6.6 View of homes in *Sundance Village.*

of homes per acre than normally allowed by FmHA, and better construction cost planning.
Time lag: Because of the solar features and financing, the homes were all pre-sold.
Added value to lots: This was evident in that the appraisal for these smaller zero lot line lots was the same as they get on a conventional lot.

Marketing Techniques

The units were marketed primarily by newspaper and the local FmHA county office. There were numerous press releases and a one-week open house for the general public to view the units. Only one unit was sold by an outside broker.

Barriers

The skepticism of local city planning and zoning officials, caused by their unfamiliarity with zero lot line and solar construction practices, was alleviated by the developer's presentation of the benefits of solar homes.

Solar Access Protection

None in this area.

Comparative Data

	Before	*After* (Solar Access Considerations)
Number of lots	27	35
Total street area	Same	Same
Total lot area	Same	Same
Average lot size	70′ × 130′	60′ × 90′
Number of solar lots	18	35
Percentage of subdivision solar	0%	85%

Comments From Experience

Orientation of homes for active and passive solar collection only took a little extra planning and thinking—the first time.

Case study information, figures, and photograph were provided by Rod Coleman, Senior Vice President, ERC Properties, Inc., 4720 Rogers Avenue, Suite C, Ft. Smith, Arkansas 72901.

CASE STUDY 4
Bridge Creek

The 400-unit Bridge Creek passive solar development near Kansas City, Missouri was originally planned as a conventional subdivision of 285 homes. An increase in the city's greenspace requirements makes the additional number of units in the solar plan even more impressive. The solar plan caused the narrower sideyards to become more acceptable because of the reduction of east and west windows. Privacy is maintained from front to back as the larger areas of glass are always to the south and either face the sixty-foot wide greenspace or the street.

Figure 6.7 shows the conventional layout of the subdivision and Fig. 6.8 shows the solar access plan. Figure 6.9 indicates typical building placement on either side of the greenspace.

General Background

Name: Bridge Creek
Location: Overland Park (Johnson County), Kansas, a suburb of Kansas City, Missouri
Climate: 4750 heating degree-days; 1100 cooling hours; on borderline of regions A and B
Credits: Developers: Bodine-Ashner Development Co., and Ambassador Development Co.
Status: First plat: February 1980, approved by City in June, 1980. Revised plat: June 1981, approved by City in July, 1981.
Size: 116 acres: 400 lots
Type: Single-family detached passive solar homes
Density: 3.4 units/acre
Solar access: 100 percent of units have solar access

Economics

Additional costs: minimal to zero for solar access planning
Density bonus considerations: the conventional plan accommodated only 285 lots (2.5

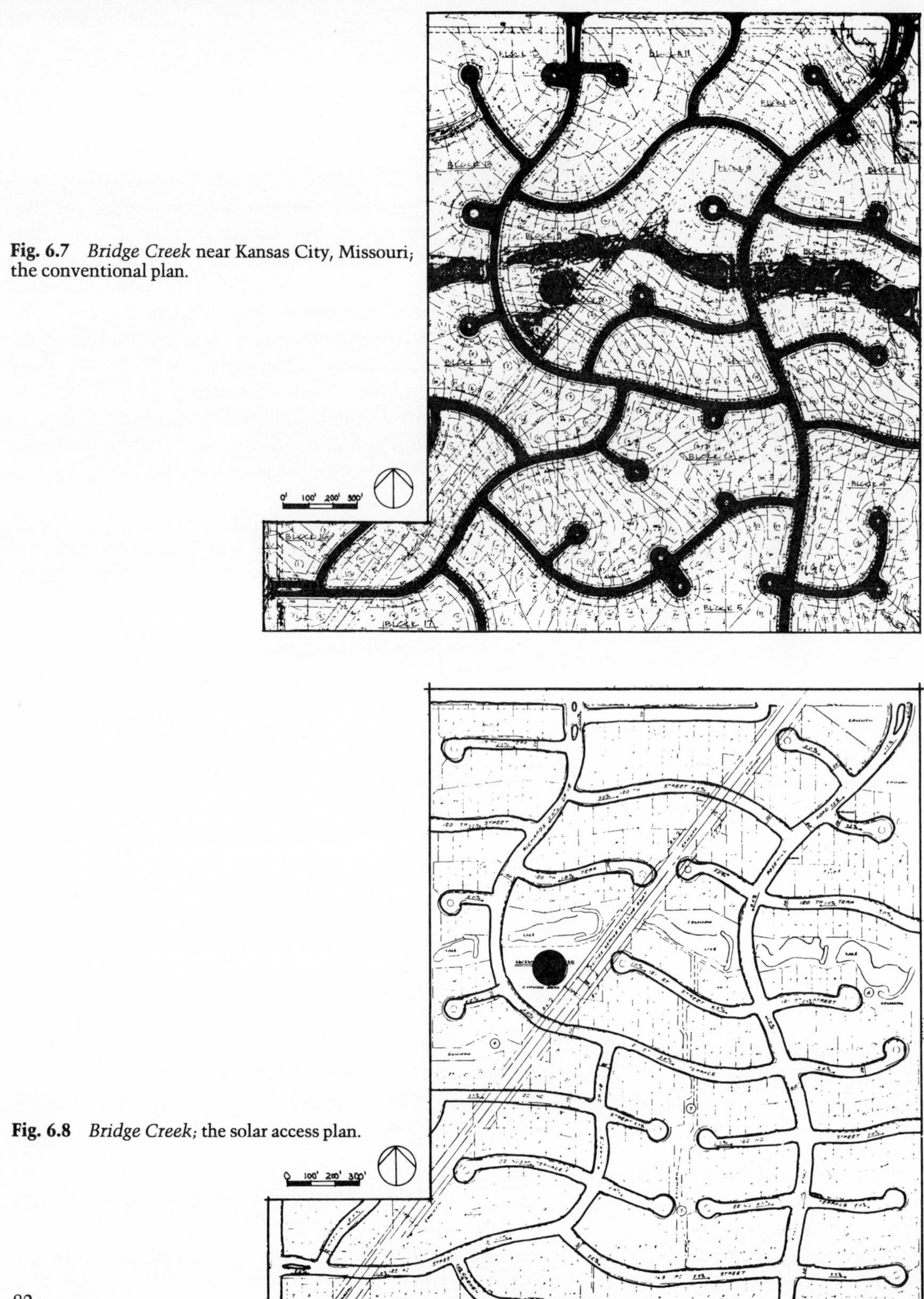

Fig. 6.7 *Bridge Creek* near Kansas City, Missouri; the conventional plan.

Fig. 6.8 *Bridge Creek*; the solar access plan.

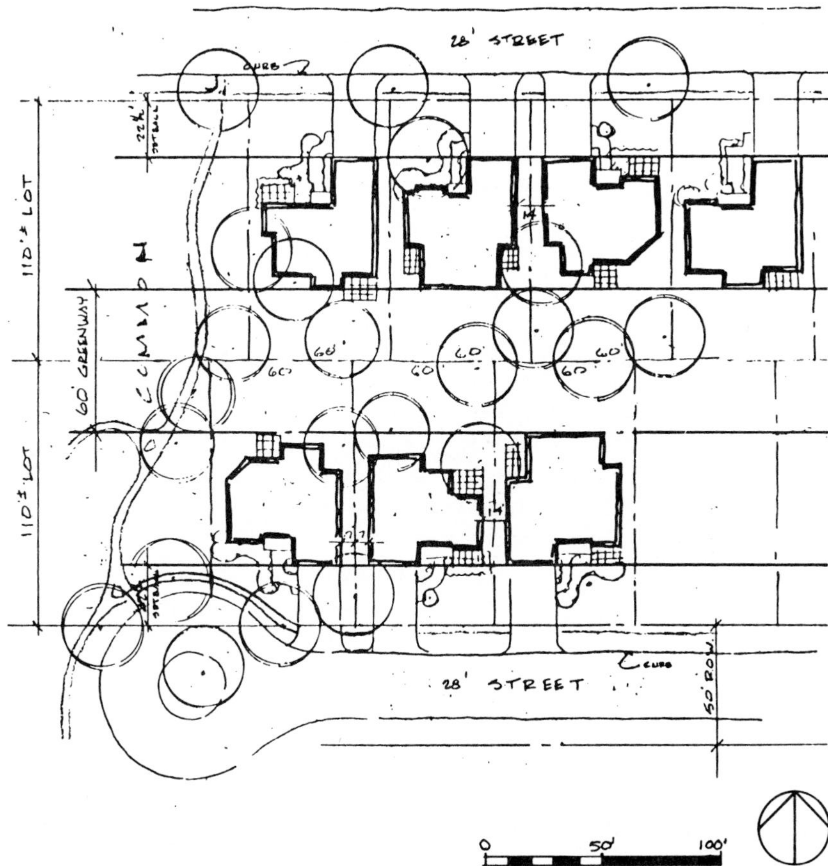

Fig. 6.9 Detail of *Bridge Creek* solar access site plan.

units/acre), whereas the solar plan accommodated 400 lots (3.4 units/acre).
Added value to lots: Expected to be considerable

Marketing Techniques
Area not yet developed

Barriers
Terrain: The terrain has a slope of 4–8 percent which was not a problem. The gas easement was effectively used to create a greenspace and to break-up the grid pattern of streets.
Zoning ordinances and officials: These presented no problems; in fact, they were eager to work with a "Solar Subdivision"
Planning board: Again, no problems. They applauded the final plat because they felt it met the needs for future development.
Land planners: The same land planner was used for the solar plan that had done the conventional plan.

Solar Access Protection
As no state, county, or city solar access legislation exists, deed restrictions will contain rules on solar access and shading, plus the

Home Owners Association will have an architectural committee to review and enforce them.

Comparative Data

	Conventional Subdivision Plan	*Solar Access Plan*
Number of lots	285	400
Total street area	23 acres	23 acres
Total lot area	83 acres	60 acres
Greenspace area	10 acres	33 acres
Number of solar lots	110	400
Percentage of subdivision solar	40%	100%

Case study information and figures were provided by Craig Eymann of Ambassador Real Estate, Inc. 1901 E. Frontier, Olathe, Kansas 66061.

CASE STUDY 5
Winding Trail Village

For over 15 years, Wonderland Hill Development Company has been building planned residential communities and has, in conjunction with its associate architectural firm Downing & Leach, pioneered the design and development of energy-efficient housing. They have developed a hierarchy of energy conserving techniques for designing housing products for the Boulder housing market. Beginning with very simple and highly cost-effective construction tightness and detailing techniques, they move to suntempering and simple sun control, and then to more expensive but more highly marketable options. After all these considerations are optimized they move into passive solar design by adding glazing in conjunction with existing mass in the structure, simple air movement systems to distribute excess solar gain, and attractive interior mass, such as brick walls, in places of maximum aesthetic impact.

Winding Trail Village in North Boulder, Colorado is an 80-unit planned development of passive solar patio homes, townhomes, and condominiums. It features open space, foot and bike paths and recreation facilities (Fig. 6.10). Ninety percent of the units have solar access. Figure 6.11 shows a view of the townhomes.

General Background

Name: Winding Trail Village
Location: North Boulder, Colorado
Climate: 6100 heating degree-days and 700 cooling hours; Region A
Credits: Builder: Wonderland Hill Development Company; Architects: Downing/Leach and Associates
Status: Planning began in March, 1977. Construction began in January 1980. Current stage of completion: 52 percent as of October 1982.
Size: The entire subdivision is approximately 38 acres. The Winding Trail Village section is 10 acres, 80 units.
Type: Passive solar patio homes and passive solar townhomes (passive solar condominiums will be built later); 1000–2200 square feet, two-bedroom and three-bedroom units; sales prices ranged from $77,000–$121,000.
Density: 8 units per acre
Solar access: 72 units or 90 percent of the units have solar access.

Economics

Interest rates and financing: Builder buy-down to 13.5 percent, two years, 30-year AML mortgage; current conventional market rate 17 percent; eight models offered under Colorado Housing Finance Authority guarantee 8.875 percent financing.
Additional costs: Solar access planning was part of the original plan consideration. It was not an extra cost.
Savings from solar planning: Again, not really, since part of initial consideration.

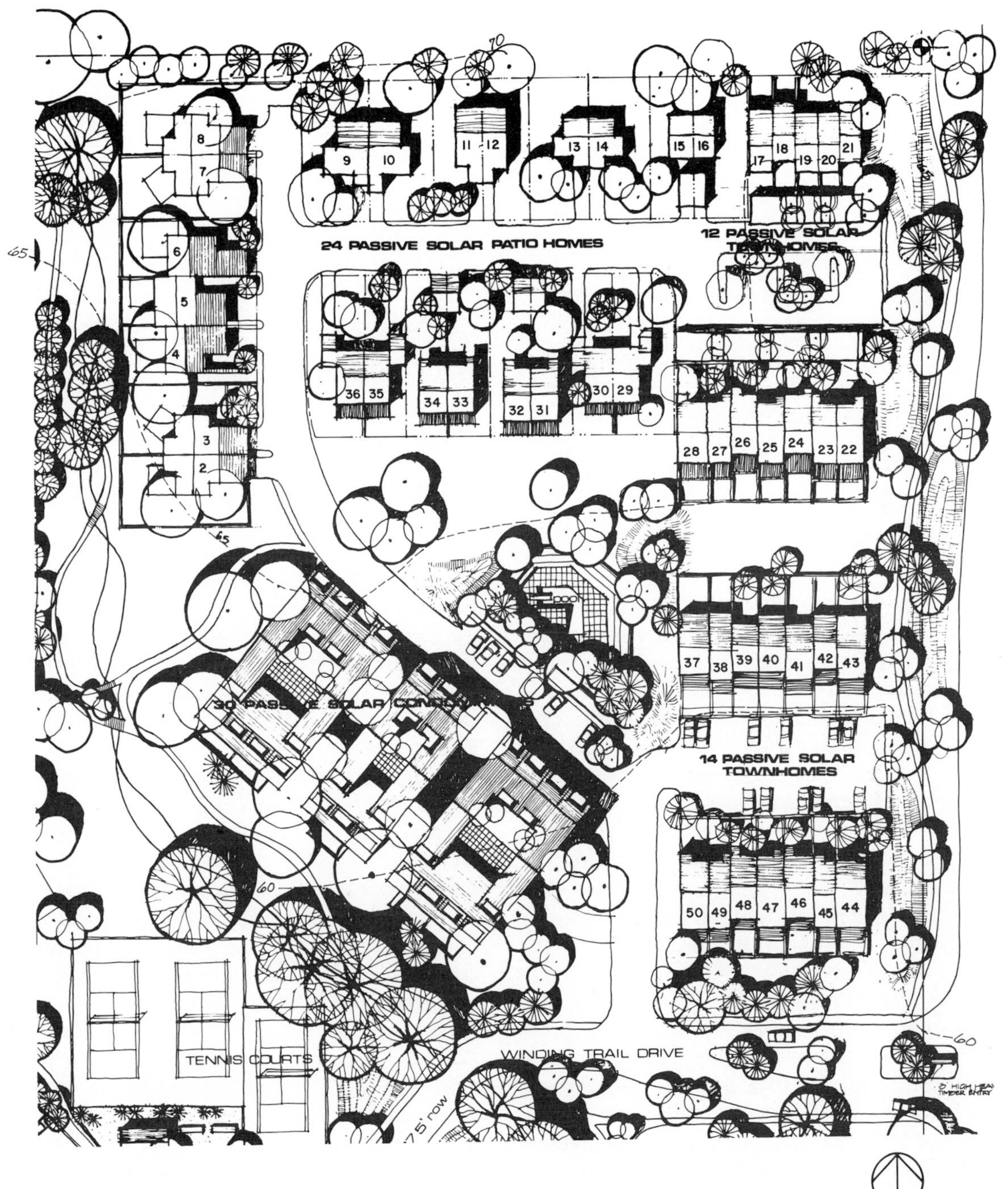

Fig. 6.10 *Winding Trail Village* in North Boulder, Colorado.

Fig. 6.11 *Winding Trail Village* townhomes.

Density bonus considerations: They were able to cluster homes which allowed for different residential unit types. In some cases this saved on utility installation, created fewer streets and used less exterior siding material. Also, it provided a density transition from surrounding lower density areas.
Time between start and sale: Average 1981 sales performance—two sales per month. Solar design and builder financing were contributing factors.
Value added to lots by solar planning: 30–40 percent over conventional lot.

Marketing Techniques
Parade of homes; solar tour of homes; press releases; comparative energy usage computer printouts; bi-monthly brokers/open house; rebates on energy usage: solar tax credits with purchase of home; and Homeowner's Pool Party and Barbeque (bring friends).

Barriers
Terrain, slope gradients: They did some overlot grading, but the site is essentially flat. There is an existing flood channel, "Wonderland Creek Drainageway," that had to be designed around.
Zoning ordinances and officials: Area was preliminarily zoned according to the comprehensive plan for the city. Annexation to the city was required. The planned unit development process was required and took about two years, involved neighborhood meetings and city processing. The process was further complicated by the fact that three major builders were/are involved in the entire subdivision.
Planning Boards: Had full support of the city planning department—main barrier/resistance was from neighbors.

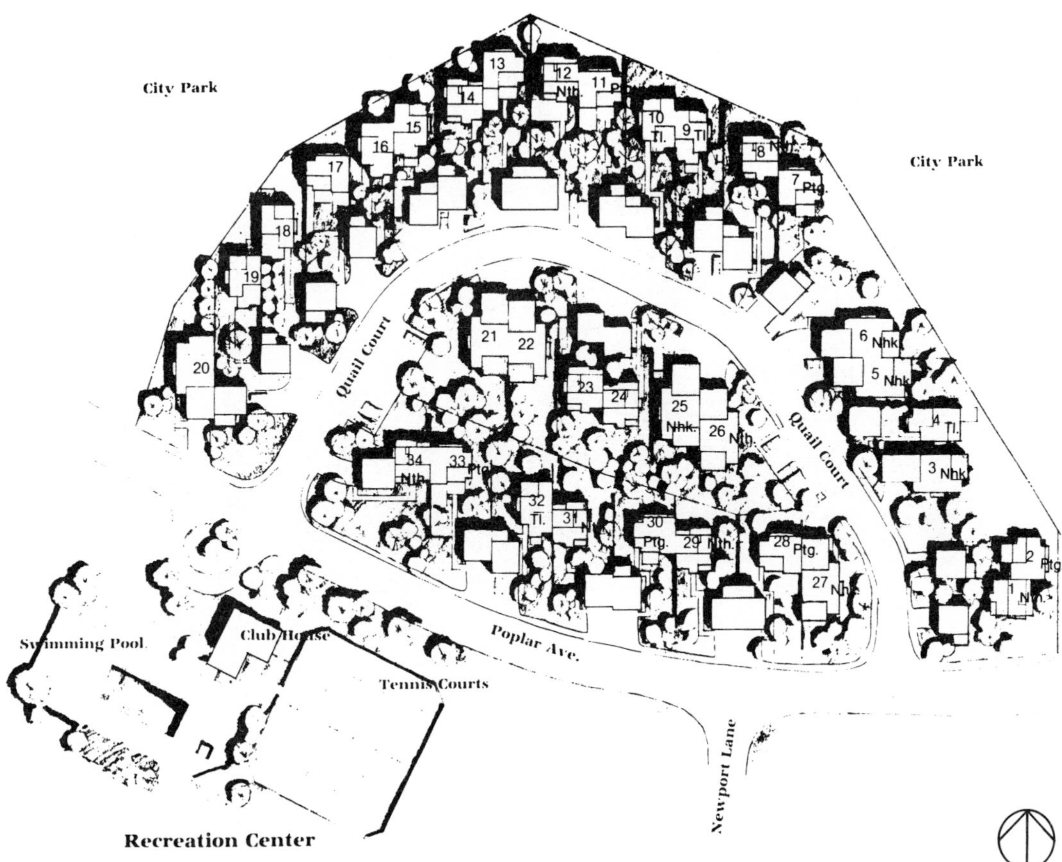

Fig. 6.12 *Wonderland Hill VI, Quail Court,* North Boulder, Colorado.

Solar Access Protection

Legislation: Currently there is some legislation being worked on, but there is nothing formal to date.

Covenants and easements: They have provided for solar easements by amendments to the covenants.

CASE STUDY 6
Wonderland Hill VI, Quail Court

Wonderland Hill is a planned unit development at the base of the North Boulder foothills. The multi-phased project initiated by the developers of Winding Trail Village, totals nearly 134 acres much of which is devoted to open space and dedicated park land. The Quail Court cluster of homes in the development is an interesting example of solar access being provided for homes along a gracefully curving street. The street follows the sloping site contours and without running east/west still provides solar access for the great majority of homes along it. Figure 6.12 illustrates the site plan of Quail Court. Figure 6.13 is a rendering of one of the homes built there.

Fig. 6.13 A *Quail Court* home.

General Background

Name: Wonderland Hill VI, Quail Court
Location: North Boulder, Colorado
Climate: 6016 heating degree-days and 700 cooling hours: Region A
Credits: Builder: Wonderland Hill Development Company; Architects: Downing/Leach & Associates
Status: Planning began in Spring 1980. Construction began in Spring 1981. Current stage of completion: 50 percent as of September 30, 1982.
Size: Quail Court is 4.5 acres of a 134 acre development.
Type: Passive solar patio homes; 1931 square feet to 2554 square feet. Three and four bedroom units; sales prices ranged from $130,000 to $180,000. New model introduced in Fall 1982 from $110,000.
Density: 7.4 units per acre
Solar access: 28 units out of 34 units have solar access.

Economics

Interest rates and financing: Builder buydown to 13.5 percent from quoted rate at closing.
Additional costs: Solar access planning was part of original plan consideration. It did not cause extra costs.
Average 1982 sales performance: 11 per month.

Marketing Techniques

General realtor campaign on biweekly basis; sophisticated brochures; models open daily.

Barriers

Irrigation ditch required by city planning department.

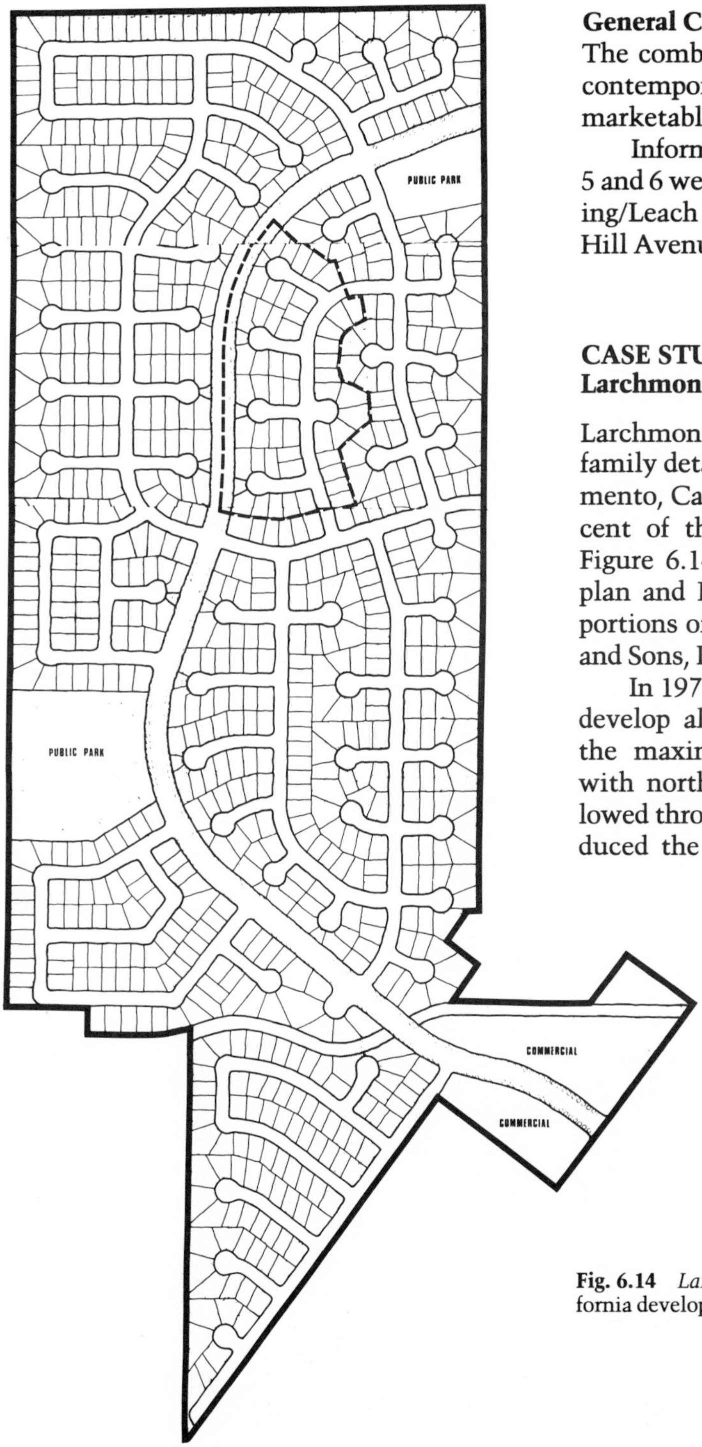

General Comments

The combination of solar concepts with the contemporary design of the product was a marketable feature of the homes.

Information and figures for Case Studies 5 and 6 were provided by James Leach, Downing/Leach and Associates, 3985 Wonderland Hill Avenue, Boulder, Colorado 80302.

CASE STUDY 7
Larchmont Summerfield

Larchmont Summerfield is an 880-unit single family detached home development in Sacramento, California designed to provide 80 percent of the units (700) with solar access. Figure 6.14 shows the overall development plan and Fig. 6.15 is a detail of one of the portions of the site developed by M. J. Brock and Sons, Inc.

In 1977 this firm made a commitment to develop all their future communities with the maximum achievable number of lots with north/south orientation and have followed through on the goal. In 1980 they introduced the "Sundial", their first production

PUBLIC PARK

PUBLIC PARK

COMMERCIAL

COMMERCIAL

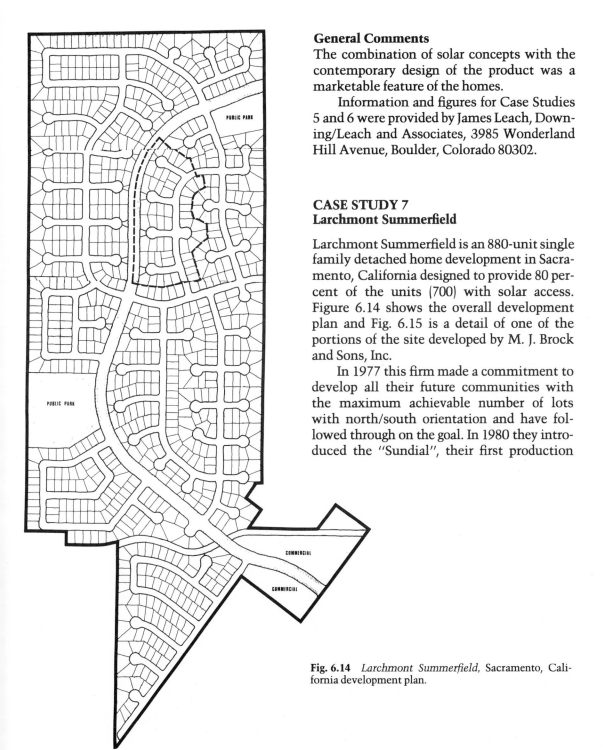

Fig. 6.14 *Larchmont Summerfield,* Sacramento, California development plan.

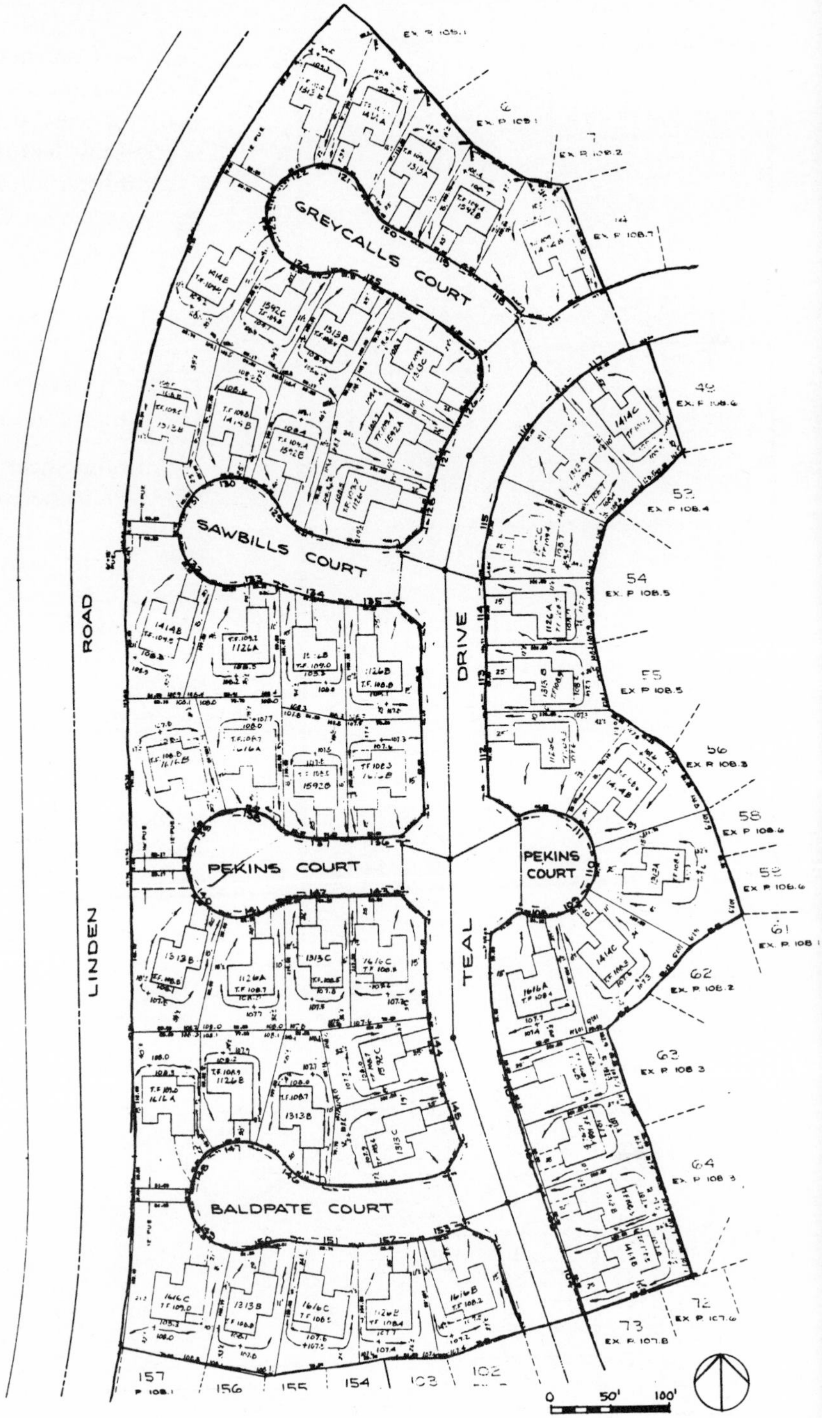

Fig. 6.15 Detail of one section of *Larchmont Summerfield*.

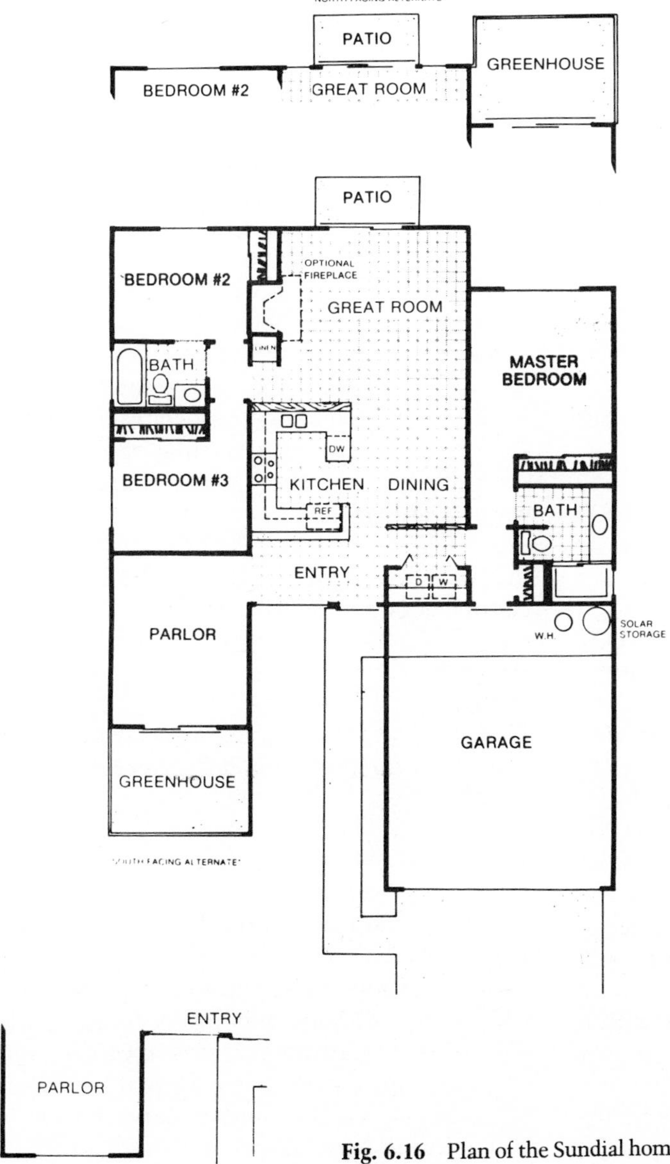

Fig. 6.16 Plan of the Sundial home.

passive solar home. The Sundial II plan shown in Fig. 6.16 is one of the most popular solar home models built in this development, among others. M. J. Brock & Sons found that by building energy-conserving passive solar homes that closely resemble standard homes, their subdivisions appealed to a much wider market.

General Background

Name: Larchmont Summerfield

Location: West Sacramento (Yolo County) California

Climate: 2700 heating degree-days and 800 cooling hours; Region B.
Credits: Carroll E. Brock, Developer, M. J. Brock & Sons, Inc.
Status: Planned, purchased and approved by 1978, with the first development activity in 1979. As of June 1982, 150 units have been constructed by M. J. Brock & Sons, Inc. plus approximately 200 units by other builders.
Size: Approximately 230 acres.
Type: 880 single family homes on 60′ × 100′ (6,000 sq. ft.) lots. (The year the subdivision was obtained, approximately half (440) of the lots were purchased for development by another Sacramento home builder.)
Density: 3.8 units/acre
Solar access: 80 percent of units (or about 700 units) have solar access.

Economics

The subdivision received approval of the U.S. Department of Housing and Urban Development qualifying it for typical Federal Housing Administration (FHA) insured loans as well as typical Veterans Administration (VA) guaranteed loans.

Due to the minimum lot size of 6,000 square feet allowed by Yolo County, the solar access and lot orientation was achieved without apparent cost. The predominance of north/south lot orientation was the only solar concern.

The time between start of construction and sale of the solar subdivision units was comparable to conventional development.

They do not believe it is possible to discern any value added to the lots by solar access planning, but the short cul-de-sac design seems to have marketing appeal.

Marketing Techniques

Parade of Homes: The subdivision has been a part of the Sacramento Building Industry Association Annual Tour of Homes.
Press releases: The original press releases mentioned the high percentage of North/South lot orientation. The addition of the Sundial Plan heralded the arrival of the "first passive solar production house by M. J. Brock & Sons, Inc." In 1980, to heighten awareness of passive solar building techniques, M. J. Brock & Sons, Inc. gave away by lottery a Sundial house built in the Summerfield development valued at $80,000.
Performance of solar homes: The Sundial (one of five model homes) was rated by Davis Alternative Technology Associates as 55–65 percent active and passive solar efficient for space heating and cooling and domestic hot water heating.
Tax credits: M. J. Brock & Sons, Inc. retained the state tax credits, allowing the buyer to claim federal tax credits.

Barriers

None
Terrain: Flat terrain (previously farmland)
Planning and zoning boards: Accepted their approach.

Comparative Data

No study was performed to compare the number of solar-oriented lots in a conventional subdivision plan for this site to the number of lots using the solar plan because M. J. Brock & Sons, Inc. has been designing subdivisions with solar access since 1977 and no longer prepares "conventional" subdivision plans. North/South orientation is a must for at least 80 percent of all units in their subdivisions.

Case Study information and figures were provided by Donald E. Reed, Executive Director, M. J. Brock & Sons, Inc. 3350 Watt Avenue, Sacramento, California 95821.

PART THREE

PASSIVE SOLAR HOME DESIGN

With rising fuel prices driving homeowner's utility bills to increasingly higher levels, builders, homeowners and mortgage lenders are giving greater attention to overall monthly housing costs.

This section presents a comprehensive assessment of the impact of windows on residential energy consumption. A considerable amount of energy waste in buildings can be attributed to windows: their thermal resistance is typically lower than that of the surrounding wall; they leak air and admit the hot summer sun into the home. Simple calculations of the thermal gain and loss attributed to windows have led to sweeping recommendations that window areas be reduced, and that windows be eliminated wherever possible.

We cannot overlook the many possible benefits that can be provided by windows, benefits not only of view and aesthetics but also of significant energy savings. When windows are used as passive solar collectors, light sources and ventilators, a very different picture of their impact upon annual energy consumption emerges. Depending upon critical decisions about design and use, windows can either greatly decrease, increase or have little effect on annual energy consumption, as illustrated throughout this book.

Windows, if properly located and managed, can reduce annual home energy consumption by up to 40 percent over an identical home located in the same climate with poorly placed and unmanaged windows.

Unmanaged east or west facing windows can significantly increase summer cooling loads and cause uncomfortable interior space temperatures.

Properly managed windows consisting of adequate summer shading, operable sash to enhance natural ventilation, and a low thermal conductance (U-value) obtained by either multiple layers of glass or operable night insulation can result in significant net annual energy savings to the home owner.

The following chapters will help the building community and mortgage lenders determine the likely energy effects of windows in new housing and thereby encourage the choice of energy efficient windows. The specific objectives of this section are:

- to convey that passive solar techniques are sound, worthwhile and relatively easy to implement;
- to explain basic principles of passive solar design;
- to present easy-to-use technical information and design tips;
- to illustrate sample homes that can face toward north or south with the same plan and only minor modifications to the elevations;
- to demonstrate how existing popular house plans can be made solar with minimal modifications.

Our discussion does have some limitations:

- Only direct gain passive solar techniques are covered; recommendations are for wood frame homes constructed on a slab, and for wood frame homes constructed on a wood floor over either a crawl space or basement. More advanced passive solar systems are not covered in this guide.
- Performance predictions are complex and time consuming; therefore, no detailed method for estimation is given. Instead, easy-to-use rules of thumb and bottom-line design recommendations are presented.
- This is not a substitute for expert advice.

Many of the guidelines and design parameters presented in Chapters 7 and 10 are derived from an extensive computer investigation of window performance in homes by the National Association of Homebuilders Research Foundation (NAHB Research Foundation), the National Fenestration Council (NFC), the Computer Computation Bureau/Cumali Associates (CCB/CA), Lawrence Berkeley Laboratories (LBL) and a variety of sources noted in the Acknowledgements and Reference Section.

CHAPTER SEVEN

The Concept of Suntempering

DEFINITION

While it is technically possible to design passive solar systems that provide greater than 90 percent of a home's heating requirement, it is more economical (given the current cost of energy and solar equipment) to design for a smaller solar contribution, and to rely on back-up heat supplied by a conventional system to make up the difference.

Suntempering is a basic application of a direct gain passive solar heating system that derives maximum benefit from the sun's energy in the most economical way, using no additional thermal storage.

Simply stated, suntempered homes use the heat capacity inherent in the materials of typical wood frame home construction for thermal storage. Suntempering can contribute from 20 to 35 percent of the space heating requirements of a home. Passive solar systems that contribute more energy than those covered in this book generally require greater amounts of thermal energy storage, at higher costs. These systems may or may not be economical, depending on local climate and energy costs. Suntempering primarily involves increasing window and glass door areas on the south side of the home to admit solar gain in winter, and also shading them properly during the summer season.

A suntempered home is well insulated and weatherized and takes advantage of good orientation. More south glazing and less east, west and north glazing increases winter heat gain and reduces summer gain because south glass can be shaded more easily.

The concept of suntempering is most clearly presented as a series of minor modifications to home designs that have already proven successful in the marketplace. The first step, best done during the initial planning of a new development, is to orient the longest elevation of each house to face south (see Orientation, Chapter 4).

In order to get a feel for the south glazing areas involved in suntempering, consider a small single family detached home with 1200 square feet of living space. Typical homes of this type have a total window area that equals 15 percent of the floor space, or $0.15 \times 1200 = 180$ square feet. Placement of 80 percent of the window area on the south side of the home yields a solar collection area of 141 square feet or nearly 12 percent of the floor area. The remaining 20 percent may be distributed on the north, east and west elevations as needed for light, view and egress. Though the cost of this approach to suntempering is small, a significant portion of the space heat-

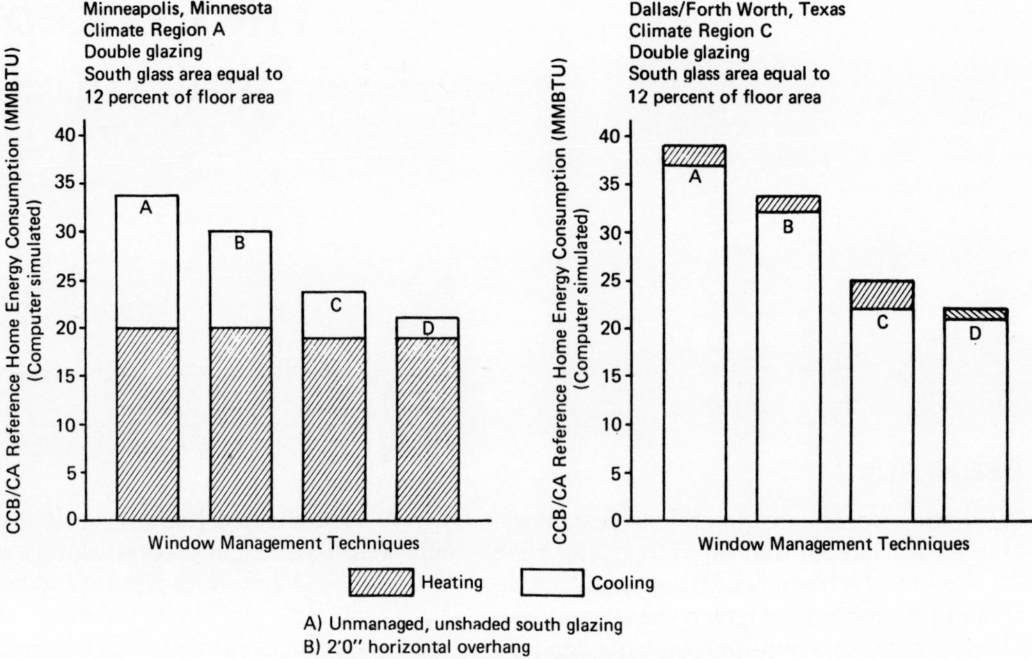

Fig. 7.1 Impact of window management techniques.

ing need will be displaced by direct solar gain, especially if proper window management techniques are also implemented (Fig. 7.1). These techniques are discussed in later sections and Chapter 11.

For a relatively modest increase in initial cost, additional properly managed glass may be added to the home to achieve greater savings. Chapter 10 describes how much glass may be added beneficially for each of three major climate regions.

Suntempered buildings fall into two very different categories, those constructed on concrete slab foundations and those constructed with crawl spaces or basements. Suppose, in the first category, that the home is built with frame construction on a concrete floor slab. The floor slab is at least 4 inches but no greater than 6 inches thick (which is the recommended mass thickness range) and will have a gross area of 1200 square feet. Even if only 30 to 50 percent of the slab area is available for thermal storage (i.e., exposed to the sun), the slab will significantly enhance the home's ability to store solar radiation during the day for use in the evening hours, thus further reducing the space heating load.

A concrete floor slab as described above is commonly called *thermal storage*. As can be seen in the tables in Chapter 10, a properly insulated floor slab substantially reduces annual energy use. The floor slab, or other equivalent forms of thermal storage such as

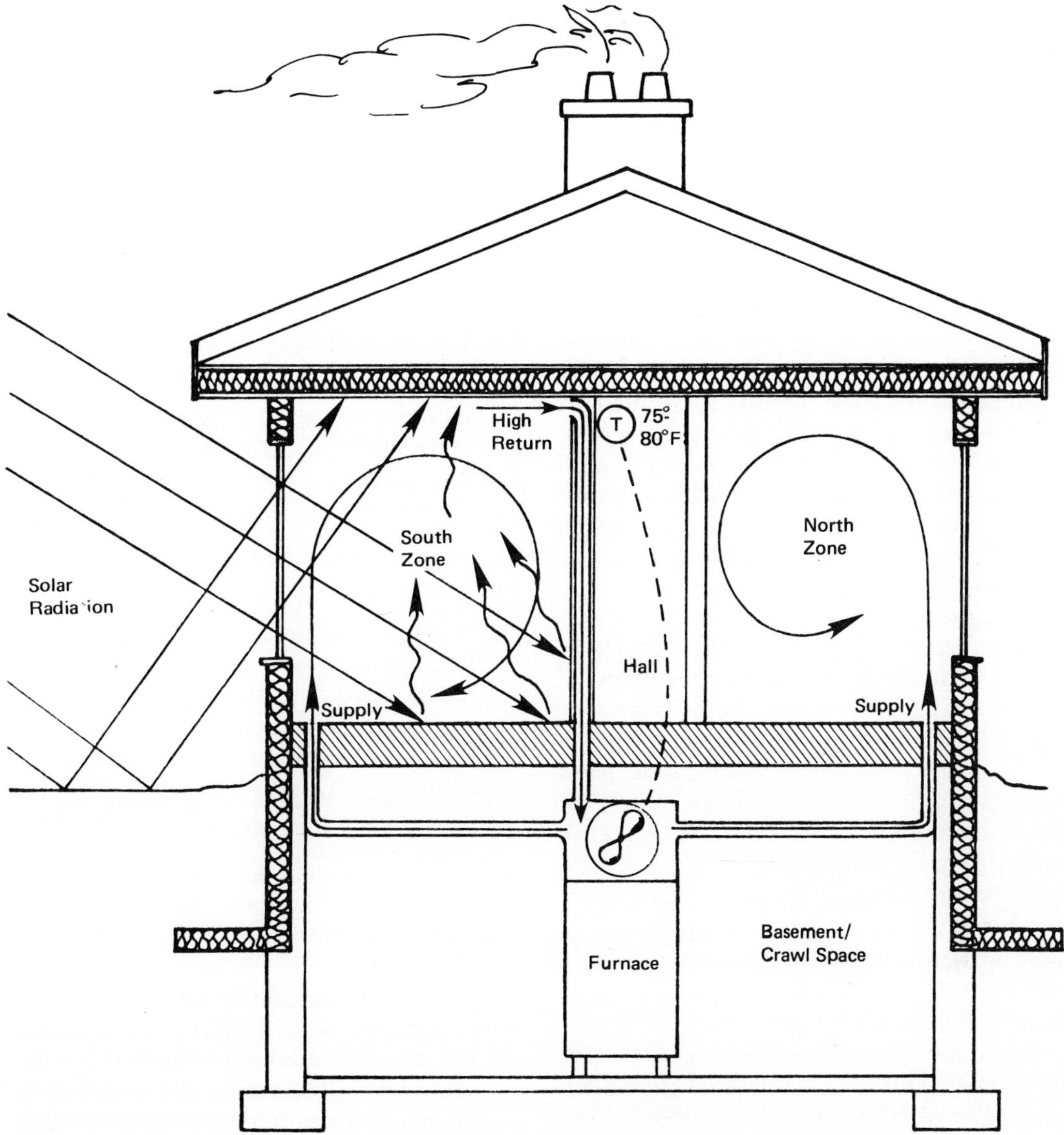

Fig. 7.2 High return and fan-on-only cycle improves solar heat distribution in a suntempered home.

exposed interior masonry walls, masonry fireplaces, 2 to 4 inches of slate or dense tile over a wooden floor, or at least one inch (two ½-inch layers sandwiched together) of gypsum board on interior wall surfaces, have four important benefits.

First, thermal storage allows for larger beneficial south glass areas in each climate region, thus reducing the need for back-up heat energy. Second, it reduces large daily temperature fluctuations, thereby increasing comfort. Third, it results in a more efficient use of the sun's energy. And fourth, by having direct contact with the ground the slab acts to reduce summer cooling loads.

If the suntempered building has a wood frame floor (over a crawl space or basement) which is not covered with 4 inches of slate or tile, and if additional gypsum board is not applied to interior wall surfaces, then this is considered a low-mass home that typifies the second category. These buildings have less thermal storage relative to the size of collection area than do slab homes. The most significant thermal storage material within the structure is the gypsum board that lines the walls and ceiling. The illustrations in Chapter 10 indicate that while the larger glazing area is beneficial (up to 15 percent of the floor area in Climate A), it does not result in as great a savings as a similar home incorporating some form of thermal storage.

The ability of a suntempered home, having a wood-floor over basement or crawl space, to store incoming solar radiation efficiently may be improved by locating return air ducts near the ceiling and by adding an air-only cycle to the heating system. This cycle utilizes a separate thermostat which operates only the furnace blower (Fig. 7.2). This technique is most easily incorporated in home designs that use a forced air distribution system. However, it can also be designed to operate as a separate air redistribution system when other types of heat distribution are planned.

These measures will have the following beneficial effects:

- minimize temperature stratification between floor and ceiling and north and south rooms;
- increase the effective storage capacity of the gypsum board and furnishings;
- reduce overheating

An air-only cycle can also improve the performance of a suntempered home containing a floor slab or other form of thermal storage.

A discussion of homes with south glass areas greater than 15 percent of the floor area is beyond the scope of this book. See Appendix IV for references on the subject.

GUIDELINES FOR INCORPORATING THERMAL STORAGE IN A SUNTEMPERED HOME

Thermal storage is the term used to describe materials which store heat energy.

- Masonry or concrete thermal storage thicknesses greater than 4 to 6 inches are not cost effective, and more than 8 inches is actually detrimental to thermal performance, due to thermal lag effects.

  "The range of thermal storage thicknesses between 2 and 4 inches can be considered a transition region. In this region solar performance penalties for reduced thicknesses are becoming significant, but in some cases may be considered acceptable depending on design and cost trade-offs."[1]

- Floor slabs in direct sun should be medium to dark in color and if covered, use a finish material that enables the sun's rays to be absorbed into the slab. Floor coverings which accomplish this include quarry tile, slate, linoleum, and vinyl tiles. These and other similar surfaces should have a matt or low reflectance finish and be dark in color.

---

[1] William Wray, *Design and Analysis of Direct Gain Solar Heated Buildings*, U.S. Dept. of Energy Contract No. LA-8885-MS, June 1981.

TABLE 7.1 R-Values of various wall and floor coverings *

Material	R-Value
Tile, asphalt, linoleum, vinyl, rubber (1/16 in.)	0.05
Terrazzo tile (1.0 in.)	0.08
Tile, asphalt, linoleum, vinyl, rubber (1/8 in.)	0.10
Cork tile (1/8 in.)	0.28
Plywood, Douglas fir (1/4 in.)	0.31
Gypsum or plaster board (3/8 in.)	0.32
Gypsum or plaster board (1/2 in.)	0.45
Plywood, Douglas fir (1/2 in.)	0.62
Wood, hardwood finish (3/4 in.)	0.68
Carpet and rubber pad	1.23
Gypsum or plaster board (3/8 in. over 1/2 in. furring strips)	1.68
Gypsum or plaster board (1/2 in. over 1/2 in. furring strips)	1.81
Carpet and fibrous pad	2.08

* *ASHRAE Handbook and Product Directory, 1977 Fundamentals*, American Society of Heating, Refrigerating, and Air Conditioning Engineers, Inc., New York, 1977, p. 22.13.

- Floor slabs covered with carpet do not work as well as exposed slabs for thermal storage, because the carpet and pad act as insulators which prevent efficient transfer of solar radiation into the floor. A maximum acceptable R-value for the floor covering would be 0.25–0.50. Heavily insulated buildings with larger amounts of south glass area should consider the lower end of the range as a recommended floor covering R-value. The R-values of various wall and floor coverings are given in Table 7.1.
- Dark colored thermal storage which is directly in view of the solar windows should have a surface area equal to three times the south glass area which charges it. Light colored thermal storage should equal five to seven times the south glass area.

TABLE 7.2 Solar absorptance of various materials *

Material	Absorptance
Flat black paint	0.95
Black lacquer	0.92
Dark gray paint	0.91
Black concrete	0.91
Dark blue lacquer	0.91
Black oil paint	0.90
Stafford blue bricks	0.89
Dark olive drab paint	0.89
Dark brown paint	0.88
Dark blue-gray paint	0.88
Azure blue or dark green lacquer	0.88
Brown concrete	0.85
Medium brown paint	0.84
Medium light brown paint	0.80
Brown or green lacquer	0.79
Medium rust paint	0.78
Light gray oil paint	0.75
Red oil paint	0.74
Red bricks	0.70
Uncolored concrete	0.65
Moderately light buff bricks	0.60
Medium dull green paint	0.59
Medium orange paint	0.58
Medium yellow paint	0.57
Medium blue paint	0.51
Medium Kelly green paint	0.51
Light green paint	0.47
White semi-gloss paint	0.30
White gloss paint	0.25
Silver paint	0.25
White lacquer	0.21

This table is meant to serve as a guide only. Variations in texture, tone, overcoats, pigments, binders, etc. can vary these values.

* G. G. Gubareff, et al., *Thermal Radiation Properties Survey*, Second Edition, Honeywell Research Center, Minneapolis-Honeywell Regulator Company, Minneapolis, Minnesota, 1960, and S. W. Moore, Los Alamos National Laboratory, Solar Energy Group, unpublished data.

The following suggestions for placement and coloring of massive and light materials near south-facing glazing are based on analyses performed by Los Alamos National Laboratories, on recommendations published by

Edward Mazria, and on common sense.

- The lightweight materials in a direct gain building should be relatively light in color, while massive materials should be relatively dark. This will assure adequate distribution of transmitted solar radiation because light colored materials reflect and diffuse the incoming light onto dark colored materials which absorb and store the solar radiation.
- The first surface struck by transmitted solar radiation should be of a light to moderate color. This will help foster uniform heating of the space receiving solar radiation directly. Light colors should only be used for massive materials if large areas of relatively dark massive materials are exposed in the same space.
- Massive materials should be distributed throughout a direct gain space as uniformly as possible. The use of masonry for interior partitions is particularly effective because both sides of the partition can face direct gain spaces, thus doubling the effective exposed surface area.

THE IMPORTANCE OF ACTIVE WINDOW MANAGEMENT

Windows provide light, views, ventilation and emergency exits for homes. When properly installed and managed they also can provide significant amounts of heating energy to the home during winter months.

A properly installed window is carefully caulked and insulated at the junction between the window frame and rough opening to minimize infiltration. For example, a poorly installed window unit may result in a triple glazed unit that performs no better than a single glazed unit, so that the potential benefits of two additional panes of glass and air spaces are offset by excessive infiltration due to inadequate seals. In order for properly installed and oriented windows to further decrease annual energy consumption, active window management by the homeowner is required.

Window management techniques range from those that are operated seasonally, such as exterior operable shade devices, to those which are operated daily (on 24-hour cycles), such as night insulation. Properly managed windows can reduce annual energy consumption by up to 35 percent (Fig. 7.4).

Unmanaged windows produce excessive solar gain in the summer, a high incidence of glare, and excessive night heat loss during the winter. A common fixed overhang is one window management technique requiring no user control, but it must be carefully designed.

A more effective summer window management technique is the use of movable exterior shade screens, blinds or awnings. This enables the homeowner to properly shade the window to meet his or her own comfort requirements. In addition, movable exterior window management has the potential for greater annual energy savings than a fixed shade device (see Chapter 11).

The use of interior located roller shades, insulated curtains, drapes and shutters can not only reduce summer heat gain but also substantially enhance winter window performance. Interior window management devices, although not as effective in preventing summer heat gain as exterior shading, can also provide privacy, security and improved comfort.

As can be seen in Figure 7.1, operable windows providing natural ventilation to the home can save additional energy that would otherwise be provided by mechanical cooling. A good rule of thumb for determining the amount of operable sash is 40 to 50 percent of the building's total window area. Efforts should be made to locate windows and doors to provide cross-ventilation throughout the home.

DWELLING FORM

Recommendations

Plan units to maintain relatively compact forms, with the least amount of exterior surface. Avoid complex projections and indentations of heated space in plan and section. The repeated use of a simple housing form may not be very attractive to purchasers, but interesting variations can be achieved by the use of unheated elements without reducing high energy efficiency. Garages, covered porches, vestibules and storage sheds are elements that can be planned around the main living space where they add not only visual interest but also shelter and, to some extent, insulate the walls to which they are joined.

Use climate controls in the form of porches, balconies or cantilevers to shade lower stories (south, west), trellises (south, west), wind screens (on prevailing windward side), awnings (east, south, west), shutters and greenhouses (south). These elements can create an improved microclimate which extends the number of days that residents may enjoy relaxing outdoors in cold climates, as well as improve the home's appearance.

Generally, the greater the exterior surface area of a building, the higher its heat losses will be. Figure 7.3 shows the relative heat losses for various forms of dwellings, all with approximately the same amount of livable floor area and all identically insulated.

The ranch, two-story, and split entry houses are all free standing. The ranch has the highest heat loss because it is relatively spread out and has the highest ratio of exposed surface area to volume. The ranch is the least energy efficient house form, but when sited with an elongated wall facing south it provides a significant portion of the living space with a south facing exposure.

The two-story house more closely approaches the shape of a cube and therefore has a smaller ratio of surface area to volume. For this reason it has a calculated heat loss rate that is nine percent less than the ranch house.

The detached split entry house is similar to the free standing two-story house in its compact shape, but it has a smaller total surface area to be heated. The split entry house should therefore be more economical to heat than a two-story house.

The semi-detached duplex is similar to the detached single family house, but since one of its walls is not exposed to the weather, it has a heat loss rate that is 20 percent less than the ranch house.

Row housing units have both long walls sheltered from the weather (except for end units), making this an extremely energy effi-

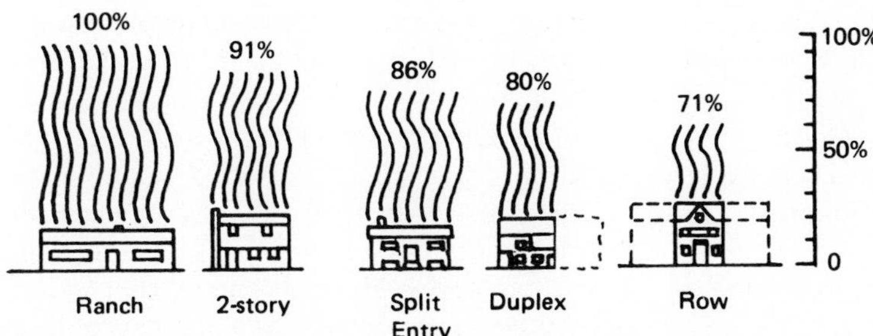

Fig. 7.3 Relative heat losses by dwelling type. Heat losses are shown as a percent of heat loss of the ranch of same habitable floor area.

cient building form. The most efficient form is stacked units, for example, a low- or mid-rise building.

Despite the wide variations in energy efficiency of these dwelling types, energy consumption is only one factor considered by purchasers in choosing a home. A number of specific measures described in this book can improve the energy efficiency of each of the dwelling forms discussed above.

CHAPTER EIGHT

Suntempered Home Design

Suntempered homes can be designed to look as similar or dissimilar to their conventional, marketable, non-solar counterparts as the builder desires, because suntempered home designs are simply modified versions of conventional home designs that have already been proven in the marketplace. The modifications are so straightforward that all types of conventional home designs can be converted to suntempered home designs. Almost every new home built today can utilize direct gain passive solar design to reduce its energy consumption without exotic technology or large cost increases.

This chapter outlines design principles for suntempered homes, describes home types, and gives plans and elevations of eight sample home designs as an illustration of how to make an existing house plan a suntempered plan. Perhaps your best selling model is ideally suited to become a suntempered home! The following design principles are characteristics to look for in your plans.

DESIGN PRINCIPLES FOR SUNTEMPERED HOMES

1. *To the extent architecturally feasible, locate the rooms most used during the day along the southern side of the home to take advantage of direct gain solar heating.*

In general, most often used rooms such as great rooms, family rooms, dining rooms, kitchen-eating areas, bedrooms and living rooms (if they are used daily) are the preferred rooms for the south side. These rooms should be spatially organized in a manner that reflects the residents' need for sunlight and ventilation throughout the day and season. For example, a breakfast area located on the southeast corner enables early morning winter sun to penetrate and warm the space, and enrich the morning routine with a play of light and shadow falling on tables, plants, walls and floor.

Identify the lifestyle of your market (i.e., family-oriented or entertainment-oriented) to determine which rooms will typically be used most during the day.

2. *Locate non-living areas away from the southern side of the home, either (a) along the northern wall or (b) internally in the home as "cores" (away from both the northern and southern walls).*

Bathrooms, closets, hallways, stairs, utility rooms, kitchen food preparation areas (non-eating areas occupied by heat generating appliances and cabinets) and living rooms (if they are rarely used) are the preferred rooms for the north side. These spaces act as a buffer against infiltration and facilitate a plan organ-

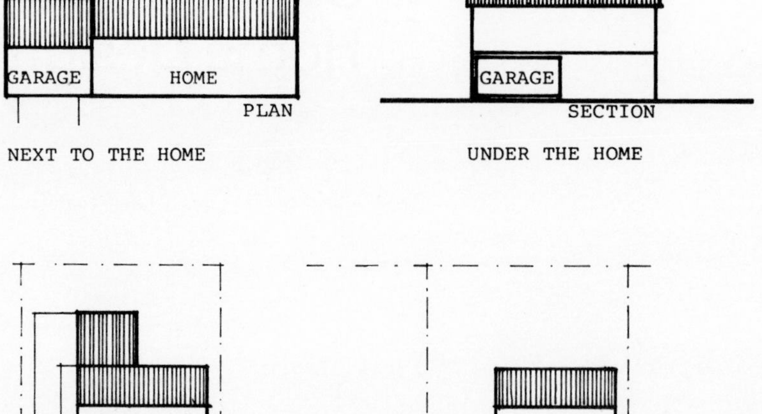

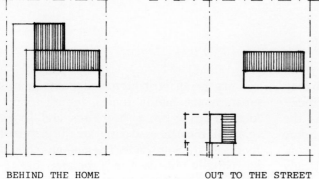

Fig. 8.1 The garage situation.

ization with the most frequently used spaces to the south where they receive ample natural light and solar radiation.

3. *Provide an open internal layout.*

Minimize partition walls, especially those running east/west which can impede the transfer of heat from the southern side of the home to the northern side.

4. *Employ more south facing glass than north, east or west facing glass to enhance beneficial solar gain and minimize excessive and unwanted radiation.*

This is the most general guideline possible. See Chapter 10, *Fenestration Guidelines: The Design and Placement of Windows,* for specific recommendations by climate region.

5. *Employ effective window shading strategies.*

Movable exterior shading devices provide the most effective protection from the sun. See Chapter 11, *Window Management Techniques,* for more specific information.

6. *Whenever possible locate garages, carports and porches so as to maximize south wall area and to either buffer north winds or shade west (or east) walls* (Fig. 8.1).

Garages and carports can block both undesirable summer solar gain *and* desirable winter solar gain. It is advisable to locate these structures so that they block summer sun on the west or east sides of a home but not attempt to shade the south with them. In situations whre the street front of a home faces south, the garage or carport would preferably go either:

- Next to the home, resulting in a wider lot;
- under a part of the home, as in a bi-level or split level;
- behind the home, resulting in a longer driveway, or
- out to the street (perhaps joined with the garage from the adjacent lot) to permit the sun to reach the south wall over it.

Porches can be built to shade the south walls of homes in hot climates in the summer only by leaving off the roof deck and growing vines on the joists. The vines will shade well in the summer, but after they lose their leaves will cause little shading in winter.

The following table lists more comprehensive planning and design principles.

SUMMARY OF DESIGN CONSIDERATIONS FOR SUNTEMPERED HOMES

Site Considerations	**Applicable seasons**	
• Avoid dead air pockets or low areas which do not receive any breeze.	Summer	
• Use natural ground cover to reduce ambient temperatures and solar glare.	Summer	
• Cut or prune trees which block solar access on the south.		Winter
• Use conifers to block or direct winter winds.		Winter
• Build close to existing trees to maximize roof shading potential. Protect roots.	Summer	
• Shade paved areas to reduce ambient temperatures near homes.	Summer	
• Where possible, use on-site materials (stone, wood, earth) for construction or berming.	Summer	Winter
• Utilize existing trees to shade hard-to-protect, east and west windows.	Summer	

Planning Principles	**Applicable seasons**	
• Proportion the home to reduce summer exposure and increase winter exposure; long axis in east-west direction.	Summer	Winter
• Zone activity spaces for summer-winter and day-night uses; living areas to the south.	Summer	Winter
• Minimize interior partitions for increased cross-ventilation and heat transfer.	Summer	Winter
• Use shading devices to protect south, east and west walls and windows from the sun.	Summer	
• Consider extended porches and verandas to shade east and west walls.	Summer	
• Place garage, service and utility spaces on north or windward side of the building.		Winter
• Locate entrances away from winter winds and use vestibules or airlocks to reduce infiltration.		Winter
• Face long side of building toward prevailing summer winds and away from prevailing winter winds.	Summer	Winter
• Balance openings for good cross-ventilation.	Summer	
• Place operable windows in each room at the level where people will benefit from them (i.e., low in sleeping spaces, medium in seating areas, and high in kitchens).	Summer	
• Locate fireplaces away from exterior walls.		Winter
• Ensure adequate natural lighting to all living spaces.	Summer	Winter
• Cluster baths, kitchens, and laundry rooms near hot water heater to reduce line losses.	Summer	Winter
• Ensure careful installation of insulation and weatherstripping.	Summer	Winter

Planning Principles (continued)	**Applicable seasons**	
• Isolate or vent heat-generating appliances in summer and utilize waste heat in winter.	Summer	Winter
Floors and Foundations		
• Insulate concrete slabs at edges to prevent heat drain to grade and subgrade earth.		Winter
• Insulate crawl spaces at perimeter or under floor.		Winter
Walls		
• Increase wall insulation to R-19 minimum.	Summer	Winter
• Use continuous caulking bead under sill plates at foundation, ground floor and upper story decks.	Summer	Winter
• If walls are brick or block, insulate on exterior to increase mass of building.	Summer	Winter
• Avoid thermal bridges. Use insulating sheathing to reduce conduction losses through framing members.	Summer	Winter
• Avoid unnecessary corners and joints.	Summer	Winter
• Insulate behind wall outlets and/or plumbing lines in exterior walls.	Summer	Winter
• Use colors which are appropriate for heat collection (dark) or rejection (light).	Summer	Winter
Windows and Doors		
• Design shading systems to protect south, east and west facing glass from undesirable heat gains in the summer.	Summer	
• Design shading systems which can be adjusted according to the season.	Summer	Winter
• Consider interior and exterior shutters to prevent summer heat gain and winter heat losses.	Summer	Winter
• Reduce glazing area on north side; increase on south side.		Winter
• Pay special attention to west facing glass which can produce the most serious overheating problems.	Summer	
• Use insulated glass and ensure that aluminum frames have a complete thermal break.	Summer	Winter
• Use triple glazing where night insulation will not be utilized to prevent excessive losses.		Winter
• Guard against excessive gains and losses on skylights.	Summer	Winter
• Design south facing glass as a solar collector. Guard against glare and fading of furnishings.		Winter
Roofs		
• Increase attic space insulation to R-38 minimum.	Summer	Winter
• Use light colored roofing materials to reduce solar heat gain.	Summer	
• Ensure adequate ventilation.	Summer	

SUNTEMPERED HOME TYPES

There are numerous ways to design a suntempered home with the south side located to match a given lot orientation. Any plan conforming to the design principles listed previously could qualify. There are also quite a few ways to design suntempered homes that, with the identical plan, can be built to face north *or* south, as lot orientation dictates.

The number of home models builders choose to design and build varies widely. Some builders prefer to build a large number of models in a given development and others prefer to build a few models repetitively on lots of different orientations. The number of lots with different orientations on which a given home can be built depends upon the number of potentially south facing sides of the home. In a home with two potentially south facing sides, the large south and small north glazing areas are merely reversed in accordance with lot orientation. Homes with south facing long front and back walls (on wider lots) or long side walls (on narrow lots) *only* are recommended (See Figs 8.2, 8.3, 8.4).

When the narrow end of a home contains the large, south facing glass area, this results in the long sides facing east and west. Even modest amounts of this difficult-to-shade east and west glazing would most likely increase the cooling cost of the home more than the increased south facing glazing would save on heating costs. For this reason, homes with south facing narrow (gable) ends are not recommended.

There are several principal approaches to the design of passive solar homes.They can be described as follows: the north buffer type, the variable elevations type, the variable dormer type and the variable main entry type.

The North Buffer Type Home

In this type of home design, most or all of the non-living spaces are located along the north wall to act as a buffer zone against north winds and to retard heat loss. The north side can be earth sheltered to reduce infiltration and decrease temperature difference through the wall. Living spaces are located along the south wall. (See Designs 1 through 4.)

The Variable Elevations Type Home

This type of home design seems both the most flexible in terms of lot orientation (can face either north or south), and the most conventional in appearance, as there are living spaces along both sides.

Basically, the rooms are laid out internally such that either the front wall or the rear wall can be chosen to face south. The identical plan arrangement serves both north facing and south facing lot orientations. Only the glazed areas on the long wall elevations vary: the largest glass area always faces south and the smallest glass area always faces north. Therefore, one basic plan provides four different long wall elevations: front elevation north and south, and rear elevation north and south. The amount of glazing on each elevation should be worked out in accordance with the rules-of-thumb given in Chapter 10. (See Designs 5 and 6).

The Variable Dormer Type Home

This type of home design is very similar to the Variable Elevations Type, but the roof dormer(s) varies location as well as the elevations. When the front of the home is built facing south, the dormer is built on the front of the home. When the rear of the home is built facing south, the dormer is built on the rear. This would also apply to second floor sun decks and balconies. (See Design 7.)

The Variable Main Entry Type Home

This type of home is designed for one particular wall to face south. Two potential main entries are provided so that the same plan can be built on lots with different orientations. The entries trade roles from being a front door to a rear door depending on the lot orientation. (See Design 8.)

SUNTEMPERED HOME DESIGNS

Eight passive solar home designs, illustrated on the following pages, demonstrate how easily the basic concepts of passive solar can be applied to conventional home designs.The designs show only a few of the numerous ways that increased south facing glazing can be employed to reduce energy consumption and provide more comfortable and pleasant places to live. See pages 144–145 for a brief description of each design.

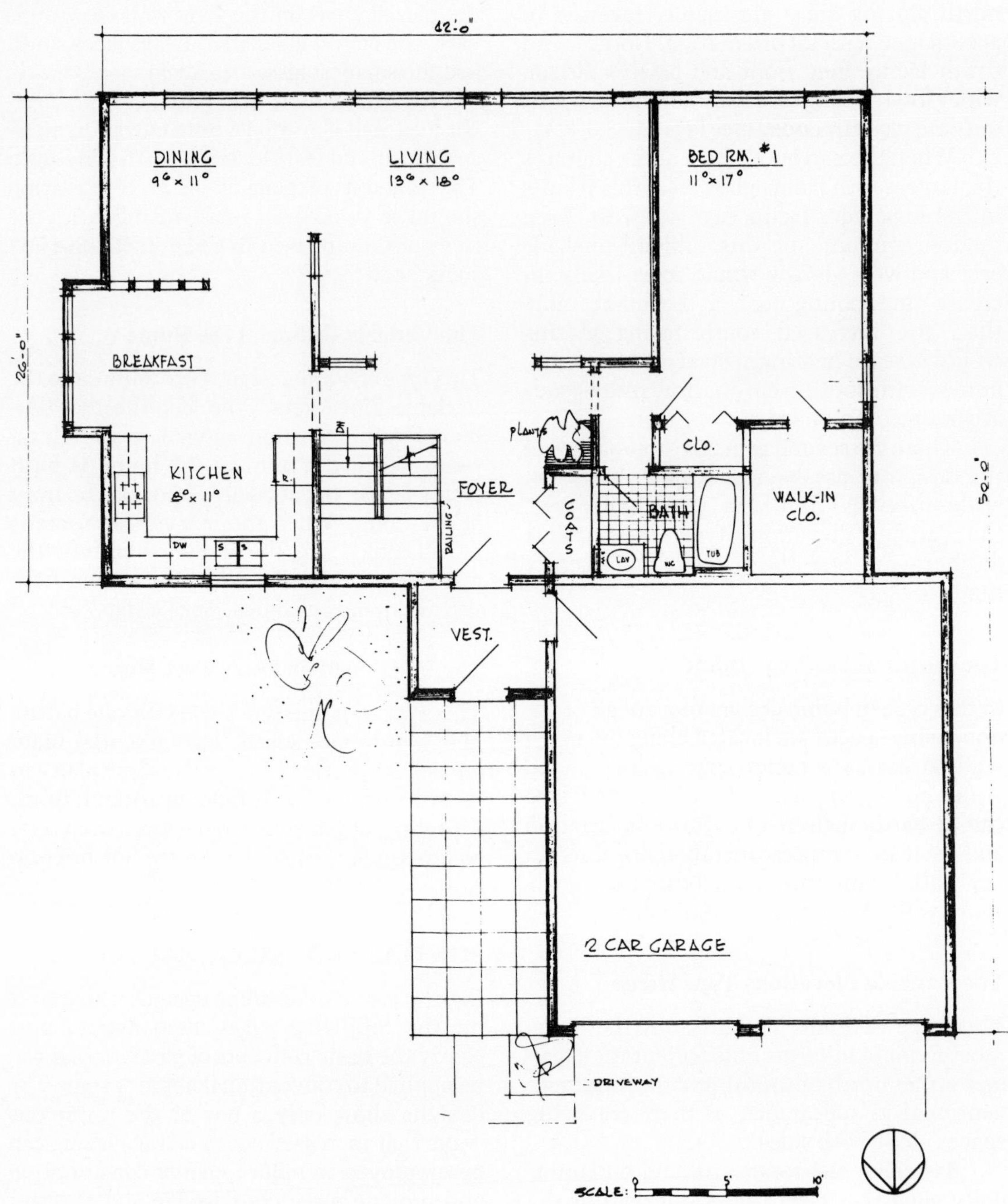

Design 1 North Buffer home for a sloping site, conditioned area 2158 sq. ft.
(a) Front toward north upper floor plan.

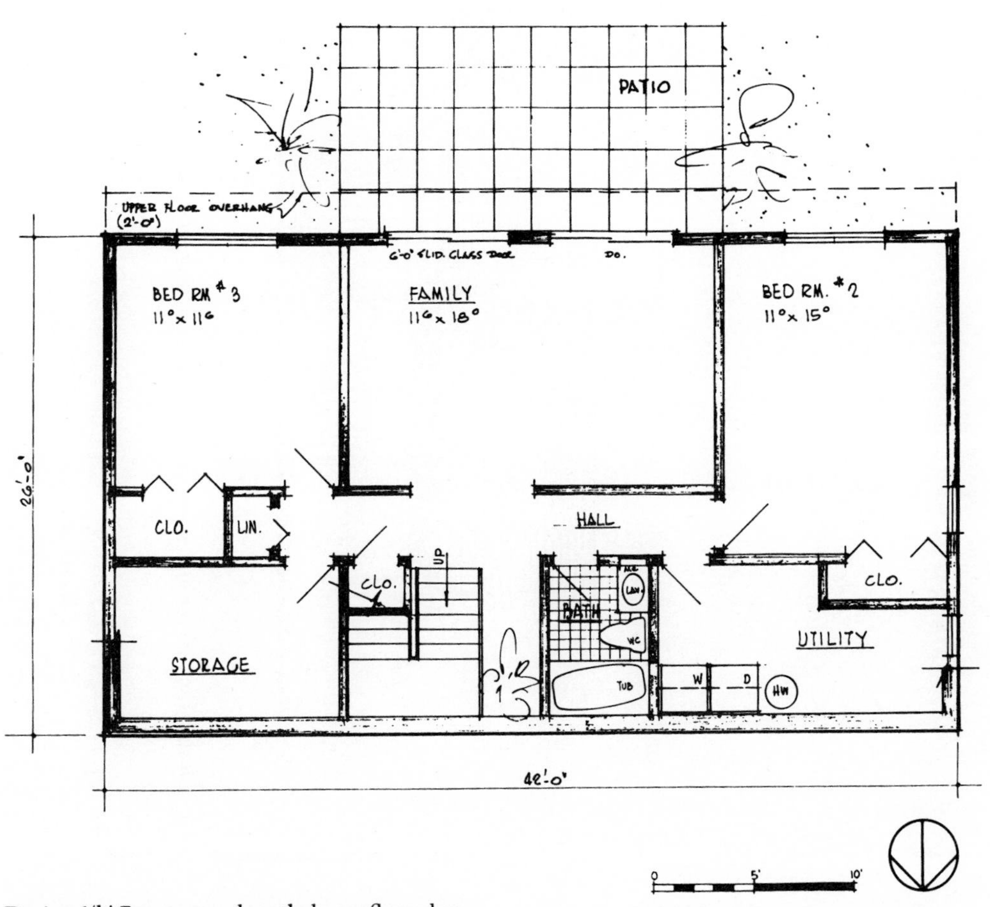

Design 1(b) Front toward north, lower floor plan.

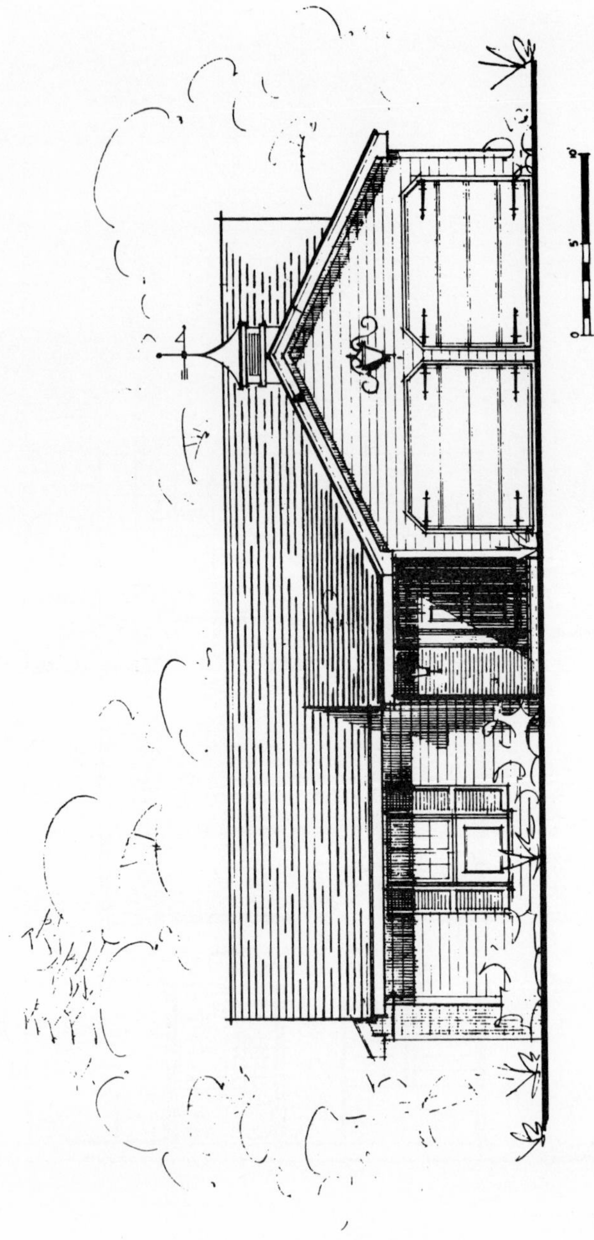

Design 1(c) North buffer home for a sloping site—front toward north, front elevation.

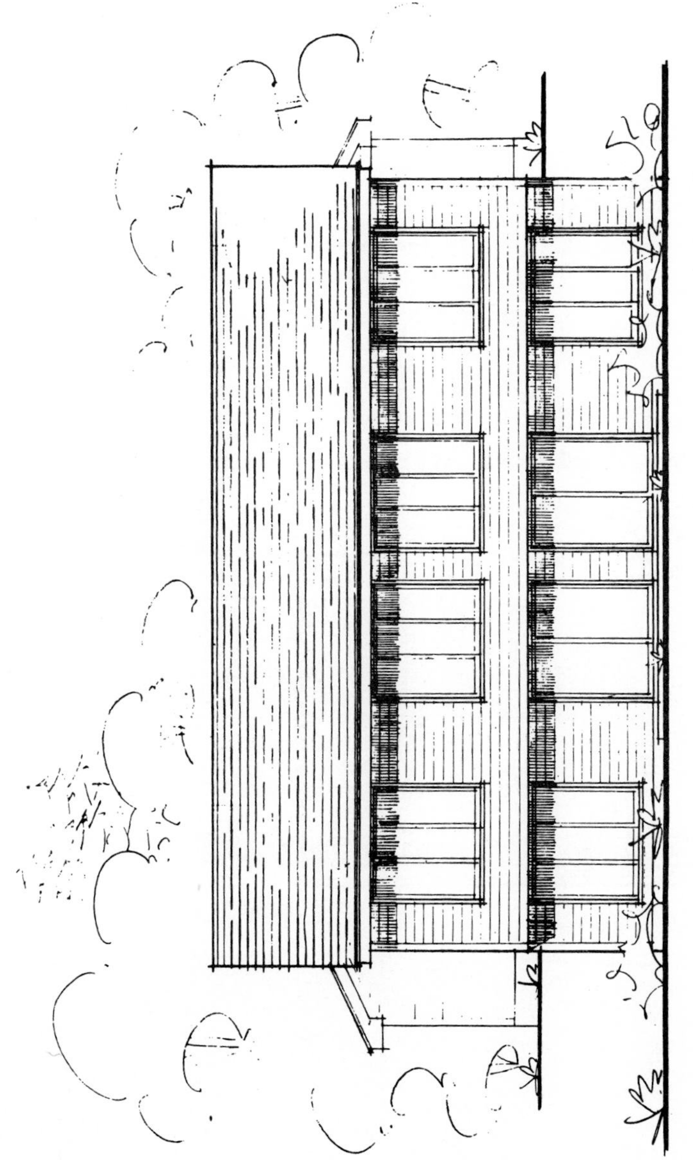

Design 1(d) Front toward north, rear elevation (south), 231 sq. ft. glass area or 10% floor area.

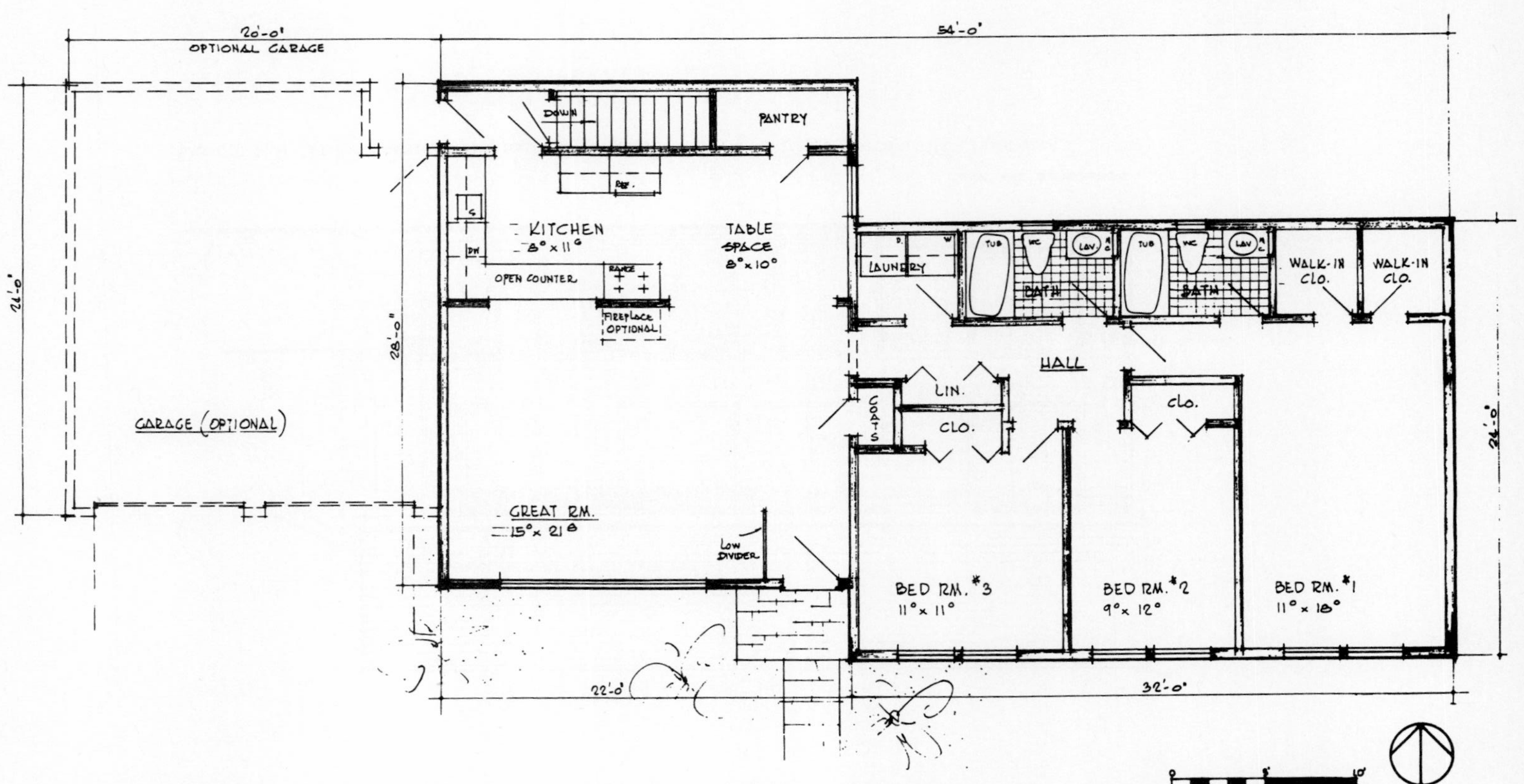

Design 2 North buffer ranch home, conditioned area 1384 sq. ft.— (a) Front toward south floor plan

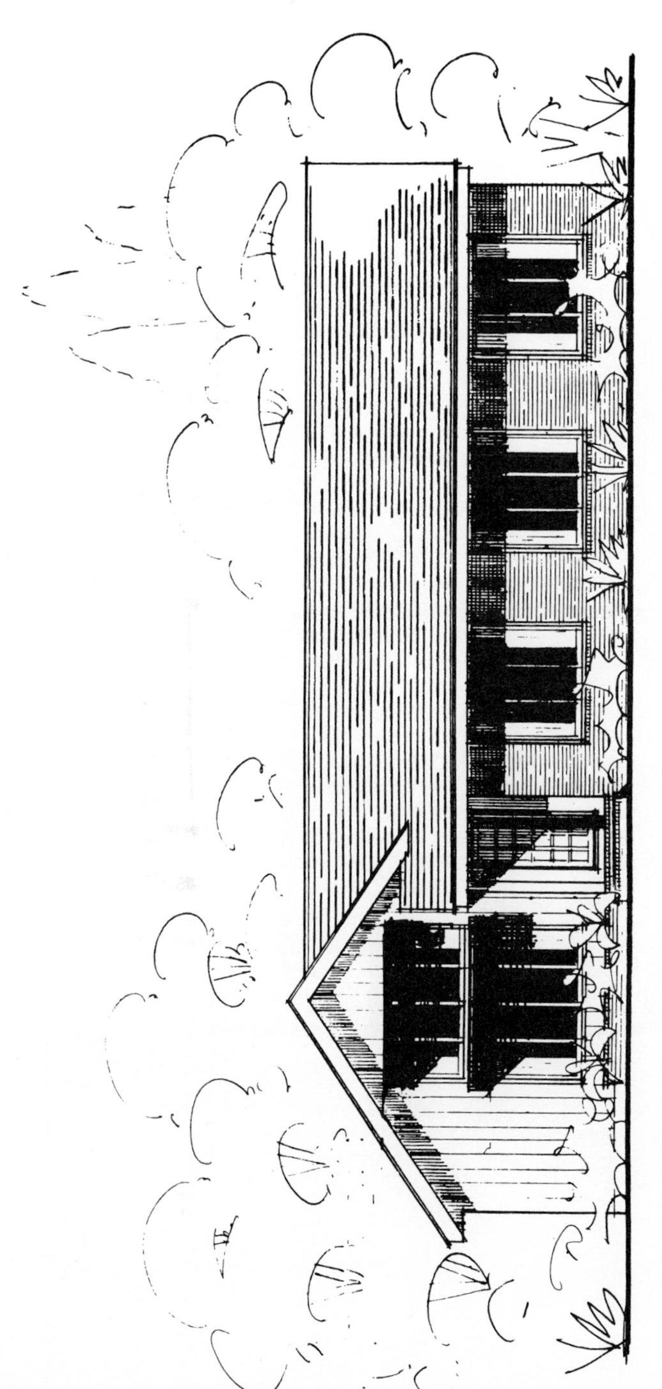

Design 2(b) Front toward south, front elevation, 143 sq. ft. glass area or 10% floor area.

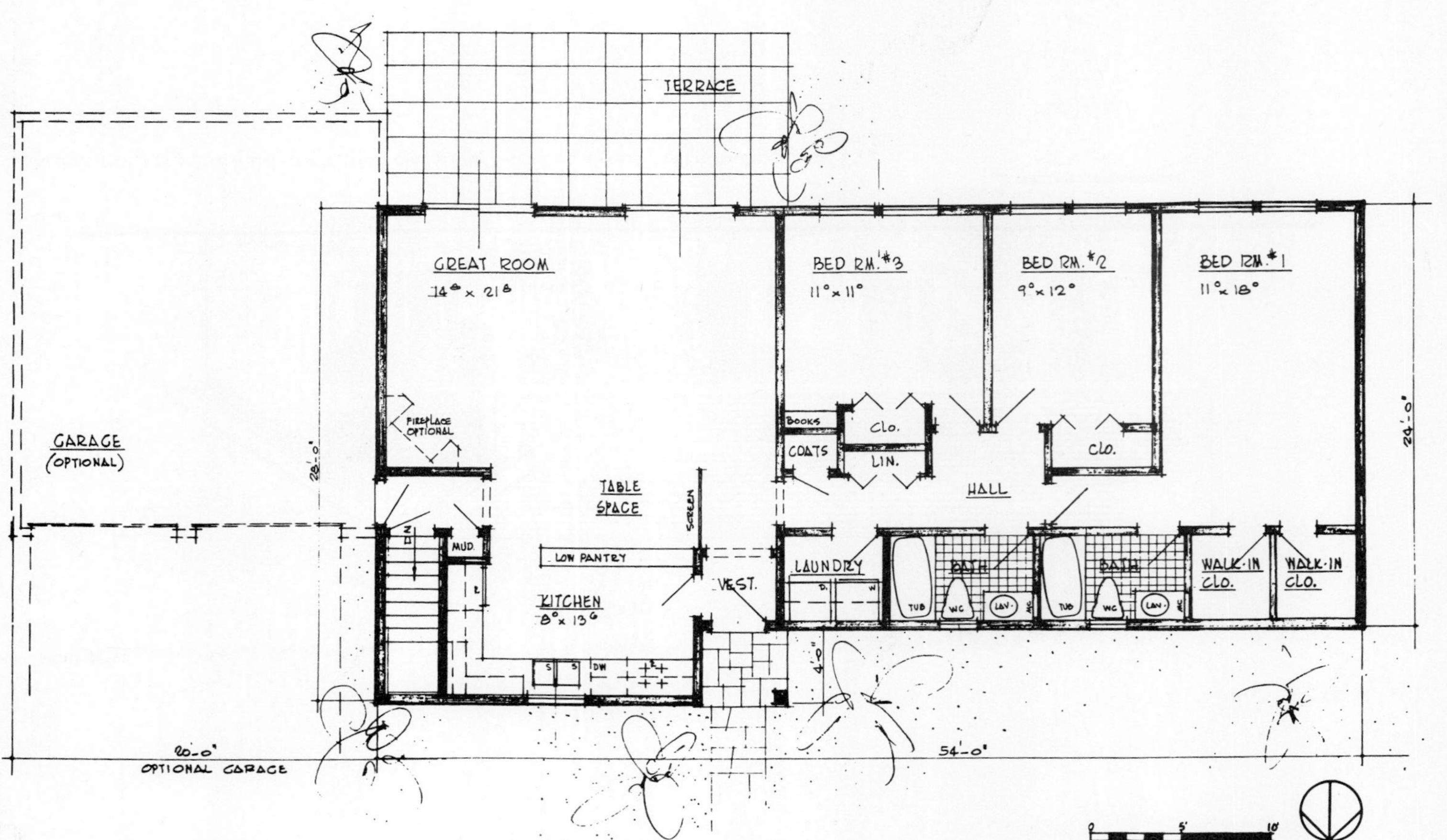

Design 2(c) North buffer ranch home—front toward north floor plan, conditioned area 1368 sq. ft.

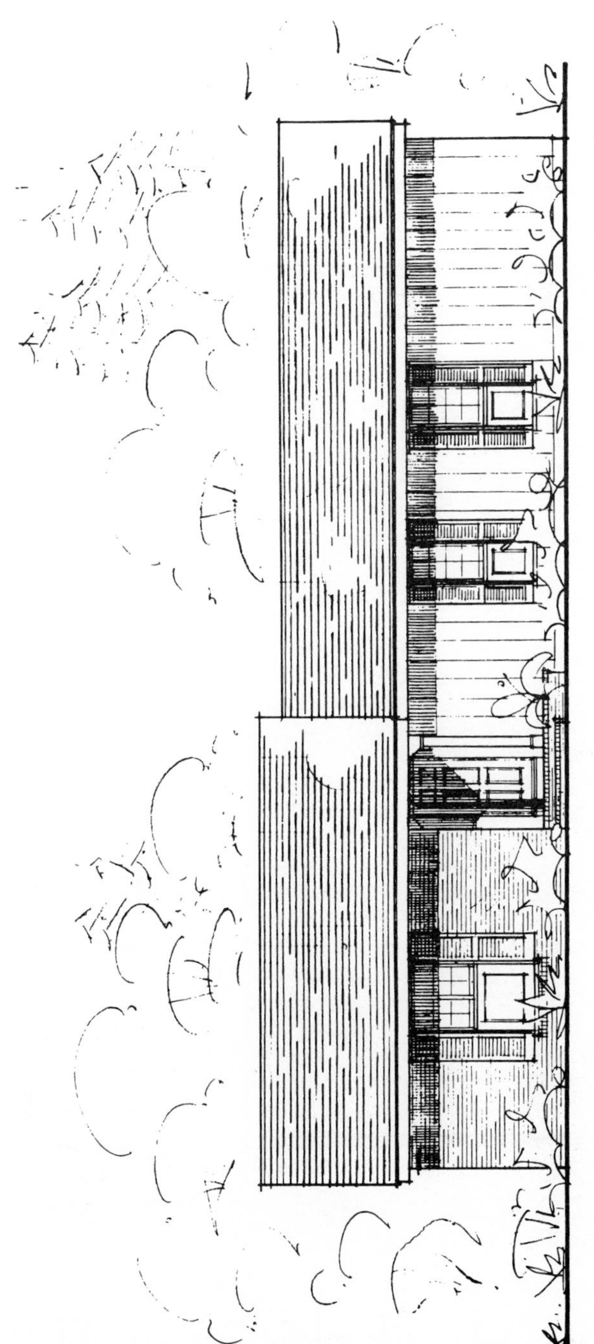

Design 2(d) Front toward north, front elevation.

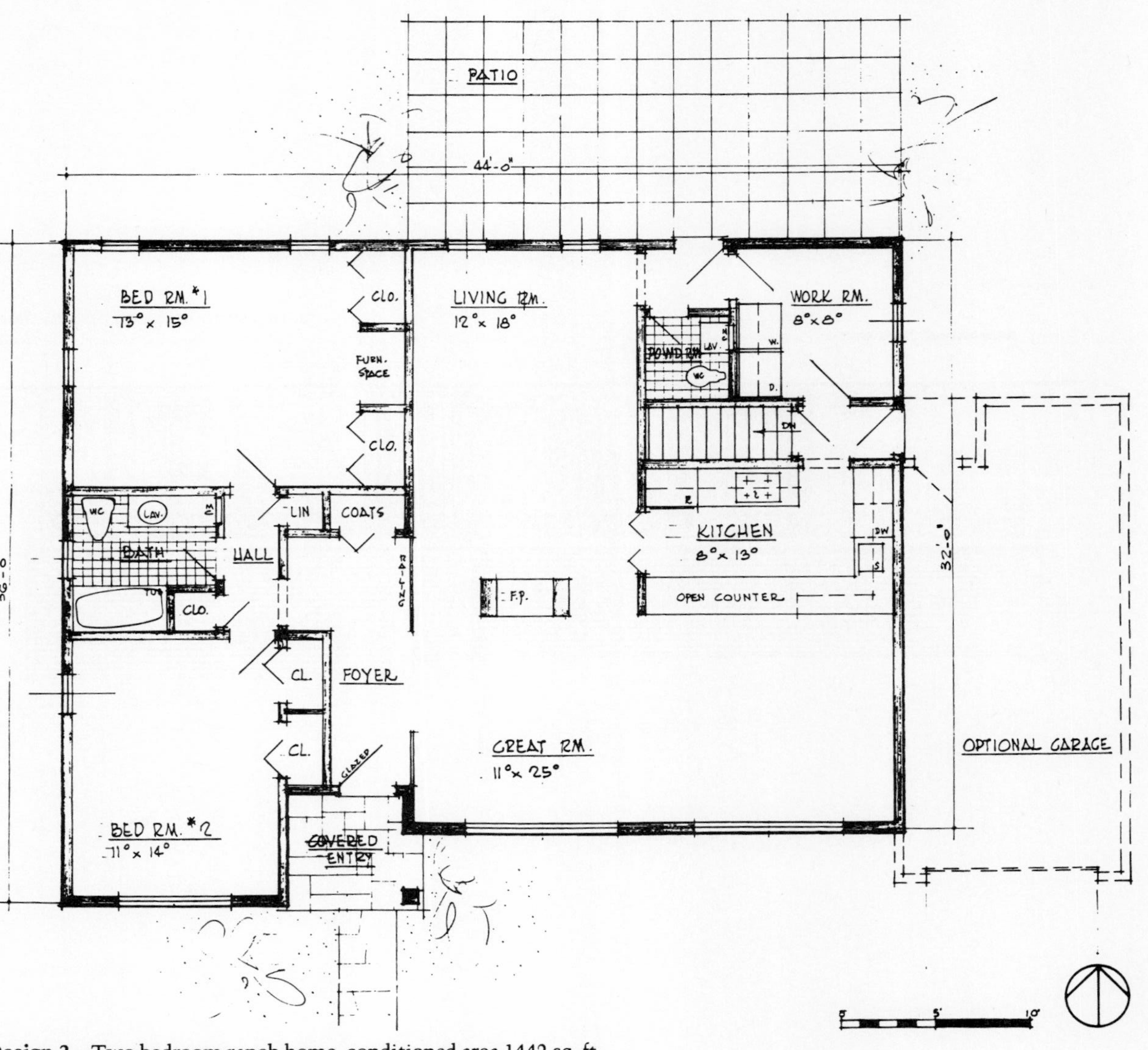

Design 3 Two bedroom ranch home, conditioned area 1442 sq. ft.
(a) Front toward south floor plan.

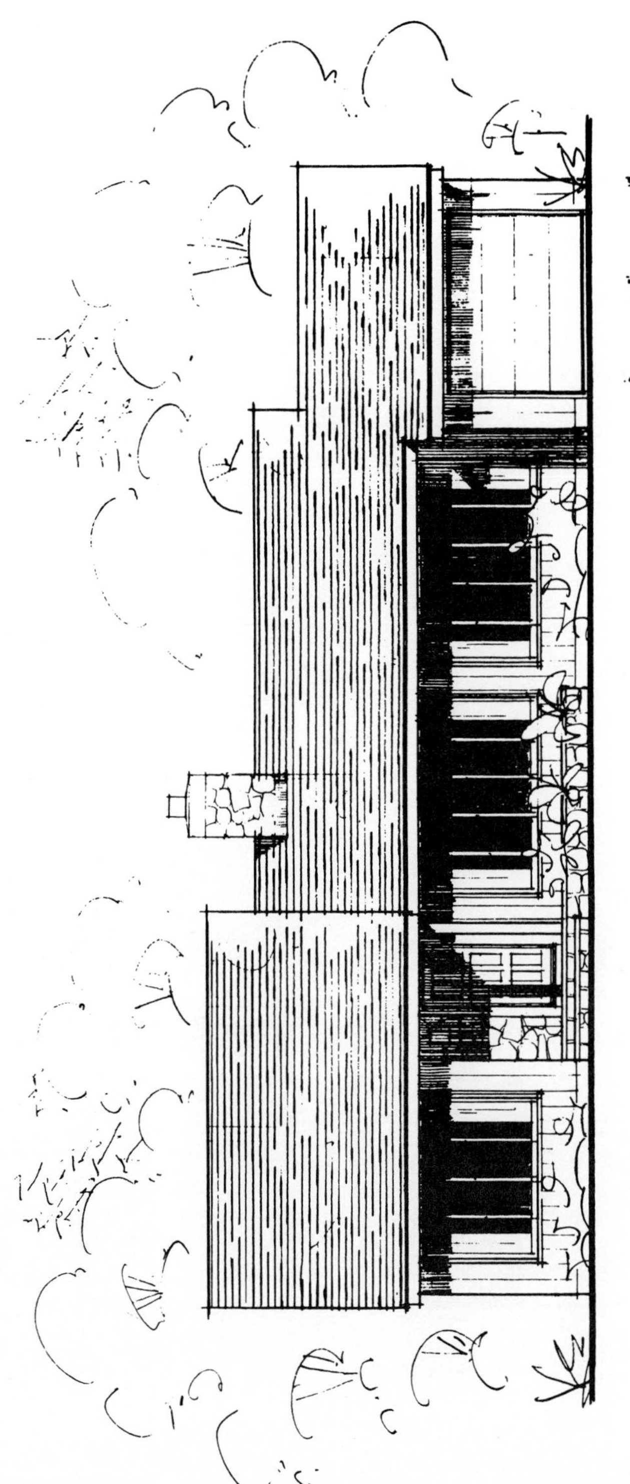

Design 3(b) Front toward south, front elevation, 129 sq. ft. glass area or 9% of floor area.

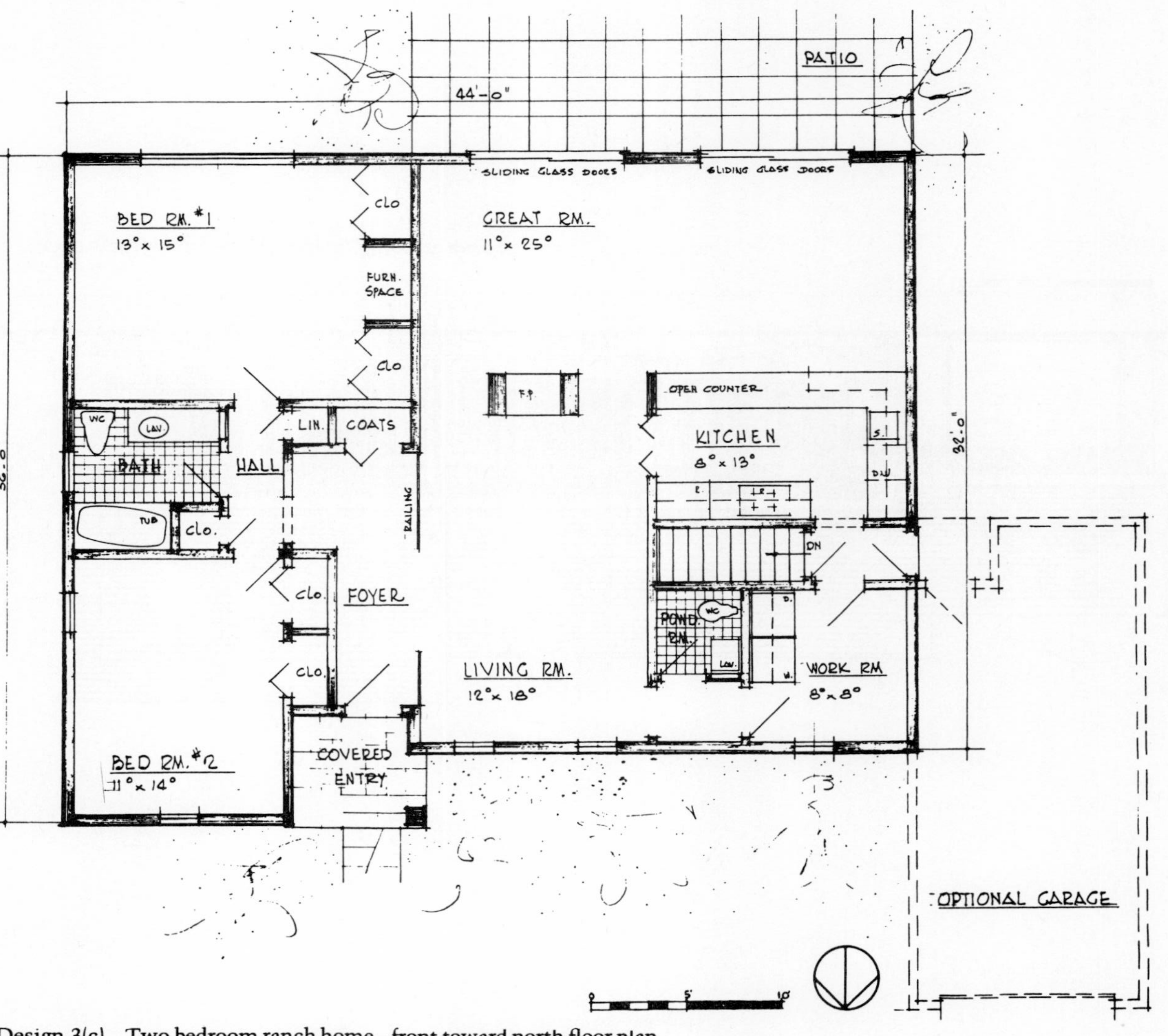

Design 3(c) Two bedroom ranch home—front toward north floor plan.

Design 3(d) Front toward north, front elevation.

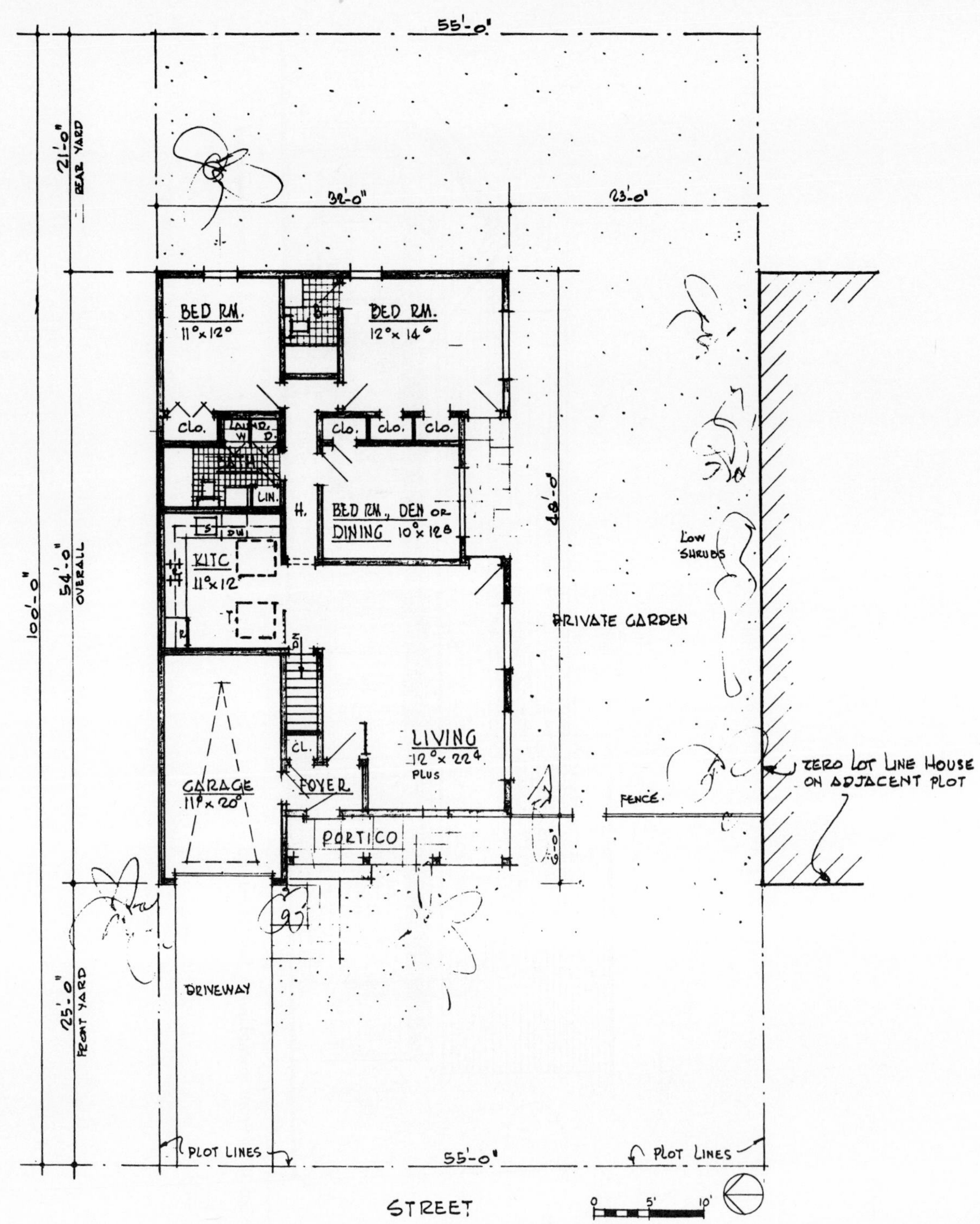

Design 4 Zero lot line home, conditioned area 1316 sq. ft.
(a) Side toward south floor plan.

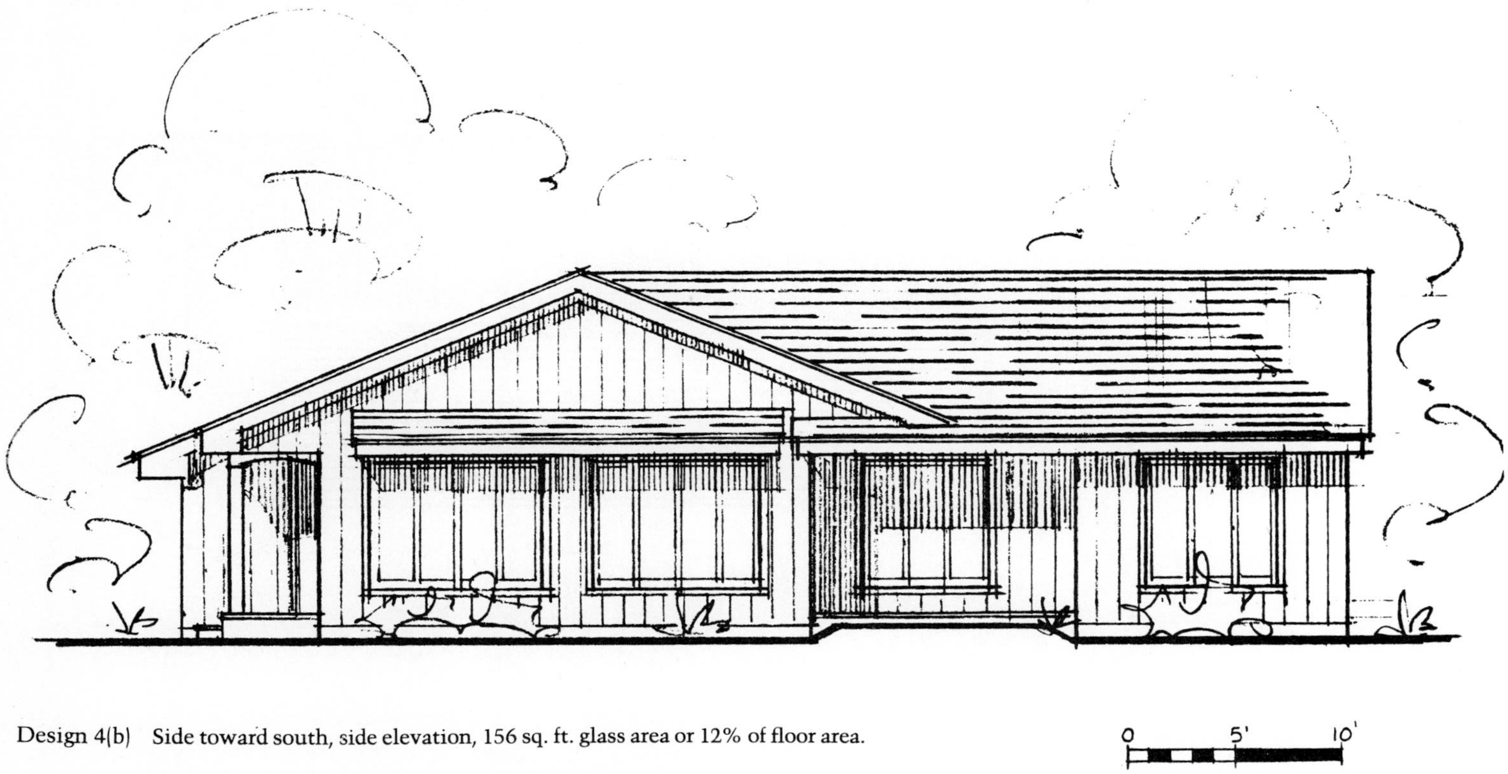

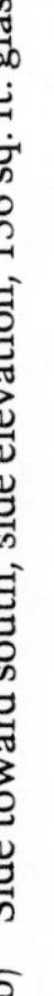

Design 4(b) Side toward south, side elevation, 156 sq. ft. glass area or 12% of floor area.

Design 4(c) Zero lot line home—side toward south, front elevation (west).

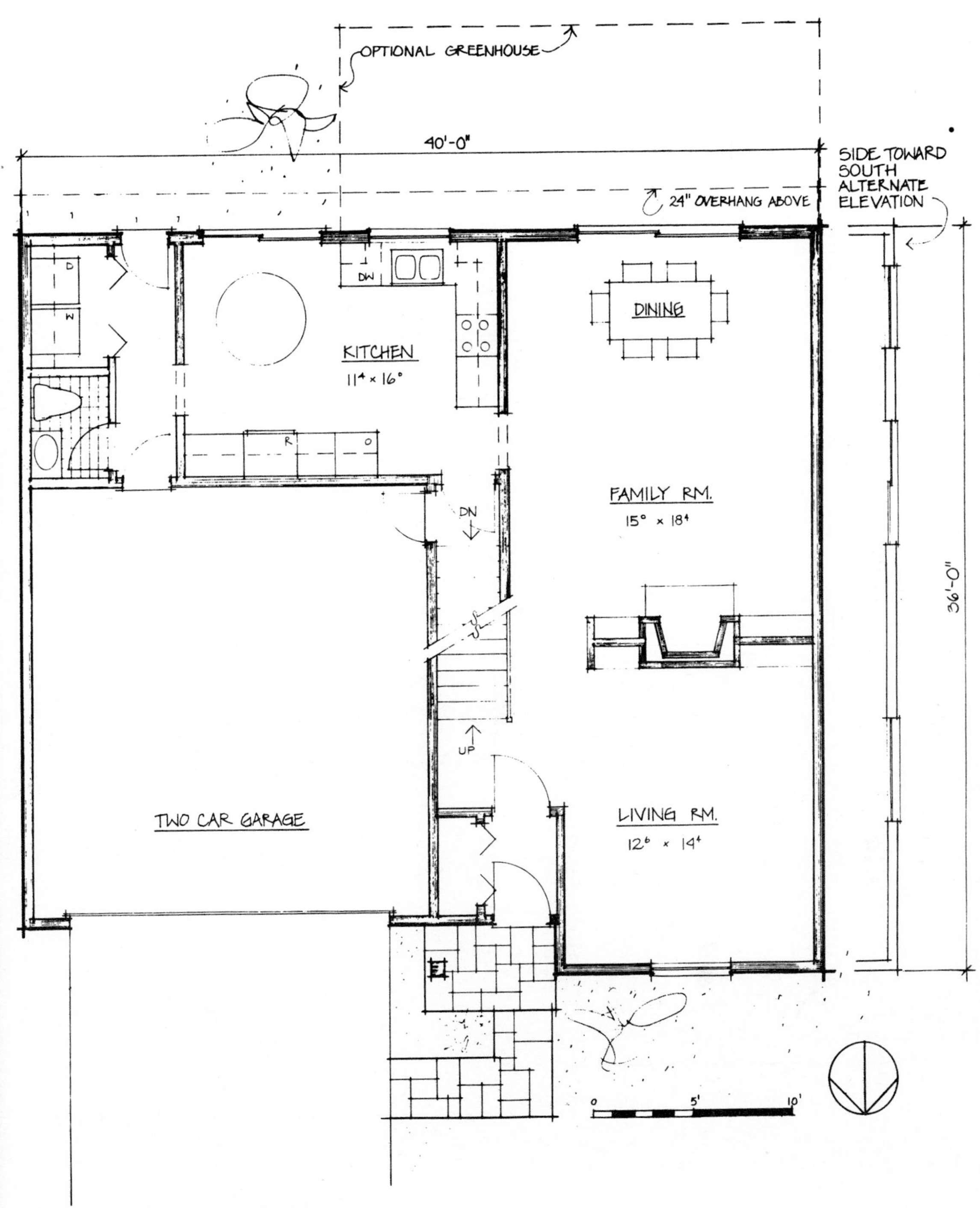

Design 5 Attachable home, conditioned area 1600 sq. ft.
(a) Front toward north first floor plan.

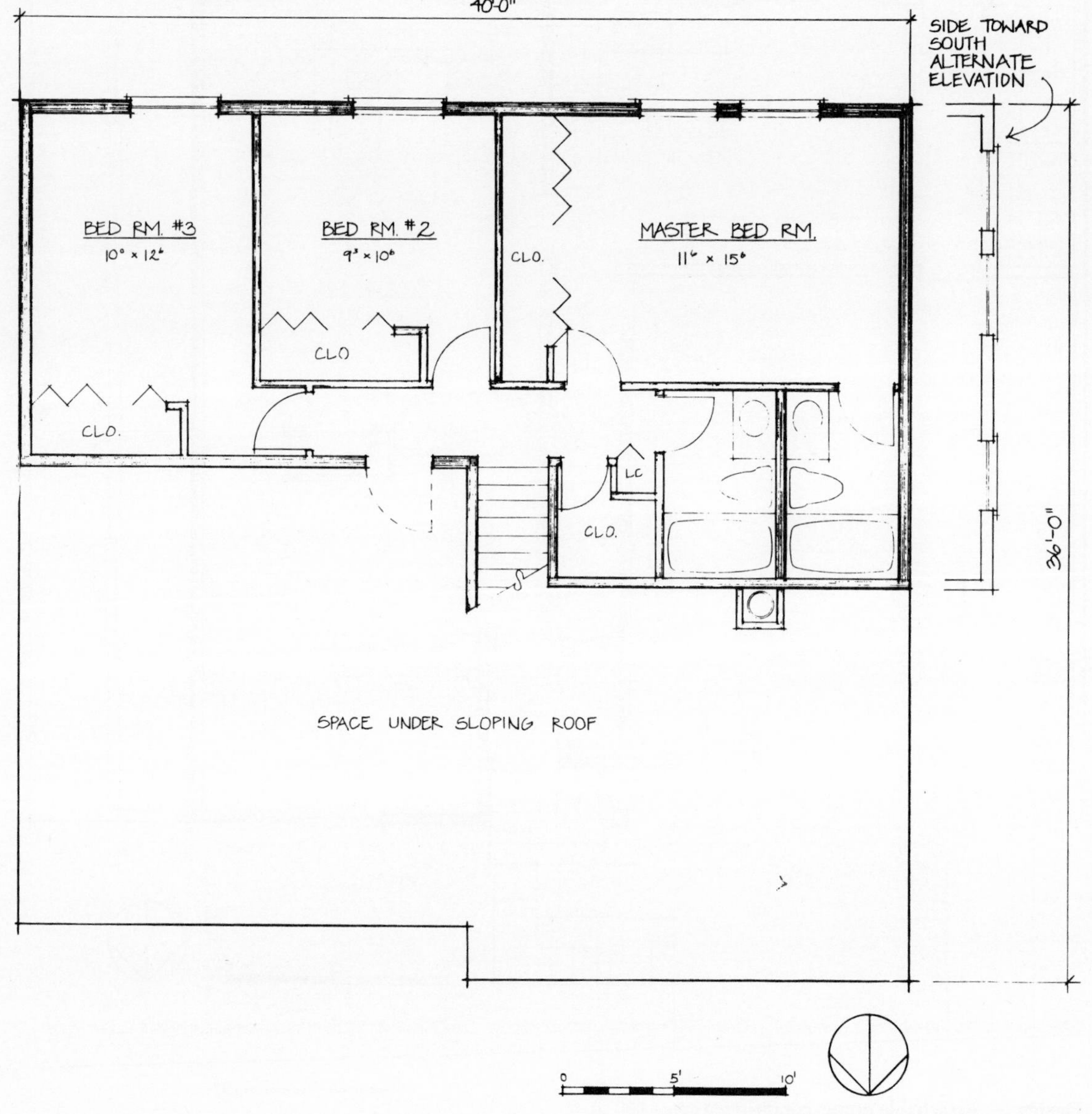

Design 5(b) Attachable home—front toward north second floor plan.

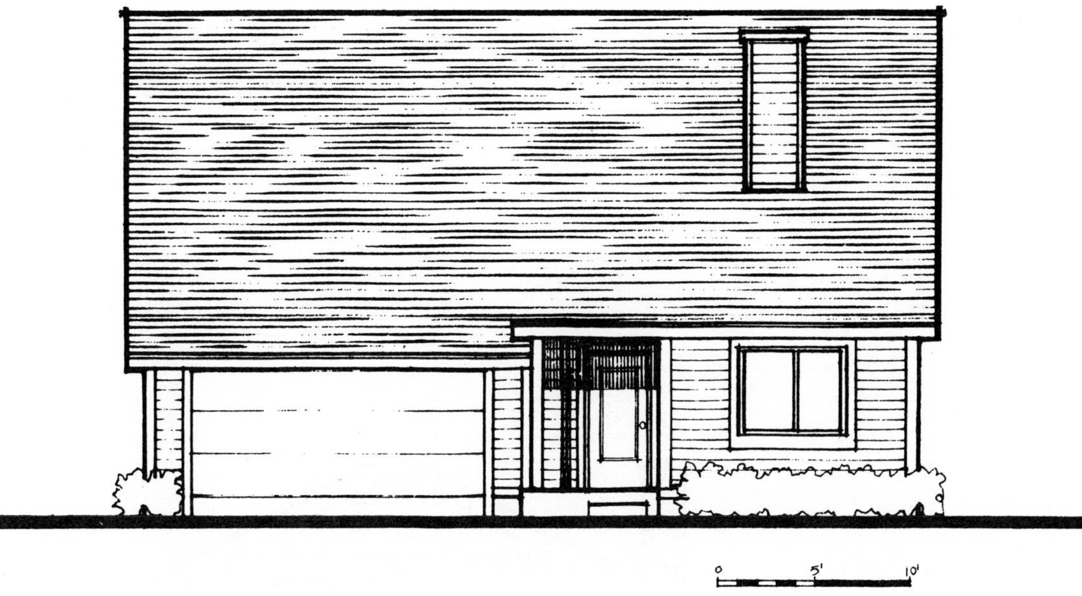

Design 5(c) Front toward north, front elevation.

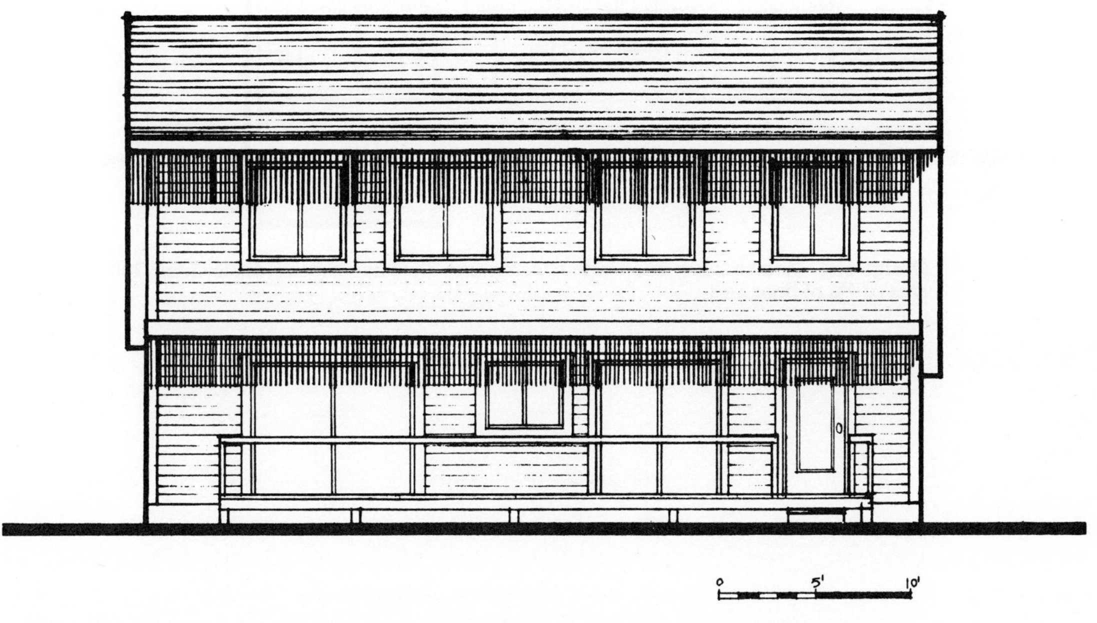

Design 5(d) Front toward north, rear elevation (south), 207 sq. ft. glass area or 13% glass area.

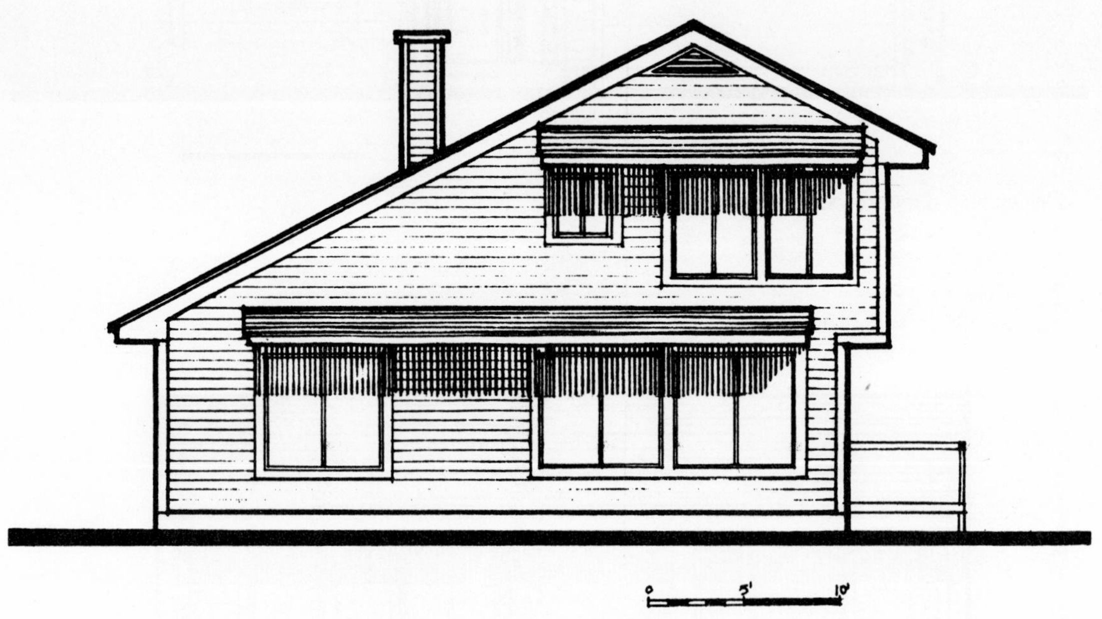

Design 5(e) Attachable home—side toward south alternate, south side elevation, 148 sq. ft. glass area or 9% of floor area.

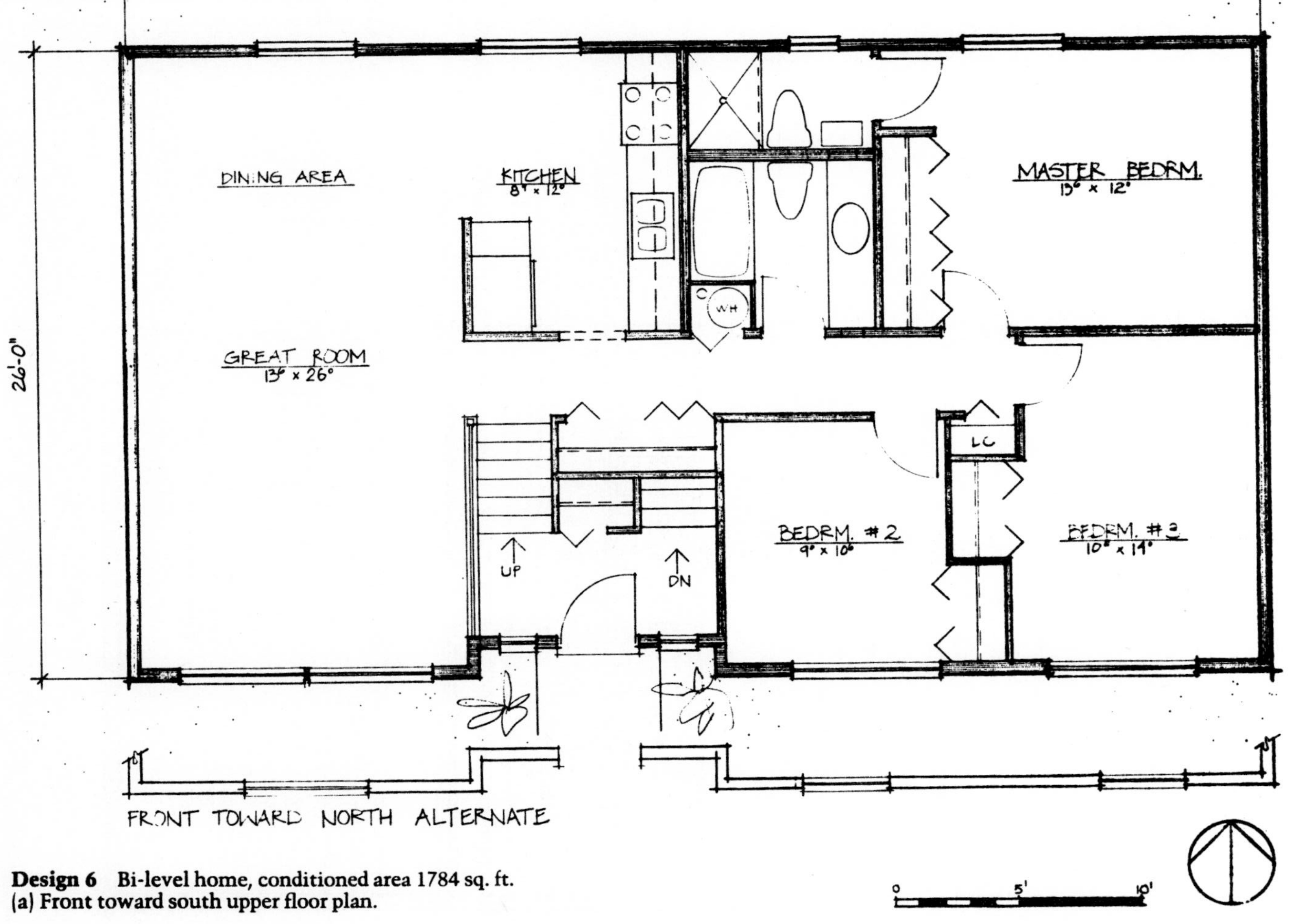

Design 6 Bi-level home, conditioned area 1784 sq. ft.
(a) Front toward south upper floor plan.

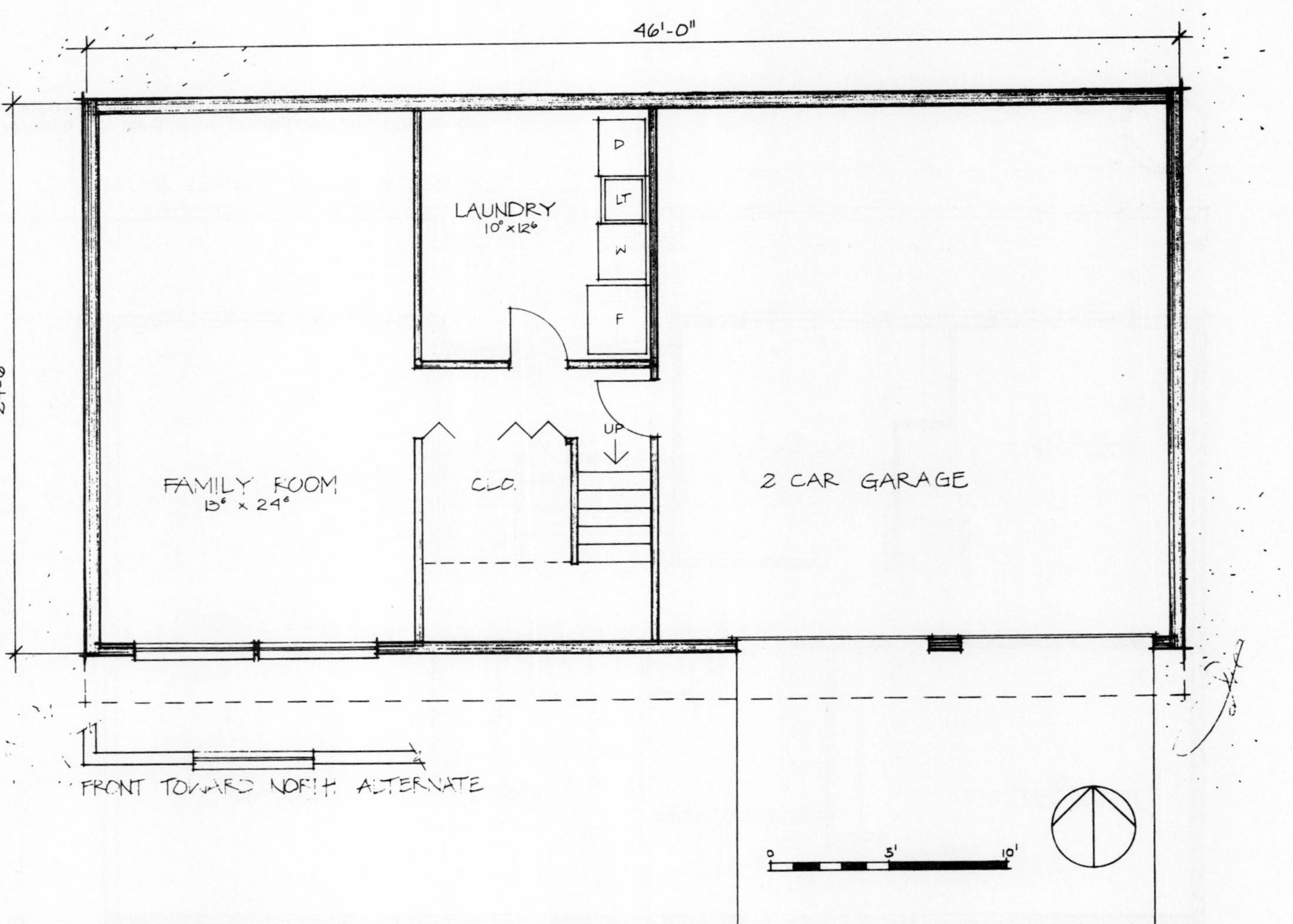

Design 6(b) Bi-level home—front toward south, lower floor plan.

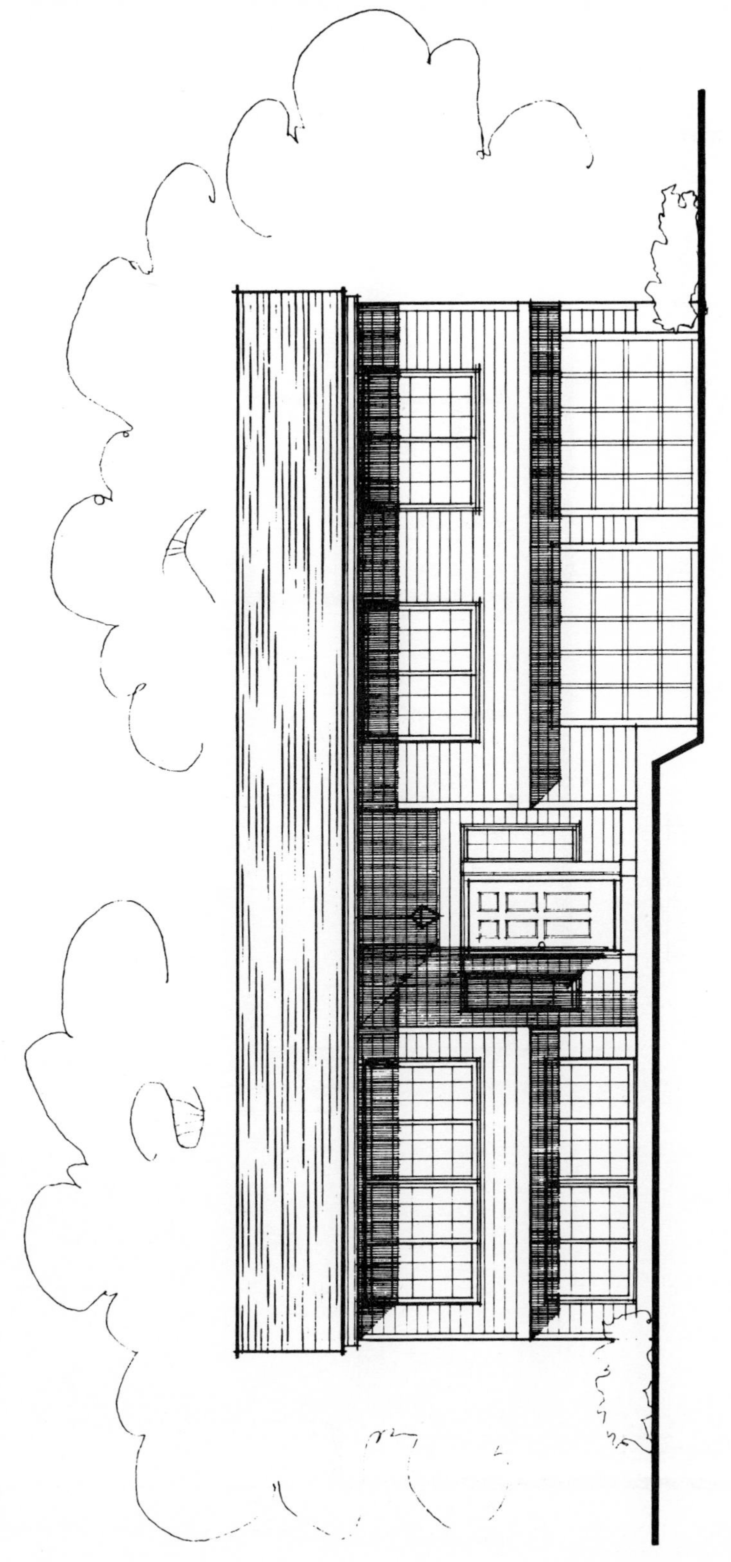

Design 6(c) Front toward south, front elevation, 165 sq. ft. glass area or 9% of floor area.

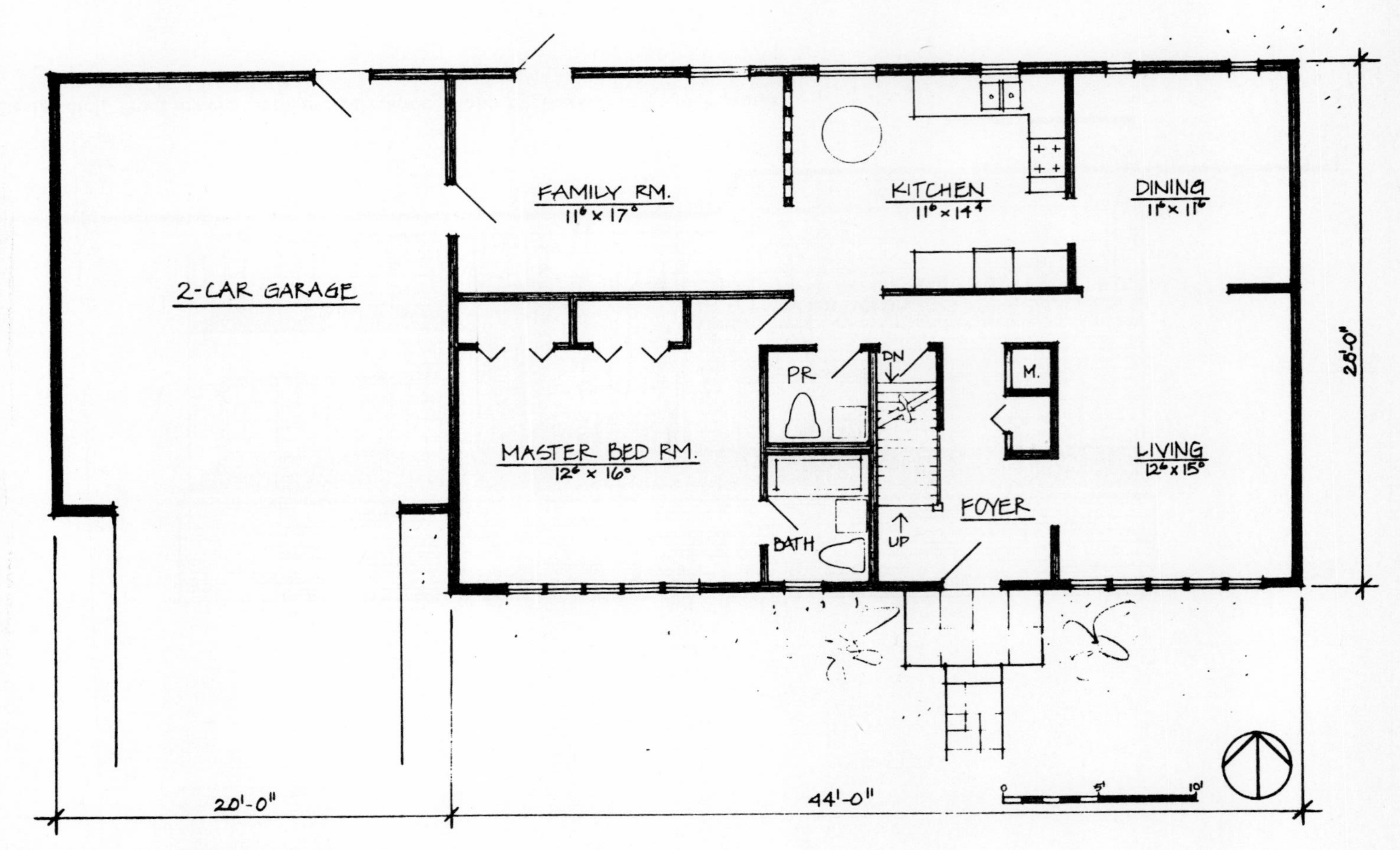

Design 7 One-and-one-half story home
(a) Front toward south, total conditioned area 1806 sq. ft., first floor plan.

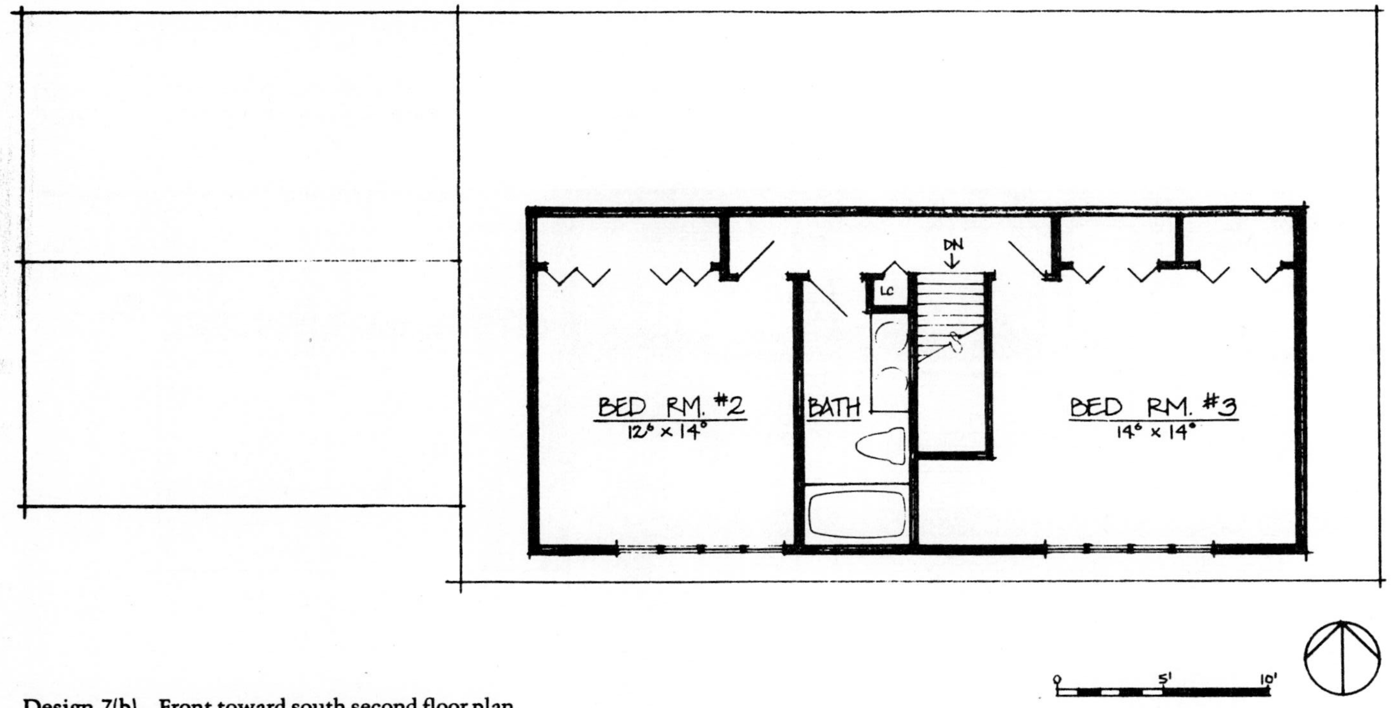

Design 7(b) Front toward south second floor plan.

Design 7(c) One-and-one-half story home—front toward south, front elevation, 170 sq. ft. glass area or 10.5% of floor area.

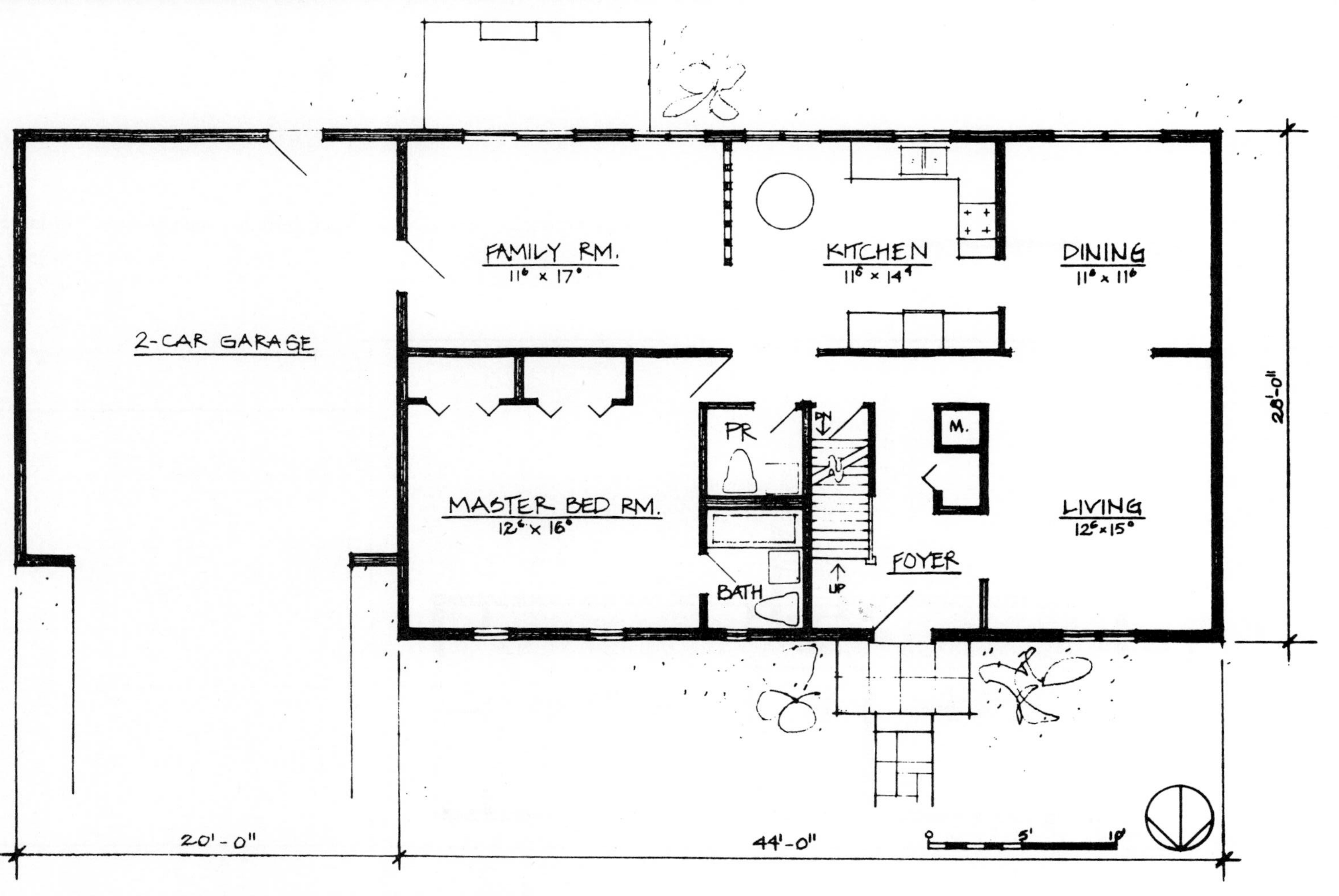

Design 7(d) Front toward north, total conditioned area 1676 sq. ft., first floor plan.

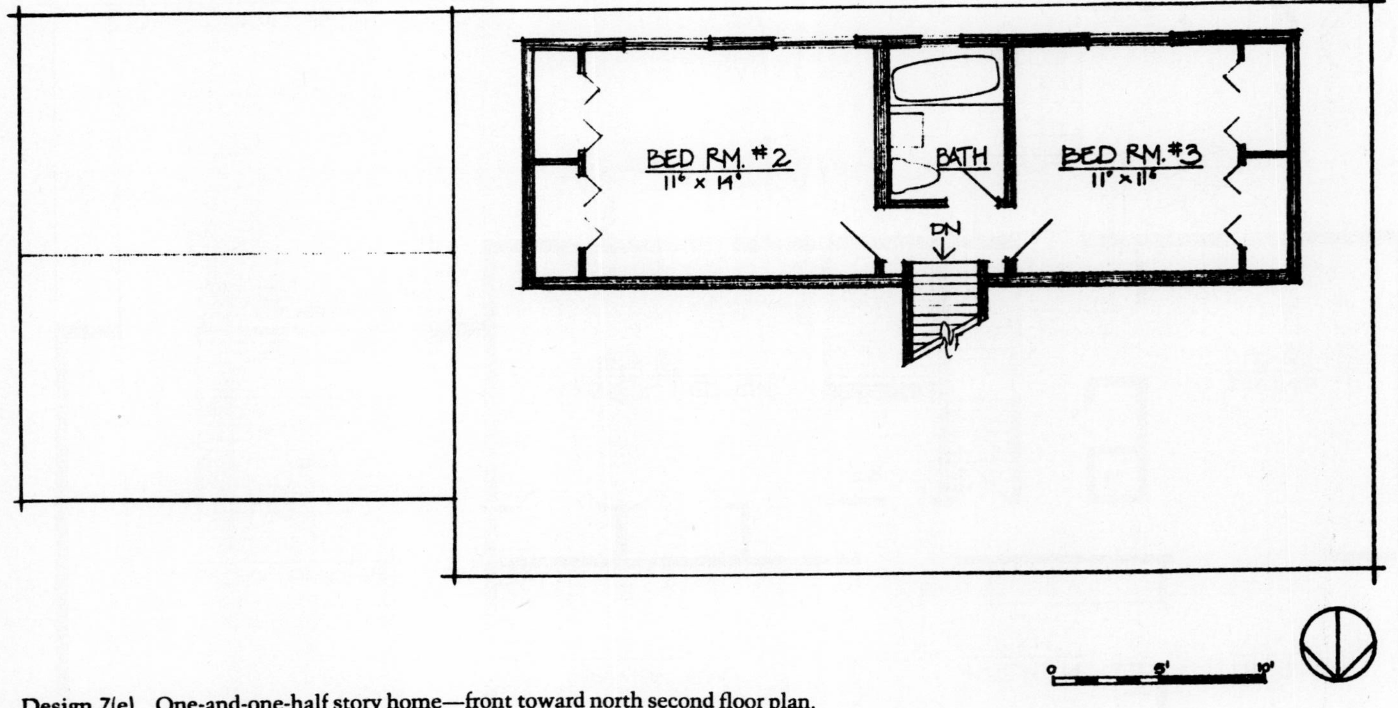

Design 7(e) One-and-one-half story home—front toward north second floor plan.

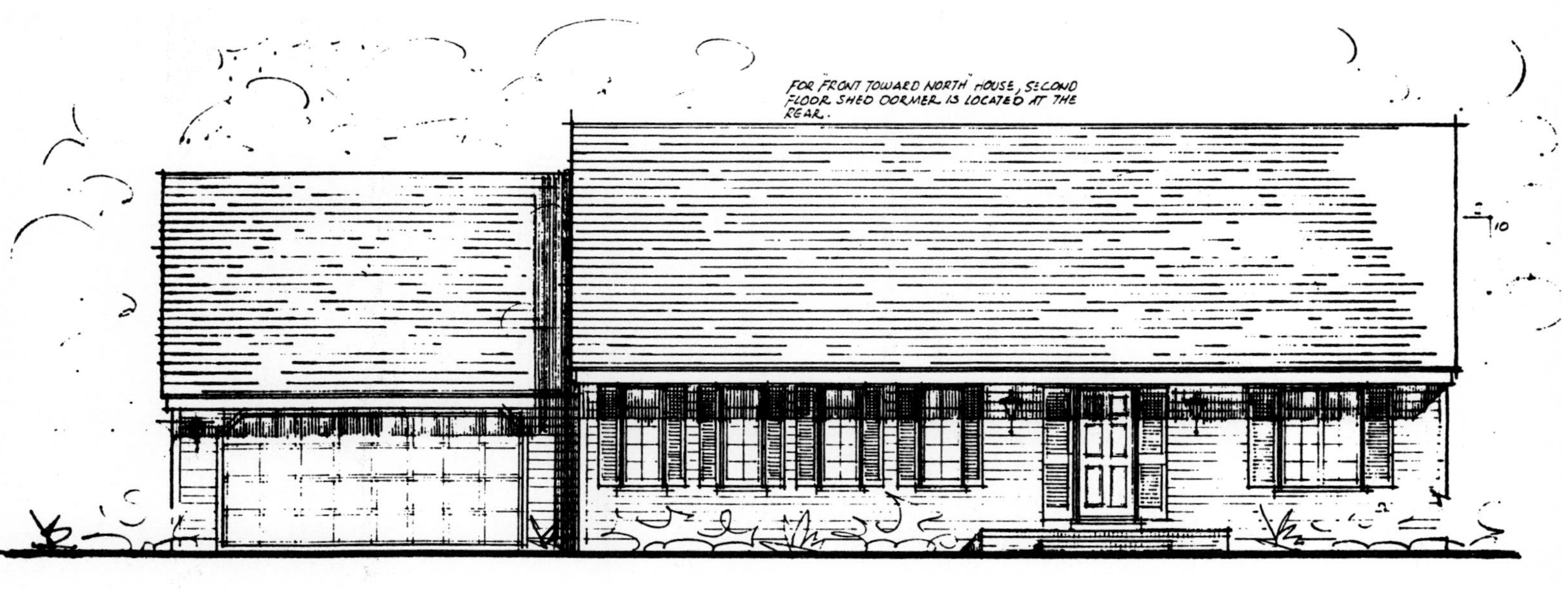

FOR "FRONT TOWARD NORTH" HOUSE, SECOND FLOOR SHED DORMER IS LOCATED AT THE REAR.
10
0
5'
10'

Design 7(f) Front toward north, front elevation.

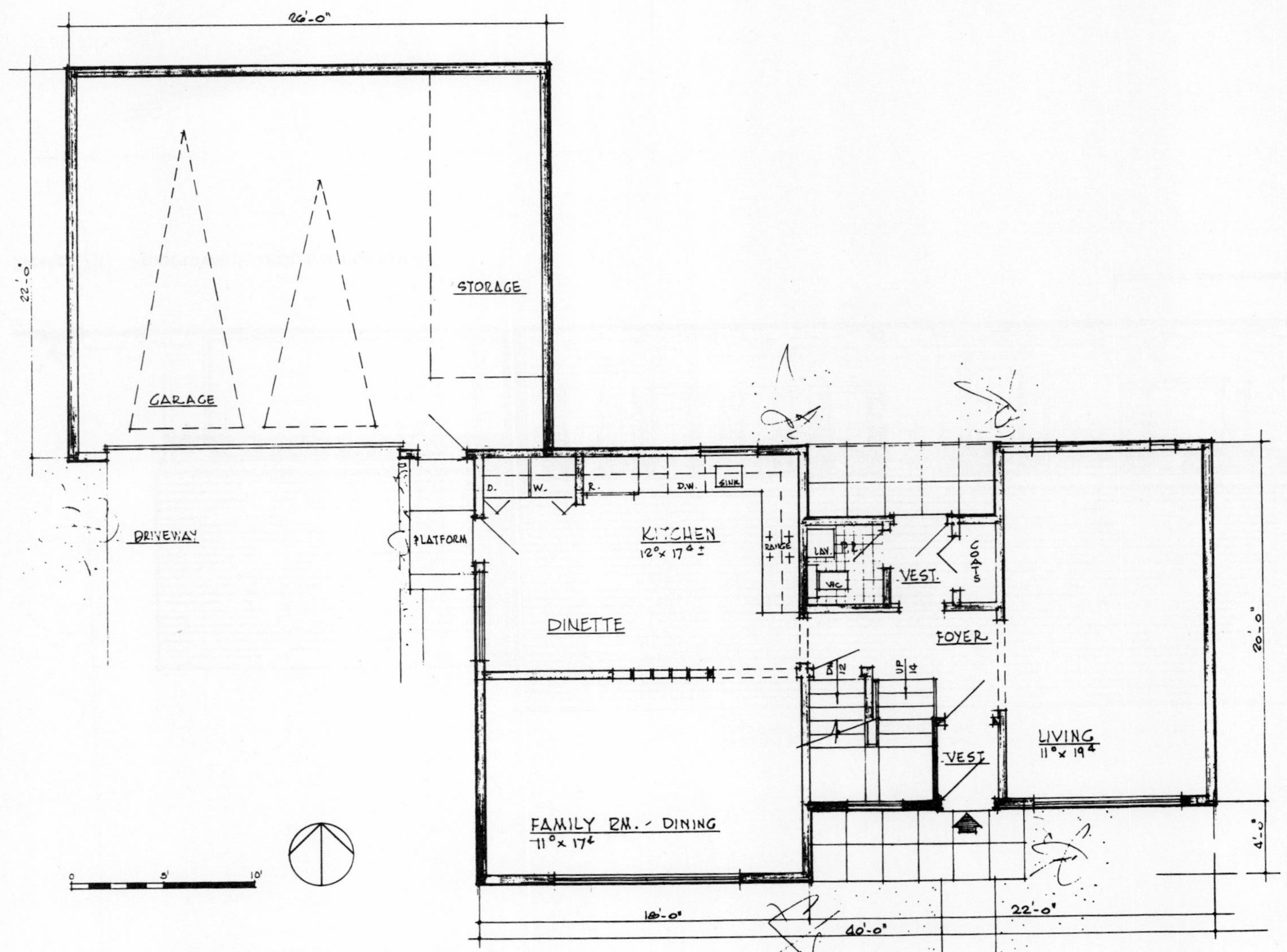

Design 8 Two story home, conditioned area 1704 sq. ft.
(a) Front toward south first floor plan.

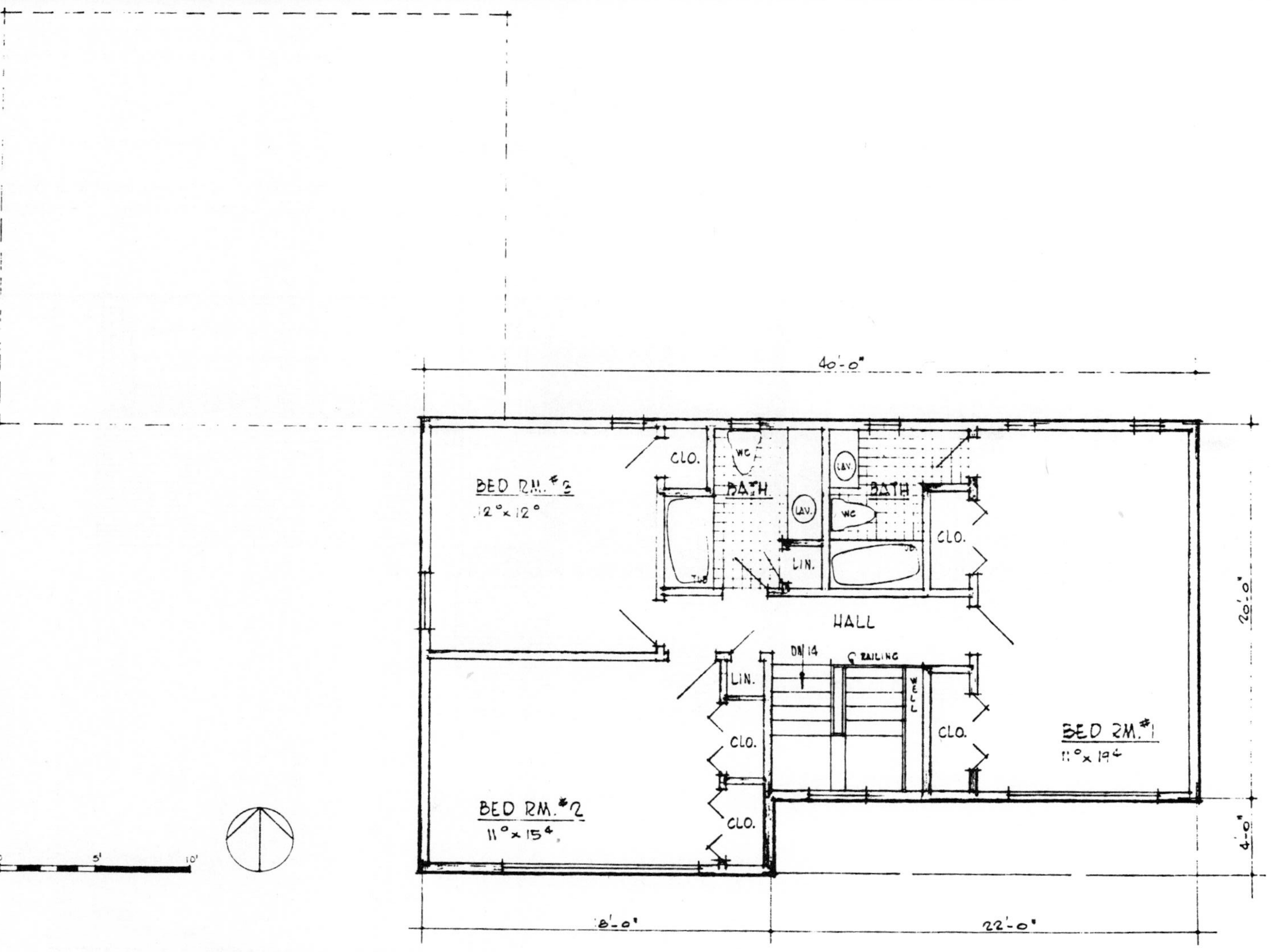

Design 8(b) Front toward south second floor plan.

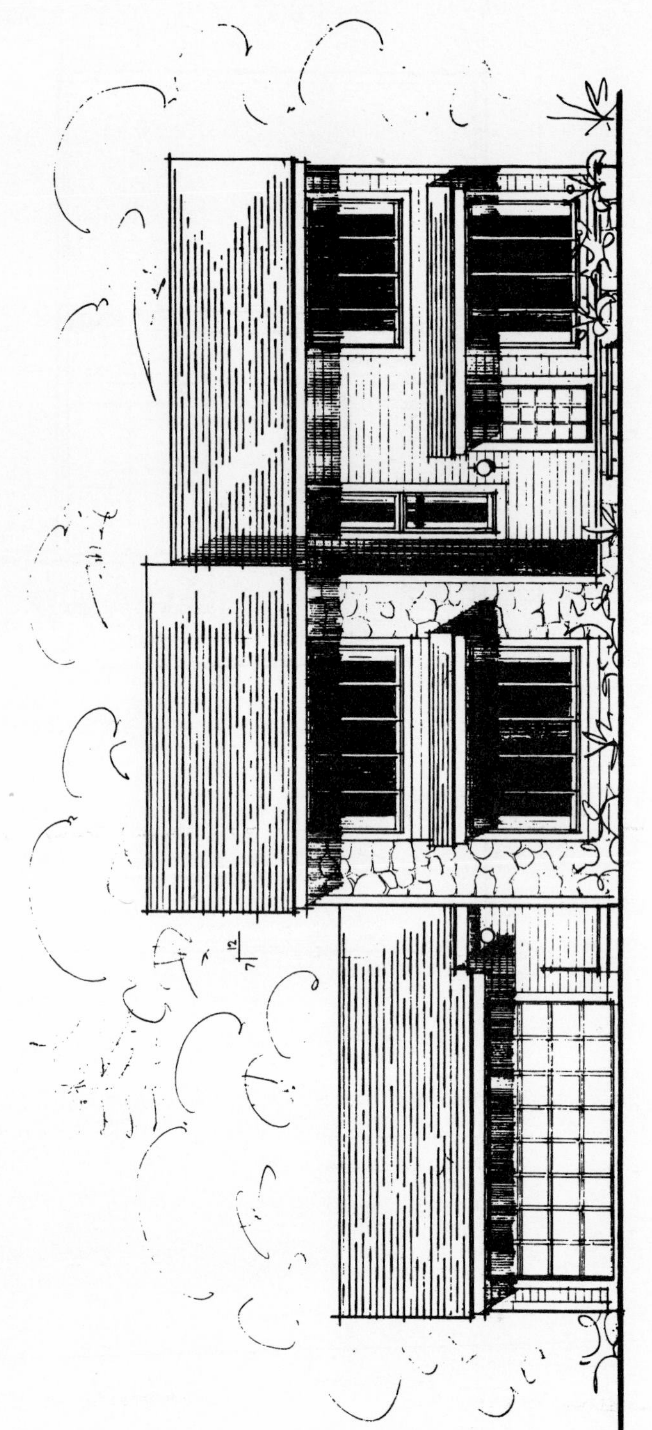

Design 8(c) Two story home—front toward south, front elevation, 208 sq. ft. glass area or 12% of floor area.

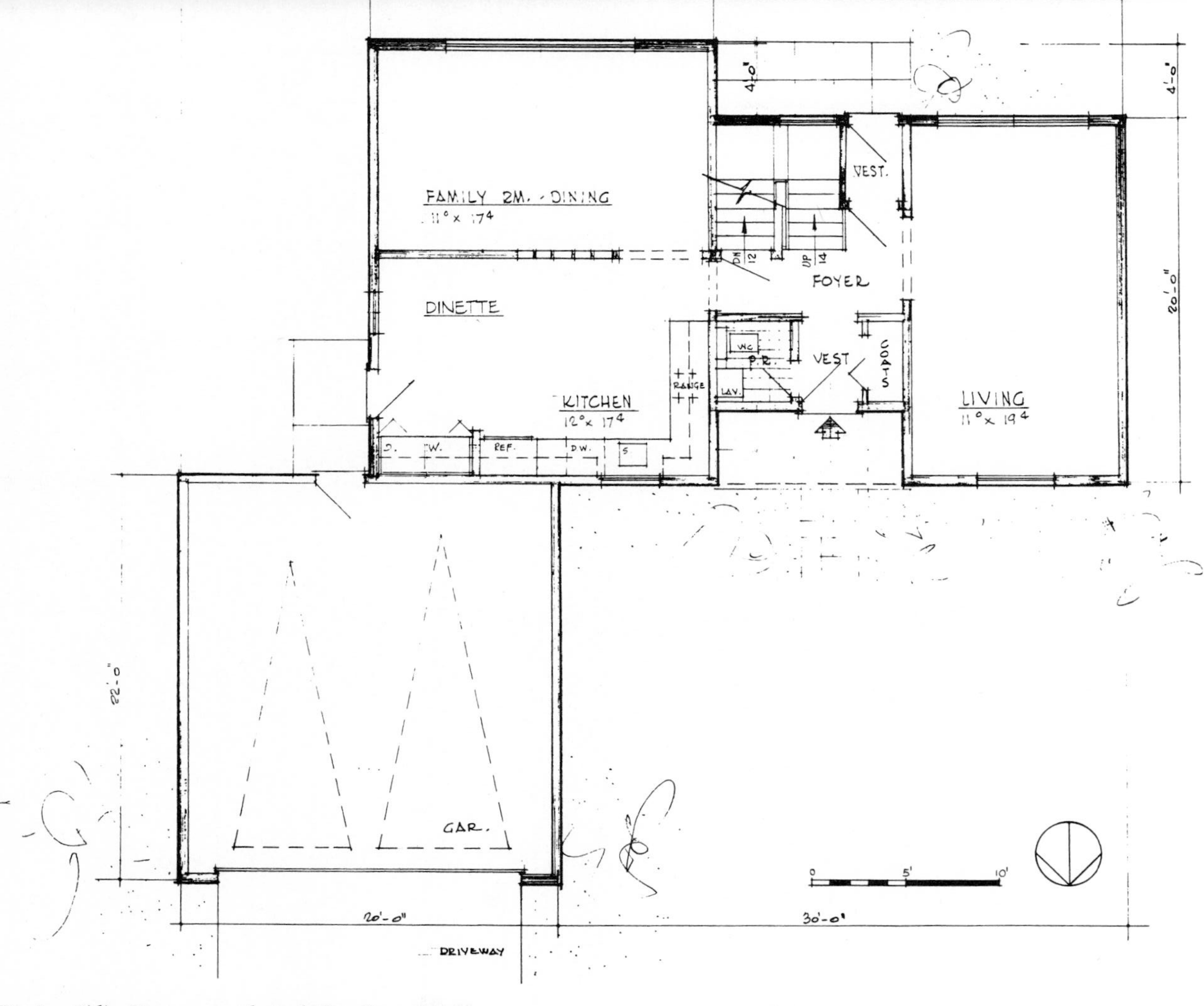

Design 8(d) Front toward north first floor plan.

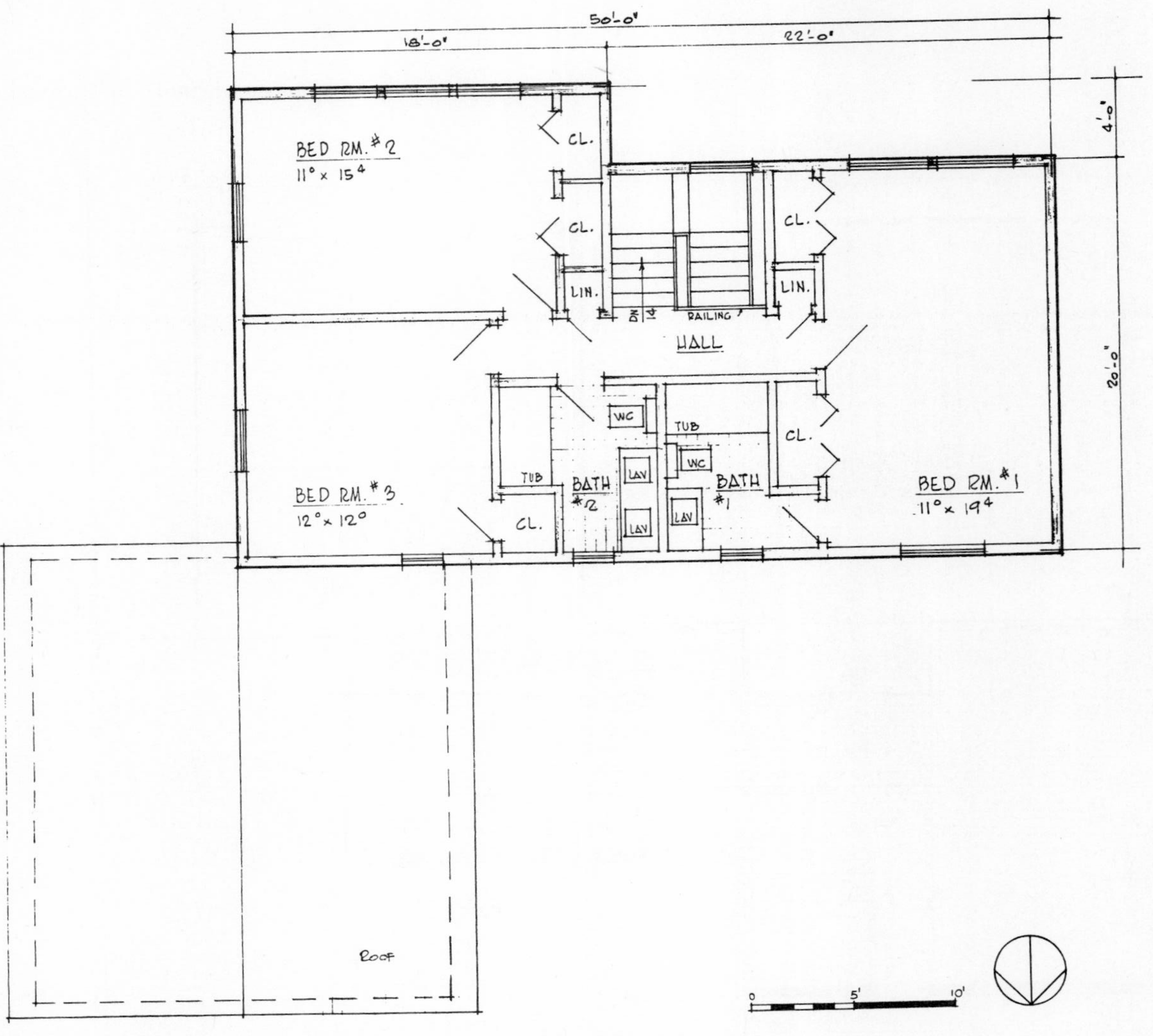

Design 8(e) Two story home—front toward north second floor plan.

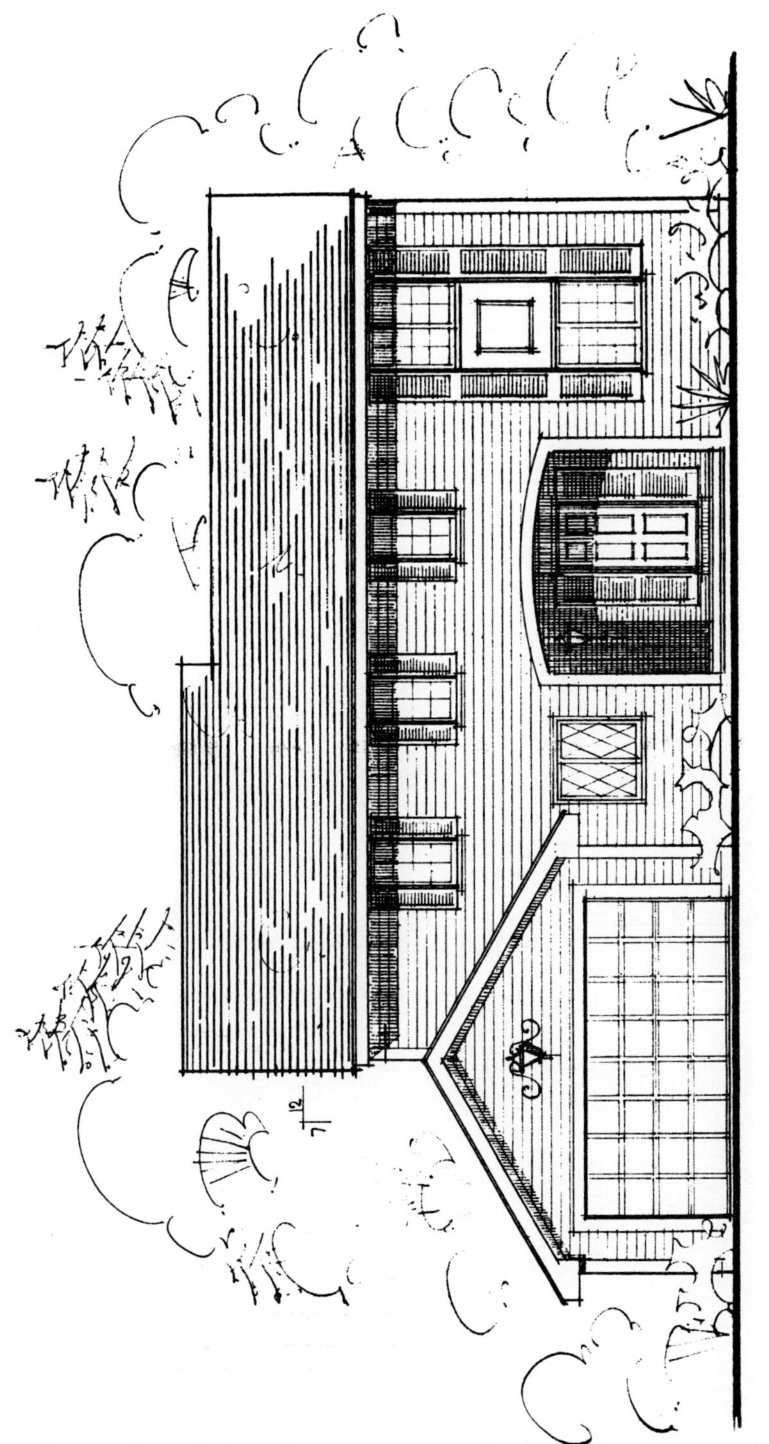

Design 8(f)   Front toward north, front elevation.

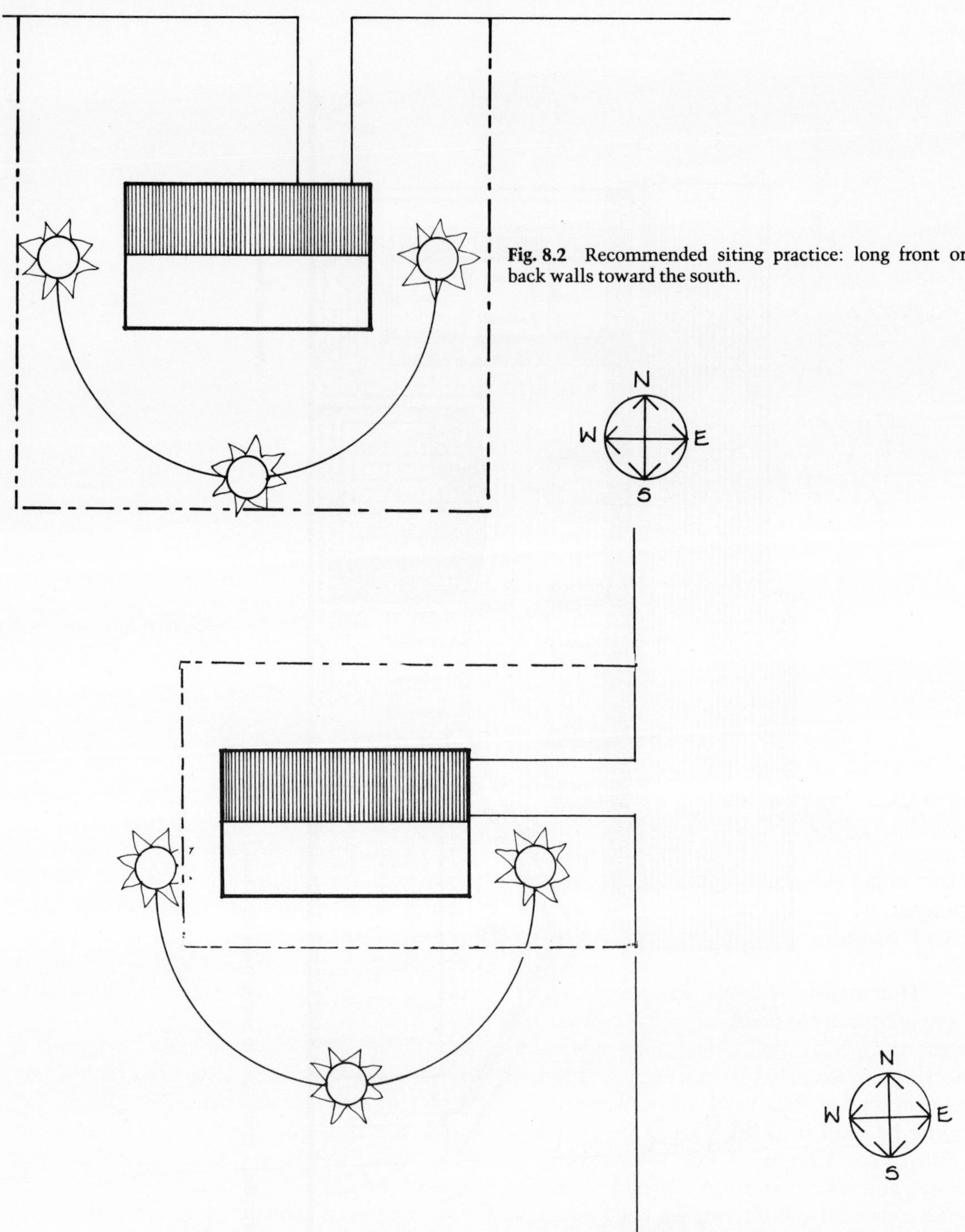

Fig. 8.2 Recommended siting practice: long front or back walls toward the south.

Fig. 8.3 Recommended siting practice for narrow lots: long-side wall toward the south regardless of street orientation.

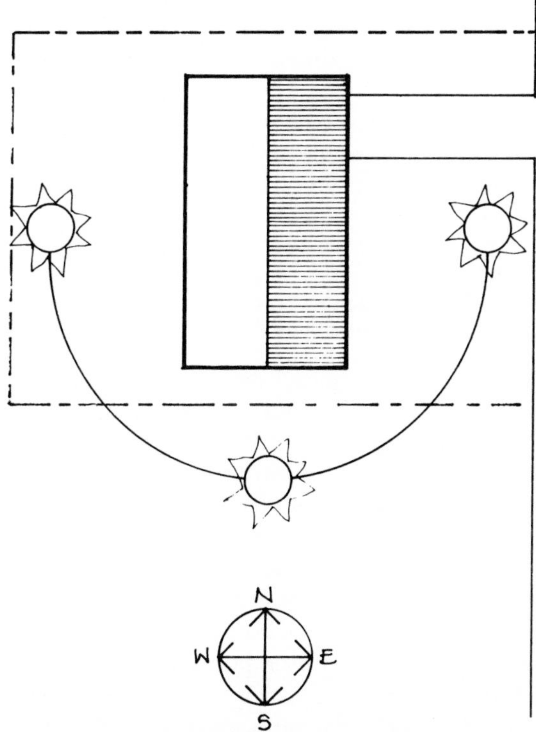

Fig. 8.4 Discouraged siting practice: short wall toward the south, long walls toward east and west.

The eight plans are representative of the many types of plans that can be converted into good suntempered homes, but they are not the only plans that will "work." The elevations also are only representative. The glass areas will vary depending on the locations in which the homes are built, and the facade styling can vary with market preference.

The majority of the designs presented here are for homes whose long axes run east/west and whose street elevations face either north or south. This is because it is strongly recommended that any type of passive solar home be built on a lot which faces north or south. (See Chapter 4 for information on street and lot orientation.) This permits the long axis of the home to run east/west and the longest sides of the home to face north and south (Fig. 8.2).

Design 4 and an alternate of Design 5 depict homes whose street elevations face west, but in all cases the long axis of the home runs east/west and long side of the home faces south. These "south sideyard" examples are appropriate for lots on north/south streets, but it is important that the north-to-south distance between homes be adequate to avoid shading of the south facing glazed areas by adjacent homes (Fig. 8.3).

No designs for homes that have narrow ends facing south and long sides facing east and west are presented here. This glazing distribution is counterproductive. A home of this type would consume more cooling energy, because of the excessive heat gain on the east and west windows—unless, of course, the long east and west sides of the home contained either virtually no glass, or an extremely effective exterior shading device such as a wide porch or carport. Such a home would not yield a very pleasant interior atmosphere or exterior appearance (Fig. 8.4).

DESIGN 1: North Buffer Home for a Sloping Site

This 2100-square-foot home has been designed for a lot sloping down toward south. The front of the home is one story and is designed to face north. The rear of the home is two stories because of the sloping site and is designed to face south. The north side buffer is composed of the kitchen food preparation area (cabinets, counters and heat generating appliances), stairway, entrance foyer, bathrooms, closets, utility and storage areas—all non-living areas. In addition, it is earth-sheltered by virtue of a sloping site. The south side of the home contains the living, dining and family rooms and all three bedrooms.

DESIGN 2: North Buffer Ranch Home

This 1384-square-foot ranch home utilizes the north buffer concept in a manner enabling the home to face north or south. In the front toward south version, the stairs, pantry, laundry, bathrooms and closets are located on the north side. In the front- toward-north version, the plan is flipped and minor modifications are made to the entry. The stairs, kitchen cabinets, laundry, bathrooms and closets comprise the north buffer.

DESIGN 3: Two Bedroom Ranch Home (Variable Elevations and Core)

This 1442-square-foot home, designed with retirees or empty-nesters in mind, has two bedrooms, one and one-half baths and ample entertainment area. The home can be built on lots facing north or south. When it is built with the front toward north, one of the bedrooms and the great room face south. When the home is built with the front toward south, one of the bedrooms and the great room again face south. In both versions, a large open counter admits light into the kitchen. A valuable concept illustrated in this plan is the core that includes the kitchen, basement stairs, powder and work rooms that can be flipped from one side of the home to the other, depending upon which side of the home faces south.

DESIGN 4: Zero Lot-Line Home (Side Toward South Type)

This 1316-square-foot home is specifically designed for narrow lots elongated along the east/west axis and can be built on a side lot line. The front of the home faces west and the long side of the home faces south. The principal rooms face south with the glazing shaded by a combination of roof and eyebrow overhangs. The garage, kitchen, bath and one bedroom form a north buffer. The west facing window is shaded by a portico, an excellent shading device for east or west glazing. Note that this home has no north facing glass and that the kitchen is illuminated by two large skylights.

DESIGN 5: Attachable Home (Variable Elevations Type)

This 1600-square-foot one-and-one-half-story home has been designed for lots facing north or west streets. It can be built as a single-family detached, an attached duplex or as a zero lot line home. Minimum amounts of glazing should always characterize the front elevation of this design.

Front toward North: This is the preferred orientation. The rooms used during the day, the eat-in kitchen, family/dining room and all three bedrooms receive south light. The south glass on the lower floor is shaded by cantilevering the second floor. The second floor is shaded by the roof overhang. The living room receives north light. The minimal need for north glazing, the absence of east and west glazing and the maximum use of south facing glazing makes this an ideal configuration.

Side toward South: This plan would work well on a corner lot. In this scheme, the family/dining room, living room and master bedroom receive south light. All three bedrooms, the eat-in kitchen and family/dining room receive morning light from the east and the living room receives evening light from the west. This plan *should not* be built with the front toward south or east, as this will result in excessive north or west glazing on the rear facade, creating an unnecessary thermal liability for the home.

DESIGN 6: Bi-Level Home (Variable Elevations Type)

This three-bedroom, two-bath, 1784-square-foot bi-level home can be sited to face north or south. The plan remains unchanged; only the amount of glazing varies. In the front toward north situation, the family room, master bedroom, kitchen and dining area receive solar radiation. With the front toward south, the family room, great room, entry foyer, and two bedrooms face south. An alternate glazing scheme for the front toward north condition is shown on the plans. This plan works particularly well when the home faces south, as the garage is tucked under the house and blocks none of the south wall's solar access.

DESIGN 7: One-and-One-Half-Story Home (Variable Dormer Type)

This 1700-square-foot home is designed to face either north or south. However, the second floor shed dormer is always located on the south side. When the front faces south, the dormer is on the front side of the home and all three bedrooms and the living room are the direct gain spaces. When the rear of the home faces south, the dormer is at the rear so that the two bedrooms, the kitchen, dining and family rooms receive solar gain. This home has been designed to make east and west glass unnecessary. North glazing should be minimized. This plan works well as an expandable home (the dormer can be added later) and as a retirement home, because the master bedroom is located on the ground floor.

DESIGN 8: Two-Story Home (Variable Main Entry Type)

This three-bedroom, two-and-one-half bath 1700-square-foot home can be sited to face north or south. It features two main entries, one on each of the long sides of the home. Depending on which side of the home is oriented toward south, one door becomes the major entry or front door and the other becomes the back door. This variability permits the living room, family/dining room, master bedroom plus one other bedroom always to be on the solar side of the home regardless of whether the front of the home faces north or south. The attached garage should be built on the north side of the home to block winter winds when the front is toward the north and moved to the side to allow full solar access when the front is toward south. This home *should not* be built with the gable end facing south (the long wall of the living room). This would make the long sides of the home face east and west. In most climate zones, the increased glazing on the east and west will so adversely affect the cooling load of the home that even the savings in heating costs obtained from glazing the south facing gable end would not offset the increased cost of cooling.

CHAPTER NINE

Conservation Comes First

Energy conservation and passive solar home design go hand in hand. The effectiveness of passive heating and cooling techniques depends greatly on a sound energy conservation commitment in the design and construction of a home. There should be a relatively high level of thermal protection in the ceilings, walls, floors, windows and doors; air infiltration (which can be very large if not given special attention) must be reduced in an energy conserving home before any solar system (passive or active) is added. First conservation, then solar!

Data on homebuilding construction practices indicates that many architects and builders already are doing a good job of designing and building energy conserving homes, but the nation's homebuilders certainly will be called on to construct homes that require even less energy.

There are literally dozens of design and construction features that can be incorporated in the home to save energy. The value of each feature must be measured against cost. Further, marketability varies depending on location, climate, price range of the home, the type and cost of fuel and the type of heating or cooling system being used. Though marketability remains a matter of judgment for each homebuilder and each home, most of the items mentioned here are thought to be economical in the long run, particularly in view of the rapidly rising price of energy.

Not all energy conserving features will add to the initial cost of the home. Some, such as using less glass area on the north orientation or reducing the temperature on the hot water heater, may either have no cost or actually lower first cost. However, even the obvious extra cost items, such as more insulation and triple glazing, have by product cost-reducing benefits that help to offset their added first cost. Such cost benefits include smaller air conditioners and furnaces, and often less duct work and smaller flues. From the marketing viewpoint energy conserving passive solar homes will be more comfortable and will have lower heating and cooling costs. The cost effectiveness of the following energy saving techniques or design tips can only be rated in a general way for all locations, because the cost effectiveness depends in large measure on local labor and material charges as well as previously mentioned factors. Energy conserving techniques should be selected on the basis of overall marketability and value in the particular market, *not* just on the basis of relative cost effectiveness.

The following design tips are ranked only

in a general way; however, the most significant energy saving techniques are at the beginning of the list. The design tips and energy conserving techniques are divided into two groups: one for homes in Climate Region A and one for homes in warmer Climate Regions B and C. Climate Region A is characterized as having more than 5000 degree-days and less than 900 cooling hours. Climate Region B has between 3000 and 5000 degree-days and between 900 and 1300 cooling hours; Climate Region C has less than 3000 degree-days and more than 1300 cooling hours. Chapter 10 provides a more detailed description of each climate region. Some techniques appear in one list and not the other because they are primarily applicable to only one climate condition. A number of the techniques have a different relative position in the two lists, depending on their relative significance in relation to climate.

The two most effective techniques in *any* climate are to reduce air infiltration and to reduce the temperature setting on the water heater.

REDUCING AIR INFILTRATION

With the high levels of thermal protection built into today's homes, ways to reduce infiltration merit increasing attention. Infiltration can be responsible for up to 50 percent of the entire home heat loss.

Infiltration takes place through any opening in the building skin—through open doors, through cracks around windows and doors, between sill plates and floors, around electrical fixtures, wiring and plumbing, and through vent openings and flues. Without resorting to unreasonable measures, it would be impossible to eliminate infiltration. Also, a certain minimum level of infiltration is desirable to bring fresh air into the building and prevent buildup of odors or potentially dangerous gases. Many carpets, furnishings,

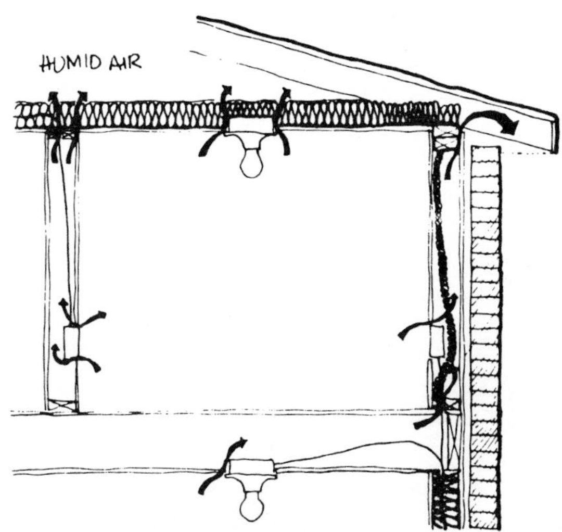

Fig. 9.1 Air leakage through holes.

and building materials emit harmful or irritating chemicals and cooking, bathing and human activity produces humidity and odors. While there has been some concern about a potential health hazard resulting from tightly sealed buildings, there is little cause for concern at infiltration rates above 0.5 air changes per hour (ACH). When special infiltration control measures and care are used during construction, infiltration may be reduced from 1.0 to 0.5 ACH. The most extensive and diligent efforts seldom reduce infiltration below 0.3 ACH in test programs. For homes constructed with infiltration rates equivalent to or less than 0.3 ACH, the installation of an air-to-air heat exchanger should be considered to ensure that adequate fresh air is introduced to the home. Reduction of infiltration is the simplest, least expensive measure to reduce energy consumption in a home (Fig. 9.1).

Problem areas and suggested solutions include:

- *leakage around recessed ceiling light fixtures* and surface mounted ceiling fixture

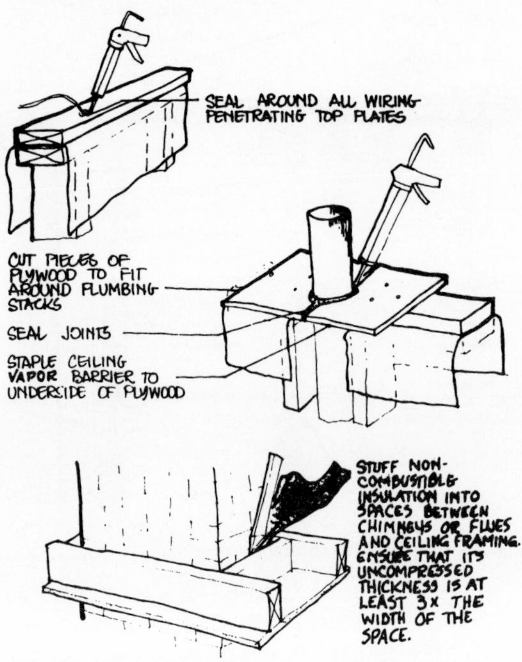

Fig. 9.2 Often overlooked leakage areas.

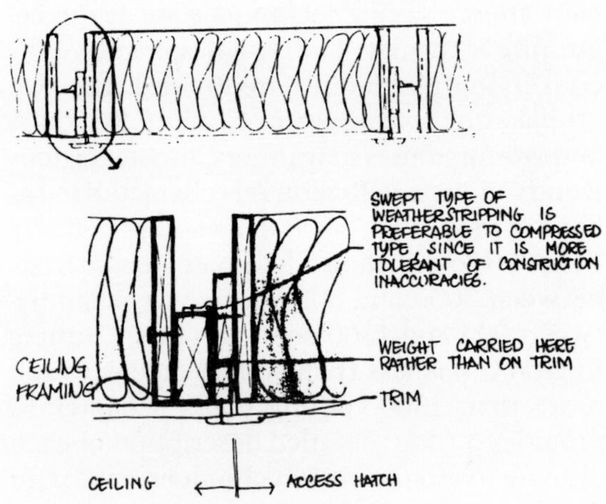

Fig. 9.3 Suggested attic access hatch detail.

wiring entrances. Before the surface mounted fixture is installed, wiring entries through walls and ceiling sections between conditioned (inside) and unconditioned (outside) areas of the home, should be caulked or sealed. To reduce heat loss and gain as well as unwanted air movement, recessed lighting fixtures should not be installed in these sections. While appeal of such fixtures cannot be denied, they may be installed judiciously in areas inside the thermal envelope, such as the kitchen, bathroom vanity and other dropped surfaces.

- leakage *where plumbing, ventilation, exhaust ducts, duct systems, piping, and wiring penetrate* the insulated ceiling section. Caulking, expanding sealants or stuffed insulation (or a combination of any and all) can be used at these points (Fig. 9.2).
- air penetration at the *attic access or scuttle.* The access panel should be "seated" on a gasket or weatherstrip to seal the periphery. Pull-down stair accesses should be checked for leakage in an upright position. Attic doors and stairways should be weatherstripped and insulated (Fig. 9.3).
- air leakage at *eaves,* where ceiling insulation is not installed over the top plate. Improperly installed baffles in loose fill applications also can leak exterior and attic air into the home. Proper application of inset stapling of batt or blanket insulation requires bringing the insulation out over the plate and stapling the vapor barrier to the inside face of the plate, or stuffing the crack at the plate with small pieces of scrap insulation to close the space (Fig. 9.4c).
- air movement *through the space between chimneys and adjacent framing.* These areas should be hand-stuffed with mineral fiber. Any vapor barrier or breather

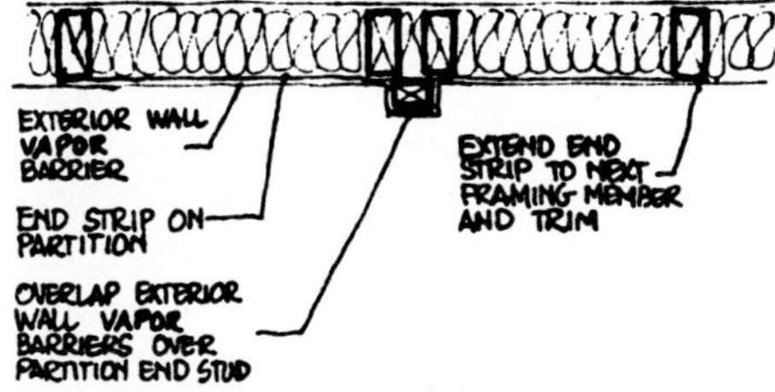

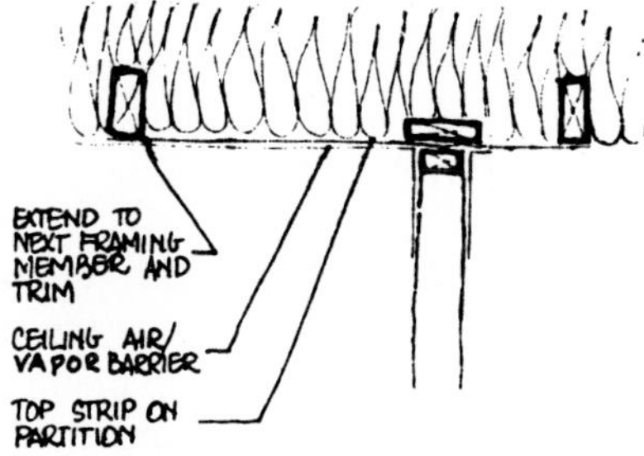

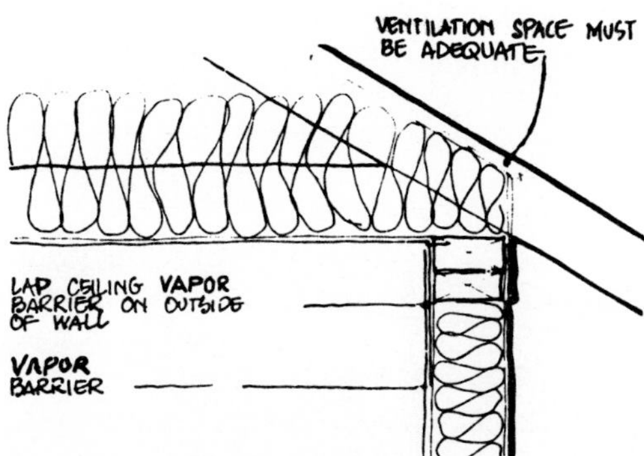

Fig. 9.4 Vapor barrier joints at intersections.

membrane papers should be removed when batt scrap is used.

- spaces *between end trusses, and common or fire walls* between units in multi-family and attached dwellings. Furring strips with gypsum board finish often are installed on these masonry unit walls. The open vertical channels between furring strips should be sealed or stuffed before insulating the ceiling section above.

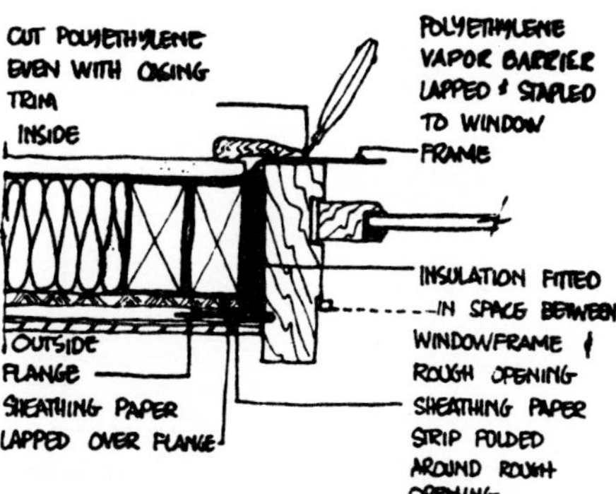

Fig. 9.5 Typical jamb section illustrating many features of good window installation practice.

- excessive infiltration at *windows and doors*. Proper fit and careful alignment of windows and doors at the time of installation is necessary. Door thresholds should fit snugly when the door is fully closed. Integral weatherstripping should be undamaged. Gaps and cavities in and around frames should be filled with sprayfoam insulation, caulked or loosely packed with fiberglass scraps. Results of national testing programs sponsored by the Architectural Aluminum Manufacturers Association and the National Woodwork Manufacturers Association that measure infiltration characteristics of commercially available windows and doors are available from their manufacturers. Also, a number of independent commercial laboratories evaluate window and door infiltration for manufacturers who do not choose to participate in the AAMA and NWMA programs (Fig. 9.5).
- leakage at *cracks in the exterior wall surfaces*. Caulking, sprayfoam or insulation stuffing may be needed at joints

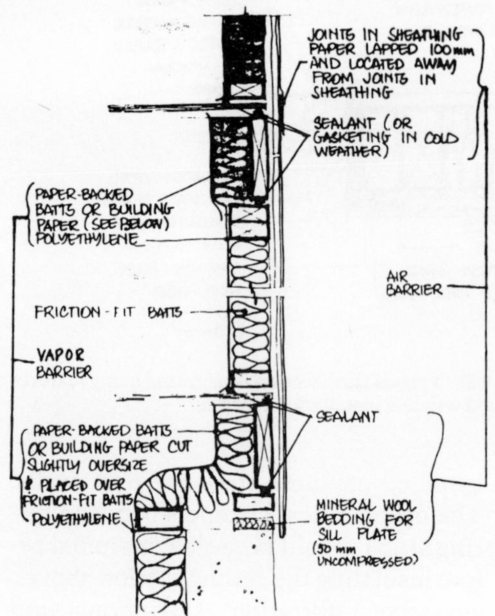

Fig. 9.6 Exterior wall/floor intersections.

around window and door casings and trim, between the slab and the bottom plate in slab-on-grade construction, between the bottom wall plate and the subfloor (where the siding or sheathing meets the foundation wall), at all internal and external corners and trim, and at any joints between dissimilar claddings or veneers (Fig. 9.6). Table 9.1 lists common caulking types and characteristics.

- all penetrations of *electrical and utility lines*, as well as hose bib lines. Depending on the size and location of the penetrations, caulking, rope caulk, sealants, sprayfoam or insulation stuffing should be used.
- leakage *where exhaust fan ducts penetrate exterior walls.* Any exhaust fan system should additionally have an insulated positive closing or double damper. The common louvre sets *do not* seal well.
- air penetration at *wall convenience outlets and switch housings.* Effective vapor barrier application is needed at these openings.

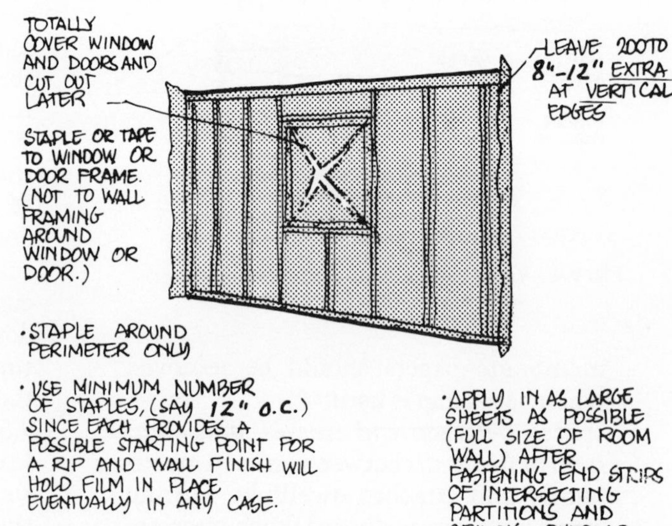

Fig. 9.7 Installation of vapor barrier on exterior walls.

TABLE 9.1 Caulking types and characteristics

Name	Cost	Adhesion	Elongation (%)	Life (yrs)	Cont. Service Temp. (°C)	Resistance to UV	Shrinkage Free	Cure time (days)	Paint	Thinner	Use Primer On
Urethane (1 part)	$2–3	Excellent	300–450	20+	−50 to 135	Good	Excellent	14	If desired	MEK, acetone, lacquer thinner	Not required
Silicone	3–4	Good (excellent w/ primer)	100–200	20+	−60 to 205	Excellent	Excellent	5	Possible difficulties	Paint thinner, Naphtha, toluol	Not required
Acrylic Terpolymers	3–4	Excellent		20+	85 maximum	Very good					Not required
Hypalon (1 part)	2	Very Good	15–50	15–20	−20 to 110	Good	Good	60–180	If desired	Toluene, xylene, xylol	Not required
Polysulfide (1 part)	2–4	Excellent	200–350 (2 part)	20+	−50 to 120	Very good	Excellent	4(	If desired	TCE, toluene, MEK	Special primer on all but metal
Butyl Rubber	1–2	Very good	75–125	7–10	−40 to 135	Fair	Fair	7	Recommended	Paint thinner, Naphtha	Not required
Acrylic Latex	1–2	Excellent except w/metal	25–60	2–1S	−30 to 100	Fair	Fair	3	Recommended	Water	Porous surfaces
Oil	1	Fair–good	5	1–7	−25 to 85	Poor	Poor	120–360	Must	Paint thinner	Porous surfaces

Source: Total Environmental Action, Inc., Harrisville, N.H.

- infiltration from *damaged sheathing.* Sheathing should be snugly nailed to the framing. Joints should be tight, and any damaged sections should be repaired or replaced.
- leakage *where fireplace constructions extend past the exterior walls.*
- at all *lateral and longitudinal joints of ducts* in unconditioned spaces.

Here are a few specific construction practices and details that help reduce air infiltration: use sill sealer, prehung and weatherstripped doors; caulk around all openings and at corners as needed; caulk or seal around wire/pipe penetrations in outer shell; caulk or seal wire/pipe holes in top wall plates; and eliminate recessed ceiling lights penetrating into nonconditioned space. Stuff mineral wool insulation in space between chimney and ceiling framing. If unfaced batts for (pressure fit) insulation are used, cover entire wall and ceiling area with a 4-mil polyethylene film for vapor barrier (Figs. 9.7, 9.8, 9.9). Do not cut window openings until trim is in place. These measures reduce air infiltration through small spaces between window frame and rough frame openings around windows.

As no two homes are alike in workmanship, supervisors are advised to schedule several "walk-arounds" as an integral part of the inspection process. Each inspection should be based on a detailed checklist and should include a review of all potential air leakage areas.

In the NAHB Research Foundation's Energy Efficient Residence (more commonly called the "EER House") built in 1976 under a HUD contract, the most cost effective technique in *any* climate was to reduce the temperature setting on the water heater. In the EER House, lowering the setting on the water heating thermostat from 160°F to 120°F accounted for most of the 49 percent decrease in energy used for water heating. Significantly, this amounted to 27.8 percent of the total energy savings in the EER.

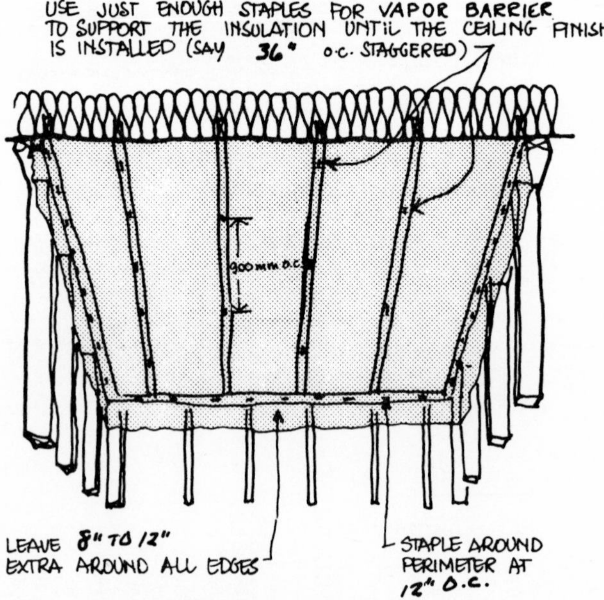

Fig. 9.8 Installation of vapor barrier on ceilings.

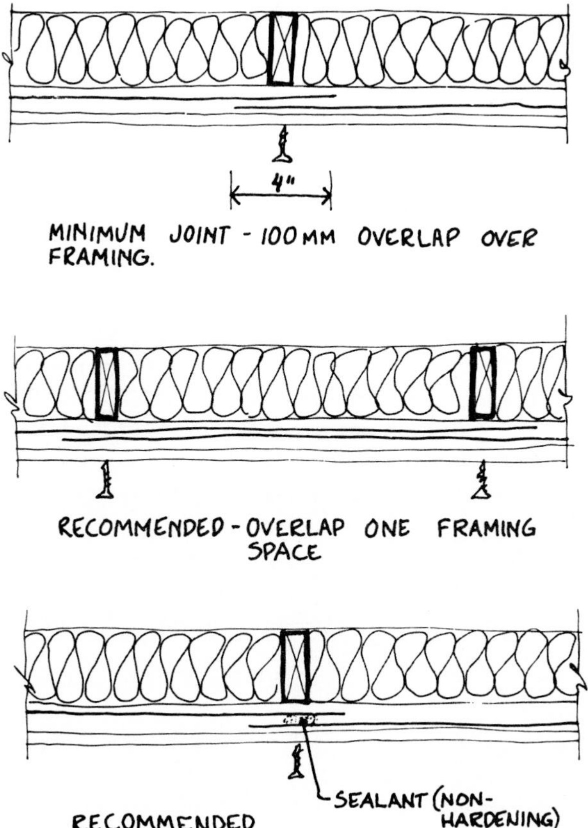

Fig. 9.9 Vapor barrier joints.

In warmer climates (Regions B and C) the saving would not be quite as great because average incoming water temperatures would be higher. Lowering the water heater setting is also very important in terms of total energy saving, since energy use for heating water is usually the second largest consumer of energy in the home, next to heating or cooling energy use.

ENERGY CONSERVING DESIGN RECOMMENDATIONS FOR HOMES IN CLIMATE REGION A

Use Clock Thermostats

Install clock thermostats so temperature can be set back at night in winter with automatic morning turn-on, or use several zones of conventional thermostats. Based on different temperature setting regimens for various climates, calculated savings have been prepared by OAK Ridge National Laboratory (ORNL). Figure 9.10 shows that a higher percentage of savings can be achieved for milder winter climates than cold climates with the same temperature setpoints. Note that an eight-hour, 8°F setback is equal to about 43 percent savings for a 3000 degree-day climate and 23 percent savings for a 7000 degree-day climate.

Buyers must be instructed in the proper use of these devices and reminded that the amount of savings to be achieved is up to them. Generally, heat savings from setbacks

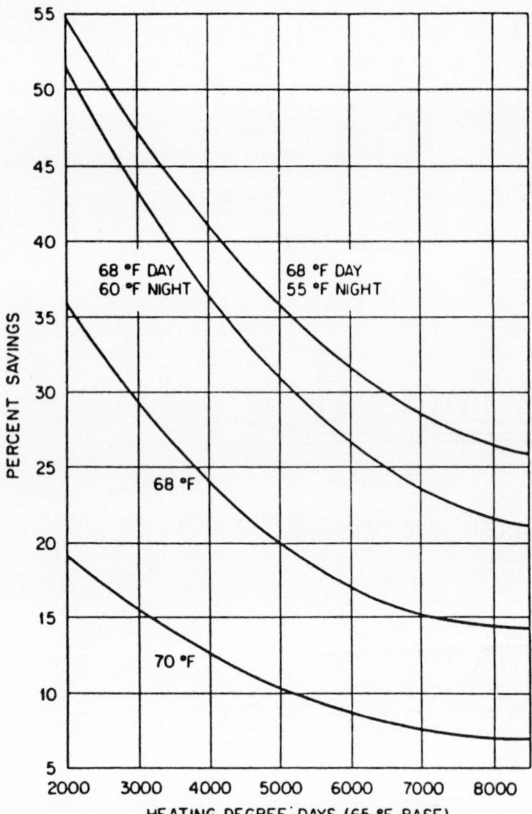

Fig. 9.10 Predicted energy savings for several thermostat settings (72° F is the reference setting and night setback is from 10 p.m. to 6 a.m.)

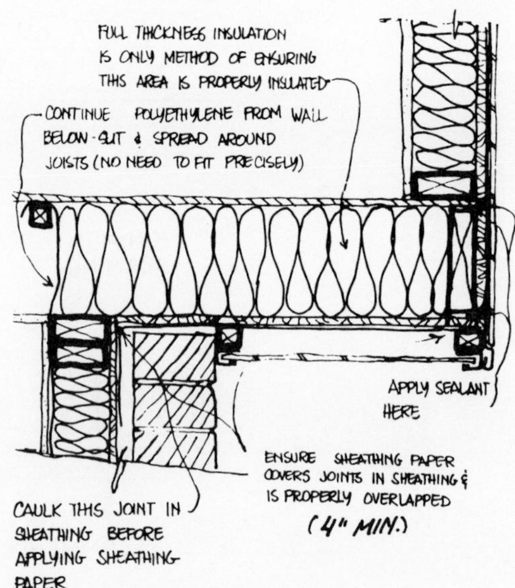

Fig. 9.11 Special care should be used to effectively insulate cantilevered floor. Place vapor barrier on warm-in-winter side. (Note: Achieving a continuous air barrier is very difficult at this location and a great deal of care must be taken in applying the sheathing and the sheathing paper to the underside of the overhang. If this is not done properly, floor may be cold, despite full thickness insulation, due to air infiltration.)

are less with heat pump systems. The local power supplier or HVAC contractor should be consulted about potential benefits and penalties of heat pump setbacks.

Require Proper Installation of Insulation

Proper installation of insulation has an important bearing on heat loss and gain. The heat loss or gain effect of a void is much greater than its proportional area. (Refer to the *Insulation Manual—Homes/Apartments*, NAHB Research Foundation, Inc., 1979, second edition.) On-site industrial engineering studies by the NAHB Research Foundation show that good quality insulation installation requires no more insulation, and from less than one additional hour of labor up to a maximum of two additional hours per house. Important installation features follow:

- When using blown-in insulation, specify the R-value desired and the number of bags required according to the product label. *Do not specify blown insulation by inches.*
- Make sure all insulated areas are covered completely.
- Extend the ceiling insulation all the way over the top plate.
- Insulate behind band joints, including those at upper floors.

Fig. 9.12 Insulation should be placed behind plumbing and wiring.

- Insulate soffits of cantilevered floor construction (Fig. 9.11).
- Stuff all cracks around doors and windows and small, odd shaped cavities with insulation and staple polyethylene (vapor barrier) over these areas.
- Cut batts to fit narrow spaces between studs and leave enough surplus to staple the flanges.
- Put insulation behind pipes, wires and electrical outlet boxes in outside walls (Fig. 9.12).
- Butt the ends of batts snugly against each other.
- Shove batts snugly against the top and bottom plates in wall cavities.

For Frame Construction Use Optimum Value Engineering (OVE) Framing Techniques

NAHB Research Foundation measurements show that this reduces the amount of solid lumber in exterior walls from about twenty to ten percent of the opaque wall, thereby reducing thermal short circuits and increasing average R-value of the wall. This reduces heat loss and gain through the walls about seven to ten percent. See *Reducing Home Building Costs with OVE Design and Construction.*[1] Examples of OVE framing include:

- Using exterior wall studs 24 inches o.c. instead of 16 inches o.c.
- Two stud corners with metal backup clips for drywall (Fig. 9.13).
- One horizontal 2x4 at the intersection of an interior wall with an exterior wall with metal backup clips for drywall (Fig. 9.14).
- Plywood box headers. Fill header cavities with insulation (Fig. 9.15).
- Engineered headers, rather than solid wood, in load bearing walls and elimination of headers in nonload bearing (i.e., gable end) walls.
- Locate doors and windows adjacent to one regularly occurring stud.

Use R-30 to R-50 Ceiling Insulation

The colder the climate and the higher the cost of energy, the more insulation can be justified.

For Frame Exterior Walls, Use R-19 Cavity Insulation and R-4 to R-8 Insulated Sheathing.

The colder the climate and the higher the price of energy, the more insulation can be justified.

For Crawl Space Designs, Insulate the Perimeter Foundation Wall.

Use R-19 on exterior walls and on two-foot to four-foot wide area on ground surface adja-

[1] United States Department of HUD, Office of Policy Development and Research, December, 1979.

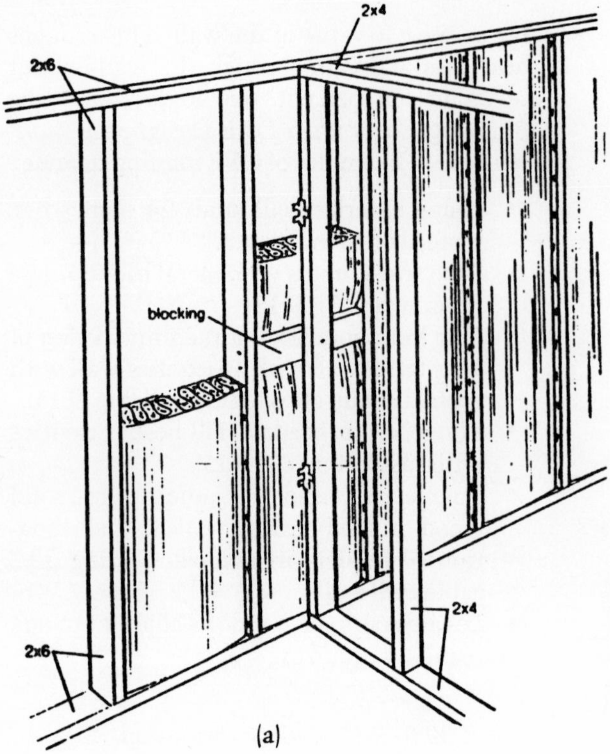

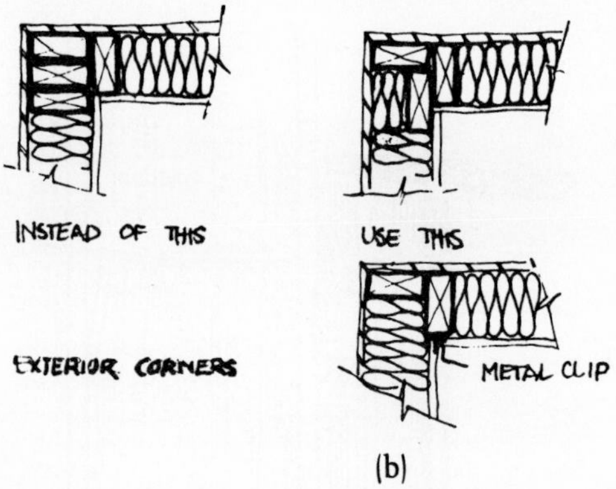

Fig. 9.13 (a) Energy efficient corner framing detail. (b) Use of a mid-height block and drywall clips in place of the traditional partition post allow this area of the exterior wall to be fully insulated.

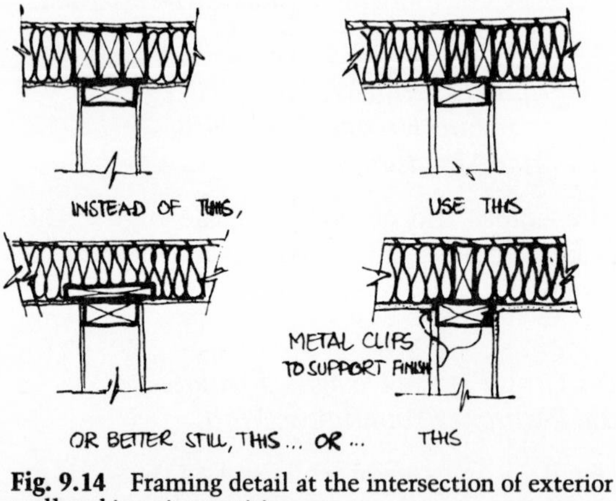

Fig. 9.14 Framing detail at the intersection of exterior wall and interior partition.

cent to exterior walls. An alternate R-19 floor installation is to use 4- to 6-mil polyethylene film on the ground throughout the entire crawl space, turned up about six inches and

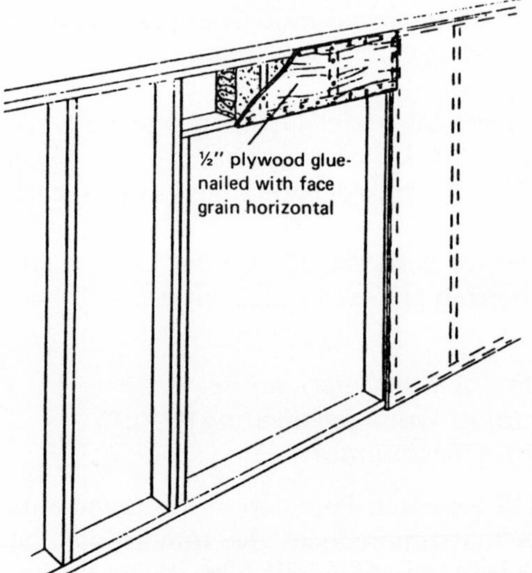

Fig. 9.15 Plywood box header provides for insulation over openings in exterior wall.

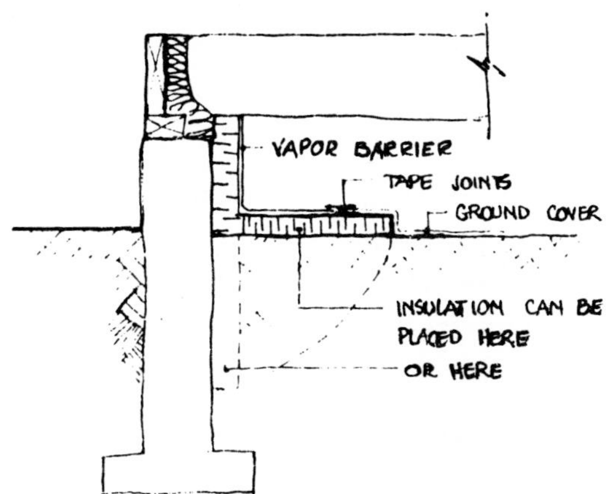

Fig. 9.16 Insulation of crawl spaces.

taped to the wall behind the insulation. Place ground cover film before insulating ground so that film is below ground cover insulation (Fig. 9.16).

Use R-11 or R-19 Basement Wall Insulation

Use 2×3s, 24 inches o.c., held either one inch away from basement wall for R-11 (batt/blanket) wall insulation or three inches away from wall for R-19 to avoid compression and reduced R-value. This appears to be the most cost effective method of installation. Use unfaced batts, low flame-spread-rating foil faced batts, or if asphalt impregnated batts are used, cover with fire retardant material such as gypsum board (Figs. 9.17 and 9.18).

Employ Edge Insulation for Slab-on-Grade Construction

Experiments with slab floors indicate that heat loss from a concrete slab is mostly from the perimeter rather than through the floor and into the ground. The total heat loss is more nearly proportional to the length of

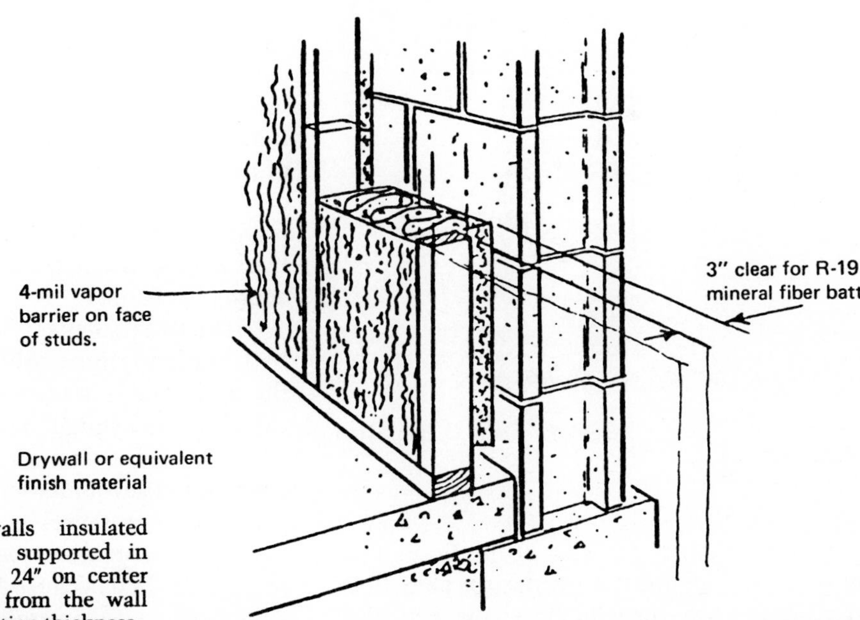

Fig. 9.17 Masonry walls insulated with insulation batts supported in nonload bearing 2×3's 24" on center that are spaced away from the wall depending on the insulation thickness.

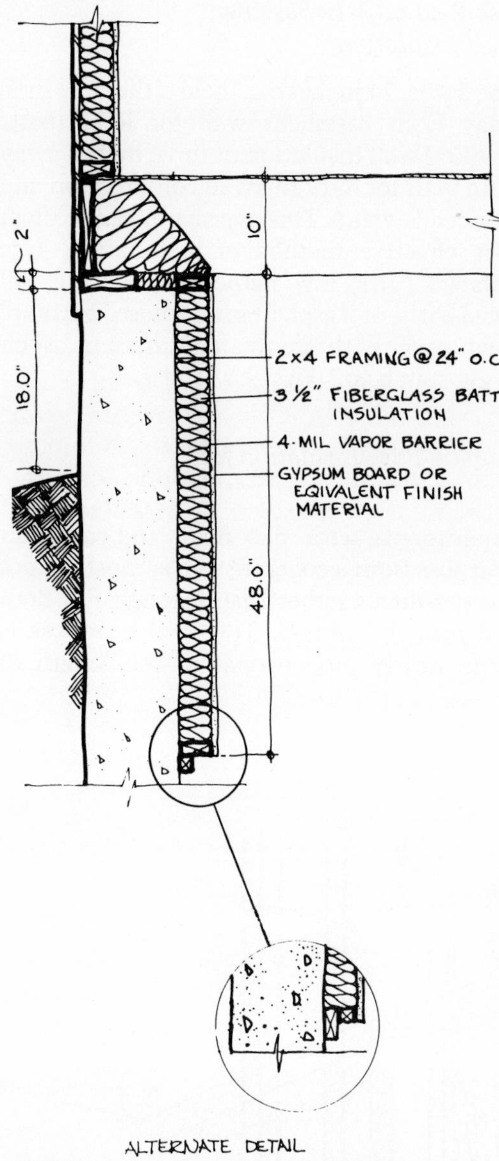

Fig. 9.18 Alternate basement wall insulation technique.

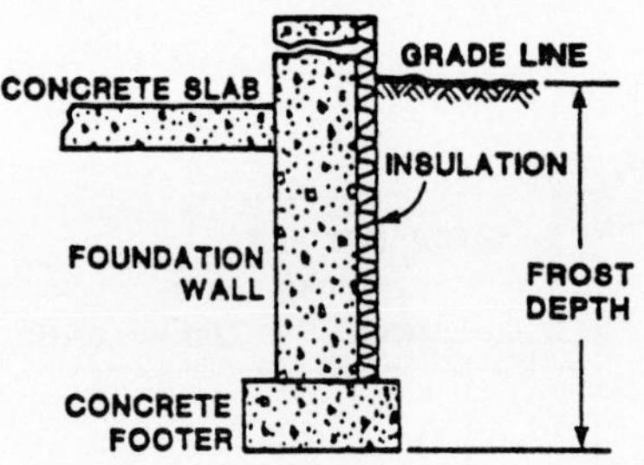

Fig. 9.19 "I" shape or vertical insulation system.

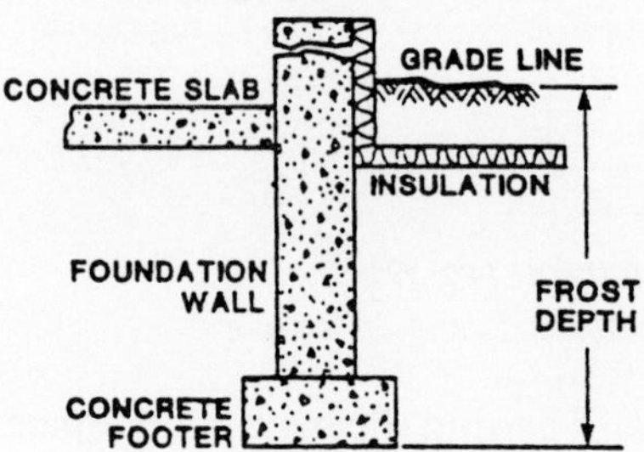

Fig. 9.20 "L" shape insulation system.

perimeter than to the area of the floor. Two common systems for insulating slab floor perimeters are vertical "I"-shape and "L"-shape systems. In the "I" system, at least two inches of rigid foam, water resistant insulation is placed vertically next to the exposed slab edge. The insulation should extend from the top of the finished slab surface to a depth equal to the local frost depth (Fig. 9.19). In the "L" system, at least two inches of rigid foam insulation should extend from the top surface of the finished slab to one half the local frost depth and horizontally outward from that point a distance that, when added to the vertical depth, is equal to the total local frost depth (Fig. 9.20).

The thermal effect is nearly the same for both configurations, when the thickness and the total length of the insulations are identical. The additional advantage of the "L" shape system is that it also prevents freezing away from the foundation, and eliminates the potential of frost heave damage. It is important to avoid breaks or joints when the insulation is installed because local thermal bridges which reduce the overall efficiency of the installation will result. In homes being constructed in climates having greater than 7,000 degree-days, three inches of rigid insulation is recommended.

For passive solar homes constructed in Climate Region A that rely on the floor slab to store transmitted solar energy, one to one-and-one-half inches of rigid foam insulation should be placed directly beneath the entire slab to eliminate excessive heat loss from the slab into the ground. The extra benefit of this additional insulation is that significantly more collected solar heat will be available to offset nighttime heat loss.

Minimize North Facing Windows to Marketable Amount and Increase South Facing Windows.

To extent feasible, minimize east and west facing glass and shade against solar heat gain. (See Chapters 10 and 11.)

Use Windows and Glass Doors with U-Value less than 0.39 (ASHRAE Calculated) on North, South, East and West Elevations.

Options include triple or quad glazing; double glazing plus night insulation; and low emittance coatings applied to the number two or three surface of a sealed insulated glass unit or applied to a polyester substrate that is suspended between the inner and outer panes of an insulated glass unit. (See Chapter 10 for specific guidelines.) If using aluminum frame windows, select those with a condensation resistance factor (CRF) greater than 50 and with complete thermal breaks (Fig. 9.21).

Use Windows and Doors that have Low Air Infiltration Characteristics.

- Select windows and doors meeting the best quality air infiltration requirements of either the Architectural Aluminum Manufacturers Association or the National Woodwork Manufacturers Association.
- Use weatherstripped operable sash (such as double-hung, casements, awnings) to enhance natural ventilation. Operable sash should be at least five percent of the home's conditioned floor area.

Use Energy-Conserving Doors.

For metal doors, important features include insulated core, thermal break, prehung, weatherstripping and low air infiltration rate. For wood doors, important features

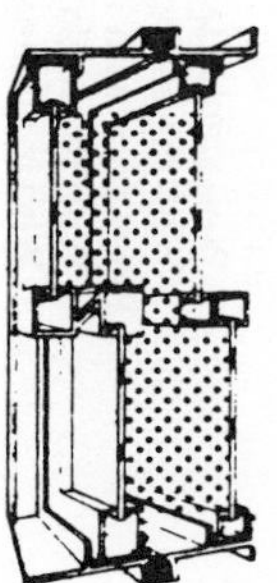

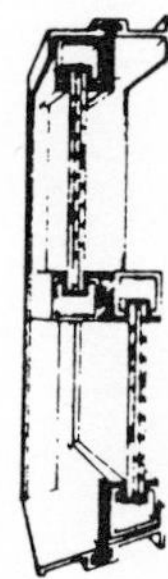

Fig. 9.21 A typical aluminum frame window with a complete thermal break.

TABLE 9.2A Coefficients of transmission (*U*) for wood doors,[a] Btu/hr · ft² · °F

Door Thickness, in.[d]	Description	Winter[b] No Storm Door	Winter[b] Wood Storm Door[e]	Winter[b] Metal Storm Door[f]	Summer[c] No Storm Door
1-3/8	Hollow core flush door	0.47	0.30	0.32	0.45
1-3/8	Solid core flush door	0.39	0.26	0.28	0.38
1-3/8	Panel door with 7/16-in. panels	0.57	0.33	0.37	0.54
1-3/4	Hollow core flush door	0.46	0.29	0.32	0.44
	with single glazing[g]	0.56	0.33	0.36	0.54
1-3/4	Solid core flush door	0.33	0.28	0.25	0.32
	With single glazing[g]	0.46	0.29	0.32	0.44
	With insulating glass[g]	0.37	0.25	0.27	0.36
1-3/4	Panel door with 7/16-in. panels[h]	0.54	0.32	0.36	0.52
	With single glazing[i]	0.67	0.36	0.41	0.63
	With insulating glass[i]	0.50	0.31	0.34	0.48
1-3/4	Panel door with 1-1/8-in. panels[h]	0.39	0.26	0.28	0.38
	With single glazing[i]	0.61	0.34	0.38	0.58
	With insulating glass[i]	0.44	0.28	0.31	0.42
2-1/4	Solid core flush door	0.27	0.20	0.21	0.26
	With single glazing[g]	0.41	0.27	0.29	0.40
	With insulating glass[g]	0.33	0.23	0.25	0.32

[a] Values for doors are based on nominal 3′8″ × 6′8″ door size. Interpolation and moderate extrapolation are permitted for glazing areas and door thicknesses other than those specified.
[b] 15 mph outdoor air velocity; 0 F outdoor air; 70 F inside air temp natural convection.
[c] 7.5 mph outdoor air velocity; 89 F outdoor air; 75 F inside air natural convection.
[d] Nominal thickness.
[e] Values for wood storm door are approximately 50% glass area.
[f] Values for metal storm door are for any percent of glass area.
[g] 17% exposed glass area; insulating glass contains 0.25 inch air space.
[h] 55% panel area.
[i] 33% glass area; 22% panel area; insulating glass contains 0.25 inch air space.

TABLE 9.2B Coefficients of transmission (*U*) for steel doors, Btu/hr · ft² · °F

Thickness	Steel Door[14]			No Storm Door
1.75 in.				
A[a]	0.59	—	—	0.58
B[b]	0.40	—	—	0.39
C[c]	0.47	—	—	0.46

[a] A = Mineral fiber core (2 lb/ft³).
[b] B = Solid urethane foam core with thermal break.
[c] C = Solid Polystyrene core with thermal break.

1981, ASHRAE Handbook of Fundamentals

include solid core, not paneled, weather-stripping, low infiltration rate and a combination storm/screen door in colder areas of this climate category (Table 9.2).

Provide Adequate Natural Attic Ventilation.

Natural attic ventilation equal to one square foot of net free vent opening area for each 300 square feet of ceiling with vapor barrier or double that amount (one square foot in 150 square feet) when there is no vapor barrier in ceiling is recommended. Except under *extreme* summer conditions power venting of attic space is not cost or energy efficient with high levels of attic insulation.

Use Whole-House Ventilation for Partial Summer Cooling.

There are a number of times when economical summer cooling can be obtained by whole-house ventilation because total outdoor enthalpy is less than indoors. In addition, the increased air movement contributes to improved summer comfort (Fig. 9.22).

Size Heating and Cooling Equipment to Match, *Not* Exceed, *the Design Load.*

According to ASHRAE, substantial reduction in seasonal heating efficiency results from oversizing gas or oil fired equipment. The seasonal efficiency decreases as the degree of oversizing increases and as the number of heating degree-days decreases.

Slightly undersizing cooling equipment (10 to 15 percent based on standard design load calculation methods) may provide better comfort, particularly in humid climates. It also may cost less to operate, have lower first cost and use less energy. Conventional sizing techniques usually are based on a maximum of a 3°F temperature rise (swing) at design conditions. Standard procedures indicate only 4.5°F temperature rise at design conditions when equipment is 15 percent undersized. Air movement from continuous fan operation and lower humidity, may produce equal or better comfort conditions, especially with high levels of thermal protection for ceilings, walls and glass which reduce mean radiant temperatures in the summertime.

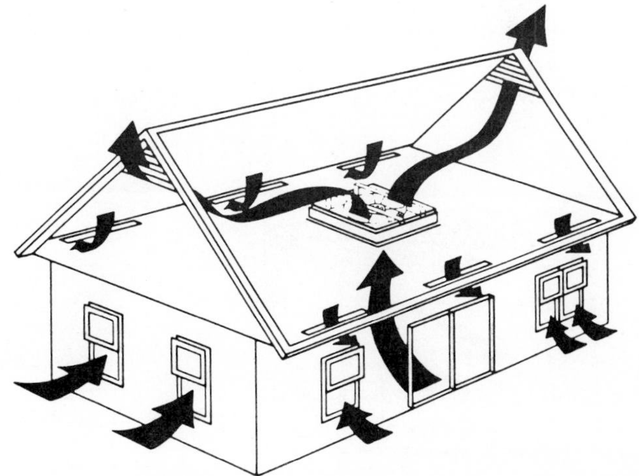

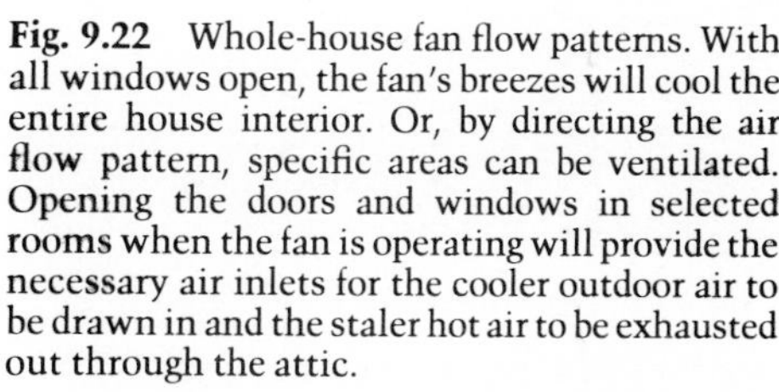

Fig. 9.22 Whole-house fan flow patterns. With all windows open, the fan's breezes will cool the entire house interior. Or, by directing the air flow pattern, specific areas can be ventilated. Opening the doors and windows in selected rooms when the fan is operating will provide the necessary air inlets for the cooler outdoor air to be drawn in and the staler hot air to be exhausted out through the attic.

Use Heat Pumps if Electricity is Used for Heating.

This is particularly appropriate if cooling also will be provided. Contact a local distributor to assist in assessing such site specific criteria as ground water availability, seasonal earth temperature, conductance and diffusivity. When electricity is used for heating, consider modulated or two-stage heat pumps, ground or water source heat pumps.

Use High Efficiency Features on Gas Fired Equipment.

Consider a multistage unit with corresponding thermostat, intermittent ignition device (IID), vent damper or othei features to improve seasonal efficiency.

Select High Seasonal Energy Efficiency Ratio (SEER) Air Conditioning Units.

A SEER-9 unit uses 22.2 percent less energy than a SEER-7 unit; SEER-10 unit uses 30 percent less than SEER-7; SEER-11 uses 36.4 percent less than SEER-7.

Use Duct Insulation.

Avoid ducts in nonconditioned spaces to the extent possible. If ducts in nonconditioned, but partially protected spaces (i.e., garages and crawl spaces) are necessary, use at least R-8 duct wrap on metal ducts or 1½-inch thick rigid insulation. If ducts are in nonconditioned spaces, use R-12 duct wrap. Tape metal duct joints and joints of duct insulation (Fig. 9.23). Avoid ducts in exterior walls. Insulate cold-in-winter side of ducts, bends or boots adjacent to outside walls (i.e., those serving floor registers at outside walls). Consider running duct work in soffits within the conditioned space. According to some recent measurements, properly taping duct joints will save five to 10 percent of heating and cooling energy, and when combined with proper insulation levels will save as much as 25 percent of heating and cooling energy when ducts are in nonconditioned spaces.

Use Insulated Skylights for Natural Daylighting and/or Passive Solar Gain.

Skylights should have provisions for external summer shading and interior winter night insulation.

Select Energy-Efficient Fireplaces and Install Properly.

For masonry and prefabricated fireplaces and wood stoves, important energy features include: locations that do not penetrate exterior walls; provision for supplying combustion air from outdoors direct to firebox; easily operated, tight closing damper; provision for

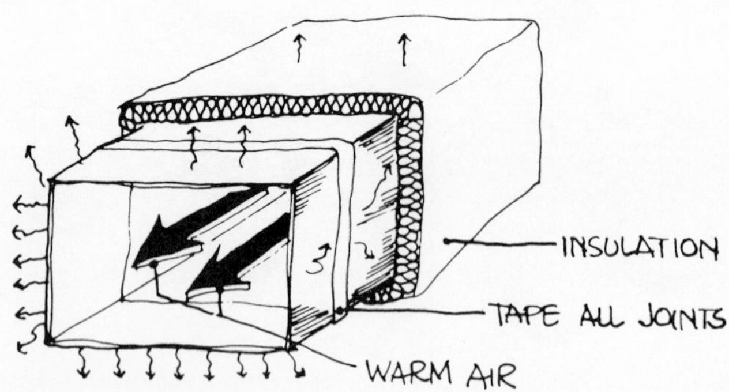

Fig. 9.23 Insulation of heating ducts.

circulation of room air around the firebox and back into the room; and glass doors or tight fitting metal panel to fit over opening when not in use. Generally, if these energy conserving features are not applied—particularly to fireplace design—the heat contribution to the home by such devices will be marginal or slightly negative. When feasible, locate masonry chimney and fireplace mass where they will receive the direct rays of the sun and provide thermal storage for passive solar heat gain.

Insulate and Weatherstrip Attic Openings.

Insulate back of attic door or scuttle (use one or more layers of foam insulation board or batts) and add weatherstripping. Locate attic scuttle in nonconditioned area, if possible.

Avoid Running Hot and Cold Water Piping through Nonconditioned Spaces.

If it is necessary to do this, insulate those pipes with at least one and one-half inches of flexible foam insulation.

Consider an Extra Heavily Insulated Water Heater.

Wrap a 3-inch thick jacket of mineral wool insulation around the water heater (Fig. 9.24). In high energy cost areas and when electricity is to be used for water heating, consider a heat pump hot water heater.

Install Water Saving Water Closet and Water Saving Devices for Kitchen and Bathroom Faucets and Shower Heads

(See Tables 9.3 and 9.4.)

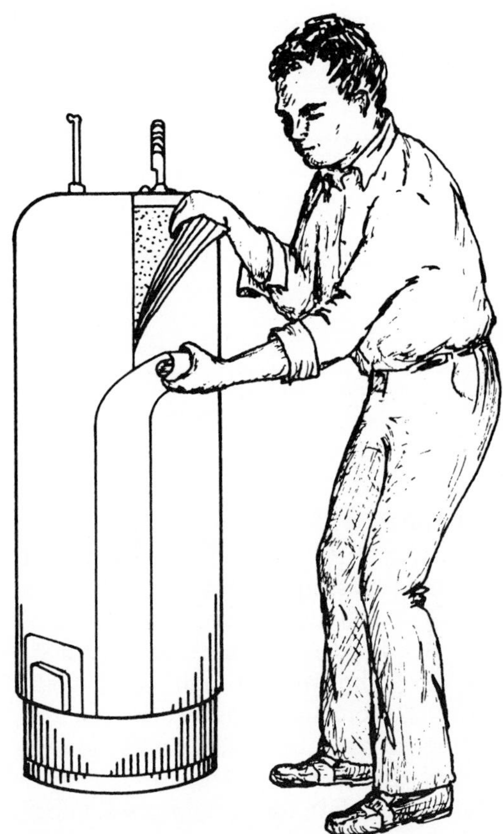

Fig. 9.24 Installation of jacket insulation.

ENERGY CONSERVING DESIGN TIPS FOR HOMES IN CLIMATES B AND C

Use Clock Thermostats.

Install clock thermostats so temperature can be set back at night in winter with automatic morning turn-on, or use several zones of conventional thermostats. Based on different temperature setting regimens for various climates, calculated savings have been prepared by Oak Ridge National Laboratory (ORNL). Examination of the graph shows that a higher percentage of savings can be accomplished for milder winter climates than

TABLE 9.3 Daily water consumption for a family of four

Activity	DHW Consumption (Gallons)
Dishwashing	10.0
Cooking	—
Kitchen Sink	8.0
Laundry	36.0
Showers and Bath	16.0
Bathroom sink	7.0
Toilet	—
	77.0 Gallons

Source: Canadian Electrical Association.

cold climates with the same temperature setpoints (Fig. 9.10). Note that an 8-hour, 8°F setback is equal to approximately 43 percent savings for a 3000 degree-day climate and 23 percent for a 7000 degree-day climate. An 8°F setback for eight hours at night in St. Louis will save 32 percent of the heating energy. The same setback in Atlanta will save 44 percent of the heating energy, according to the Oak Ridge National Laboratories. Clock thermostats are not recommended for use with heat pumps unless thermostat has a manual cut-off or bypass switch for resistance heating. Check with local power company.

Use R-30 to R-38 Ceiling Insulation.

The warmer the climate and the higher the cost of energy, the more insulation can be justified.

For Frame Exterior Walls, Use R-11, R-13 or R-19 Cavity Insulation and R-4 Sheathing.

The warmer the climate and the higher the cost of energy, the more insulation can be justified.

Require Proper Installation of Insulation.

See discussion of Climate Region A above for specific strategies.

Table 9.4 Options for reduced domestic hot water consumption.

Conservation Device		Annual Energy* Savings MBTU** ($)	Cost, $	Payback, Yrs
Shower:	Flow Restrictor	3–5 ($22–15)	3–4	Under 1
	Adjustable Volume Control	3–4 ($22–15)	8–12	Under 1
Faucets:	Flow Restrictor	1–2 ($7–6)	1–3	Under 1
	Restrictor Aerator	1–2 ($7–6)	5–7	1
	Spray Tap	1–2 ($7–6)	8–10	1–2

* Annual energy savings will depend on annual consumption. The left hand column assumes electric water heaters and the right hand column assumes gas water heaters.
** MBTU = Millions of Btu's.

For Frame Construction Use OVE Framing Techniques.

See Climate Region A for details.

Employ Edge Insulation for Slab-on-Grade Construction.

- It is recommended that one to two inches of rigid insulation be used to insulate against slab-edge losses in the southern sections of Climate Region B and all of Climate Region C. See discussion of Climate Region A for installation options.
- For homes in the southern sections of Climate Region B and all of Climate Region C, the use of insulation beneath the slab is not recommended. A slab in direct contact with the earth has greater benefit in reducing annual cooling loads than the marginal benefit achieved in winter if it were fully insulated. Slabs with direct earth contact in these regions have the advantage of ameliorating indoor daily temperature swings during the cooling season by acting as massive heat sinks or diffusers.

Insulate Basement Walls to R-11 or R-19.

Use 2×3s, 24 inches o.c., held either one inch away from basement wall for R-11 (batt/blanket) wall insulation or three inches away from wall for R-19 to avoid compression and reduced R-value. This has proven to be the most cost effective method of installation. Use unfaced batts, low flame-spread-rating foil faced batts, or if asphalt impregnated batts are used, cover with fire retardant material such as gypsum board.

For Crawl Space Designs, Insulate Perimeter Foundation Wall.

Use R-19 on exterior walls and on 2-foot to 4-foot wide area on ground surface adjacent to exterior walls. An alternate R-19 floor installation is to use 4- to 6-mil polyethylene film on the ground throughout the entire crawl space, turned up about six inches and taped to the wall behind the insulation (Fig. 9.16). Place the ground cover film before insulating the ground so that the film is below the insulation covering the ground.

Shade South Facing Glass Against Direct Summer Sun.

For two-story houses, second story balconies or a cantilevered second floor may provide adequate shade. (See Chapter 11 for specific recommendations.)

- Exterior shading is the most effective approach; exterior shades block both direct and diffuse radiation.
- Double glazing reduces both solar and conduction gains.
- Natural ventilation is a particularly simple and effective method of passive cooling.

Minimize East and West Facing Glass and Shade Properly.

(See Chapter 11 for specific guidelines.)

Use Glazing with a U-Value Equivalent To or Less Than 0.58 (ASHRAE Calculated) on North, South, East and West Elevations.

- A medium quality double glazed window can achieve this recommendation.
- If using aluminum frame windows, select those with a condensation resistance factor (CRF) greater than 50 and complete thermal breaks (Fig. 9.21). (See Chapter 10 for additional details.)

Select Windows and Doors Having Low Air Infiltration Characteristics.

- Select windows and doors which meet the best quality air infiltration requirements of either the Architectural Aluminum Manufacturers Association or the National Woodwork Manufacturers Association.

- Use weatherstripped operable sash (such as double-hung, casements, awnings) to enhance natural ventilation. Operable sash should be at least five percent of the home's conditioned floor area.

Take Advantage of Prevailing Summer Breezes for Natural Cooling When Feasible.

Orient the home and relatively larger amounts of operable glass to receive these breezes.

Employ Whole-House Ventilation for Partial Summer Cooling.

There are a number of times when economical summer cooling can be obtained by whole-house ventilation because total outdoor enthalpy is less than indoors. In addition, the increased air movement contributes to improved summer comfort. This recommendation has limited applicability in southern regions having exceptionally high relative humidity in the spring and fall. Check local climate data and distributors for details (Fig. 9.22).

Size Heating and Cooling Equipment to Match, *Not* Exceed, *the Design Load.*

According to ASHRAE, substantial reductions in seasonal heating efficiency result from oversizing gas or oil fired equipment. The seasonal efficiency decreases as the degree of oversizing increases and the number of heating degree-days decreases. Slightly undersizing cooling equipment (10 to 15 percent based on standard design load calculation methods) may provide better comfort, particularly in humid climates. It may also cost less to operate, have lower first cost and use less energy. Conventional sizing technique is usually based on a maximum of a 3°F temperature rise (swing) at design conditions. Standard design procedures indicate only 4.5°F temperature rise at design conditions when equipment is 15 percent undersized. Air movement from continuous fan operation and lower humidity may produce equal or better comfort conditions, especially with high levels of thermal protection for ceilings, walls and glass which reduce mean radiant temperature in the summertime.

Select High Seasonal Energy Efficiency Ratio (SEER) Air Conditioning Units.

A SEER-9 unit uses 22.2 percent less energy than a SEER-7 unit; SEER-10 unit uses 30 percent less than SEER-7; SEER-11 uses 36.4 percent less than SEER-7.

Use a Cooling Season Thermostat Set-Forward, for Cases Where Air Conditioning is Used.

Setting the cooling point up 5°F (e.g., 78°F to 83°F) yields a 53 percent cooling energy savings. Thermostat set-forward strategies for times when occupants are not at home yields even greater savings. Automatic set-point adjustment controls are recommended for convenience and comfort (i.e., clock thermostats).

Use Heat Pumps if Electricity is Used for Heating.

This is particularly appropriate if cooling is also to be provided; however, they are not usually recommended in very hot climates, so check with the local power supplier. Also consider using modulated or two-stage heat pumps or ground or water source heat pumps in areas with high energy costs.

Use High Efficiency Features on Gas Fired Equipment.

Consider a multistage unit with corresponding thermostat, intermittent ignition device (IID), vent damper or other features to improve seasonal efficiency.

Use Duct Insulation.

Avoid ducts in nonconditioned spaces. If ducts in nonconditioned but partially protected spaces (i.e., garages and crawl spaces) are necessary, use at least R-8 duct wrap on metal ducts or 1½-inch thick rigid insulation. If ducts are in nonconditioned spaces, use R-12 duct wrap. Tape metal duct joints and joints of duct insulation, and avoid ducts in exterior walls. Insulate cold-in-winter side of ducts, bends or boots adjacent to outside walls (i.e., those serving floor registers on outside walls). Consider running duct work in soffits within the conditioned space. According to some recent measurements, properly taping duct joints will save five to 10 percent of heating and cooling energy and when combined with proper insulation levels will save as much as 25 percent of heating and cooling energy when ducts are in nonconditioned spaces (Fig. 9.23).

Consider a Heavily Insulated, High Efficiency Hot Water Heater.

Heat loss from a water heater can add substantially to the summer cooling load. Wrap a 3-inch thick jacket of mineral wool insulation around the water heater (Fig. 9.24). For the warmest areas of this climate category, consider placing the hot water heater in garage or similar nonconditioned space that is closed during cold or cool weather. Also, if feasible, locate clothes washers and dryers in nonconditioned spaces to further reduce cooling load. In high energy cost areas and when electricity is to be used for water heating, consider a heat pump hot water heater.

Install Water Saving Water Closet and Water Saving Devices for Kitchen and Bathroom Faucets and Shower Heads (Tables 9.3 and 9.4).

Avoid Running Hot and Cold Water Piping Through Nonconditioned Spaces.

If it is necessary to do this, insulate those pipes with at least one-and-one-half inches of flexible foam insulation.

Consider Solar Assisted Water Heating.

In the warmer climates, solar assisted water heating is cost effective, particularly in those locations with high year-round levels of solar radiation where the conventional fuel price for water heating is high, and in states having high financial incentives for solar installations. Try to select experienced, reputable dealers and installers and insist on good supervision of installation. The experience of HUD in the installation of several thousand solar assisted water heating systems shows that a large percentage of failures or disappointing results were due to faulty installation.

Use Energy-Conserving Exterior Doors.

For metal doors, important features include insulated core, thermal break, prehung, weatherstripping and low air infiltration rate. For wood doors, important features include solid core, not paneled, weatherstripping, low infiltration rate and a storm door in colder areas of these climate categories with removable panel for screens in summer (Table 9.2).

CHAPTER TEN

Fenestration Guidelines: The Design and Placement of Windows

THE IMPORTANCE OF CLIMATE

The specific guidelines for window orientation, type and area that may be beneficially used in a conventionally constructed home are closely linked to the climate in which a home is to be located. Energy conscious design decisions take into account regional and local variations of four primary climatic factors: sun, wind, temperature and humidity.

The United States is composed of hundreds of localized climates. The division of the country into climate regions for building design has been performed by a number of researchers according to diverse criteria and has resulted in several classification schemes. The variability among the schemes results from differing degrees of emphasis upon various meteorological factors and from the fact that the division of any particular factor into several categories is largely arbitrary.

The four broad climate regions used in this book were determined by examining climatic classification schemes developed by the American Institute of Architects Research Corporation,[1] and Wilmont and Vernon,[2] and monthly heating degree-day, cooling hours and solar insolation contour maps (Fig. 10.1). The regions were then compared to computer studies for a typical reference home's energy consumption (See Appendices I and II) in 25 geographically distributed United States cities to confirm that the classification system was appropriate for the energy conservation and passive solar measures recommended in this book. The climatic characteristics of each region are not uniform. They may vary both between and within regions. In fact, it is not unusual for one region to exhibit at one time or another the characteristics associated with every other climatic region. However, each region has an inherent weather pattern that distinguishes it from the others. The boundary between regions is not as sharp as indicated, each different climatic region merges gradually and almost invisibly into the next one.

The following descriptions of the four climatic regions will identify the general conditions to which solar dwelling and site designs in those regions must be responsive.

---

[1] AIA Research Corporation, *Regional Guidelines for Building Passive Energy Conserving Homes*, 1980.

[2] C. Willmot and M. Vernon, "Solar Climates of the Contiguous U.S." *Solar Energy*, Vol. 24, No. 3, 1980.

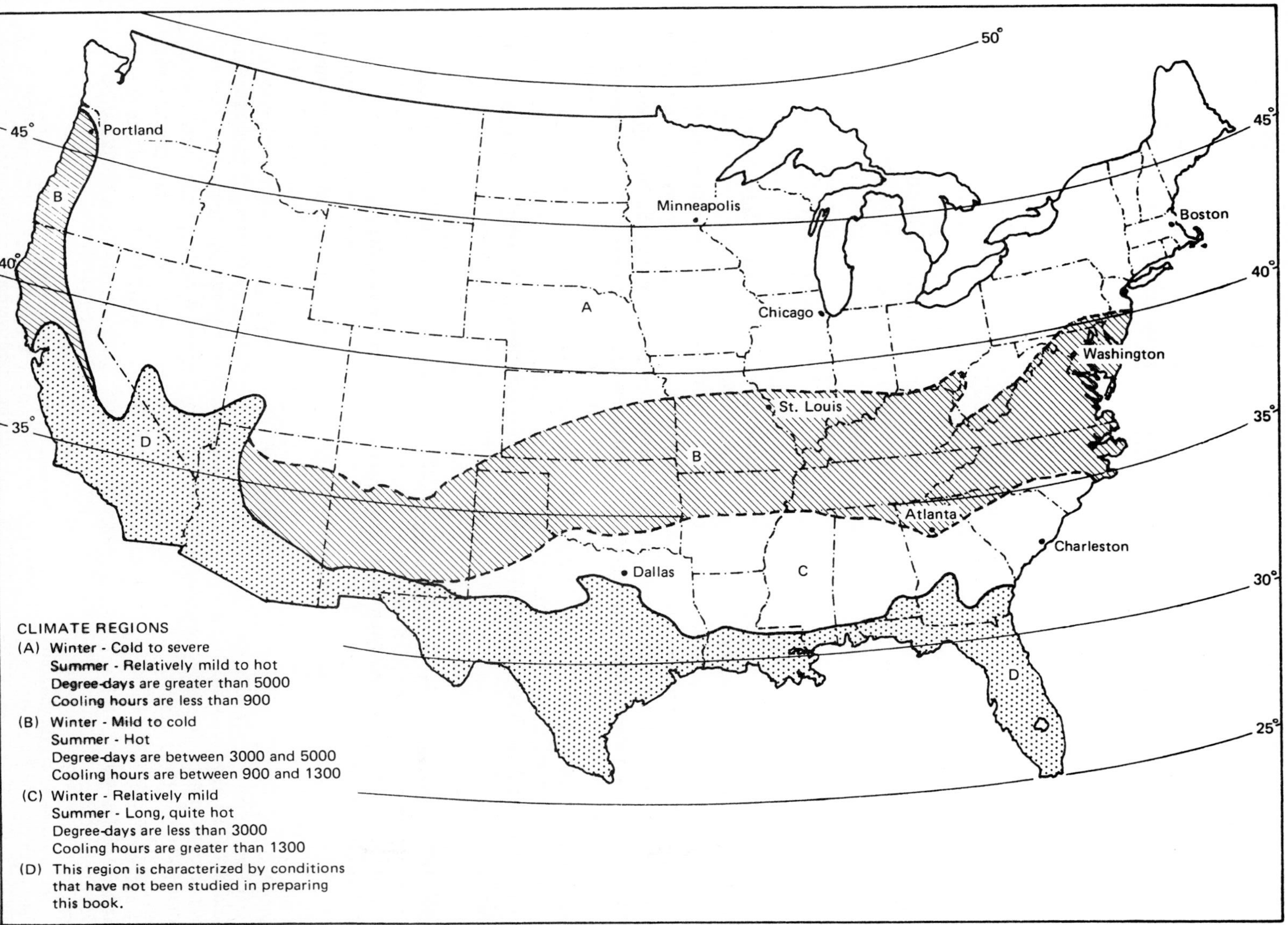
50°
45°
40°
35°
30°
25°
Portland
Minneapolis
Boston
Chicago
Washington
St. Louis
Atlanta
Charleston
Dallas
A
B
C
D
CLIMATE REGIONS
(A) Winter - Cold to severe
Summer - Relatively mild to hot
Degree-days are greater than 5000
Cooling hours are less than 900
(B) Winter - Mild to cold
Summer - Hot
Degree-days are between 3000 and 5000
Cooling hours are between 900 and 1300
(C) Winter - Relatively mild
Summer - Long, quite hot
Degree-days are less than 3000
Cooling hours are greater than 1300
(D) This region is characterized by conditions
that have not been studied in preparing
this book.

Fig. 10.1 Climate regions.

- Climate Region A is characterized by cold to severe winters (more than 5000 heating degree-days) and mild to hot summers (less than 900 cooling hours) with only occasional need for mechanical cooling.
- Climate Region B is characterized by mild to cold winter temperatures (between 3000 and 5000 heating degree-days) and a hot summer (between 900 and 1300 cooling hours), making mechanical cooling desirable.
- Climate Region C is characterized by a relatively mild winter (less than 3000 heating degree-days) and long, quite hot summers (more than 1300 cooling hours). Mechanical cooling is seen by most homeowners as a necessity.
- Climate Region D is characterized by conditions which were not examined in this study. To receive the latest design information for these areas, contact either the Florida Solar Energy Center for the eastern section of the United States or the California Energy Commission for the western section of the United States.

To choose the correct design guidelines, determine in which climate region the building site is located and then refer to the appropriate window orientation, type and area sections, respectively.

INCREASED GLASS AREA: BENEFIT OR LIABILITY?

In the last few years homes with large glass areas, though marketable and aesthetically pleasing, have been seen as having a significant energy liability. However, large glass areas comprised of today's significantly improved glazing systems with southern orientation and proper window management can produce greater savings than a well insulated opaque wall.

Glazing is usually considered to be a weak point in a building's insulated shell, a place through which heat passes easily. In fact, new energy codes have moved toward restricting the amount of glazing to the minimum required for lighting, ventilation and emergency exit. While glazing does offer relatively minimal insulation, it can be a net energy source

TABLE 10.1A Comparison of calculated net energy gain between a south-facing window and an opaque wall (all units in Btu/sq. ft/year; 2′-0″ overhang for shading)

Climate Region A (Heating season from October to April)

	Triple Glazed Units with Varying U-Values		Opaque Wall
	R-2.60 or U = 0.39	(R-3.4 or U = 0.29)	(R-20 or U = 0.05)
Boston			
Solar Gain	+105,055	+105,055	—
Heat Loss	−52,603	−38,851	−6,745
Added A/C Energy	−4,872	−4,872	−636
Net Energy Gain	*+47,580*	*+61,332*	*−7,381*
Minneapolis			
Solar Gain	+113,737	+113,737	—
Heat Loss	−77,220	−56,394	−9,790
Added A/C Energy	−4,342	−4,343	−678
Net Energy Gain	*+32,175*	*+53,000*	*−10,468*

The heat loss, heat gain and summer air conditioning load are considered separately. Heating credit is given for the seven coldest months. An air conditioning Coefficient of Performance (COP) of 2.5 (SEER 8.5) is assumed. Glazing is assumed to be actively managed, vertical south facing and shaded by a fixed overhang.

for the home. In order to be effective, it must be properly oriented, installed and managed. The optimum window orientation for solar gain is true south; however, moderate variations to the east or west of south reduce performance only slightly. Large variations, though, can reduce window performance substantially. Specific recommendations for each climate region follow our discussion of general guidelines for all climate regions.

South facing vertical glazing receives large amounts of solar radiation during winter, yet is easily shaded during summer. To illustrate the value of south facing glazing, compare its thermal performance to that of an R-20 wall (Table 10.1 A through C). The glazing is assumed to be vertical, south facing with a fixed overhang.

TABLE 10.1B Comparison of calculated net energy gain between a south-facing window and an opaque wall

Climate Region B (Heating season from October to March)	Double Glazed Window (R-1.9 or U = 0.53)	Opaque Wall (R-20 or U = 0.05)
Washington		
Solar Gain	+123,510	—
Heat Loss	−56,896	−5,000
Added A/C Energy	−8,015	−1,145
Net Energy Gain	*+58,599*	*−6,145*
Atlanta		
Solar Gain	+131,798	—
Heat Loss	−36,932	−3,464
Added A/C Energy	−9,796	−1,400
Net Energy Gain	*+85,070*	*−4,864*

The heat loss, heat gain and summer air conditioning load are considered separately. Heating credit is given for the six coldest months. An air conditioning Coefficient of Performance (COP) of 2.5 (SEER 8.5) is used. Glazing is assumed to be actively managed, vertical south facing and shaded by a fixed overhang.

TABLE 10.1C Comparison of calculated net energy gain between a south-facing window and an opaque wall

Climate Region C (Heating season from November to March)	Double Glazed Window (R-1.9 or U = 0.53)	Opaque Wall (R-20 or U = 0.05)
Dallas/Fort Worth		
Solar Gain	+115,800	—
Heat Loss	−28,151	−2,600
Added A/C Energy	−17,373	−2,694
Net Energy Gain	*+70,276*	*−5,294*
Charleston, South Carolina		
Solar Gain	+110,921	—
Heat Loss	−27,303	−2,575
Added A/C Energy	−11,356	−1,622
Net Energy Gain	*+72,262*	*−4,197*

The heat loss, heat gain and summer air conditioning load are considered separately. Heating credit is given for the five coldest months. An air conditioning Coefficient of Performance (COP) of 2.5 (SEER 8.5) is used. Glazing is assumed to be actively managed, vertical south facing and shaded by a fixed overhang.

TABLE 10.2 Overall coefficients of heat transmission (U-Factor) of windows, sliding patio doors, and skylights (Btu/h·ft²·°F)

Part A. Exterior[a] vertical panels

	No Storm Sash				Glass Outdoor Storm Sash 25-mm (1-in.) Air Space[b]			
	No Shade		Indoor Shade		No Shade		Indoor Shade	
	Winter	Summer	Winter	Summer	Winter	Summer	Winter	Summer
Flat Glass[c]								
Single Glass,	6.2(1.10)	5.9(1.04)	4.7(0.83)	4.6(0.81)	2.3(0.50)	2.8(0.50)	2.5(0.44)	2.8(0.49)
Insulating Glass; Double[c]								
5-mm (3/16-in.) air space[f]	3.5(0.62)	3.7(0.65)	3.0(0.52)	3.3(0.58)	2.1(0.37)	2.3(0.40)	1.7(0.29)	2.1(0.37)
6-mm (1/4-in.) air space[f]	3.3(0.59)	3.5(0.61)	2.7(0.48)	3.1(0.55)	2.0(0.35)	2.2(0.39)	1.6(0.28)	2.0(0.36)
13-mm (1/2-in.) air space[g]	2.8(0.49)	3.2(0.56)	2.4(0.42)	3.0(0.52)	1.8(0.32)	2.2(0.39)	1.4(0.25)	2.1(0.30)
13-mm (1/2-in.) air space low emittance coating[h]								
$e = 0.60$	2.4(0.43)	2.9(0.51)	2.2(0.38)	2.7(0.48)	1.7(0.30)	2.0(0.36)	1.4(0.24)	2.0(0.35)
$e = 0.40$	2.2(0.38)	2.6(0.48)	2.0(0.36)	2.5(0.43)	1.5(0.27)	1.9(0.39)	1.3(0.22)	1.8(0.32)
$e = 0.20$	1.8(0.32)	2.2(0.38)	1.7(0.30)	2.1(0.37)	1.4(0.24)	1.7(0.30)	1.1(0.20)	1.6(0.28)
Insulating Glass; Triple								
6-mm (1/4-in.) air space[f]	2.2(0.39)	2.5(0.44)	1.8(0.31)	2.3(0.40)	1.5(0.27)	1.8(0.32)	1.3(0.22)	1.7(0.30)
13-mm (1/2-in. air space[i]	1.8(0.31)	2.2(0.39)	1.5(0.26)	2.0(0.36)	1.3(0.23)	1.8(0.31)	1.1(0.19)	1.7(0.29)

	Glass Indoor Storm Sash 25-mm (1-in.) Air Space[b]				Acrylic Indoor Storm Sash 25-mm (1-in.) Air Space[b]			
	No Shade		Indoor Shade		No Shade		Indoor Shade	
	Winter*	Summer**	Winter*	Summer**	Winter*	Summer**	Winter*	Summer**
Flat Glass[c]								
Single Glass,	2.8(0.50)	2.8(0.50)	2.5(0.44)	2.8(0.49)	2.7(0.48)	2.7(0.48)	2.4(0.42)	2.7(0.47)
Insulating Glass; Double[e]								
5-mm (3/16-in.) air space[f]	2.1(0.37)	2.3(0.40)	1.7(0.29)	2.0(0.36)	2.0(0.35)	2.2(0.39)	1.6(0.28)	2.0(0.35)
6-mm (1/4-in.) air space[f]	2.0(0.35)	2.2(0.39)	1.6(0.28)	2.0(0.36)	(1.9(0.34)	2.2(0.38)	1.5(0.27)	1.9(0.34)
13-mm (1/2-in.) air space[g]	1.8(0.31)	2.2(0.38)	1.4(0.25)	2.0(0.35)	1.7(0.30)	2.1(0.37)	1.4(0.24)	1.9(0.33)
13-mm (1/2-in.) air space, Low emittance costing[h]								
$e = 0.60$	1.7(0.29)	2.0(0.36)	1.4(0.24)	1.9(0.33)	1.6(0.28)	2.0(0.35)	1.3(0.23)	1.8(0.32)
$e = 0.40$	1.5(0.27)	1.9(0.33)	1.3(0.22)	1.8(0.31)	1.5(0.26)	1.8(0.32)	1.3(0.22)	1.7(0.30)
$e = 0.20$	1.4(0.25)	1.7(0.29)	1.1(0.20)	1.5(0.26)	1.4(0.24)	1.6(0.28)	1.1(0.20)	1.5(0.27)
Insulating Glass; Triple[e]								
6-mm (1/4-in.) air space[f]	1.5(0.27)	1.8(0.32)	1.3(0.22)	1.7(0.30)	1.5(0.26)	1.8(0.31)	1.3(0.22)	1.7(0.29)
13-mm (1/2-in.) air space[i]	1.3(0.23)	1.7(0.30)	1.1(0.19)	1.6(0.28)	1.3(0.22)	1.7(0.29)	1.0(0.18)	1.6(0.28)

Part B. Exterior[a] horizontal panels (skylights)

Description	Winter[i]	Summer[j]
Flat Glass[e]		
Single Glass	7.0 (1.23)	4.7 (0.83)
Insulating Glass; Double[c]		
5-mm (3/16-in.) air space[d]	4.0 (0.70)	3.2 (0.57)
6-mm (1/4-in.) air space[d]	3.7 (0.65)	3.1 (0.54)
13-mm (1/2-in.) air space[e]	3.4 (0.59)	2.8 (0.49)
13-mm (1/2-in.) air space, low emittance coating[f]		
$e = 0.20$	2.7 (0.48)	2.0 (0.36)
$e = 0.40$	3.0 (0.52)	2.4 (0.42)
e = 0.60	3.2 (0.56)	2.6 (0.46)
Plastic Domes[k]		
Single Walled	6.5 (1.15)	4.5 (0.80)
Double Walled	4.0 (0.70)	2.6 (0.46)

Part C. Adjustment factors for various window, sliding patio door, and skylight frame types (multiply U-factors in Parts A and B by these factors)

Description	Single Glass	Double or Triple Glass	Storm Windows
Windows			
All Glass[h]	1.00	1.00	1.00
Wood Sash; 80% Glass	0.90	0.95	0.90
Wood Sash; 60% Glass	0.80	0.85	0.80
Metal Sash; 80% Glass	1.00	1.20[m]	1.20[m]
Sliding Patio Doors			
Wood Frame	0.95	1.00	—
Metal Frame	1.00	1.10[m]	—

[a]See Part C for adjustments for various windows and sliding patio doors.
[b]Emissivity of uncoated glass surface = 0.84.
[c]Double and triple refer to number of lights of glass.
[d]3-mm (1/8-in.) glass.
[e]6-mm (1/4-in.) glass.
[f]Coating on either glass surface facing air space; all other glass surfaces uncoated.
[g]Window design: 6-mm (1/4 in.) glass, 3-mm (1/8 in.) glass, 6-mm (1/4 in.) glass.
[h]Refers to windows with negligible opaque areas.
[i]For heat flow up.
[j]For heat flow down.
[k]Based on area of opening, not total surface area.
[m]Values will be less than these when metal sash and frame incorporate thermal breaks. In some thermal break designs *U* values will be equal to or less than those for the glass. Window manufacturers should be consulted for specific data.
[i]24 km/h (15 mph outdoor air velocity; −18°C (0 F) outdoor air; 21°C (70 F) inside air temp. natural convection.
[j]12 km/h (7.5 mph) outdoor air velocity; 32°C (89 F) outdoor air; 21°C (75 F) inside air natural convection; solar radiation 782 W/m² (248.3 Btuh/ft²).

The reciprocal of the above *U*-factors is the thermal resistance, *R* for each type of glazing. If tightly drawn drapes (heavy close weave), closed Venetian blinds, or closely fitted roller shades are used internally, the additional *R* is approximately 0.05 m² · °C/W (0.29 ft² · F Btuh). If minature louvered solar screens are used in close proximity to the outer fenestration surface, the additional *R* is approximately 0.04 m² · °C/W (0.24 ft² · F/Btuh).

Source: 1981 ASHRAE Handbook of Fundamentals, Chapter 23.28.

In all cases, south facing glazing provides a significant net energy contribution for the year. The R-20 wall constitutes a net loss. This is not an argument for glass houses, but it does point out the potential of properly designed suntempered and passive solar houses.

GLAZING AND SASH TYPE GUIDELINES FOR ALL CLIMATE REGIONS

Climate-specific recommendations for window U-values are given based on ASHRAE thermal transmittance calculations. There are currently a number of methods for determining thermal performance of windows and doors. The various methods yield quite different results with regard to a particular glazing unit's performance. Therefore, when evaluating the efficiency of different window and door systems, be sure to compare values that were determined using the same method. The U-values recommended throughout this chapter may be achieved through the use of one of the following combinations: double glazing or triple glazing; double glazing with night insulation; double glazing plus storm sash or low emissivity coatings and films (Table 10.2). Chapter 11, *Window Management Techniques*, describes window night insulation applications that achieve the recommended U-values.

To ensure selection of energy efficient windows or doors, carefully evaluate the following characteristics:

1. thermal transmittance (U-value) or resistance (R-value)
2. air and water infiltration resistance
3. condensation resistance (CRF), (aluminum sashes only)
4. net ventilation area

The lower the thermal transmittance (U-value), or the higher the thermal resistance (R-value), the more efficient the window will be in reducing winter heat loss and summer heat gain. Recommended U-values for each climate region are presented later in this chapter.

The window unit sash design and material composition can significantly influence a unit's overall thermal transmittance. Properly designed wood and aluminum sash windows will have comparable performance. Wood as a sash material acts effectively to impede heat flow through a window unit's perimeter. Wood is a relatively good insulator (R = 1.25 per inch of thickness) compared to aluminum, which is an excellent conductor of energy. An aluminum sash can be designed to perform comparably to a wood sash through the use of a thermal break located in the aluminum sash. Thermal break aluminum sash windows have the outside aluminum completely separated from the inside aluminum window surface by an insulating material such as closed cell vinyl foam, or a high strength polymer resin such as polyurethane. This means that the entire window frame has a continuous thermal barrier separating inner and outer aluminum extrusions, thus inhibiting thermal conductance through the sash. A thermal break also substantially reduces the incidence of condensation formation on the interior side of the frame.

	Frame U-Value
2-inch thick aluminum frame—no thermal break	1.18
2-inch thick aluminum frame—with thermal break	0.60

A thermal break is extremely important in preventing a short circuit for heat flow through the frame.

Thermal break windows are rated by condensation resistance factor (CRF). This rating, developed by the Architectural Aluminum Manufacturers Association, is a guide to which windows are designed for good protec-

TABLE 10.3

Condensation Resistance Factor (CRF)	Outside Temperature (°F) where 30% relative humidity will cause condensation on the inner sash
46	+8°F
47	+7°F
50	+3°F
54	−3°F
55	−4°F
61	−15°F
63	−20°F
65	−25°F

Based on AAMA Test Procedure 1502.6.

tion against condensation; the higher the CRF the lower the likelihood of condensation forming on the interior sash. Window units having condensation resistance factors greater than 50 are easily achievable and are recommended. Table 10.3 illustrates at what outdoor temperature with the relative humidity at 30 percent, windows with particular CRFs will cause excessive condensation on the inside sash.

Select operable glazing units that are well weatherstripped. The greater a window unit's resistance to air and water infiltration, the more efficiently it will perform. Window units having infiltration rates equal to or less than 0.10–0.20 cubic feet per minute (CFM) per linear foot of operable sash perimeter (which also ensures a sufficiently high resistance to water infiltration) should be used. Numerous aluminum and wood sash window manufacturers are presently marketing units with infiltration rates in the range of 0.04 to 0.09 CFM per foot of operable sash perimeter (with sash closed and in the locked position) under a static pressure drop equivalent to a wind velocity of 25 miles per hour (American Society of Testing Material Air Infiltration Test E-283-73).

Infiltration is one of the primary ways that energy is lost through windows. Air leakage through cracks occurs when there is a difference in air pressure between the inside and outside of the building. In homes this pressure difference most frequently occurs when the wind blows. Wind creates a positive pressure against the windward side of a building and a negative pressure on the downwind side. This causes infiltration to occur through windward windows and exfiltration through downwind windows. Air leakage caused by wind pressure can be diminished effectively with weatherstripping because of its ability to accommodate changing joint sizes. Weatherstripping works to reduce water and snow penetration as well.

- The net window and door ventilation area should be five to seven percent of a home's floor area to adequately ventilate the home and reduce the demand on mechanical cooling.
- The National Woodwork Manufacturers Association (NWMA) and the Architectural Aluminum Manufacturers Association (AAMA) have developed window evaluation procedures in accordance with ASHRAE, ASTM and ANSI testing standards to evaluate the energy efficiency of each window manufactured. Request the results of these evaluations from the window supplier or manufacturer when selecting window units for your application.
- Wood sash window and door units are evaluated using the ANSI/NWMA Industry Standard I.S.2-80 for air and water infiltration resistance and thermal transmittance.
- Aluminum sash window and door units are evaluated through the AAMA certification program for air and water infiltration, condensation resistance and thermal transmittance.
- The addition of a tightly fitting night window insulation system or thermal shade can enhance solar performance

and reduce total energy use by 10 to 15 percent.

The glazing area recommendations that follow for Climate Regions A through C are for the net clear area, not including sash and mullions or external and internal devices which permanently shade a portion of the glass. An additional factor that should be considered when selecting a window unit for any climate is its overall size, as smaller units generally have a larger ratio of sash area to glass area, thus reducing the total net area useful for collecting solar energy. Larger units have a smaller sash to glass area ratio, making them more efficient solar collectors per gross unit area. Larger operable units have the benefit of greater net vent area as well.

ORIENTATION AND ANNUAL ENERGY CONSUMPTION

Studies performed by Victor Olgyay, the Small Homes Council, Lawrence Berkeley Laboratory (LBL), and Computer Computation Bureau/Cumali Associates (CCB/CA) report a range of orientation recommendations for homes. The key factors influencing orientation guidelines are climate region, level of thermal protection of the home, the amount of thermal storage, window management strategies employed, and the amount of south facing glass area.

True south is the preferred orientation for homes in all climate regions. As orientation varies toward east or west of south, the amount of solar radiation received in winter decreases and the amount of radiation received in summer increases. Thus, as orientation deviates from true south, less sun is available to offset heating costs in winter and more sun is available to increase cooling costs in summer.

In warmer climates where cooling loads are higher, annual energy consumption becomes increasingly sensitive to building orientations off true south, therefore, the orientation recommendations are narrowed with respect to true south. An east-of-south variation is always preferable to one west of south, because morning air and home temperatures generally are cooler than afternoon temperatures. Thus, solar radiation received from the east can be more easily accommodated without causing overheating. In colder climates where summer cooling is not as great a concern, the orientation recommendations off true south are more liberal, though with still a preference for east over west variations.

ORIENTATION SENSITIVITY FACTORS

- The better insulated a home or the more thermal storage it contains, the more sensitive its annual energy consumption becomes to orientation variations off true south. Because these homes can more efficiently utilize solar radiation in winter, variations off south that cause reductions in the amount of solar radiation available, noticeably detract from these homes' energy performance.
- The less managed a home's windows, the more sensitive its energy consumption becomes to orientation. A home with unshaded glazing on the east, west and south elevations with an orientation west of south will have an unnecessarily high cooling load. Conversely, if the glazing is well managed, the home can tolerate a greater orientation variation off true south.
- The greater the area of south facing glazing on a home, the more sensitive the home becomes to orientation variations off true south. Homes with a large area of south facing glazing should be very well insulated and employ thermal storage and window management techniques.

Reductions in the amount of solar radiation available due to non-true-south orientation will detract from annual energy performance. If a home with a large south facing glass area does not utilize these techniques, orientation variations off true south will increase annual energy consumption by excessive heat gain through the glass in summer and heat loss in the winter.

The orientation recommendations given for each climate region are only approximations, many factors affect the orientation guidelines for a particular home on a particular site. Use the preceding list as a general guide.

WINDOWS: CLIMATE REGION A

- Winters are cold to severe.
- Summers are mild to hot.
- Annual heating degree-days are greater than 5,000.
- Annual number of cooling hours are less than 900.

Window Orientation

The major (largest) area of glazing on a home should face south or within 35° east or 20° west of true south for optimum solar performance. Homes designed with a long wall exposure to face south, within the parameters stated, will permit a larger degree of window placement flexibility than with a short south facing wall. A home that is oriented within 22.5° east or west of true south in this climate region will receive 92 percent of the radiation available on a true south facing wall in winter.

Figure 10.2 illustrates the effect of orientation on annual energy consumption based on CCB/CA computer simulations of the well-insulated 1232-square-foot reference home. For the three cities analyzed, when the major area of glazing faces east or west, the home consumes 25 to 35 percent more total heating and cooling energy than when the major area of glazing faces south. When the major area of glazing is facing north, the home consumes 35 to 40 percent more total heating and cooling energy than when the major area of glazing faces south. The range of percentage differences is primarily attributable to the effect of local climate variations within the region.

The more actively managed a glazing system, the greater the difference in energy consumption between homes with the major glazing area oriented south versus east/west or north. This is due to the fact that well managed windows—those having proper shading and sufficient natural ventilation— are more energy efficient than unmanaged windows.

Computer simulations by Lawrence Berkeley Laboratory (LBL) show their reference home (See Appendix II), with the major area of glazing facing east or west, in Climate Region A consumes 12 to 22 percent more heating and cooling energy than the same home having the major area of glazing facing south. The LBL reference home with the major area of glazing facing north in Climate Region A consumes 8 to 17 percent more total heating and cooling energy than the same home having the major area of glazing facing south (Table 10.4).

The differences in the effect of orientation of the major glass areas on annual heating and cooling energy consumption between the CCB/CA and LBL computer simulations are due to: (1) the numerous differences in assumptions; (2) the differences in the size and configuration of the two homes: (3) the different cities in which the homes were analyzed; and (4) the fact that the LBL assumptions included no glazing management, not even common controls such as drawing shades. In any event, both sets of analyses show that the orientation of the major area of glazing can significantly affect annual energy consumption for heating and cooling.

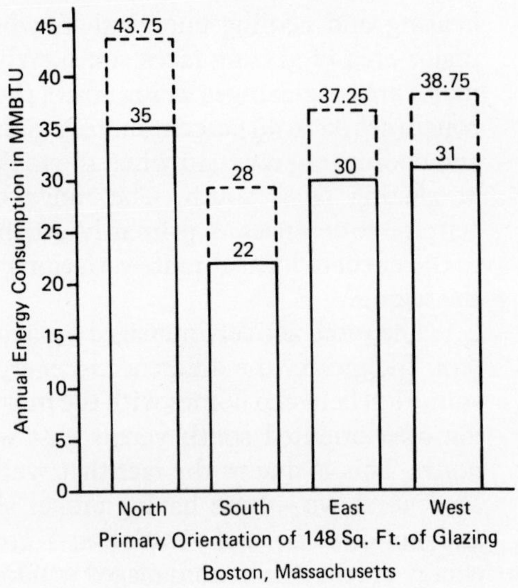

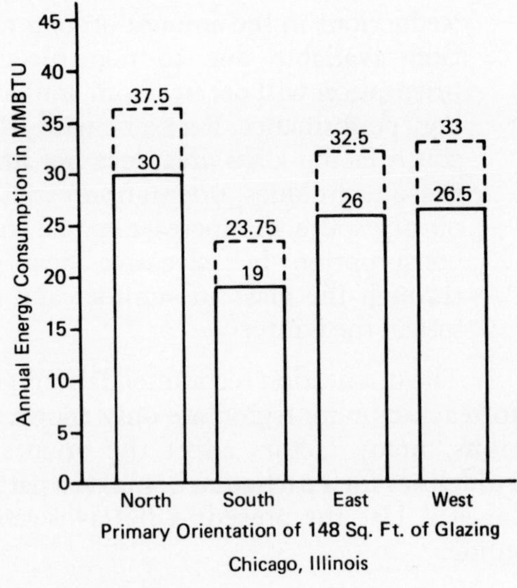

Foundation Type: Slab on grade———

Wood floor over crawl space------

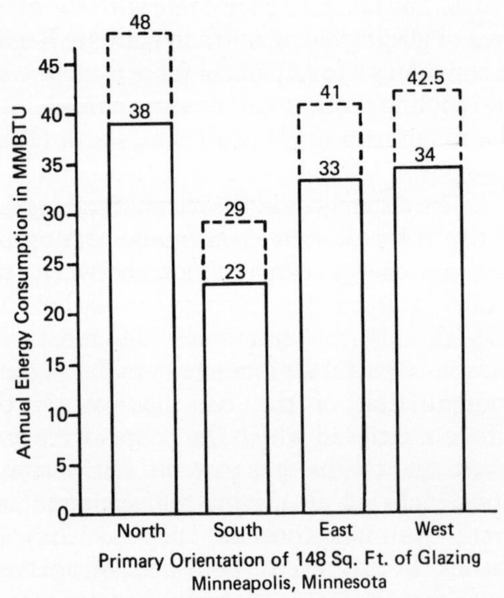

Foundation Type: Slab on grade———

Wood floor over crawl space------

Fig. 10.2 Comparison of annual energy consumption with respect to home orientation for 1232 square feet (computer simulated reference home, climate region A). Glazing type—triple U = 0.29; amount of glazing—148 square feet on primary orientation (12 percent of floor area of reference home); and window management strategy—active. (Note: See Appendix I for reference home characteristics.)

TABLE 10.4 The impact of building orientation on a typical residential building* annual heating and cooling loads

Climate Region A

City	State	% of Total Annual Load that is Heating, South Facing Home	MMBtu	% Increase in Total Annual Load of East or West Facing over South Facing Home	% Increase in Total Annual Load of North Facing over South Facing Home
Caribou	ME	99	43.7	12	14
Seattle	WA	97	19.1	12	12
Bismarck	ND	93	43.1	15	14
Great Falls	MT	93	30.2	20	17
Madison	WI	92	33.3	18	15
Boston	MA	92	27.4	18	15
New York	NY	87	23.5	19	16
Medford	OR	78	16.6	22	8

* Residence has 1176 sq. ft. of conditioned floor space and 132 sq. ft. (11.2% of floor area) of glazing on primary orientation. See Appendix for detailed building and computer simulation description.

Source: Lawrence Berkeley Laboratory paper, "The Impact of Orientation on Residential Heating and Cooling" by Brandt Anderson, Ronald Kammerud and Wayne Place, Passive Solar Analysis and Design Group, Spring 1982.

Window Type

In this climate region use on all elevations a glazing system that has a thermal transmittance (U-value) of less than 0.39 or a thermal resistance (R-value) greater the 2.6, as determined by ASHRAE thermal transmittance calculations.

It is important to note that in all of the charts and graphs in this book derived from computer simulation, the U-values used for double and triple glazing (double, U = 0.53 and triple, U = 0.29), are based upon average local annual wind speeds derived from actual long term weather observations. These values differ from ASHRAE calculated values which are computed using a constant 15 MPH wind speed. If an exterior film resistance resulting from a 15 MPH wind (0.17) was used in place of the actual wind speed observations used in this study, the U-values reported here would be equivalent to those in the ASHRAE *Handbook of Fundamentals*. It is believed these values, ones normally used in annual computer simulations, are more representative of actual field performance of windows in houses than calculated values.

The computer simulation results presented in Figure 10.3 comparing glazing systems with year-long average, dynamic U-values of 0.29 and 0.53 show that an improved glazing system can reduce annual energy consumption (heating and cooling combined) by 23 to 29 percent. The greatest savings are achieved by homes having relatively little thermal storage located in the northern sections of Climate Region A. The economic benefits, payback period, or cost-benefit ratio of triple versus double glazing depend on the cost of the windows selected, local fuel prices, interest rates and project budget.

A glazing system with a U-value in the recommended range also increases the interior glass surface temperature, resulting in a higher mean radiant temperature in the adjacent space. The mean radiant temperature is the average of all surface temperatures within a particular thermal zone. The higher the average surface temperatures, the lower the space air temperature may be to maintain a comfortable environment. A radiant floor slab works on the principle of increasing the

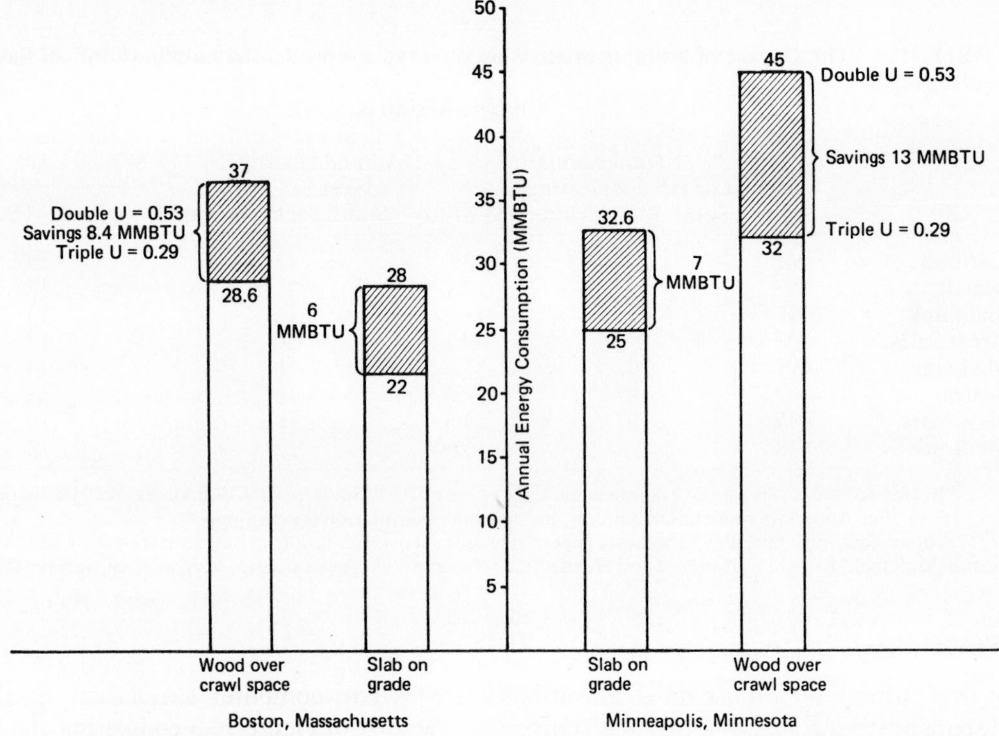

Fig. 10.3 Comparison of annual energy consumption with triple versus double glazing in climate region A. (Note: South glazed area on reference home used in computer simulation is 12 percent of conditioned floor area.)

mean radiant temperature. The use of low emissivity coatings and films or movable insulation can further enhance this effect, thereby improving thermal comfort, especially during the nighttime hours when radiation and conduction losses through windows are greatest.

There are currently a number of methods (ASTM, ASHRAE, AAMA and NWMA) for determining thermal performance of windows and doors. The various methods yield rather different results with regard to a particular window unit's performance; when evaluating the efficiency of different window and door systems, be sure to compare values that were determined using the same method. The U- and R-values recommended in this region may be achieved through the use of triple glazing, double glazing with night insulation, or double glazing plus storm sash or low emissivity coatings and films. See Chapters 9 and 11 for additional details on techniques.

For buildings located in climate zones with more than 7500 degree-days, U-values lower than 0.39 are especially desirable. Lower values may be achieved with quad glazing, low emissivity glass coatings and films or a combination of double glazing and movable night insulation.

The choice of glazing should not be based upon thermal transmittance alone. Selected glazing configurations also must admit sufficient amounts of solar radiation to provide heat and light to the space. Most existing buildings in Climate Region A are either single or, more commonly, double glazed. The solar transmission of the configurations is relatively high but thermal transmission losses are substantial. In order to reduce these

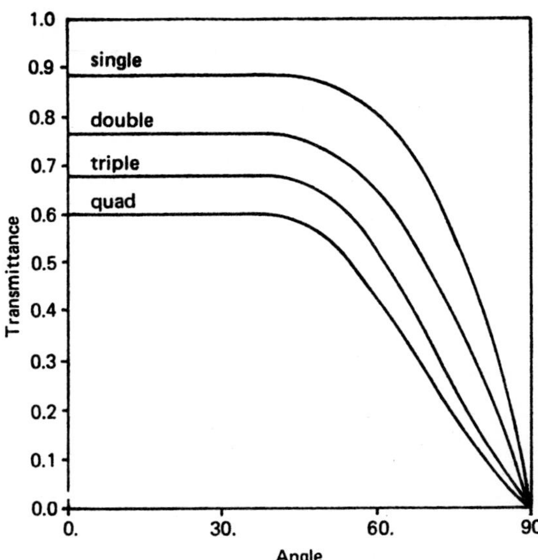

Fig. 10.4 Transmittance as a function of angle of incidence for 1-, 2-, 3-, and 4-pane glass windows.

losses, the use of windows incorporating three or more layers of clear glass or plastic and/or night insulation is recommended.

Solar gain is a function of the following factors: transmittance of the glazing system itself; the angle at which the sun is striking the glazing system (commonly called the angle of incidence) and, as previously mentioned, orientation, latitude and local climate conditions.

The transmission value most often given in product literature for a particular glazing system is one which is measured at a 90° angle of incidence, meaning the sun's rays are exactly perpendicular to the glass (commonly referred to as normal to the glass). This value is useful for comparing the relative transmittance of various glazing configurations; however, when you perform even simplified calculations of solar heat gain, this normal value should be replaced by an averaged value which takes into account daily and seasonal variations of solar radiation striking the glass. Figure 10.4 gives solar transmittance values for four types of glass windows as a function of angle of incidence. For simplified heat gain calculations a 60° average angle of incidence is recommended. Such calculations are not intended to replace annual load calculation methods, but can provide a quick assessment as to the relative performance of a variety of glazing systems.

Window Area

The amount of beneficial south facing glass that may be incorporated into a home in Climate Region A is based upon the following design considerations, as well as the recommendations discussed in the preceding sections of this chapter.

- large rooms or "open plan" to the south and preferably the long axis of the home oriented east/west.
- sufficient external shading during the cooling or summer season. An in-depth discussion of this consideration is located in Chapter 11.
- provision for natural ventilation to reduce the need for mechanical cooling.

Slab-On-Grade Homes

For homes in this region that use a properly insulated slab-on-grade (See Chapter 9) foundation system or an equivalent amount of thermal storage (for example, exterior masonry walls, insulated on the outside surface, or interior masonry partitions or fireplaces) south facing glazed areas of up to 15 percent of the conditioned space floor area can significantly reduce annual energy consumption [Figs. 10.5(a), (c), and (e)]. This recommendation presumes at least 30 to 50 percent of the floor slab is exposed to direct sunlight and is covered with a finish material that has a thermal resistance (R-value) no greater than 0.25 (i.e., no carpeting). Common floor materials that fulfill this requirement are quarry, asphalt, linoleum, vinyl rubber and terrazzo tile. Table 7.1 lists the R-values

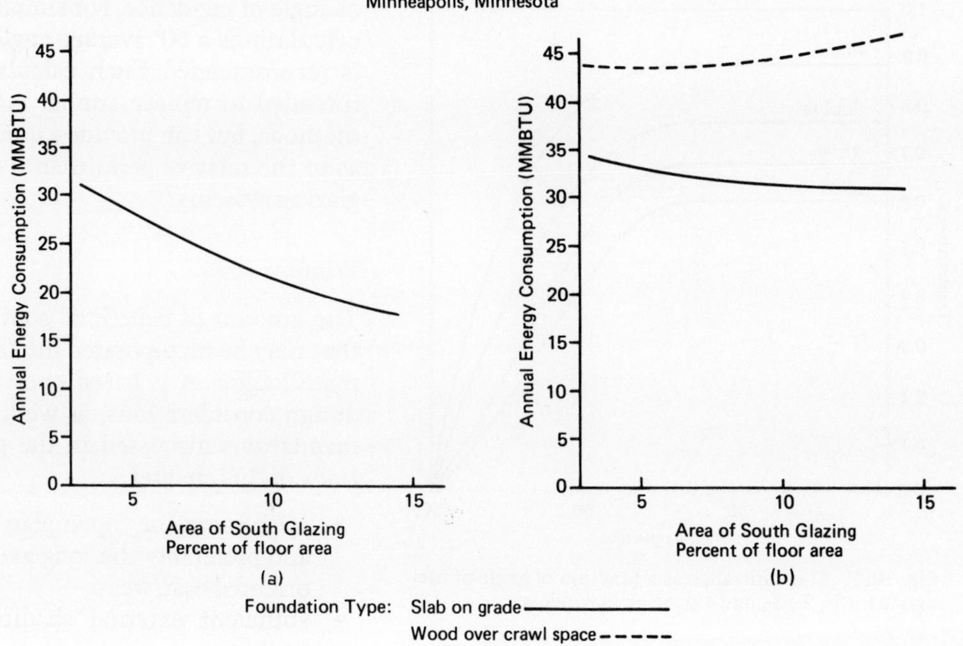
Minneapolis, Minnesota
Annual Energy Consumption (MMBTU)
45
40
35
30
25
20
15
10
5
0
5
10
15
Area of South Glazing
Percent of floor area
(a)
(b)
Foundation Type: Slab on grade
Wood over crawl space

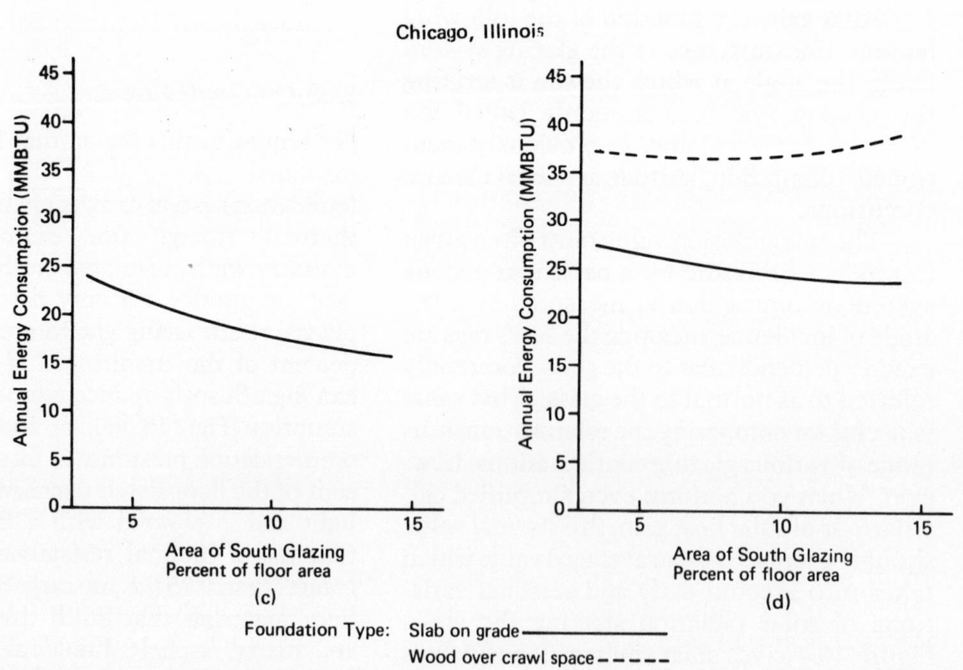
Chicago, Illinois
Annual Energy Consumption (MMBTU)
45
40
35
30
25
20
15
10
5
0
5
10
15
Area of South Glazing
Percent of floor area
(c)
(d)
Foundation Type: Slab on grade
Wood over crawl space

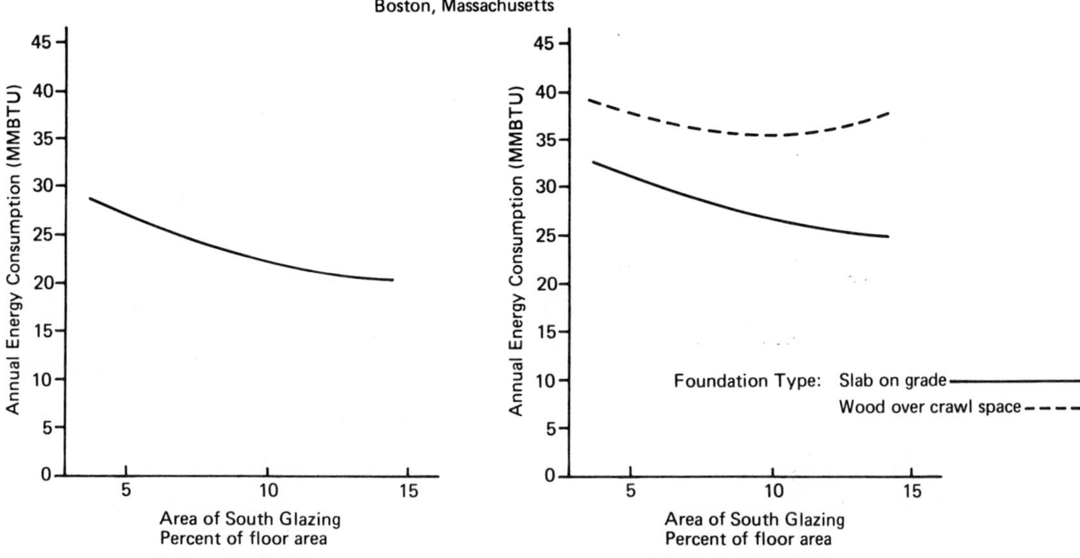

Fig. 10.5 Climate Region A: Annual energy consumption reduction as a function of south glazing areas, based on the following building characteristics:
Single story, 1232 square feet
Shading: two-foot fixed overhang and roller shades
North glass area = 0
East and west glass area = 85 square feet
Heating: gas furnace at 0.60 seasonal efficiency
Cooling: electric—COP = 1.8 (SEER—6.1)
Heating temperature: 68°, no setback
Cooling temperature: 80°
(Note: See Appendix I for detailed building characteristics.)

of various common floor and wall surface materials.

A slab-on-grade home design with a glazing system having a U-value equivalent to double glazing can incorporate south facing glass areas of up to 12 percent of the conditioned space floor area. This glazing system design approach will moderately reduce annual energy consumption [Figs. 10.5(b), (d), and (f)].

Wood-Floor-Over-Crawl-Space Homes

In Climate Region A, south facing glazed areas of up to ten percent of the floor area can moderately reduce annual energy consumption if the design considerations discussed earlier in this chapter are implemented. To increase the area of glazing much beyond ten percent of the floor area without causing overheating, a wood-over-crawl-space home should incorporate additional exposed thermal storage to effectively absorb and store the excess incoming solar radiation [Figs. 10.5(b), (d), and (f); also Chapter 7].

For a wood-floor-over-crawl-space home constructed with a glazing system having a U-value of 0.58, south facing glass areas of up to seven percent can moderately reduce annual energy consumption, if design considerations outlined at the beginning of this section are implemented.

Although home designs having a full basement foundation were not specifically examined, we believe the energy performance of a home which uses a wood-floor-over-crawl-space foundation is a sufficiently close approximation to a home design with a full basement that the pertinent window recom-

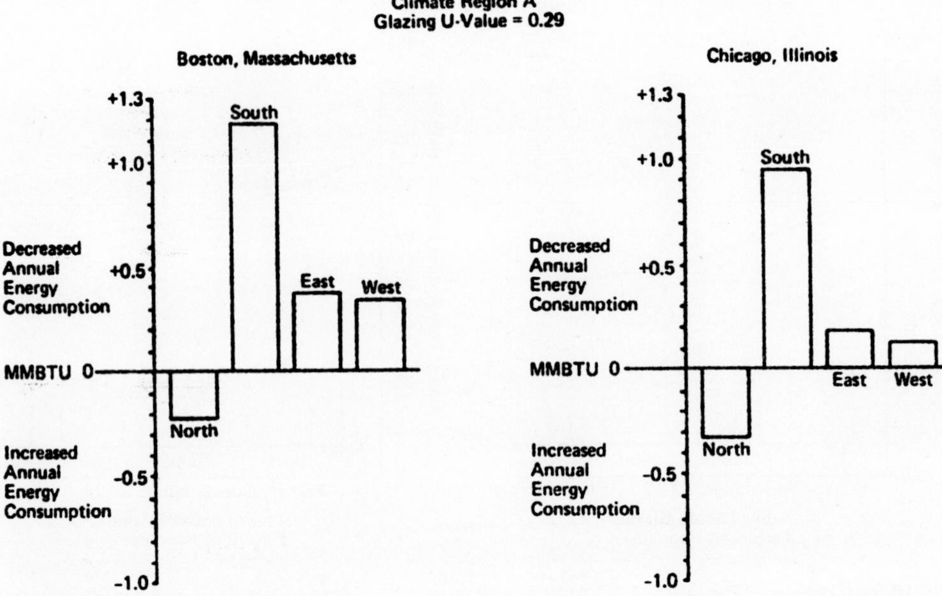

Fig. 10.6 Effect on annual energy consumption of adding an actively managed 20-square-foot window to each elevation respectively of the reference home. The home is 1232 square feet, slab-on-grade. The wall being added to already contains 105 square feet of glazing (or 8.6 percent of the floor area). Addition of 20-square-foot window brings glazing up to 10 percent of the floor area. Glazing is actively managed. (Note: See Appendix I for detailed characteristics.)

mendations in this chapter are directly applicable.

East and West Glazing

For slab-on-grade, wood-floor-over-crawl space and basement homes, well managed east glazing, including summer shading, shows a modest benefit toward reducing annual energy consumption in Climate Region A. Unmanaged east glazing shows a modest penalty and should be used with caution. Well managed west glazing modestly decreases annual energy consumption and should be used only if well shaded during the summer months (Fig. 10.6). Unmanaged west glazing should not be used, because it can increase energy consumption significantly.

North Glazing

Regardless of construction type, north glass offers little or no thermal benefit in this climate and is recommended only to satisfy natural light and ventilation, egress and architectural requirements. A modest amount of north glazing that has a sufficiently low thermal transmittance will not egregiously affect annual energy consumption.

WINDOWS: CLIMATE REGION B

- Winters are mild to cold.
- Summers are hot.
- Annual heating degree-days are between 3000 and 5000.
- Annual cooling hours are between 900 and 1300.

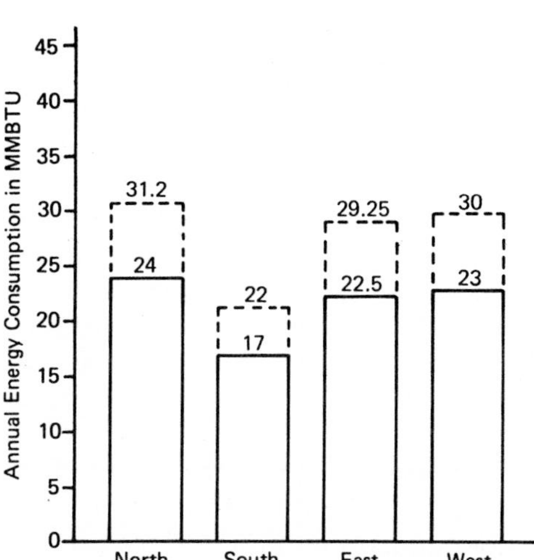

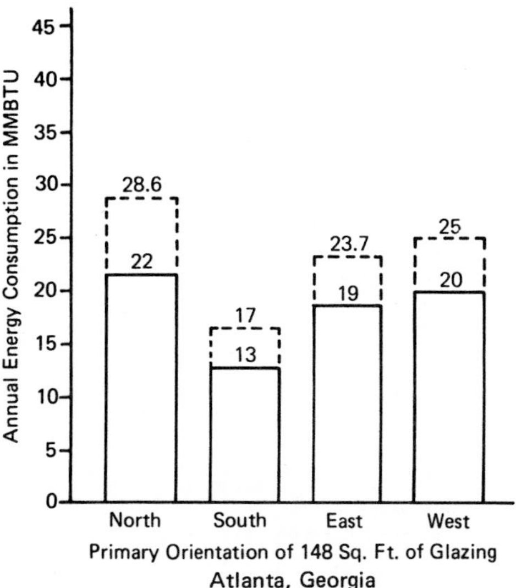

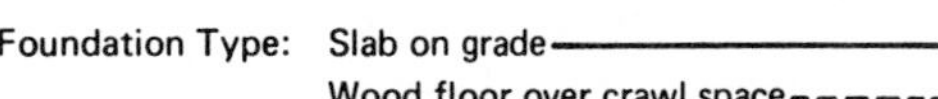

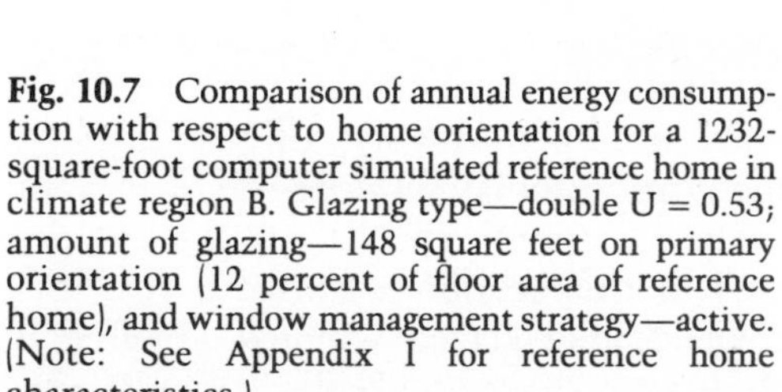

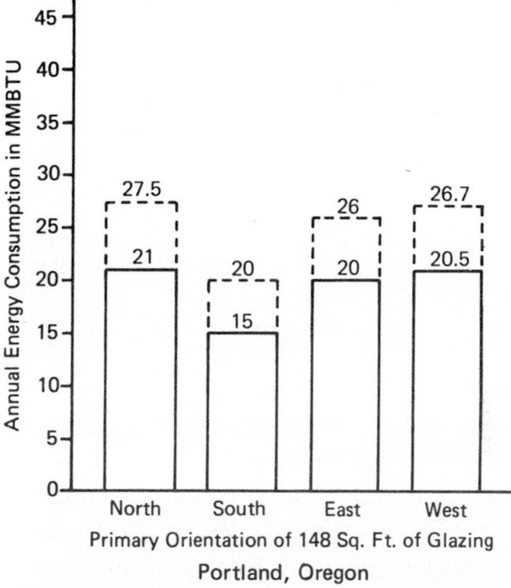

Fig. 10.7 Comparison of annual energy consumption with respect to home orientation for a 1232-square-foot computer simulated reference home in climate region B. Glazing type—double U = 0.53; amount of glazing—148 square feet on primary orientation (12 percent of floor area of reference home), and window management strategy—active. (Note: See Appendix I for reference home characteristics.)

Window Orientation

The major area of glazing on a home should face south or within 30° east or 15° west of true south to receive maximum benefit from solar radiation in the winter and the least radiation during the summer months.

Figures 10.7 and 10.8 (from CCB/CA simulations) show that when the major area of glazing is facing east or west in four Climate Region B locations, the homes consume 25 to 32 percent more heating and cooling energy than for the same homes having the major area of glazing facing south. When the major glazing area is facing north from 29 to 40 percent more heating and cooling energy is used than when the major area of glazing faces south.

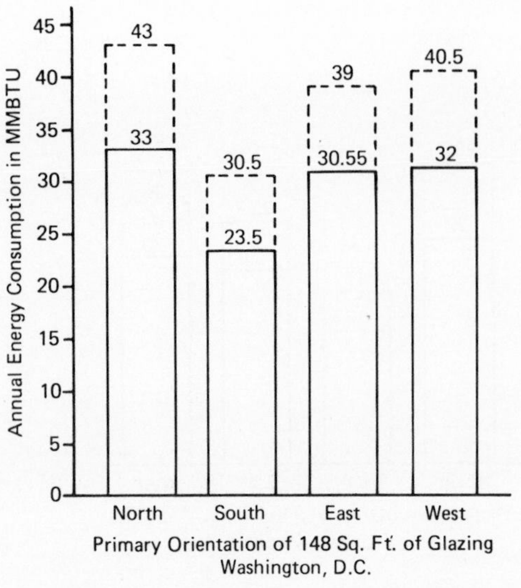

Fig. 10.8 Comparison of annual energy consumption with respect to home orientation for 1176-square-foot computer simulated reference home in climate region B. Glazing type—double U = 0.53; amount of glazing—141 square feet on primary orientation (12 percent of floor area of reference home), and window management strategy—unmanaged. (Note: See Appendix II for reference home characteristics.)

The LBL simulations for Climate Region B show that when the major area of glazing is facing east or west versus south, the reference home consumes 24 to 72 percent more heating and cooling energy. When the major area of glazing faces north instead of south in the LBL analysis, the reference home consumes 12 to 45 percent more total heating and cooling energy (Table 10.5).

For a discussion of the differences in results of CCB/CA and LBL simulation analyses, refer to the earlier discussion of Climate Region A. Both sets of analyses show that the orientation of the major area of glazing can significantly affect annual energy consumption for heating and cooling.

Window Type

In Climate Region B, use a glazing system that has a thermal transmittance (U-value) of less than 0.58 or one which is typical for double glazing as determined by ASHRAE thermal transmittance calculations. Table 10.2 gives ASHRAE thermal transmittance values for a variety of glass and sash configurations that meet or surpass this guideline.

It is important to note that in all of the charts and graphs in this book derived from computer simulation, the U-values used for double and triple glazing (double, U = 0.53 and triple, U = 0.29), are based upon average local annual wind speeds derived from actual long term weather observations. These values differ from ASHRAE calculated values which are computed using a constant 15 MPH wind speed. If an exterior film resistance resulting from a 15 MPH wind (0.17) was used in place of the actual wind speed observations used in this study, the U-values reported here would be equivalent to those in the ASHRAE *Handbook of Fundamentals*. It is believed these values, ones normally used in annual computer simulations, are more representative of actual field performance of windows in houses than calculated values.

The computer simulation results presented in this section assumed a year-long average double glazed window U-value of 0.53, interior shades, and solar transmittance normal to the window plane of 0.74. Transmittance normal to the window is defined as the condition when solar radiation is striking the window plane perpendicularly (90°). This is the value most often listed in manufacturers' literature. A more detailed discussion pertaining to windows and sash type selection can be found at the beginning of this chapter in the earlier discussion of Climate Region A.

TABLE 10.5 The impact of building orientation on a typical residential building* annual heating and cooling loads

Climate Region B

City	State	% of Total Annual Load that is Heating, South Facing Home	MMBtu	% Increase in Total Annual Load of East or West Facing over South Facing Home	% Increase in Total Annual Load of North Facing over South Facing Home
Columbia	MD	74	26.3	29	16
Dodge City	KS	71	23.5	43**	25**
Washington	DC	69	23.2	25	15
Albuquerque	NM	61	11.6	71**	45**
Nashville	TN	53	22.0	24	12
Cape Hatteras	NC	37	18.8	33	13

* Residence has 1176 sq. ft. of conditioned floor space and 132 sq. ft. (11.2% of floor area) of glazing on primary orientation. See Appendix for detailed building and computer simulation description.

** Figures for the desert climate are often much higher than comparable areas because the cold night and hot, sunny days are ideal for reduction of both heating and cooling loads by proper orientation and appropriate levels of thermal mass.

Source: Lawrence Berkeley Laboratory paper, "The Impact of Orientation on Residential Heating and Cooling" by Brandt Anderson, Ronald Kammerud and Wayne Place, Passive Solar Analysis and Design Group, Spring 1982.

Window Area

The amount of beneficial south facing glass that may be incorporated into a home in Climate Region B is based upon the design recommendations in the preceding sections, as well as the following considerations:

- large rooms or "open plan" to the south and preferably the long axis of the home oriented east-west.
- sufficient external shading during the cooling season. An indepth discussion of sufficient shading can be found in Chapter 11.
- provision for natural ventilation to reduce the need for mechanical cooling.

Slab-On-Grade Homes

For homes constructed in this region that use a properly insulated slab-on-grade (see Chapter 9) foundation system or an equivalent amount of thermal storage (for example, exterior masonry walls, or interior masonry partitions or fireplaces), south facing glazed areas of up to 15 percent of the conditioned space floor area can beneficially reduce annual energy consumption (Fig. 10.9). This recommendation presumes at least 30 to 50 percent of the floor slab is exposed to direct sunlight and is covered with a finish that has a thermal resistance (R-value) no greater than 0.25. Table 7.1 lists the R-values of various common floor and wall surface materials.

Wood-Floor-Over-Crawl-Space Homes

In Climate Region B, south facing glazed areas of up to eight to ten percent of the floor area moderately affect annual energy consumption if the design considerations discussed at the beginning of this section are implemented. To increase the area of glazing much beyond ten percent of the floor area

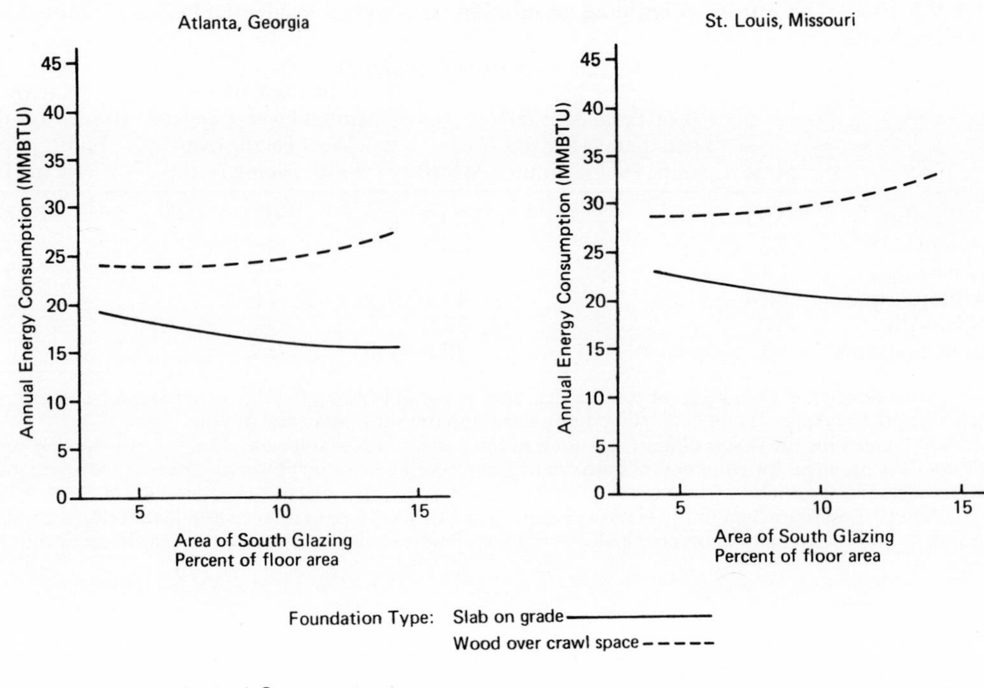

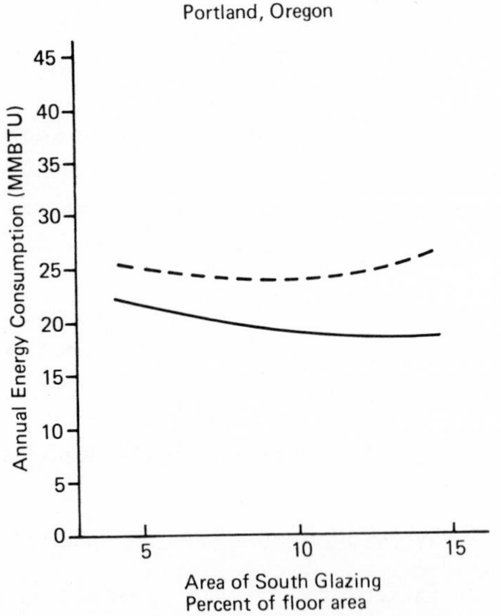

Fig. 10.9 Climate Region B: Annual energy consumption reduction as a function of south glazing areas, are based on the following building characteristics:

Single story, 1232 square feet
Shading: two-foot fixed overhang and roller shades
North glass area = 0
East and west glass area = 85 square feet
Heating: gas furnace at 0.60 seasonal efficiency
Cooling: electric—COP = 1.8 (SEER—6.1)
Heating temperature: 68°, no setback
Cooling temperature: 80°

(Note: See Appendix I for detailed characteristics.)

without causing overheating, a wood-over-crawl-space home should incorporate additional exposed thermal storage to effectively absorb and store the incoming solar radiation (Fig 10.9; also see Chapter 7). Although home designs having a full basement foundation were not specifically examined, we believe the energy performance of a home design

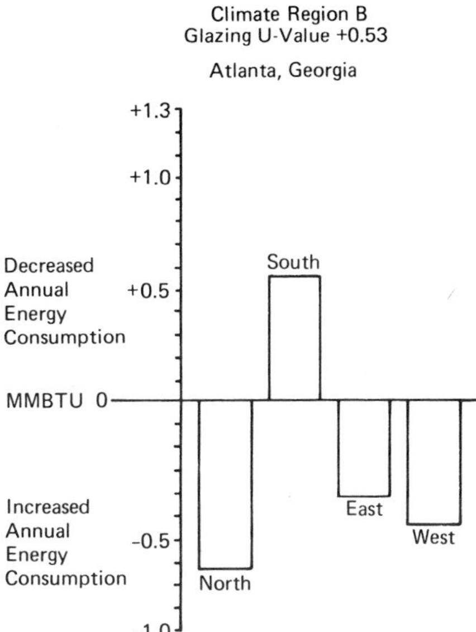

Fig. 10.10 Effect on annual energy consumption of adding a 20-square-foot window to each elevation respectively of the reference home. The home is 1232 square feet, slab-on-grade. The wall being added to already contains 105 square feet of glazing (or 8.6 percent of the floor area). Addition of 20-square-foot window brings glazing up to 10 percent of the floor area. Glazing is actively managed. (Note: See Appendix I for detailed characteristics.)

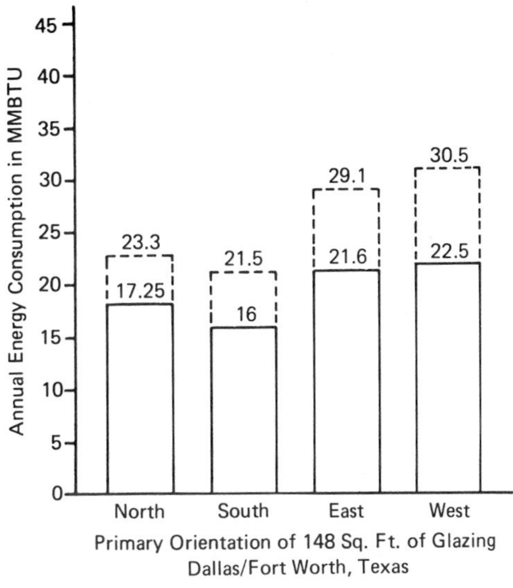

Fig. 10.11 Comparison of annual energy consumption with respect to home orientation for 1232-square-foot computer simulated reference home in climate region C. Glazing type—double U = 0.53; amount of glazing—148 square feet on primary orientation (12 percent of floor area of reference home), and window management strategy— unmanaged. (Note: See Appendix I for reference home characteristics.)

which uses a wood-over-crawl-space foundation is a sufficiently close approximation to a home design with a full basement that the pertinent window recommendations in this chapter are directly applicable.

East and West Glazing

For slab-on-grade, wood-floor-over-crawl-space and basement homes, well managed east and west glazing modestly increases annual energy consumption and should be used only if well shaded, generally during the months of April through September (Fig. 10.10). Partially managed or unmanaged east or west glazing should not be used, because it can increase energy consumption significantly. Unmanaged east or west glazing has a greater effect on increasing the annual energy consumption in Climate Region B than in Climate Region A, as would be expected.

WINDOWS: CLIMATE REGION C

- Winters are relatively mild.
- Summers are long and quite hot.
- Annual heating degree-days are less than 3000.
- Annual cooling hours are greater than 1300.

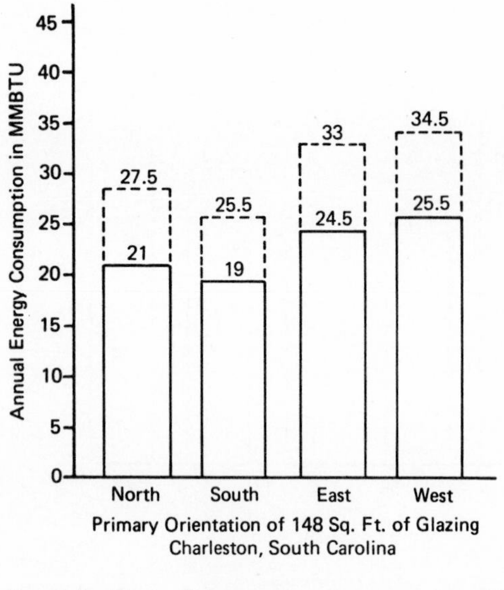

Fig. 10.12 Comparison of annual energy consumption with respec to home orientation for 1176-square-foot computer simulated reference home in climate region C. Glazing type: double U = 0.53; amount of glazing—141 square feet on primary orientation (12 percent of floor area of reference home), and window management strategy—unmanaged. (Note: See Appendix II for reference home characteristics.)

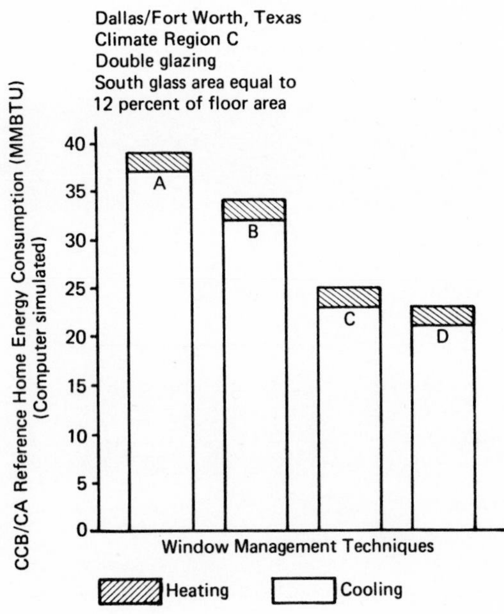

Fig. 10.13 Impact of window management techniques.

Window Orientation

The major area of glazing on a home should face true south or within 20° east or 5° west of true south for optimum solar performance (Figs. 10.11, 10.12).

In Climate Region C, east or west facing homes consume 30 to 42 percent more total heating and cooling energy than those having a south orientation with identical glass area distributions on each elevation. The better managed a window system, the greater the difference in energy consumption between south oriented and east/west oriented homes. This is attributable to the fact that well managed windows, those having proper external shading and natural ventilation, are more efficient than unmanaged windows (Fig. 10.13). Homes with the major area of glazing facing north in Climate Region C consume 8 to 11 percent more total heating energy than those having south orientations with identical glazing distributions on each elevation. The small difference in annual energy consumption between the reference home facing north and facing south is due to the combination of a mild winter climate (less than 3000 heating degree-days), and long cooling season (a minimum of 1300 cooling hours). In this region larger amounts of south facing glass may reduce by a large percentage the total heating requirement, but in absolute units of energy the quantity is small due to the mild winters. Larger amounts of south glass also increase the cooling energy requirement be-

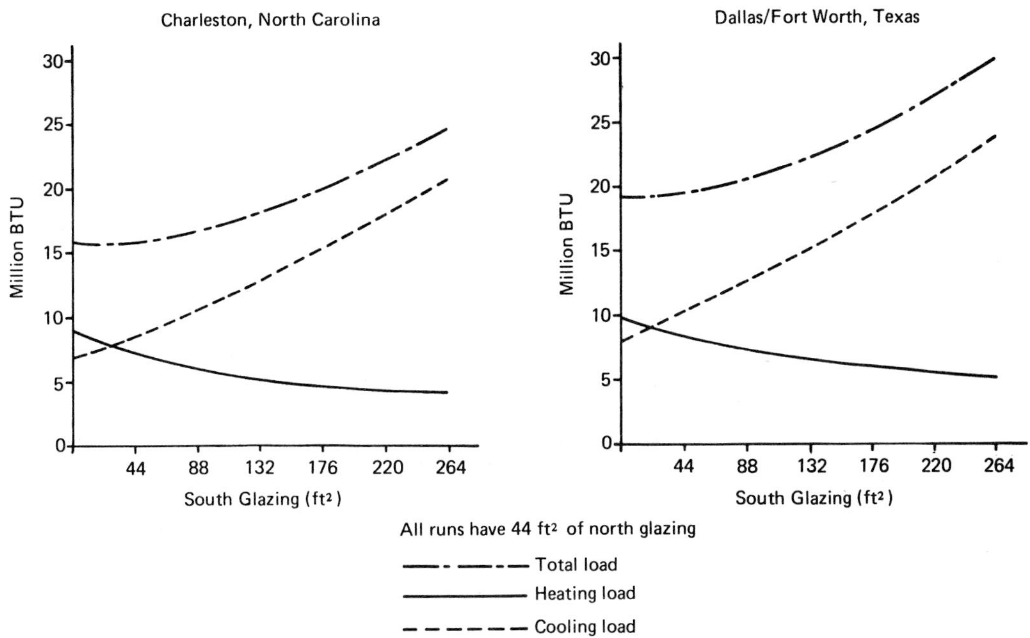

Fig. 10.14 Annual energy consumption as south facing glass area is increased.

cause the average cooling season extends sufficiently into the spring and fall seasons that a substantial amount of solar radiation strikes the south wall well in advance of the heating season. Figure 10.14 illustrates the relationship of annual heating and cooling energy consumption as the glass area increases.

Like those presented for Climate Regions A and B, these recommendations also are derived from extensive computer simulations performed by LBL and CCB/CA. The work of both organizations is in general agreement with results from the Los Alamos National Laboratory, the Solar Energy Research Institute and data from the field (See Chapter 12).

Window Type

In Climate Region C, use a glazing system that has a thermal transmittance (U-value) of less than 0.58 or one which is typical for double glazing as determined by ASHRAE thermal transmittance calculations. Table 10.2 gives ASHRAE thermal transmittance values for a variety of glass and sash configurations that meet or surpass this guideline.

It is important to note that in all of the charts and graphs in this book derived from computer simulation, the U-values used for double and triple glazing (double, U = 0.53 and triple, U = 0.29), are based upon average local annual wind speeds derived from actual long term weather observations. These values differ from ASHRAE calculated values which are computed using a constant 15 MPH wind speed. If an exterior film resistance resulting from a 15 MPH wind (0.17) was used in place of the actual wind speed observations used in this study, the U-values reported here would be equivalent to those in the ASHRAE *Handbook of Fundamentals*. It is believed these values, ones normally used in annual computer simulations, are more representative of actual field performance of windows in houses than calculated values.

The computer simulation results presented in this section assumed a year-long average double glazed window U-value of 0.53, interior shades, and solar transmittance normal to the window plane of 0.74. Transmittance normal to the window is defined as the condition when solar radiation is striking the window plane perpendicularly (90°). This is the value most often listed in manufacturers' literature. A more detailed discussion pertaining to windows and sash type selection can be found at the beginning of this chapter in the earlier discussion of Climate Region A.

Window Area

The amount of beneficial south facing glass that may be incorporated into a home in Climate Region C is based upon the following design considerations and the guidelines presented in the preceding sections:

- large rooms or "open plan" to the south and preferably the long axis of the home oriented east/west.
- sufficient external shading during the cooling or summer season. (See Chapter 11).
- provision for natural ventilation to reduce the need for mechanical cooling.

Indigenous home design practices of the eighteenth and nineteenth centuries can provide some valuable tips for today's designer and builder. Such vernacular features include: wide verandas to shade and keep rain out of the indoor living space; floor-to-ceiling windows and doors that provide maximum ventilation area; raised floors to enhance ventilation and keep moisture out of the home; and floor plans that are spread out to increase exterior wall area and, hence, a narrower building cross-section to improve air movement through the home. Breezeways, often incorporated in nineteenth century homes, channeled breezes through the home and provided valuable outdoor living space sheltered from the sun.

Slab-On-Grade Homes

For homes in this region that use a properly insulated slab-on-grade (See Chapter 9) foundation system or an equivalent amount of thermal storage (for example, exterior masonry walls insulated on the outside surface, or interior masonry partitions or fireplaces), south facing glazed areas of up to 10 percent of the conditioned floor area can modestly decrease annual energy consumption (Fig. 10.15). However, also note that larger, well managed glazed areas do not appreciably increase the energy consumption for slab-on-grade type homes. This recommendation presumes at least 30 to 50 percent of the floor slab is exposed to sunlight during the winter months and is covered with a finish material that has a thermal resistance (R-value) no greater than 0.25 (i.e., no carpeting). Common materials that fulfill these criteria are quarry, asphalt, linoleum, vinyl rubber or terrazzo tile. Table 7.1 lists the R-values of various floor and wall surface materials. As can be observed in Figures 10.13 and 10.14 adequate thermal storage and well managed windows have the greatest effect on reducing annual energy consumption in Climate Region C.

Wood-Floor-Over-Crawl-Space Homes

In Climate Region C, south facing glazed areas of up to five percent of the floor area do not appreciably increase annual energy consumption if the design considerations outlined at the beginning of this section are im-

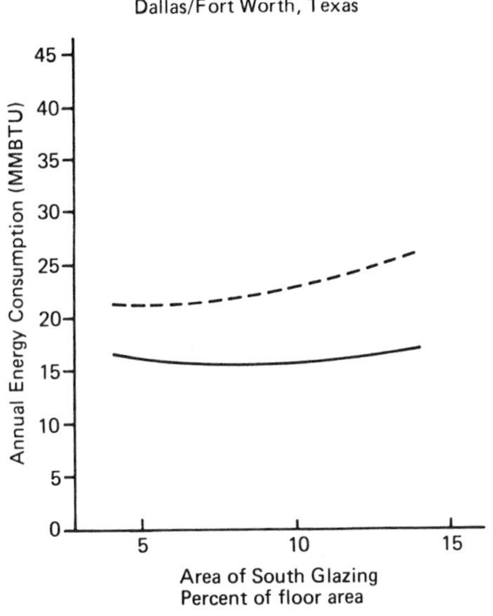

Fig. 10.15
Single story, 1232 square feet
Shading: two-foot fixed overhang and roller shades
North glass area = 0
East and west glass area = 85 square feet
Heating: gas furnace at 0.60 seasonal efficiency
Cooling: electric—COP = 1.8 (SEER 6.1)
Heating temperature: 68°, no setback
Cooling temperature: 80°
(Note: See Appendix I for detailed building characteristics.)

plemented. Figure 10.15 clearly illustrates the benefit of constructing homes with at least an amount of thermal storage equivalent to a floor slab. To increase the area of south facing glazing much beyond five percent of the floor area without causing overheating, it is recommended that a wood-over-crawl-space or full foundation home incorporate additional exposed thermal storage to effectively absorb and store the incoming solar radiation. Chapter 7 provides guidelines for adding this thermal storage material.

East and West Glazing

For slab-on-grade, wood-floor-over-crawl-space and basement homes, well managed east and west glazing moderately increases annual energy consumption and should be used only if shaded, generally, during the months of April through September. Partially managed or unmanaged east or west glazing should not be used since it will increase energy consumption significantly. Unmanaged north glazing does not result in as great a thermal liability in Climate Region C as unmanaged east or west glazing. Figures 10.11 and 10.12 compare the annual energy consumption of the four cardinal orientations for two cities in Climate Region C. Importantly, a north facing home has a 20 to 25 percent lower annual energy consumption than an east or west facing home with identical glazing areas on each elevation. The home is simply rotated 90° to the east or west.

CONCLUSION

In each of the climate regions discussed, building orientation, availability of thermal storage within the dwelling and effective window management techniques together largely determine the amount of window area that beneficially affects annual energy consumption. Issues of building orientation and its relationship to land planning have been extensively discussed in Part Two.

Window management, which includes exterior and interior shading, movable night insulation and natural ventilation is an essential component of a comfortable energy conserving passive solar home.

CHAPTER ELEVEN

Window Management

Windows and operable glass doors provide light, views, ventilation and emergency exits for homes. When properly oriented, installed and managed, they also can help provide significant amounts of heat to a home during winter months. Window management strategies improve window performance through summer sun control, winter heat loss control and enhancement of natural ventilation.

A properly installed window is well caulked, insulated and sealed at the junction between the window frame and the rough opening to minimize infiltration. A poorly installed triple glazed window, for example, might be no better thermally than a properly installed single glazed unit. The potential benefits of two additional panes of glass and air spaces might be offset by excessive infiltration due to inadequate seals. Depending upon critical decisions about design and use, windows can either significantly decrease, increase or have little impact on annual energy consumption. The actual impact depends upon the window management strategy employed as well as climate, orientation, shading and quality of installation. Properly oriented, installed and actively managed windows can reduce the annual energy consumption of a home by approximately 40 percent over an identical home located in the same climate with poorly oriented, installed and unmanaged windows (Fig. 11.1).

An *actively* managed window is characterized by:

- Properly engineered exterior summer shading devices which minimize the amount of direct sunlight passing through the window throughout the summer cooling season without significantly reducing winter solar gain.
- Daily operation of operable sash (when indicated) and interior shading or night insulation devices.
- A large amount of ventilation area.

An *unmanaged* window is characterized by:

- Little or no exterior summer shading.
- Few or no interior shading or night insulation devices.
- A small amount of ventilation area.

Unmanaged windows produce excessive solar gain in the summer, a high incidence of glare and excessive night heat loss during the winter. Window management is the second most important design consideration after proper building orientation. Window man-

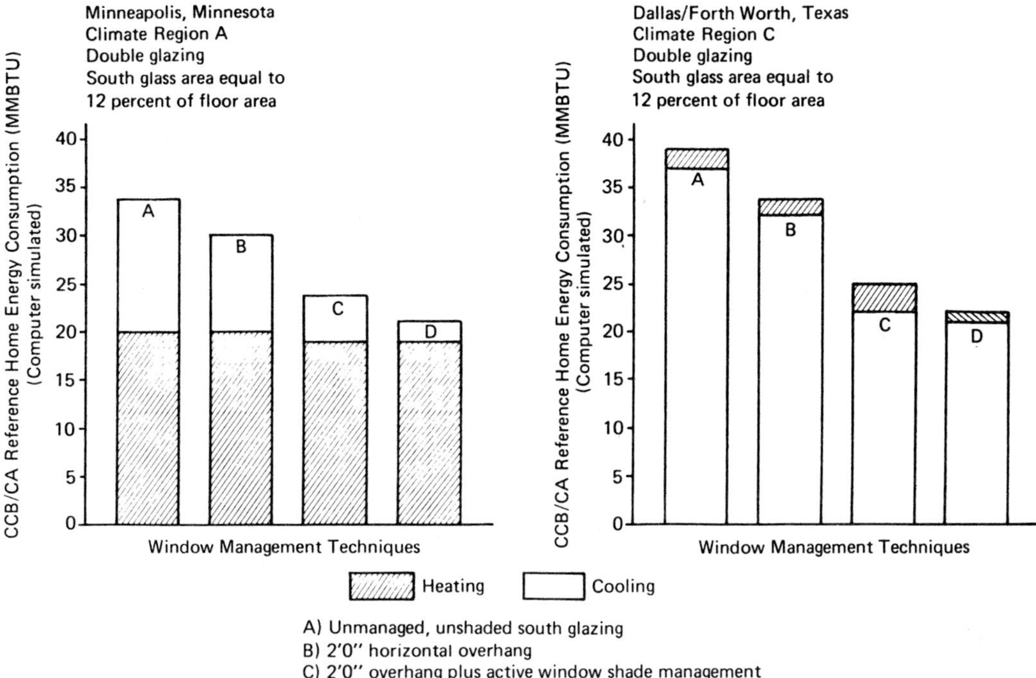

Fig. 11.1 Impact of window management techniques.

agement determines the efficiency with which a residential building will use the sun and breezes to reduce its demand for purchased energy. During the heating season, windows must be managed to capture as much solar energy as possible while simultaneously minimizing the flow of heat energy from the building. The cooling season demands a window design and management response that holds summer heat gain to a minimum while encouraging heat loss. Appropriate responses to both of these principles and seasonal uses demonstrate a balance between functional, aesthetic and economic considerations.

Window management techniques range from those that are operated seasonally, such as exterior operable shading devices, to those which are operated daily, such as night insulation. A common fixed overhang is a window management technique requiring careful design, but no user control. A better summer window management technique is the use of movable exterior shade screens, blinds or awnings, enabling the homeowner to shade the window properly to meet his or her own comfort requirements. Movable exterior window management may be more or less energy conserving than fixed overhangs depending on the action of the occupants; however, it has the potential for greater annual energy savings.

The use of interior roller shades, insulated curtains, drapes and shutters is a window management approach that can not only reduce summer heat gain but also substantially enhance winter window performance. Interior window management devices also can provide privacy, increased security and improved comfort.

Operable windows provide natural ventilation which can save additional energy for cooling that would otherwise be provided by mechanical equipment. A good rule-of-thumb is to provide operable sash equal to five to seven percent of a home's habitable floor area.

The relative importance of various window management techniques depends on the climate region in which a home is to be built. In warmer climates during the spring, summer and fall, exterior or interior shading is by far the most important window management strategy, though effective natural ventilation can also reduce the need for mechanical cooling. In colder climates, winter heat loss reduction is the most important window management strategy, but summer shading is essential to prevent daytime overheating. Effective natural ventilation in spring and fall is also important in helping to maintain comfortable interior conditions.

This chapter presents a number of strategies for successfully balancing the seasonally conflicting requirements of a building's fenestration. Once a designer or builder becomes familiar with the virtues and shortcomings of various window management strategies, he or she can select a combination which will provide a thermally comfortable environment for the building's residents.

EFFECTIVENESS OF VARIOUS TYPES OF SHADING

Shading a home and its glazed areas during late spring, summer and fall is essential to comfort in an energy conserving passive solar home.

The relative economic importance of effective seasonal shade control becomes clear when we compare the solar heat gain through 150 square feet of shaded and unshaded south facing double glazed window area. A typically constructed home located at 40° north latitude receives approximately 112,000 Btu's on the exterior surface of each square foot of south facing glass from June 1 to September 30. The unshaded double glazed windows will absorb and transmit approximately 86,000 Btu/ square foot. The same window area shaded with an exterior mounted shading device such as a fiberglass shade screen will absorb and transmit approximately 24,000 Btu/square foot of the solar radiation striking the outer surface of the shade. Presuming a homeowner of the described home is paying $15 for each million Btu's of electricity purchased from the local utility and his or her mechanical cooling system has a coefficient of performance (COP) of 2.5, the increased cost of cooling energy for the same area of unshaded and shaded glass would be approximately $87.00 and $26.00, respectively. This more than three-fold difference between the two approaches only underscores the importance of proper design and operation of window management devices.

Shading the glass and selected exterior building surfaces affects the quantity of transmitted solar radiation and reduces both the heat flow to a building's interior and the indoor temperature. The amount of reduction depends on the location of the shade control device, either natural or fabricated, with respect to the glass, whether internal or external. Shading that intercepts solar radiation external to the glass (such as an awning) is the most effective type because some radiation is reflected outwards and some inwards while the balance is absorbed, raising the temperature of the shading device. This causes heat flow away from the shade by radiation and convection (Fig. 11.2).

Wind or gentle breezes also act to remove heat from the exterior shading, with the result

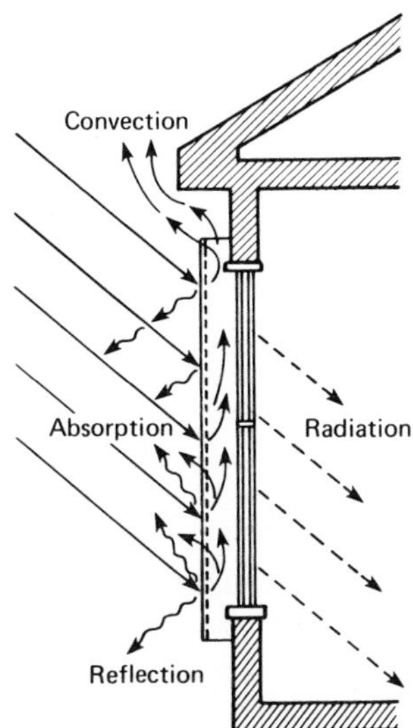

Fig. 11.2 Shading external to the glass/window.

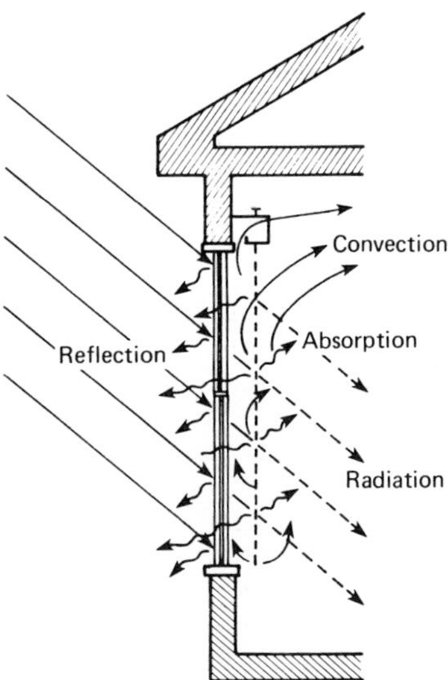

Fig. 11.3 Shading on interior side of the glass.

that only a small portion of the incident solar radiation penetrates the glazing and, hence, the conditioned space. Shading on the interior side of the glass, such as venetian blinds or roller shades, intercepts solar radiation only after it has been transmitted through the glazing (Fig. 11.3). The radiation that strikes the shade is absorbed and re-released almost entirely as heat to the interior space. Only a small fraction of the radiation initially transmitted is reflected outwards from the shade, because when solar radiation is intercepted by a material, its wavelength is altered in such a way that the resulting longer wave length radiation (heat energy) cannot pass back through the glass. This is often referred to as the "greenhouse effect." The effectiveness of internal shading to re-radiate solar radiation through the glass once it is inside the building is largely determined by the reflectivity of its exterior-facing surface. Generally, this approach to solar control is much less effective than external shades.

Various types of shading systems block different amounts of the sun's heat. The effectiveness of a system is measured by its "shading coefficient." This measurement compares the relative heat gain of a window equipped with a shading device to the heat gain of an unshaded single glazed window of clear 1/8-inch glass; the lower the shading coefficient, the higher the effectiveness of the shading device (Table 11.1). The highest shading coefficient possible is 1.0 which is defined as the condition in which 100% of the sun's heat energy incident on the glass is transmitted to the adjacent interior space, even though in reality, a small fraction of this energy is reflected, absorbed and re-radiated by the glass itself.

An exterior shutter, for example, can have a shading coefficient of 0.04; 96 percent of the heat that would pass through a single pane of glass is intercepted and dissipated by the shutter. In contrast, a single pane unshaded window has a shading coefficient of 1.0; 100 percent of the heat is admitted to the interior space.

Shading coefficients as low as 0.25 can be achieved by using reflective glass. Heat ab-

TABLE 11.1 Performance comparisons of various shading devices

Type	Shading Coefficient
Clear glass 1/8″ thick	1.00
Insulated double glazed clear glass unit	0.88
Triple glazed clear glass	0.78
Low emissivity glass	0.40–0.75
Clear glass with interior dark venetian blind, closed	0.75
Interior light roller shade, half drawn	0.71
Heat absorbing insulated glass, 1/4″	0.56
Interior medium-color venetian blind, closed	0.65
Interior white venetian blind, closed	0.53
Tinted film on roller shade, closed	0.51
Reflective aluminum interior venetian blinds or drapes	0.45
Exterior venetian blind, white, 2/3 closed	0.43
Interior white roller shade, closed	0.39
Woven fiber glass exterior sun screen	0.34
Exterior vertical fixed fins	0.31
Exterior canvas awning, opaque, medium color*	0.25
Continuous overhang on south side*	0.25
Dense shade trees—heavy shade	0.25
Exterior 40° mini-louvers**	0.18
Reflective interior roller shade, closed	0.18
Exterior venetian blind, light color, fully extended	0.15
Exterior movable vertical louvers on east or west	0.15
Exterior movable horizontal louvers	0.15
Exterior roll-up/roll-down louvered shutters	0.04

*Ineffective at low sun angles

**Cannot be rolled up

Source: Olgyay, *Design with Climate*, 1963 and independent laboratory test data.

To determine the total shading coefficient of a particular glazing system, multiply the shading coefficient of the glazing by the shading coefficient of the shade device selected.

sorbing or tinted glass can have a shading coefficient of approximately 0.5. When used in a double glazed unit, the heat absorbing glass should be on the exterior so the heat is dissipated to the outside. Most glass manufacturers provide complete tables of shading coefficients. Reflective glass is especially recommended for east and west facing windows in southern climates if adequate exterior shading is not part of the design.

B. Givoni in *Man, Climate and Architecture*[1] draws several conclusions from research studies assessing the effectiveness of various types of internal and external adjustable shading devices:

1. External devices are much more efficient than internal ones.
2. The differences in efficiency between external and internal devices increase as the color of the shades darken.
3. For external devices, the efficiency increases as the color darkens.
4. For internal devices, the efficiency increases as the color lightens.
5. With efficient shading, such as external shutters, it is possible to eliminate more than 90 percent of the heating effect of solar radiation.
6. With inefficient shading, such as dark colored internal devices, approximately 75 to 80 percent of the solar radiation impinging on the window may be expected to enter the building.
7. The increased efficiency of external shading when the color is darker exists only when the windows are closed. With open windows the effect of color shading depends to a great extent on orientation with regard to wind direction.

TYPES OF SHADING

Three approaches to shading will be discussed, in order of effectiveness: first, movable exterior shading devices; second, fixed

[1] B. Givoni, *Man, Climate and Architecture*, Van Nostrand Reinhold Company, New York. Copyright 1969, 1976.

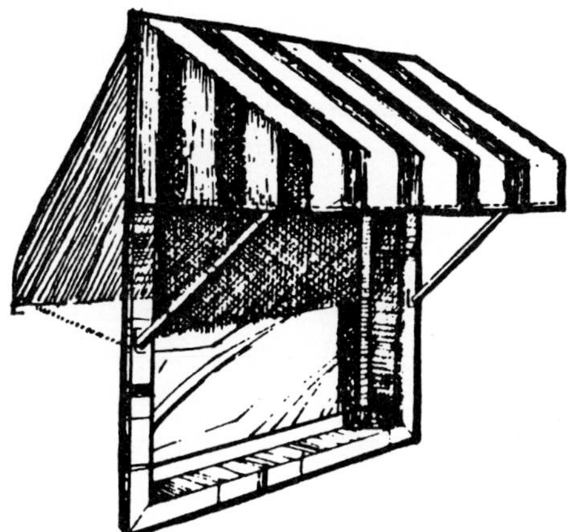

Fig. 11.4 Seasonal awning

Fig. 11.5 Roller awning (self-storing).

exterior shading devices; and third, interior movable shading devices, the least effective sun control technique.

MOVABLE EXTERIOR SHADING DEVICES

Exterior shading systems are far more effective than interior devices because they block the sun's heat before it enters a building.

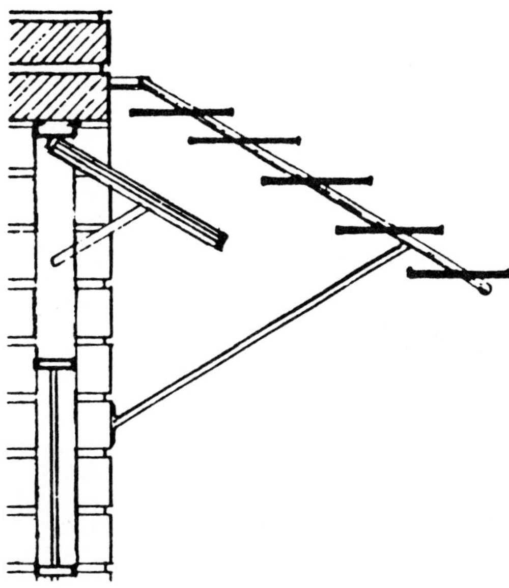

Fig. 11.6 Operable louver awning.

Movable shading devices can be adjusted on a seasonal or daily basis; they allow for maximum beneficial use of solar heat during the winter if fully retracted and work effectively in the extended position to prevent unwanted heat gain during late spring, summer and early fall. Examples of such devices are listed below.

Retractable Awnings

Awnings are an old solution to the shading problem (Figs. 11.4 and 11.5). However, today's awnings with hinged support arms, weather- and fade-resistant synthetic fabrics, and automatic roll-up controls are more reliable and colorful. The effectiveness of an awning for shading depends on the color and opaqueness of the awning material. Materials which transmit little direct sunlight and are light in color to minimize the amount of heat absorbed by the fabric and re-radiated to the window are recommended. An awning can provide shade without heat build-up underneath if it is installed with a provision for air

Fig. 11.7 Exterior mounted sunscreen.

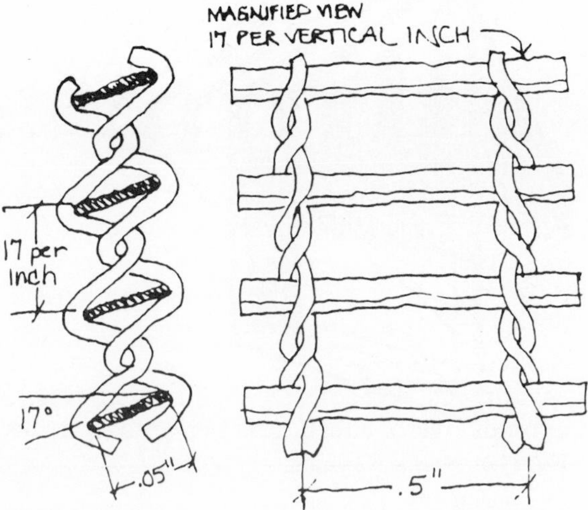

Fig. 11.8 Exterior mounted mini-louver sun screen (close-up view).

(a)

(b)

(c)

Fig. 11.9 (a) View from interior looking out through deployed fiberglass sunscreen. (b and c) Typical installation details.

to circulate between it and the window (Fig. 11.6). Awnings allow reflected light from exterior surfaces and the ground to provide some daylighting to the home. They also reduce glare and ultraviolet radiation discoloration of fabrics and carpets when extended.

To be effective, an awning must be designed to provide adequate coverage of the glass for the specific orientation of the window. A south facing window requires only a modest horizontal projection to be completely shaded throughout the cooling season. An east or west window needs an awning which extends over a substantial percentage of the window height in order to provide protection from low sun angles in early morning and late afternoon. In addition, the sides of such an awning should be closed to prevent solar radiation from angling in behind it.

Sun Screens and Mini-Louvers

Woven fiberglass sun screens (Fig. 11.7) similar to conventional wire screens, and aluminum mini-louvers (Fig. 11.8) provide effective exterior shading, some natural light, and view and ventilation to the living space. They also afford privacy from the outside while only slightly obscuring the view from the inside

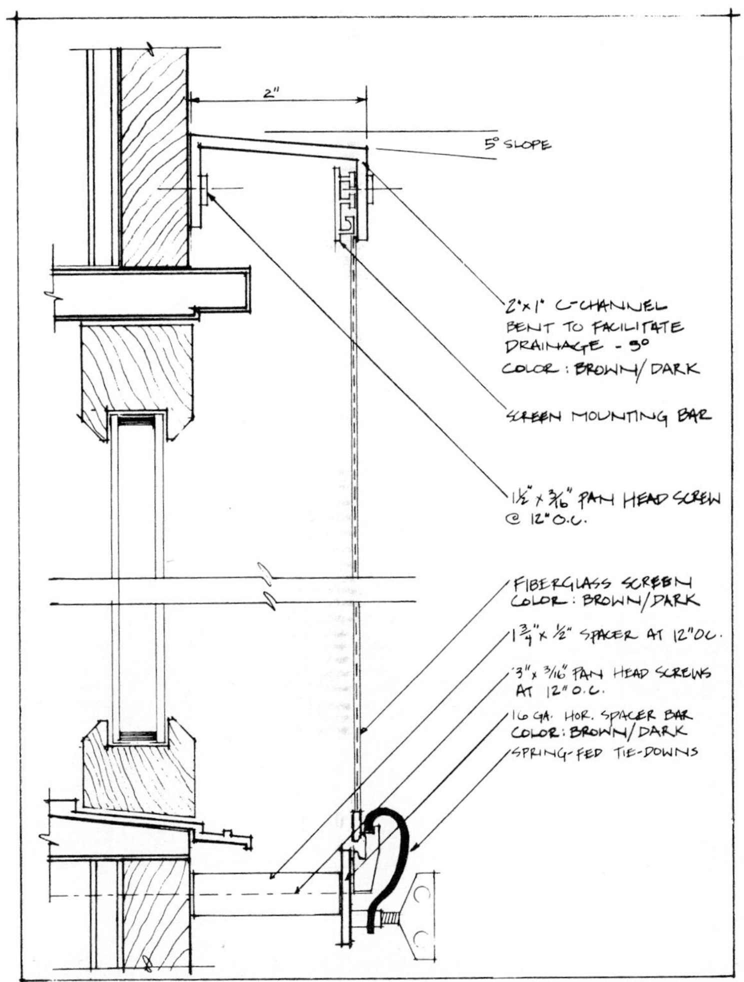

Fig. 11.10 Section through window with fiberglass sunscreen in place.

(Fig. 11.9). If fiberglass sun screens or mini-louvers are installed approximately two inches out from a window with the edges left open, natural convection will minimize heat build-up resulting from absorption of solar radiation by the shading device and reduce the amount of energy which would otherwise be re-radiated to the glass unit (Figs. 11.10). Sun screens and mini-louvers are especially well suited for shading east and west glazing against the morning and afternoon sun. Sun-screens may be left in place throughout the cooling season and easily rolled up and stored above a window or removed for storage during the heating season. These type devices also reduce glare, UV decoloration of fabrics and carpet, and provide a high level of daytime privacy and a view out simultaneously. Woven fiberglass screens are an especially cost-effective approach for substantially reducing solar radiation penetration during the cooling season. Mini-louvers, usually a more costly approach, are most commonly used on residential projects with more flexible budgets. They are also specified for commercial building shade control.

Exterior Shutters

Louvered, operable shutters installed outside a window provide shade in the summer during the day and reduce heat loss and infiltration in the winter during the night (Fig. 11.11). Unlike awnings, sun screens and mini-louvers, shutters must be operated on a daily basis. Hinged, sliding and roll-up shutters

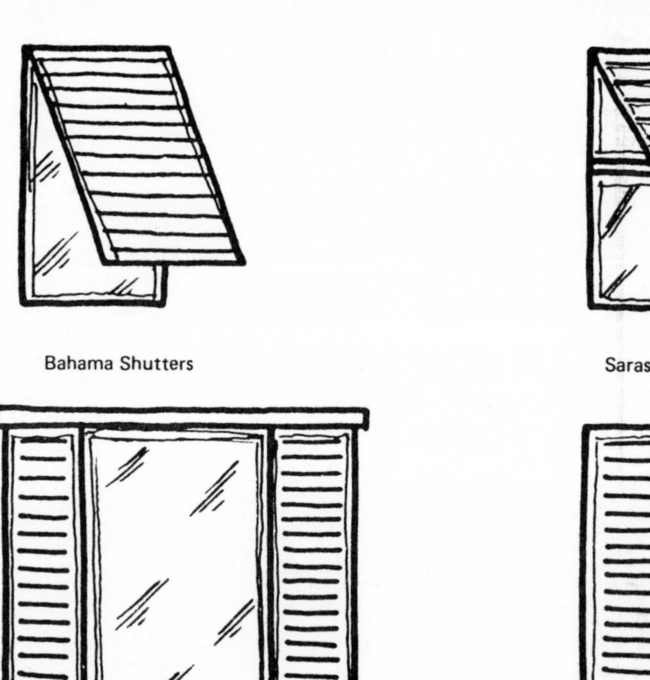

Fig. 11.11 Types of exterior shutters commonly available throughout the United States.

can be controlled from inside a home. The shading performance of a closed exterior shutter depends upon how well the heat absorbed by the shutter itself is dissipated to the outside air. Operable louvers adjusted to block the sun and permit air circulation improve a shutter's ability to keep heat out of a home. Light colored shutters which reflect much of the sunlight rather than absorb it are more effective.

Heat loss through a window with closed shutters in winter is reduced because the air space and surface film between the shutter and the glass provide additional resistance to the flow of heat. The effectiveness of the shutter in reducing heat loss depends on the airtightness of the space between the window and the shutter and on the insulating value of the shutter itself. Even louvers fixed in an open position reduce heat loss through the window by sheltering the insulating film of air at the outer surface of the window unit from the scouring action of the wind. In warmer climate regions, shutters installed a few inches away from a window are preferable to those positioned against the window because they can better dissipate summer heat. In cooler climates, more tightly fitting shutters are preferred because of their better winter insulation performance.

Fixed shutters are considered by many homeowners to be an important decorative feature of windows. The designer, homebuilder, and owner should consider the valuable energy conserving functions as well as the aesthetic virtues of operable exterior shutters. If their benefit is once again realized, perhaps operable exterior shutters may become an option selected by home builders and buyers alike.

FIXED EXTERIOR SHADING

Fixed shading devices, by definition, cannot be adjusted according to variations in sun position or conditions such as rain, snow or glare which may change from season to season or day to day. Therefore, the relationship between a fixed shading device at a particular orientation and the annual and daily paths of the sun determine the effectiveness of such a device in keeping solar radiation from reaching behind the shading device when it is undesirable.

An assessment of the anticipated performance of a planned fixed shading device prior to construction is highly recommended to ensure satisfactory performance of the device and a comfortable indoor thermal environment. Several methods for such an assessment exist. One is to construct a model and test it under artificial or natural irradiation conditions. Figure 11.12 illustrates one evaluation technique using a *heliodon*. A heliodon is simply an artificial light source and a model base, either or both of which are moved to simulate the sun's position. The heliodon pictured in Figure 11.12 is called a "moving earth-moving sun" type where the model base is tilted to an angle equal to 90° minus the site latitude and the artificial sun (a light source)

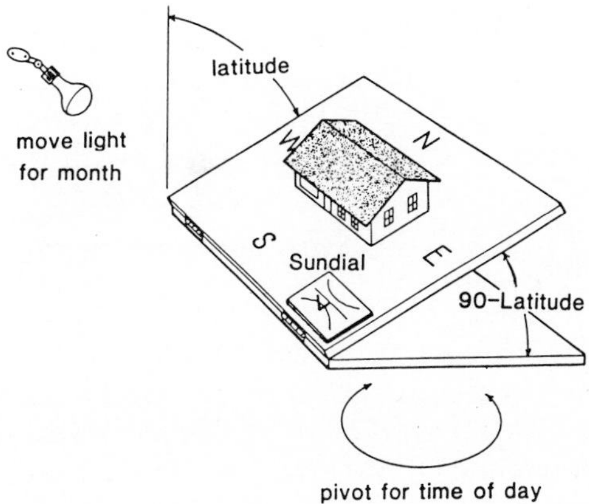

Fig. 11.12 A moving earth-moving sun-type heliodon.

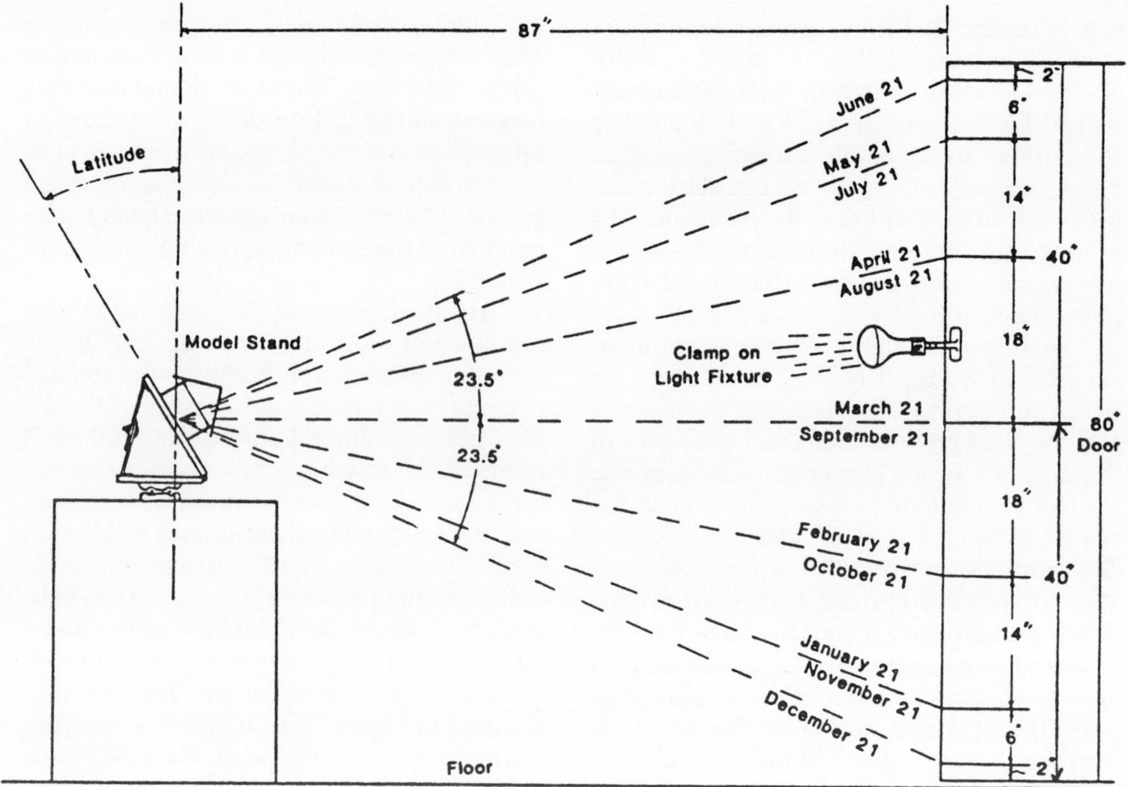

Fig. 11.13 The model is tilted to the latitude of the building site and the light source is positioned at the indicated locations above to assess solar penetration for each month.

is adjusted for the season of the year (declination). A common approach using this method is to move an artificial light source on a vertical staff to adjust for declination, with the result that the model base and tilt table requires only one angular adjustment for each hourly setting (Fig. 11.13).

A variety of other modeling techniques for determining the effectiveness of a fixed shading device are described in detail in the *Solar Control Workbook* by Donald Watson and Raymond Glover (Yale University, available from ACSA, 1735 New York Avenue, N.W., Washington DC 20006).

Several graphical methods for examination of expected fixed shading device performance also exist. One commonly used method which was first proposed by Olgyay and Olgyay is a *shading mask*. A shading mask is an easy way of locating on a sun path diagram the dates and times when a window is either fully or partially shaded by a proposed solar control device. The Olgyay shading mask construction technique can be used in conjunction with the LOF Sun Angle Calculator described in Part One, *Solar Fundamentals*. The method is detailed in *Design with Climate*. The Olgyay method projects

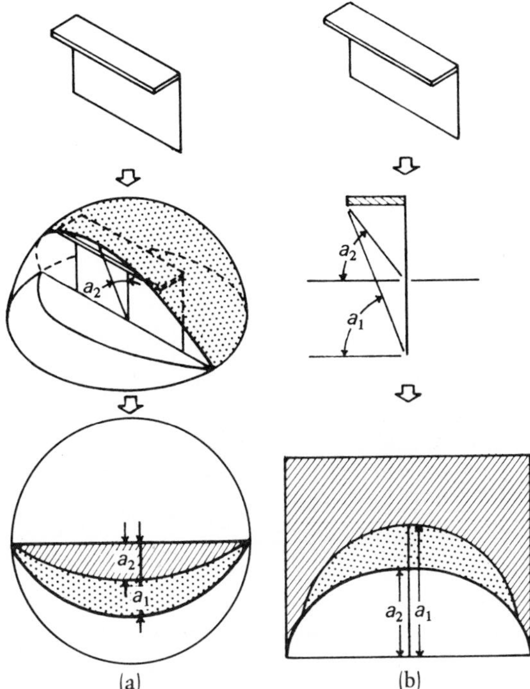

Fig. 11.14 (a) Horizontal plane shading mask for a simple overhang projection. (b) Vertical plane shading mask for a simple overhang projection.

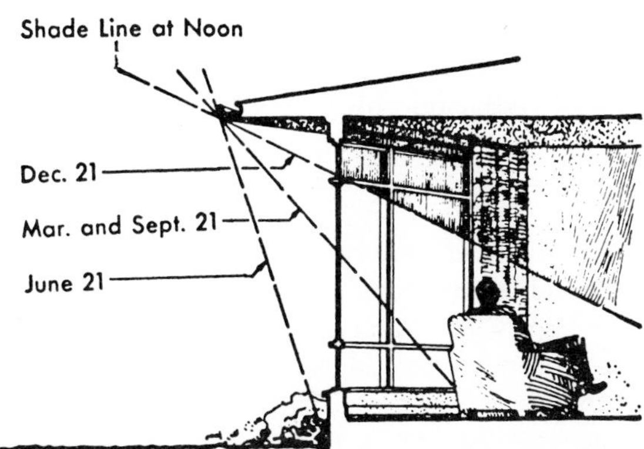

Fig. 11.15 Roof overhang admits winter sun, blocks summer sun.

the shading mask on a LOF horizontal plane sun path diagram using a shading mask protractor (Fig. 11.14a). A second method proposed by Mazria and detailed in *The Passive Solar Energy Book* (Rodale Press) utilizes vertical cylindrical sun charts in which a vertical plane shading mask results (Fig. 11.14b). Both methods yield a shading mask that can be placed over a sun path diagram to provide the time and dates when shading is preventing solar radiation from striking surfaces and causing an uncomfortable thermal environment for the users. The horizontal and vertical mask methods are both in common use, so the designer or builder should select the method with which he or she feels most comfortable for designing fixed shading.

Fixed Exterior Overhangs

Fixed overhangs for south facing glazing provide effective shading during summer months but may cause undesirable shading during spring and/or fall. While fixed overhangs have some shading limitations, they do not require any action by the occupant and can be designed to accommodate the dominant heating or cooling load in relation to the latitude.

Overhangs can shade south facing windows during the summer months and leave them unshaded during winter months because of the seasonally changing altitude angle of the sun (Fig. 11.15).

The maximum and minimum shading provided by an overhang coincides with the summer and winter solstices (June 21 and December 21). However, maximum cooling and heating loads normally occur 30 to 45 days after the respective solstice. The symmetry of shading around the solar cycle can lead to problems during spring and fall. For a specific home design, especially one to be located in Climate Region A, shading may be desired during August but not in April. Although these months occur at the same point in the solar cycle, they do not have comparable heating and cooling demands. Consequently, an overhang designed to allow solar radiation through south windows on April 21 will also allow it to penetrate on August 21. In Climate Region B, however, since the maximum cooling load occurs six to eight weeks after the summer solstice, it is desirable to design the overhang to provide shading for the glazing in September. In that case, the sun would be excluded for heat gain purposes in March. That probably would be the wisest energy conservation choice assuming the September cooling load is higher than the March heating load. As can be seen from this example, fixed overhangs present a compromise situation. Movable shading is an alternative which, although it requires some user involvement, provides maximum flexibility toward achieving satisfactory solar control year-round.

Of all the shading options available to designers and builders, fixed overhangs are the most commonly used. These are constructed as extended soffits on flat and pitched roof homes or as extended floor framing soffits to shade lower level glazing on multi-story homes. Although they are not perfect, fixed overhangs can be designed to shade effectively a large portion of south facing glazing. The amount of projection of fixed overhangs for south facing exposed windows depends on site latitude and the position of the overhang relative to the glazing.

SIZING FIXED OVERHANGS

Overhangs sized by the following method will provide effective shading for the five most severe hours on August 1. With this method we may assume that on this date complete protection from direct solar radiation is provided. Therefore, only the diffuse solar component and conduction will contribute to heat gain. In cooling load calculations, this is the equivalent of assuming that the glazing faces north. This method applies only to overhangs which are considerably wider than the windows they shade. For example, a three-foot-wide overhang centered over a three-foot-wide window would allow morning and afternoon sun to strike the window. The effective length of the shadow provided by an overhang may be found by the following steps (Fig. 11.16).

1. Locate the latitude of the site on the vertical scale by using the map or by reading directly on the scale.
2. Select the appropriate curve for the direction which the window faces.
3. From the latitude scale, read horizontally to the right to the direction curve and then down to the shadow length scale. The value on the shadow length scale is the length of effective shadow provided by each foot of overhang. Multiply this number by the length of the overhang (in feet) to obtain the total effective shadow length (in feet). If the windows on the south wall are not all the same height, determine either the average height or most commonly occurring window height to size the overhang.

Example: Chicago, Illinois; very near the 42° latitude line.

Coming straight across the graph to the heavy curved lines, it may be seen that for each foot of overhang on the south side, approximately 2.2 feet of vertical wall will be in shade. Similarly, for walls facing southeast, approximately 1.2 feet of vertical shade corresponds to a one-foot overhang. Note that east and west walls will experience a constant 0.8 feet of shade per foot of overhang regardless of latitude.

For a south facing window in summer with the bottom of the glass located five feet below the overhang, the desired shading could be provided by a 2.3 foot overhang (5.0 feet divided by 2.2 feet of shade per foot equals 2.3

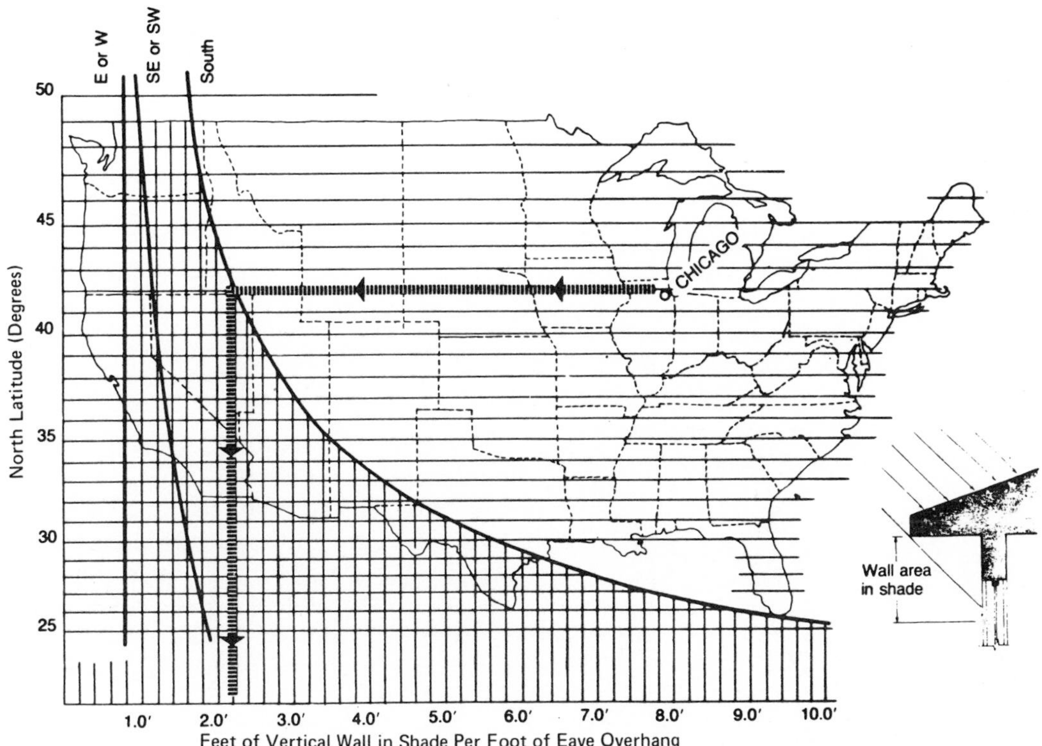

Fig. 11.16 Overhang sizing chart.

feet). To maximize potential for heat gain in winter using a 2.3 foot overhang, locate the top of the window's glass out of the area of shade in winter, or 0.8 feet or more below the overhang.

In addition to the overhang's horizontal projection, the space between the top of the window and lowest point of the overhang projection (the "overhang gap"), determines the efficiency of an overhang shading device. Figure 11.17 shows that as the window height increases the overhang gap as well as the horizontal projection are also increased to provide a correctly dimensioned shading device. Table 11.2 gives overhang gap and projection dimensions for five common window heights. The values listed in the overhang sizing table for each window height and latitude will result in fully unshaded windows from November 11 to January 31 and fully shaded ones from May 12 to August 1. These values produce an overhang more closely aligned with the annual heating and cooling cycle than one more commonly designed for December 21 and June 21, the solar cycle.

To use the tables, first determine the window height and site latitude. Second, enter the appropriate table and determine the overhang gap and projection. For site latitudes that fall between those listed simply interpolate between the nearest two in the table. If the windows on the south wall are

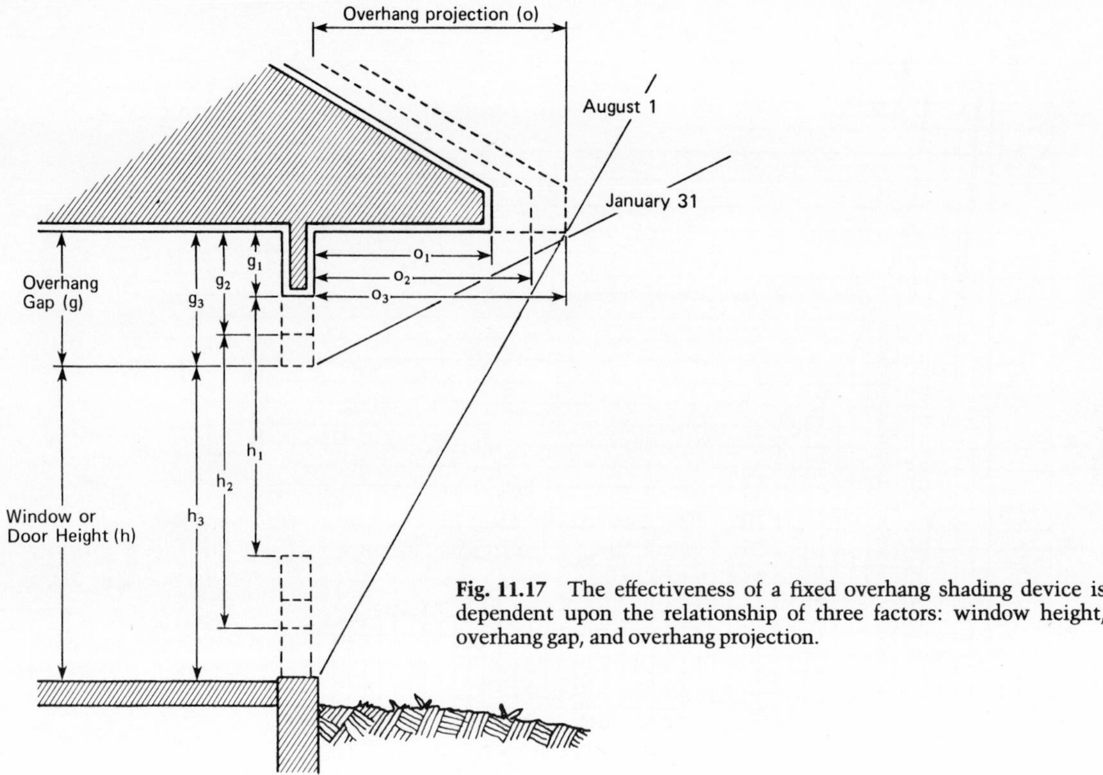

Fig. 11.17 The effectiveness of a fixed overhang shading device is dependent upon the relationship of three factors: window height, overhang gap, and overhang projection.

not all the same height, determine either the average height or most commonly occurring window height to size the overhang. For example, at a site latitude of 40° a 4′-0″-high window will be optimally shaded by an overhang projection of 2′-0″ and gap of 1′-4″. If there are windows on the wall with a height greater than 4′-0″ and an equivalent overhang gap, they will be less than optimally shaded during the summer season. In climates where air conditioning is desired a supplemental movable shading device is recommended. In general, if a proper fixed overhang cannot be designed to effectively shade the south windows during the summer months and allow penetration during the winter, then a movable shading system should be used.

In more extreme climates it may be desirable to increase or decrease the number of days that south windows are shaded or unshaded, or to use window sizes other than those covered by the table. A detailed method for determining the proper overhang characteristics for such alternate cases is described in "A Simple Method for Sizing Overhangs" by Michael Utzinger (*Solar Age Magazine*, July, 1980, pg. 37–39).

The length of an overhang or distance from the soffit to the top of the glazed area may be partially determined by wall, roof framing, roof trim and rain gutter details. The details, however, should be developed with an awareness of solar control. Roof overhangs can be created with appropriate rafter tail designs, added-on framing or properly designed roof trusses that place the bottom out-

TABLE 11.2 Overhang sizing table for common window sizes

Window Height	Latitude (degrees)	Overhang Gap (feet)	Overhang Projection (feet)
4′-0″	30	.92	1.10
	35	1.16	1.56
	40	1.32	2.16
	45	1.36	2.76
	50	1.32	3.28
4′-6″	30	1.04	1.22
	35	1.30	1.76
	40	1.50	2.43
	45	1.53	3.10
	50	1.50	3.70
5′-0″	30	1.15	1.35
	35	1.45	1.95
	40	1.65	2.70
	45	1.70	3.45
	50	1.65	4.10
6′-0″	30	1.38	1.62
	35	1.74	2.34
	40	1.98	3.24
	45	2.00	4.14
	50	1.98	4.92
6′-8″	30	1.53	1.80
	35	1.93	2.60
	40	2.20	3.60
	45	2.26	4.60
	50	2.20	5.50

side corner of the facia board into the proper position, which yields the appropriate overhang gap. Horizontal soffit framing, called "lookouts," may be attached to each rafter and toenailed into a ledger that has been securely nailed to the side wall (Fig. 11.18). This detail can also be used for roof overhangs attached to sidewalls on multi-story buildings. These "eyebrow" overhangs must be integrated properly with exterior siding, flashing and other roof and wall trim details.

Fixed Vertical Fins

Fixed vertical fins may be used effectively for shading east and west glazing in all climates. East and west windows get one-and-one-half times as much direct sunlight as south facing

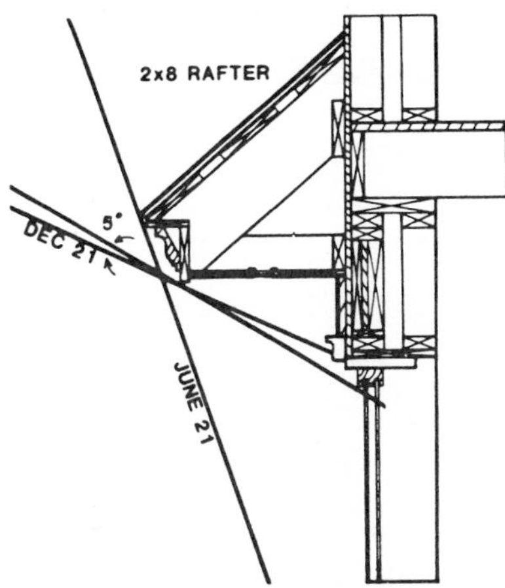

Fig. 11.18 Eyebrow overhang.

windows in summertime. For these windows, a system which entirely shades the glazed surface is recommended. Only *very* wide overhangs, approximately eight feet, such as a wide covered porch or carport are effective for east and west glazing. East and west glazing usually requires some sort of vertical element or movable device for adequate shading.

To size a vertical fixed fin shading device accurately, construct a simple shading mask to determine the width of and spacing between fins. As previously described, a shading mask is a graphical description of the shading characteristics of a particular device or obstruction, and when superimposed over a sun path diagram, accurately determines the time direct sunlight is blocked from reaching the glazing. *The Passive Solar Energy Book* by Edward Mazria shows how to design a correctly proportioned east or west vertical fin or combination vertical/horizontal fin device for all climates.

INTERIOR MOVABLE SHADING DEVICES

Interior movable shading devices can intercept only the solar energy which has passed through the glass surface and can eliminate

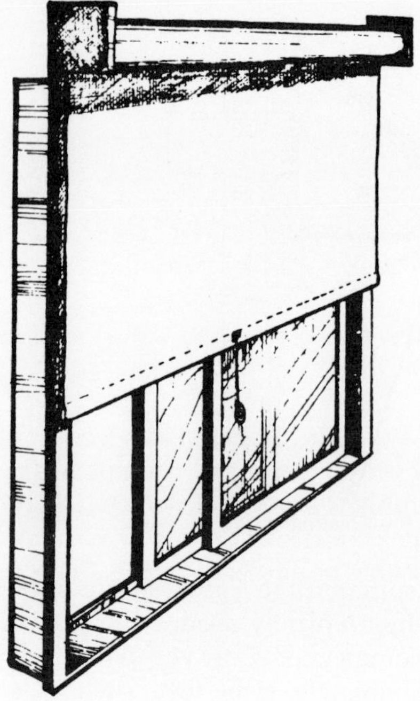

Fig. 11.19 Interior translucent roller shade with magnetic or velcro edge seals.

only that portion of the energy which can be radiated and conducted back through the glass. Much of the energy striking an interior shading device is absorbed, convected and reradiated into a home.

Although interior shading devices are easily controlled, reduce glare and prevent direct radiation from striking deep into the interior, they trap a substantial amount of heat within a home. If interior devices are used, the side facing the window should be a light-to-white color or reflective (such as bright aluminum) and tightly fitting at top, sides and bottom. Interior shade protection devices include light-to-white-colored roller shades (Fig. 11.19), venetian blinds (Fig. 11.20), light colored or reflective draperies and movable night insulation (Fig. 11.21). Movable night insulation may be effectively used in both the cooling and heating season.

Fig. 11.20 Interior venetian blinds.

Fig. 11.21 Interior insulated bifold shutters or other movable night insulation devices can be used to reduce summer heat gain.

However, the disadvantage when opaque winter night insulation becomes summer day insulation is that there is little or no view or daylight during the day when summer heat gains are greatest.

Table 11.1 compares the expected performance for various shading devices in terms of shading coefficients. As defined earlier, the shading coefficient is a relative measure of the amount of solar radiation a particular shade will prevent from being transmitted through itself as compared to a single sheet of clear double strength 1/8-inch thick glass. In order to determine the total shading coefficient of a window system, multiply the shading coefficient (s.c.) of the glazing by the shading coefficient of the shading device being considered. For example, insulated double glazing has a 0.88 s.c. and an interior medium-white-colored blind in the closed position has a s.c. equal to 0.65. The product of these is that total shading coefficient for the window system, 0.57. However, a large amount of radiation intercepted by the shade will be converted to heat and will have to be removed through mechanical means.

NATURAL VENTILATION

The purpose of ventilation is to provide thermal comfort by augmenting heat loss from the human body through convection and sweat evaporation and from the home by removing heat from equipment and natural processes. Ventilation is a common form of passive cooling. Before mechanical cooling, this was the only reasonable way to keep a building cool. When mechanical cooling became commonplace a conflict arose between mechanical and natural cooling, as it was difficult to decide which approach to use during certain times of the year.

In addition to providing thermal comfort, ventilation is required to maintain the air in a home above a certain minimum quality index by replacing indoor air with fresh outdoor air. This requirement should be ensured under all climatic conditions and is discussed in more detail in Chapter 9.

Ventilation also can be used to cool the structure and denser thermal storage-type materials of a building when the temperature indoors is higher than outdoors. This approach is especially effective in dry climates which have a relatively large diurnal temperature swing. In such locations, a home is opened at night to allow breezes to pass through and cool the air as well as building materials. In the morning before the outdoor temperature begins to climb, the home is closed up tightly to contain the coolness of the massive materials within the building envelope. These cooled materials act as a thermal flywheel and moderate the indoor temperature throughout the day. In many situations, it is possible to close up a home completely in the morning when it is cool, to exclude as much solar gain as possible with shading, and to allow the home to coast through the entire day without need for mechanical cooling. If the home becomes uncomfortably hot, it should be opened up to provide maximum ventilation or, if such a strategy cannot provide comfortable conditions, mechanical cooling can be used. This night ventilation strategy does not work well in humid climates, where evening temperatures may not be comfortable. Additionally, many people do not like to have their home closed up during a hot day, especially if there is a breeze. Therefore, ventilating at night and closing the house up during the day works best in climates having a large daily temperature variation.

BASIC PRINCIPLES OF VENTILATION

Pressure differences across a home induce air flow. These differences are caused by two forces: external wind forces, and thermal forces caused by temperature gradients between indoor and outdoor air. Air movement in a home results from the combined effect of these forces. The two forces may work in the same or opposite directions, depending upon the direction of the wind and on whether the internal or external temperature is higher.

Ventilation caused by thermal forces depends on the product of the indoor/outdoor temperature difference and the vertical distance between the inlet and outlet opening, and is successful only when these two factors are sufficiently large. In homes the average effective vertical distance between inlet and outlet is very small, usually less than ten feet, so for an air flow of any practical value to be caused by thermal force there must be a sizable difference between indoor and outdoor temperatures. Differences large enough to induce sufficient ventilation are present only during the winter; in the summer, ventilation induced by thermal force usually is too insignificant for any practical residential application. It is also important to note that even the slightest breeze can overcome thermal forces if the openings are high and low on the walls, so location of ventilators with respect to prevailing breezes is extremely important. Otherwise, the two forces, wind and thermal, may work against each other.

Air flow induced by wind pressure, when windows are opened in both the windward and leeward sides of a building, can bring about a satisfactory air flow across the entire home. The pattern, and thus the cooling effectiveness of such an air flow, is largely determined by the inertia of the incoming air mass. This inertia can be controlled and beneficially directed through the orientation, type and location of inlet and outlet openings, usually windows or doors.

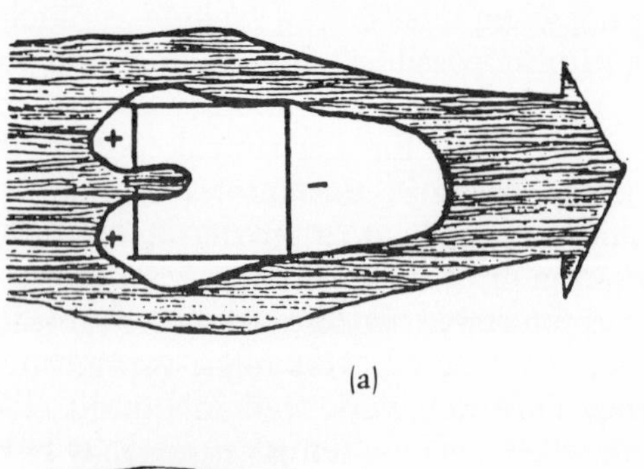

(a)

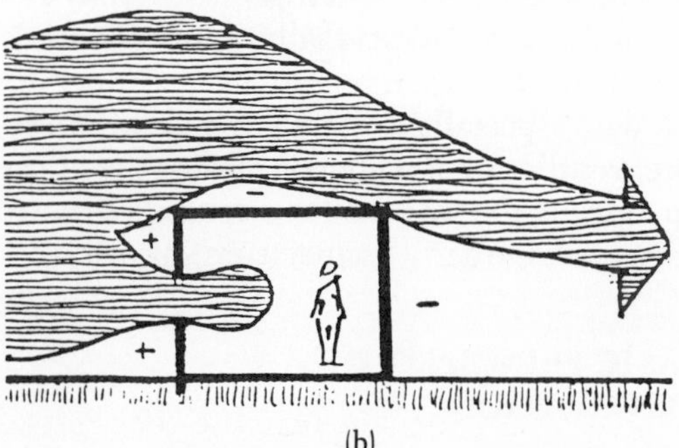

(b)

Fig. 11.22 (a) One opening in windward side results in poor ventilation, in plan. (b) One opening in windward side results in poor ventilation, in section.

WINDOW VENTILATION DESIGN GUIDELINES FOR ORIENTATION, LOCATION AND SIZE

- When the wind is oblique (45°) to the inlet opening of the same room, most of the air volume takes up a turbulent, circling motion around the room, increasing the air flow along the side walls and corners. The outlet is assumed to be in the opposite wall. (Givoni)

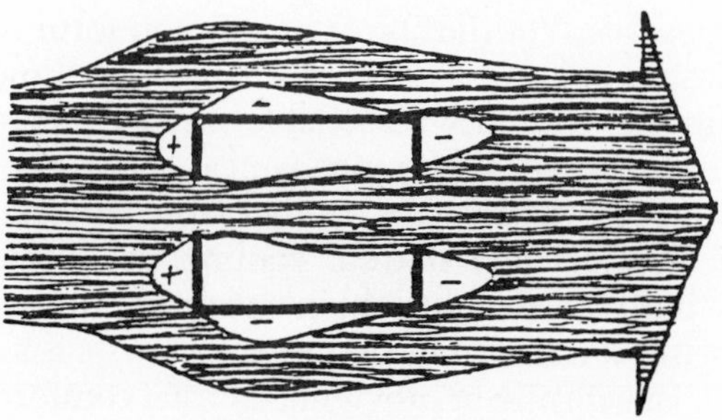

Fig. 11.23 Small inlet and large outlet increases velocity of airflow through interior space.

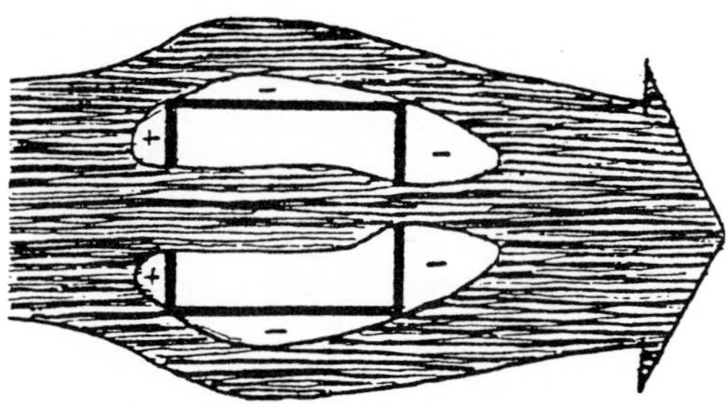

Fig. 11.24 Large inlet and small outlet reduces velocity of airflow through interior space.

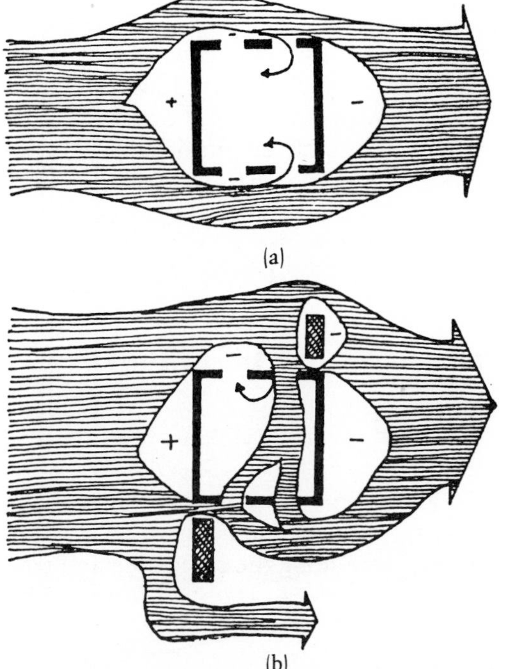

Fig. 11.25 (a) A poor cross-ventilation pattern. (b) A poor cross-ventilation pattern may be improved by the strategic locations of wind barriers.

- Better ventilation conditions are obtained when the air stream has to change direction within the room than when the flow is direct from inlet to outlet. (Givoni)
- One window in a windward side of a room results in poor ventilation (Fig. 11.22).

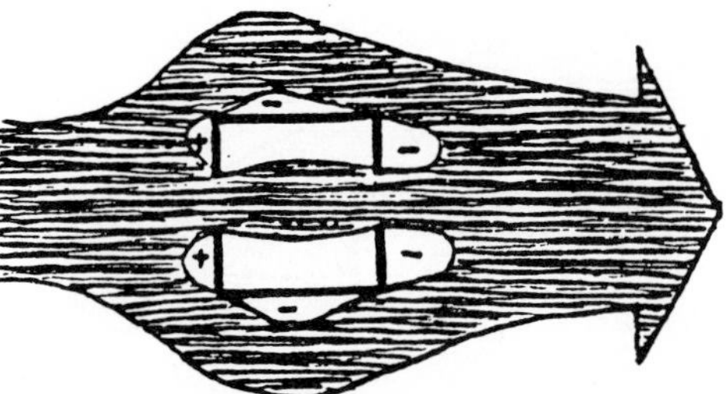

Fig. 11.26 Openings on opposite walls relieve high pressure on the windward side, permitting good cross-ventilation of interior space.

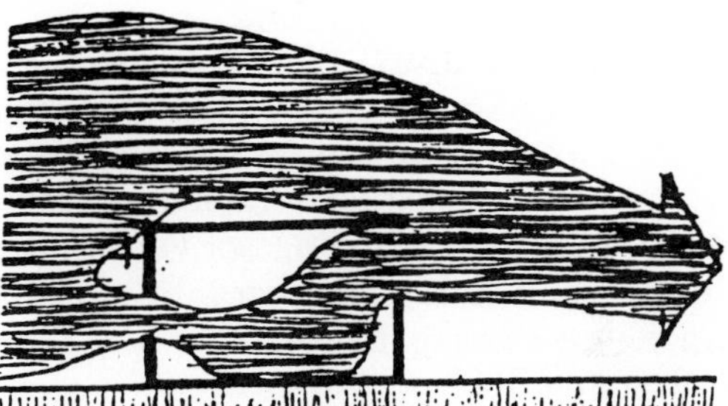

Fig. 11.27 Medium height inlet and high outlet provide an acceptable downward flow despite the high outlet.

- A small inlet and large outlet increases velocity of air flow through interior spaces (Fig. 11.23).
- Poor cross-ventilation may be improved by the strategic locations of wind barriers (Fig. 11.25).
- Identical inlet and outlet at body height yields good cross-ventilation cooling patterns (Fig. 11.26).
- A medium-height inlet and high outlet provides an acceptable downward flow despite the high outlet (Fig. 11.27).
- A low inlet and medium-level outlet provides acceptable cross-ventilation (Fig. 11.28).

One can conclude that the location of inlets are more important than of outlets. Inlets should be located near the average height of the object, person or activity being

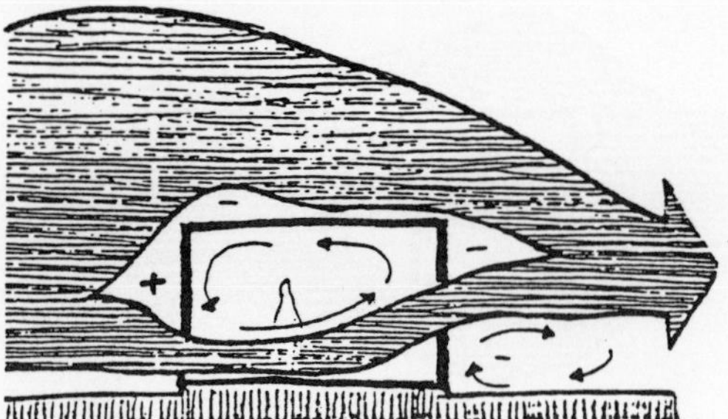

Fig. 11.28 Low level inlet with medium level outlet, sweeps a room floor before exiting.

ventilated. Generally, the recommended inlet sill height for providing sufficient ventilation is approximately two feet above the floor for seated sedentary resident activity and three feet for standing activity. If the height of the window or other inlet sill in a room is above that of the sedentary user, then ventilation will be poor in most of the occupied zone of the room.

When a room is not cross-ventilated, the average indoor velocity is quite low, especially when the wind is perpendicular to the inlet. Provision for cross-ventilation in a room or home has the effect of doubling the average maximum air flow velocities according to studies reported by Givoni in *Man, Climate and Architecture.*

WINDOW INSULATION: MATERIALS, COMPONENTS AND PRODUCTS

In addition to multiple glazing and storm windows, a wide variety of window insulating options are now available to designers, builders or owners for both new and existing buildings.

The selection of available window insulating options continues to grow as numerous new products enter the market each year. Some of these are fixed devices; others are designed to be deployed on a daily or seasonal basis. Many of the new products are descendants of traditional roller shades, shutters or storm windows (Fig. 11.29). Recently two new groups of products have appeared: roll-up insulating shutters (Fig. 11.30), which have been marketed for years in Europe and are now available here; and low emissivity plastic films and coatings on glass, sometimes called

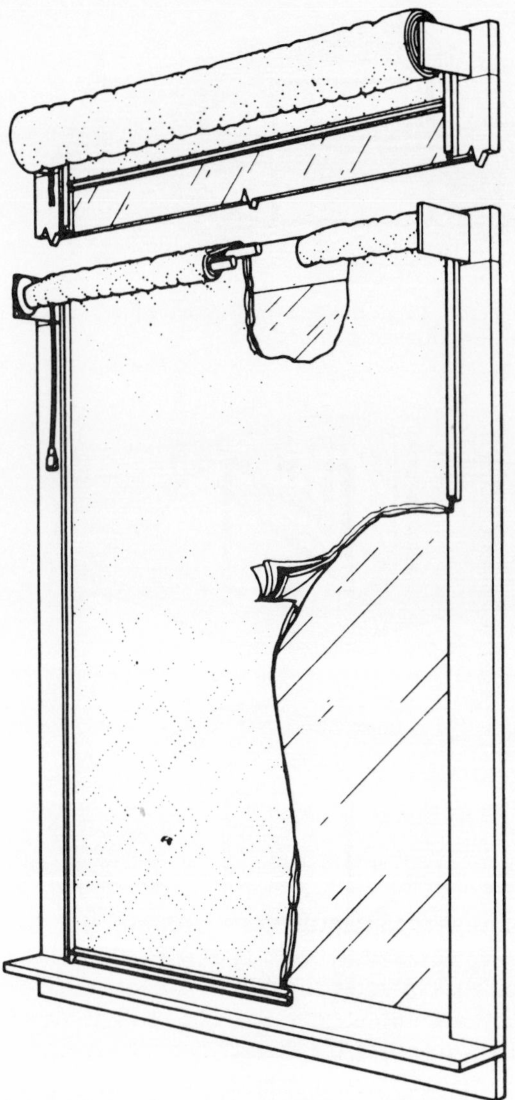

Fig. 11.29 Interior insulated fabric pull-down shade with PVC edge tracks.

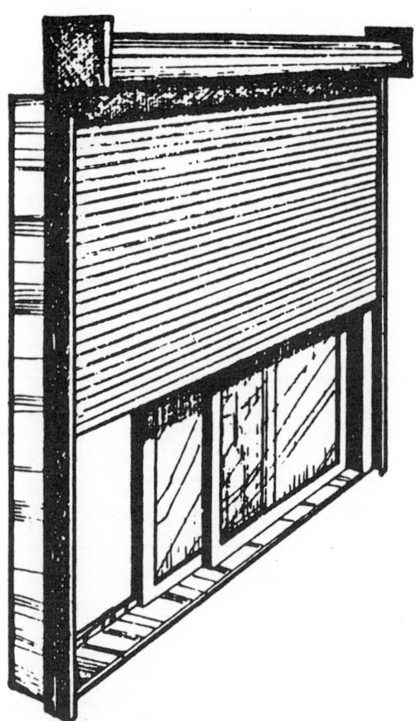

Fig. 11.30 Exterior pull-down shutter with wooden edge track.

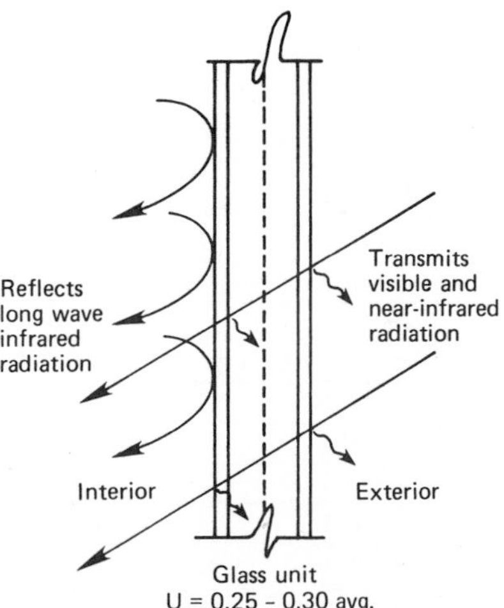

Fig. 11.31 Low emissivity glazing systems reflect heat energy (long wave radiation) back into the room. Low emissivity glazing material may be applied directly to glass surface or as a film suspended between two lights of glass.

"selective transmitters," which are being marketed by several solar control film and coatings manufacturers.

Low emissivity films or coatings reduce heat loss by reducing radiative heat transfer. They are sometimes thought of as infrared reflectors or mirrors because of their opaqueness to radiation in the far-infrared (heat energy) wavelength spectrum (Fig. 11.31). Most important, these materials can boost the inner glazing surface temperature by as much as 9° F over normal double glazing (assumes 0° F outside temperature, 70° F inside temperature, and a 15 mile per hour wind), resulting in a higher mean radiant temperature for the adjacent living space. A double glazed selective transmitter can have a U-value as low as 0.22 if the low emissivity coating is applied to a polyester film, suspended in a sealed double glazed window and has a solar transmittance of 70 percent. A low emissivity coating applied directly to the third glass side of a sealed double glazed window can achieve U-values as low as 0.30 and a solar transmittance of 70 percent.

Window insulating materials and devices have a number of common characteristics. An insulating layer (air gap, rigid board, multilayer films) reduces heat loss through conduction, convection and radiation. The insulating layer can be positioned in three locations relative to the window: internally, externally or between the layers of glass. Window insulating devices may be installed permanently, as is often the case with exterior or interior storm sash or low emissivity films located between two layers of sealed glass, or they may require active window management on a daily basis. When not in use, movable or regularly operated devices slide, roll, collapse or fold out of the way of the window to provide view, ventilation and solar penetration. Control of such devices may be though manual or automatic means.

TABLE 11.3 Comparison of available window thermal barriers

KEY:

D: Daily
S: Seasonal
Sec: SECurity
Pr: PRivacy
*: Not Available

NA: Not Applicable
VAR: Varies widely depending upon specific materials and designs
A: Based upon ASHRAE calculation procedures

M: Manufacturer's data
EM: Estimated from manufacturer's data
ES: Estimated from other sources

Product Type	Description	Trade Name	Manufacturer	Functions: Sun Control	Functions: Thermal Insulation	Functions: Infiltration Barrier	Functions: Security/Privacy	Management & Control: Static	Management & Control: Movable	Management & Control: Manual	Management & Control: Automatic	Applications: Window (vert.)	Applications: Skylight (horiz.)	Applications: Prime/Replacement	Applications: Add-on/Retrofit	Installation by: Homeowner	Installation by: Contractor	Thermal performance Btu/hr-ft²-°F (winter value): Device Conductance	U Value: Device plus single glass	U Value: Device plus double glass	Shading coefficient
More detailed information about products listed in this comparison matrix can be found in the product descriptions on the preceding pages of Windows, Vol. 1, No. 3.																					
Interior storm window	Acrylic glazing with a plastic frame	Thermatrol® storm window	Perkasie Industries Corp. 50 East Spruce St. Perkasie, PA 18944 (215) 257-6581		•	•			S	•		•			•	•	•	NA	.50 A	.32 A	a
Interior storm window	Vinyl film in an aluminum frame	Vinyl Therm	Insulated Pane Industries 2227A Heybourne Road Minden, NV 89423 (702) 782-5479		•	•			S	•		•			•	•		NA	.50 A	.32 A	a
Interior storm window	Glass in an aluminum frame	Kent Air Control Panel	Kent Air Control, Inc. 19 Belmont St. South Easton, MA 02375 (617) 238-1453		•	•			S	•		•			•	•		NA	.50 A	.32 A	a
Interior storm window	Acrylic glazing	Insulite, Magnetite	Northeast Energy Corp. 11 Beacon St. Boston, MA 02108 (617) 523-5632		•	•			S	•		•			•	•		NA	.50 A	.32 A	a
Interior storm window	Polyester film with plastic frame	Window Film™	Thermotech Corp. 410 Pine St. Burlington, VT 05401 (802) 658-6230		•	•			S	•		•			•	•		NA	.60- .50 A	.36- .32 A	a
Interior storm window	Plastic glazing with plastic frame	In-Sider® storm window	Plaskolite, Inc. P.O. Box 1497 Columbus, OH 43216 (800) 848-9124		•	•			S	•		•			•	•		NA	.50 A	.32 A	a
Interior storm window	Plastic film with aluminum frame	Flexigard storm window	3M Company Special Enterprises Dept. Bldg. 223-2, 3M Center St. Paul, MN 55101 (612) 733-0306		•	•			S	•		•			•	•		NA	.50 A	.32 A	a
Conventional multiple glazing	Window incorporating two or more glazing layers	Various	Various	•	•	•		•				•	•	•			•	.50: double .32: triple A, b, c			VAR

Low conductance insulating glass assembly	Sealed insulating glass with low emissivity coating and low conductivity gas fill	Thermoplus	Flachglas AG Auf der Reihe P.O. Box 669 D-4650 Gelsenkirchen, West Germany	●	●			●				●		●			●	.28- .32 M,c	NA	NA	.17- .55 M
Translucent sandwich panel	Two sheets of fiberglass bonded to aluminum frame	Kalwall®	Kalwall Corp. 1111 Candia Road P.O. Box 237 Manchester, NM 03105 (603) 627-3861	●	●		PR	●				●	●	●		●	●	.06- .40 M,c	NA	NA	.84- .04 M
Double wall plastic glazing	Extruded double wall glazing panel	Alkcobar, Acrylite	Alkco Manufacturing Company 734 North Pastoria Ave. Sunnyvale, CA 95086 (408) 733-3344; CY/RO Industries Wayne, NJ 07470	●	●			●				●	●	●		●	●	.58 M,c	NA	NA	.25- .88 VAR
Retrofit insulating glass system	Glass with aluminum frame dessicant and seal	Energy Seal Thermal Add-A-Pane System	Energy Seal Thermal Add-A-Pane 1 N. Wacker Drive Chicago, IL 60606 (312) 263-3132		●			●				●			●		●	NA	.49 A	.31 A	a
Insulating window film	Vacuum-deposited aluminum on a polyester film	Various. See accompanying text.	Various. See accompanying text.	●	●			●				●	●		●	●	●	NA	.83- .76 EM,d	.44- .42 EM,d	.25- .22 M
Drapery (conventional)	A wide variety of fabrics	—	Various	●	●		PR		D	●		●			●	●	●	NA	.83 A	.43 A	VAR A
Drapery, quilted	Polyester filled cotton	windowBlanket™	windowBlanket Co., Inc. Route 1 - Box 83 Lenoir City, TN 37771 (615) 986-2115	●	●		PR		D	●		●			●	●		.50 M	.34 EM	.25 EM	*
Drapery liner/shade	Metallized plastic film	Wind-N-Sun Shield	Commercial Drape & Design 464 N. Harbor City Blvd. P.O. Box 1434 Melbourne, FL 32935 (305) 725-7291	●	●		PR		D	●		●			●	●	●	*	*	*	*
Insulating drapery lining	Metallized polyester drape lining	NRG Shield	NRG Shields, Inc. 288 Willow Drive Levittown, PA 19054 L0700 (215) 943-8850	●	●		PR		●	D		●			●	●		*	*	*	*
Drapery gasket	Self-adhesive flexible gasket	Fluff Gasket	D. Russell & Associates 110 Riverside Drive Jacksonville, FL 32202 (904) 356-2654			●			●	D		●			●	●		NA	NA	NA	NA
Insulation panel	Manufacturing instructions	Solar Insolator/ Insulator Panel	Solpub Co. P.O. Box 2351 Gaithersburg, MD 20760	●	●	●			●	D		●			●	●		.33 M,e	.26 EM,f	.19 EM,f	*

(Continued)

TABLE 11.3 *(Continued)*

KEY

D:	Daily	NA:	Not Applicable	M:	Manufacturer's data
S:	Seasonal	VAR:	Varies widely depending upon specific materials and designs	EM:	Estimated from manufacturer's data
Sec:	SECurity			ES:	Estimated from other sources
Pr:	PRivacy				
*:	Not Available	A:	Based upon ASHRAE calculation procedures		

Product Type	Description	Trade Name	Manufacturer	Functions				Management & Control				Applications				Installation by		Thermal performance Btu/hr-ft²-°F (winter value)			
																			U Value		
				Sun Control	Thermal Insulation	Infiltration Barrier	Security/Privacy	Static	Movable	Manual	Automatic	Window (vert.)	Skylight (horiz.)	Prime/Replacement	Add-on/Retrofit	Homeowner	Contractor	Device Conductance	Device plus single glass	Device plus double glass	Shading coefficient
Insulation panel	Rigid foam insulation panels held in place by magnetic clips	Nightwall	Zomeworks Corp. P.O. Box 712 Albuquerque, NM 87103 (505) 242-5354	•	•		PR		•	D		•			•	•		.29 M,g	.27 EM,h	.21 EM,h	*
Interior folding shutter	Folding wood shutter with foam core for interior use	Insul Shutter	Insul Shutter, Inc. Box 338 Silt, CO 81652 (303) 876-2743	•	•	•	PR SEC		•	D		•			•	•		.16 EM	.14 EM,f	.12 EM,f	*
Sliding window insulating panel	Window incorporating a sliding interior insulating panel which is stored in a pocket in the wall	Sunflake Window System	Sunflake Window 625 Goddard Avenue P.O. Box 676 Ignacio, CO 81137 (303) 563-4597	•	•	•	PR, SEC		•	D		•		•		•	•	NA	.07 EM,f	NA	*
Shutter/heater	Hollow interior shutters	Window Solar Heater/Thermal Barrier	Solar Master, Inc. 223 East Knight Ave. Collingswood, NJ 08108 (609) 854-2960	•	•	•	PR		•	D		•			•	•		*	*	*	*
Skylight shutter	Aluminum skin over insulating core	Skylid	Zomeworks Corp. P.O. Box 712 Albuquerque, NM 87103 (505) 242-5354	•	•		PR, SEC		•		D		•		•	•	•	.33 M	.26 EM	.20 EM	*
Insulating window	Polystyrene beads in a double-glazed window	Beadwall	Zomeworks Corp. P.O. Box 712 Albuquerque, NM 87103 (505) 242-5354	•	•		PR		•	D	D	•		•			•	.13 M	NA	.11 EM	*
Roll-down shade (conventional)	Made from a variety of fabrics & plastics	—	Various	•	•		PR		•	D		•	•		•	•		NA	.85 ES	.43 ES	.25–.70 ES
Roll-down shade	Shade with metallized films	Various, see accompanying text	Various, see accompanying text	•	•		PR		•	D		•			•	•		NA	.52 ES,i	.33 ES,i	.16–.5 ES
Roll-down shade (side tracks)	Interior roller shade with side tracks	NRG Shade	NRG Shields, Inc. 288 Willow Drive Levittown, PA 19054 (215) 943-8850	•	•	•	PR		•	D		•			•	•		NA	.51 ES	.32 ES	.28–.51 ES

Interior Roller Shades (tape seals)	Interior roller shade with tape sealing to reduce air leakage	Minute Man storm windows adjustable™	Minute Man Anchors Co. 305 W. Walker Street East Flat Rock, NC 28726 (704) 692-0256		•	•			•	D S		•			•	•		NA	.5 A	.32 A	a
Roll-down shade	Roll-down shade system	Printaroll	MRS, 1800 New Highway Farmingdale, NY 11735 (212) 895-4788	•	•		PR		•	D	D	•			•		•	NA	.85 ES	.43 ES	*
Roll-down shade	Plastic or fabric shade system	Electro Shade	Electro Shade System Joel Berman Associates, Inc. 102 Prince St. New York, NY 10012 (212) 226-2050	•	•	•	PR		•	D	D	•			•		•	NA	.60- .85 M,j	.38- .48 EM,j	.25- .69 M,j
Roll-down shade	Vinyl-coated fiberglass	Sol-R-Veil®	Sol-R-Veil, Inc. 60 West 18th St. New York, NY 10011 (212) 924-7200	•	•		PR		•	D	D	•			•		•	NA	.90 ES	.44 ES	.12- .47 M,k
Roll-down shade	Multiple shade system with frame	Insealshaid™	Ark-tic Seal Systems, Inc. P.O. Box 428 Butler, WI 53007 (414) 276-0711	•	•	•	PR		•	D	D	•			•	•	•	.25 EM,m	.20 EM,m	.14 EM,m	.25 EM
Roll-down shade	Five layers of aluminized plastic with air spaces	High-"R" Shade™	Insulating Shade Co., Inc. P.O. Box 282 Branford, CT 06405 (203) 481-2337	•	•	•	PR		•	•		•			•	•	•	.08 EM	.07 EM	.07 M	*
Roll-down shade	Aluminized nylon	Curtain Wall	Thermal Technology Corp. P.O Box 130 Snowmass, CO. 81654 (303) 963-3185	•	•		PR		•	D	D	•			•	•	•	.11 M	.10 EM	.09 EM	.2 ES
Roll-down shade	Five layer quilt	Window Quilt	Appropriate Technology Corp. P.O. Box 975 Brattleboro, VT 05301 (802) 257-4501	•	•	•	PR		•	D		•			•	•	•	.31 EM	.24 M	.19 EM	*
Roll-down shade	Manufacturing instructions for quilted shade	—	Rainbow Energy Works 2324 Moraine Circle Rancho Cordova, CA 95670	•	•	•	PR		•	D		•			•	•		*	*	*	*
Interior roll-down slat shade	Hollow PVC slats	Thermo-Shade	Solar Energy Construction Company P.O. Box 718 Valley Forge, PA 19481 (215) 783-7735	•	•	•	PR, SEC		•	D	D	•			•	•	•	*	.40 ES	.30 ES	*
Venetian blind (conventional)	Plastic, metal or wooden slats	—	Various	•	•		PR		•	D		•	•		•	•	•	NA	.83 A	.43 A	.55- .64 A

(Continued)

TABLE 11.3 *(Continued)*

KEY

D:	Daily	NA:	Not Applicable	M:	Manufacturer's data
S:	Seasonal	VAR:	Varies widely depending upon specific materials and designs	EM:	Estimated from manufacturer's data
Sec:	SECurity			ES:	Estimated from other sources
Pr:	PRivacy	A:	Based upon ASHRAE calculation procedures		
*:	Not Available				

				Functions				Management & Control				Applications				Installation by		Thermal performance Btu/hr-ft²-°F (winter value)			
																			U Value		
Product Type	Description	Trade Name	Manufacturer	Sun Control	Thermal Insulation	Infiltration Barrier	Security/Privacy	Static	Movable	Manual	Automatic	Window (vert.)	Skylight (horiz.)	Prime/Replacement	Add-on/Retrofit	Homeowner	Contractor	Device Conductance	Device plus single glass	Device plus double glass	Shading coefficient
Venetian blind	Black/white slats	Solar Heating Venetian Blinds	Solar Master, Inc. 223 East Knight Ave. Collingwood, NJ 08108 (609) 854-2960	●	●		PR		●	D		●			●	●	●	NA	.83 A	.43 A	*
Storm windows (conventional)	Single glazing in metal or wood frame	—	Various		●	●		●	●	S		●			●	●	●	NA	.5 A	.32 A	a
Exterior roll-down shutter	PVC or aluminum double reinforced slats	Rolladen	American German Industries 14611 N. Scottsdale Rd. Scottsdale, AZ 85260 (602) 991-2345	●	●	●	PR, SEC		●	D	D	●			●		●	.92 EM	.45-.50 M	.29-.32 M	.04-.07 M
Exterior roll-down shutter	Hollow PVC slats	Roll-Awn	Abox Corp. 629-3 Terminal Way Costa Mesa, CA 92627 (714) 645-0623	●	●	●	PR, SEC		●	D	D	●			●		●	.63 EM	.40 M	.30 M	.04-.07 ES
Exterior roll-down shutter	Extruded hollow PVC slats	Rolsekur	The Rolsekur Corp. Fowler's Mill Road Tamworth, NH 03886 (603) 323-8834	●	●	●	PR, SEC		●	D	D	●			●		●	.92 ES	.45-.50 ES	.29-.32 ES	.04-.07 ES
Exterior roll-down shutter	PVC slats with aluminum track	Everstrait Rolling Shutter	Pease Co. Ever-Strait Division 7100 Dixie Highway Fairfield, OH 45023	●	●	●	PR, SEC		●	D	D	●			●		●	.92 ES	.45-.50 ES	.29-.32 ES	.04-.07 ES
Exterior roll-down shutter	Wood or plastic slats	Serrande Shutter	Serrande of Italy P.O. Box 1034 W. Sacramento, CA 95691 (916) 371-6960	●	●	●	PR, SEC		●	D	D	●			●		●	.92 EM	.50 M	.32 EM	.04 -.07 M
Exterior roll-down shutter	Wooden slats	Solex Wood Roll Shutters	Solex Div. of ELR, Inc. 244 San Lorenzo Ave. Coral Gables, FL 33134 (305) 443-1053	●	●	●	PR, SEC		●	D	D	●			●		●	NA	.63 ES	.40 ES	*

Exterior roll-down reefing-blind/shutter	Enameled aluminum louvres; pantograph mechanism	Guardian Shutter-Blind	Nichols-Homeshield, Inc. 1000 Harvester West Chicago, IL 60185 (312) 231-5600	•	•	•	PR, SEC	•	D	D	•	•		•		•	NA	.89 EM	.45 M	.13-.27 M
Exterior sliding or hinged shutter	Steel or aluminum panels	Willard Shutters	Willard Shutter Co. 4420 N.W. 35th Court Miami, FL 33142 (305) 633-0162	•	•		PR, SEC	•	D		•			•	•	•	NA	*	*	*

NOTE

Product descriptions, performance claims and data are reproduced from information supplied by the manufacturers. No claims are made concerning the validity or completeness of any product descriptions. The mention of certain company names or brand-name products is not intended as a recommendation of them over other companies or similar products on the market. Before purchasing or ordering any materials, it is sound practice to contact the manufacturer directly (or appropriate distributors and retailers) for complete information regarding a proposed application. Inclusion in this document does not constitute endorsement by the Lawrence Berkeley Laboratory, The University of California, or the U.S. Department of Energy.

[a] Reduces S.C. of prime window by 0.1–0.15
[b] Nominal value, 1/2″ air space, uncoated glass, no sash, frame.
[c] U value.
[d] Based upon reported emissivity of 0.2–0.3.
[e] Assumes 11/16″ polystyrene.
[f] Assumes air tight fit to window.
[g] Assumes 1″ beadboard.
[h] Assumes 5/64″ air gap between glass and panel.
[i] Assumes tight fitting shade.
[j] Single shade U = 0.85, double shade U = 0.68, double shade, metallized U = 0.60.
[k] Lower range for exterior application
[m] All three layers deployed.

1981, ASHRAE *Handbook of Fundamentals*

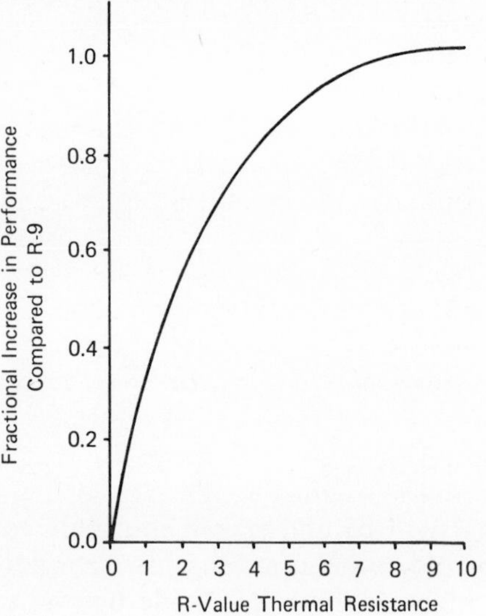

Fig. 11.32 Effectiveness of night insulation.

Photosensors, heat sensors or timers may be incorporated to control automatically devices requiring daily operation.

WINDOW INSULATION DESIGN CONSIDERATIONS

Effectiveness of Night Insulation

Climate Region A, as you may recall, recommends windows and glass doors with a U-value equal to or less than 0.39 or an R-value greater than 2.6. Generally, a lower U-value will provide better performance if the glazing system's net solar transmittance is not significantly below 60 to 65 percent. However, note that the law of diminishing returns plays a significant role in determining the most beneficial R-value and effectiveness of night insulation. As shown in Figure 11.32, a window system having a thermal resistance (R-value) of 4.5 achieves 80 percent of the performance of an R-9 window or door system.

The actual incremental savings for window insulation systems with R-values greater than 5 is quite small and R-values as low as 3 provide 62 percent of the benefit of an R-9 window insulation system.

An effective night insulation system first should provide a good seal to the window or frame to minimize convection losses. If air is allowed to leak around the insulation, then the resulting heat losses will severely reduce the value of the insulation system. Good seals between the insulation device and the window are more important than high R-values. The best return-on-investment should occur with window and door systems having a total R-value of 3.5 to 5.0 and tight seals.

Condensation

Insulating materials and devices positioned on the interior side of a window will reduce glass temperatures and increase the likelihood of condensation forming on the glass and window sash. The magnitude of this effect will be determined by the amount of air leakage around the insulating device and the window. Significant condensation may be caused either by excessive leakage of warm air into the cold air cavity between the window insulation and window or by excessive humidity in the home.

Infiltration

Air leakage through poorly engineered, badly installed or ill-fitting windows can be a substantial energy loss in new and existing homes alike. Properly installed, tight fitting thermal barriers can reduce this loss significantly. As previously mentioned, air leakage around the edge of an insulating device can dramatically reduce or completely negate its insulating value. Many window insulation products have numerous moving surfaces; therefore, seals and potential air leakage problems should be studied carefully.

Overheating

It is not inconceivable that many insulating devices may be either left in place or used year round. If the device seals tightly, preventing air leakage into or out of the cavity between the glass and device, overheating may occur when the sun strikes the window and the insulating device is in a closed position. This is particularly true if the window insulation is opaque or semi-transparent. Unless a venting option is part of the window management strategy the insulating device, window and all adjacent components must be designed to withstand the resultant high temperatures without failure.

Fire Safety

A number of window insulating assemblies are comprised of varying quantities of synthetic fibers, plastic foams and other materials containing potentially unhealthy compositions. If used improperly these could result in a smoke or fire hazard. Therefore, material properties, flame spread and toxic gases from inflamed devices are important considerations in evaluating the fire safety of window insulation devices.

Operational Reliability

The cost-effectiveness of movable window insulation devices is dependent upon three principal factors: cost of the device, local fuel prices and reliable operation by the occupant. The degree of user responsibility is critical because a fixed solution, such as multiple glazings or low emissivity films and coatings, with a higher thermal transmittance (U-value) will perform better than a device with a lower thermal transmittance which is deployed only occasionally. Although automated or motorized devices at first glance can overcome this potential barrier, cost constraints make it unlikely that individual windows can be automated cost effectively. Movable insulating devices must be opened and closed conscientiously to produce savings. One promising approach is to link the deployment of the thermal insulating equipment with an action that will be undertaken routinely to achieve privacy, such as pulling down a roller shade at night. If the roller shade has good insulating qualities, the occupant will be accruing thermal benefits while engaging in a very traditional routine, that of closing the shades at night.

Available Products

Table 11.3 compares some commercially available window thermal barriers. The list is by no means complete; sources for more extensive listings are noted in Appendix IV. The numerical performance data in the table have been assembled from calculations and data reported in manufacturers' literature. The source of the information is a comparative report prepared by the Lawrence Berkeley Laboratory Energy Efficient Windows Program in 1980. Due to the variety of sources, test procedures and calculation techniques, these relative values should be used with caution.

CHAPTER TWELVE

Case Studies

Two projects are presented in this chapter that were developed to assess the benefits and associated costs of certain energy conservation and passive solar design opportunities. The techniques implemented in the two projects fall within the framework of the recommendations put forth in the previous chapters.

The results are based on actual data collected over the past six years. Particularly valuable is the incremental cost information which gives a realistic perspective about the economic benefits of the recommendations presented throughout the previous eleven chapters. The following summaries are abstracted and adapted from papers published by the organizations responsible for the design, engineering, construction, and instrumentation of each case.

CASE STUDY 1—Energy Efficient Residence and Conventional Comparison Home

A comparative study of two homes designed and constructed by the NAHB Research Foundation, Inc.

The objective of this investigation was to demonstrate and measure residential energy conservation potential through the design, construction, and evaluation of a typical new home compared with an energy efficient modification of that (comparison) home using readily available products and techniques. The appearance and size of the home was not to be changed. The homes were designed and built in 1976–77 on adjacent lots in Mt. Airy, Maryland, about 40 miles north of Washington, D.C. Both lots sloped downward sharply to the south so that the basement in each home was completely below grade at the front (north) elevation and completely above grade at the rear (south) elevation.

Conventional Comparison Home (CCH)

The home selected for the CCH model was a best-selling model of a local Maryland builder. It had three bedrooms, two baths, and a full walkout basement. The 26-foot × 46-foot home (see Fig. 12.1) provided 1196 square feet on each level.

From an energy efficient standpoint, the rectangular one-story CCH model was already rather well protected thermally. The rectangular shape provided nearly the minimum ratio of exterior wall area to enclosed space and is more efficient than an L-, T-, U-, or H-shaped home.

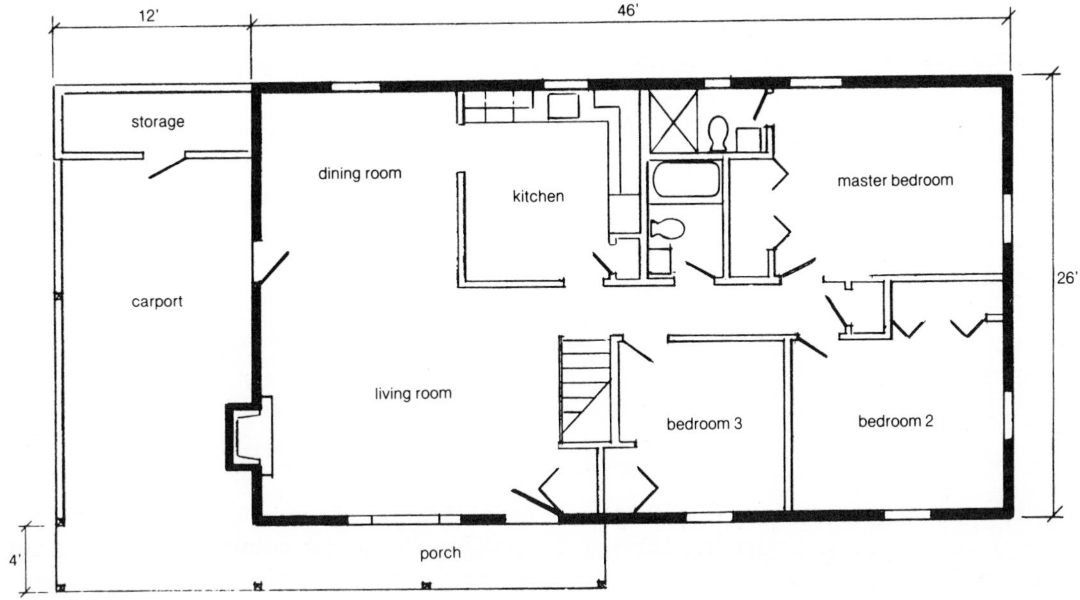

Fig. 12.1 Conventional comparison home floor plan

The general level of thermal protection was essentially equal to or better than similar homes in that section of the country in 1976. The home was oriented south to take advantage of passive solar gain. It had a roof overhang to shade south facing glass against the summer sun, R-19 insulation on the ceiling, R-11 in the walls, and tight fitting storm sash. In addition, the basement wall area above grade and for two feet below grade had R-11 insulation.

The total amount of glass area was 8.5 percent of the conditioned floor area, and the construction was such that the measured rate of air infiltration was quite low (average of 24-hour wintertime measurements was a 0.35 air change per hour). The home was equipped with an electric resistance furnace which is not as efficient in that climate as a heat pump. The basement area in both homes was well lighted by south facing windows and was conditioned to essentially the same temperature as the first floor.

The principal energy related features of the comparison home were as follows:

Design and Planning Features

- Compact rectangular plan (26-feet × 46-feet)
- South-facing windows provide passive solar gain in winter
- East-facing glass shaded by carport and west-facing glass only 1.5 percent of floor area
- Single story
- Full basement, about 50 percent below grade with south wall fully exposed above grade

Foundation/Floor

- Dry basement construction
- Gravel and sump with drainage to daylight under slab
- 6-mil polyethylene film under slab and behind concrete block walls where they are backfilled

- Exposed walls parged to seal concrete block against air infiltration and rain
- R-11 unfaced insulation attached with stick clips to basement walls above grade and 2 feet below grade
- Glass fiber sill sealer between foundation and sill plate
- R-11 band joist insulation
- Basement aluminum storm windows

Exterior Walls

- Conventional 2-inch × 4-inch wall framing 16 inches on center—approximately 20 percent of the opaque wall area is framing lumber
- R-11 kraft vapor barrier faced insulation
- R-1.22 insulation board sheathing
- Aluminum siding without backer
- Small amount of brick veneer (wainscoting) on front elevation

Doors/Windows

- Standard wood double hung windows, medium quality
- Standard aluminum storm windows, tight fitting
- Paneled wood front entrance door with two small glazed openings
- Field installed weatherstripping on the exterior doors
- Total window area 8.5 percent of floor area

Roof/Ceiling

- Conventional 2-inch × 4-inch trusses
- Gable end vents provide 1 square foot of ventilation for each 430 square feet of ceiling area
- R-19 blown fiberglass insulation
- Continuous 6-mil polyethylene vapor barrier below insulation
- 12 inch soffit overhang provides partial summer shading for south-facing windows

Heating/Cooling System

- Electric resistance furnace—forced air system
- Uninsulated ducts located within the conditioned space
- Masonry fireplace penetrating exterior wall

Water Heating/Appliances

- Standard electric resistance 52-gallon capacity water heater
- Frost-free refrigerator
- Range hood vented to outside
- Standard model dishwasher, clothes washer and dryer
- Standard electric range and oven

Energy-Efficient Residence (EER)

The energy efficient home dimensions were modified slightly by adding a vestibule and an outdoor storage space to one end of the house (see Fig. 12.2). Although this did not add to habitable space, the roof-covered porch area was greatly reduced in size which helped to offset some of the increased cost of the outdoor storage space and vestibule. The appearance was changed slightly by moving thc front door from the center to one end of the home. Exterior cladding and colors are the same as on the CCH (Figs. 12.3 and 12.4).

The interior plan was modified by converting the kitchen and living room/dining room space into two areas that could be separated—a living room and a family or retreat area somewhat like a country kitchen. The kitchen and eating space were separated from the retreat area by a low divider wall.

Although the amount of glass area was increased only slightly to 9.4 percent of the floor area, the amount of south-facing glass was increased, and triple glazing was used throughout. The measured rate of air infiltration was lower than in the CCH (average of

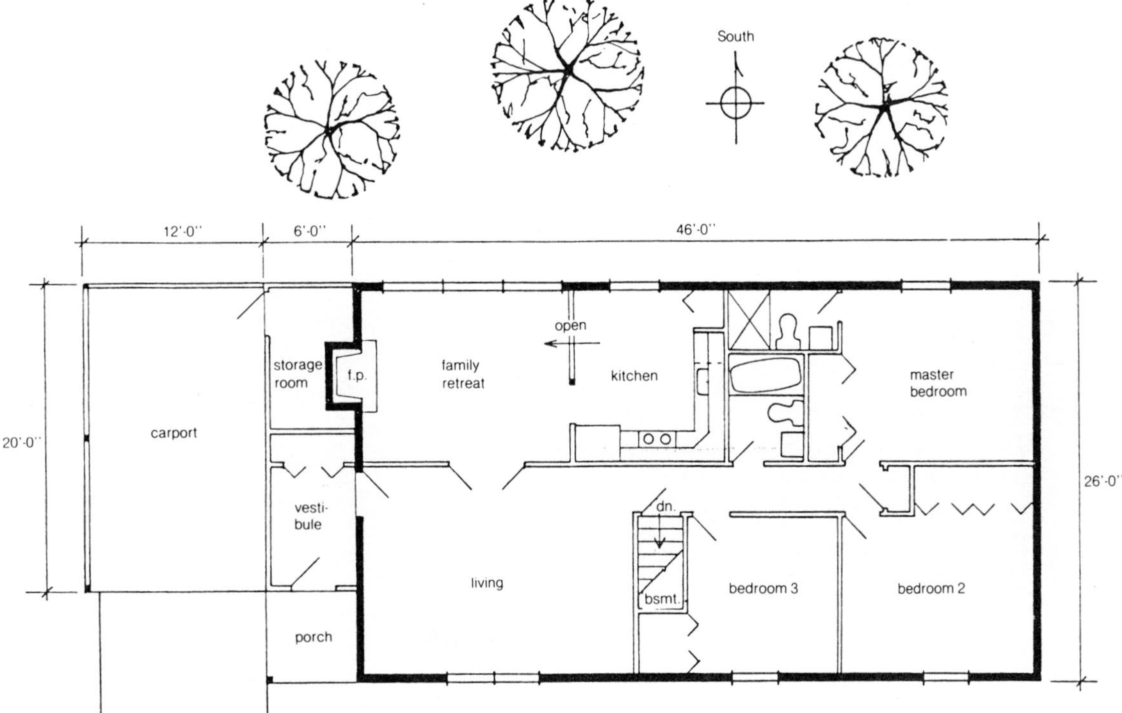

Fig. 12.2 Energy efficient residence floor plan.

Fig. 12.3 Photo of CCH.

Fig. 12.4 Photo of EER.

24 wintertime measurements was 0.19 air changes per hour). A triple split heat pump with a projected SPF in the Maryland climate of 1.9 was used.

The principal energy related features of the Energy Efficient Residence were as follows:

Design and Planning Features

- Compact rectangular plan (26-feet × 46-feet for habitable area)
- Unconditioned vestibule/storage room buffers end wall
- Vestibule "air lock" entrance isolates conditioned space
- 7 foot-6 inch ceiling height[1] reduces exterior wall area
- Family retreat room can be closed off for comfort conditioning
- Special fireplace has glass doors, damper, outdoor combustion air duct and a provision for circulating room air around fire box
- Increased area of south facing windows on main floor provides passive solar gain in winter
- Roof overhang designed to completely shade south facing windows in summer
- Deciduous trees on south side of home provide summer shading for basement wall and basement glass
- North facing window area reduced, and east and west facing windows eliminated

Foundation/Floor

- Dry basement construction with gravel and sump drainage to daylight under slab
- 6-mil polyethylene film beneath slab and behind concrete block walls to top of backfill

[1]Not a single visitor (including builders, architects, engineers, appraisers and mortgage lenders, as well as more than a thousand general public visitors) commented on the 7 foot-6 inch ceiling height.

- Exposed walls parged and painted to seal concrete block against air infiltration and rain
- 2-inch × 3-inch-24 inches on center basement wall studs set out 3 inches from wall to accommodate full thickness of R-19 insulation with no insulation compression
- R-19 pressure fit insulation batts on south, east and west basement walls
- R-11 pressure fit insulation batts on north basement walls
- 2 inch thick plastic foam perimeter insulation 2 feet wide, at exposed slab edges
- 1 inch glass fiber sill sealer between foundation and sill plate
- R-19 band joist insulation
- All utility entrances sealed with heavy caulk
- Basement storm windows

Exterior Walls (Fig. 12.5)

- Optimum Value Engineered (OVE) wall framing including 2-stud corners reduces lumber area to about 10 percent of opaque wall area
- Bottom plate sealed to deck with construction adhesive
- R-19 unfaced pressure fit insulation batts in walls, compressed to 5.5 inches equals R-17.9
- Continuous 6-mil polyethylene vapor barrier behind drywall
- R-5 plastic foam sheathing also covers band joist
- Plywood box-header over openings—insulated same as walls
- 2-stud corner posts with drywall backup clips and drywall clips at partition intersections
- Surface mounted electrical outlets with wiring beneath floor to avoid penetrating exterior walls

Doors/Windows

- Insulated steel entrance door with small double glazed openings and magnetic weatherstrip
- Mechanical door closer on outside entrance door
- Insulated steel, weatherstripped inner vestibule door
- Interior doors permit closing off family retreat area for comfort conditioning
- Well weatherstripped high quality windows with double insulating glass plus storm windows (triple glazing)
- Insulating drapes used at windows to reduce winter heat loss and summer heat gain
- Cracks around door and window frames filled with insulation and sealed with caulking
- Window area adjusted to 6.7 percent of floor area facing north and 12.2 percent of floor area facing south—average 9.4 percent

Roof/Ceiling

- Trusses cantilevered over wall top plate to allow full thickness of insulation at exterior wall
- 12 inch thick R-38 pressure fit insulation batts installed from below
- Continuous 6-mil polyethylene vapor barrier below insulation
- Gable end vents provide 1 square foot of ventilation for each 216 square feet of ceiling
- 24 inch soffit overhang provides summer shading for south facing windows
- Attic access door located in vestibule outside of conditioned area
- Only one surface mounted ceiling lighting fixture (kitchen), others wall mounted to avoid penetrating ceiling

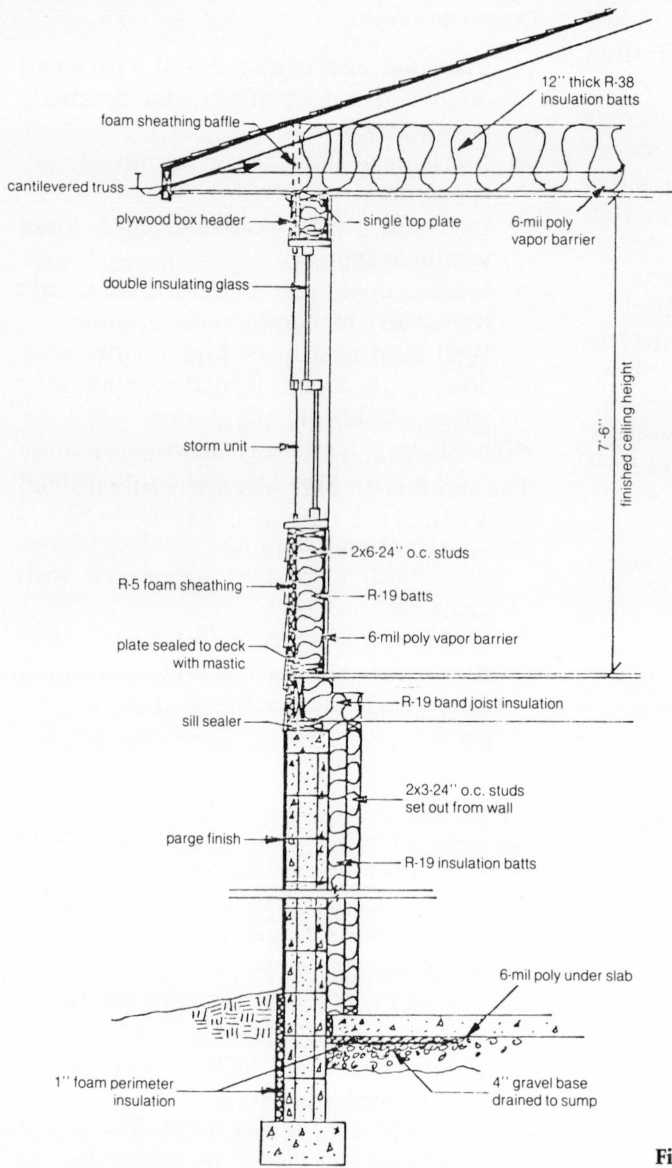

Fig. 12.5 Energy efficient residence wall section.

Heating/Cooling System

- Triple split heat pump, 240 volt 5 kW, two stage supplemental heat. Capacity at 47°F, 17,000 Btuh; COP 2.7; capacity at 17°F, 8,000 Btuh, COP 1.5. 6000 cfm at 0.5 inches static pressure. Compressor installed indoors.
- Simplified duct system with low inside registers and low central return—very short branch runs
- All ducts within conditioned space and trunk duct lined with ½ inch fiberglass duct liner (to maintain temperature of air delivered to habitable rooms)

- Controlled bypass on condenser coil for improved summer dehumidification
- Heat exchanger (desuper heater) on heat pump compressor to supplement domestic water heating energy
- Separate dehumidifier to control winter humidity without introducing outdoor air
- Manually controlled bathroom resistance heaters for increased comfort (if needed)
- Prefabricated circulator fireplace as noted above
- Large south-facing windows in family retreat area contribute passive solar heating in winter

Water Heating/Appliances

- Heavily insulated water heater with temperature set back to 120°F
- Hot and cold water pipes insulated to reduce heat loss and control summer condensation
- Low water use devices on kitchen faucet, bathroom faucets and shower heads
- High efficiency refrigerator with improved insulation, energy saving features
- Electric range with heavily insulated standard oven plus microwave oven
- Energy saving dishwasher uses less water and air circulation drying
- Front loading clothes washer uses less water, has load size scale and selector switch
- Bathroom vent fans with double damper, one at bathroom and one at exterior wall
- Fluorescent lighting, four times as efficient as standard incandescent bulbs, used whenever appropriate

Energy Use

Both homes were occupied with similar families—two young adults with two young school age children. Both families were asked to keep the thermostat at 70° in the winter and to set the thermostat at 78° when operating the air conditioner. Temperature measurement checks indicated that these instructions were well followed. Both families knew that energy consumption measurements were being taken but both were asked to live as they normally would in any home.

Numerous energy consumption measurements were made in both homes over a period of one calendar year, February 1, 1978 to January 31, 1979. In addition, local climate data was measured.

The winter climate was considerably colder than the estimated average at the site, 5460 degree-days versus 4600 degree-days. The summer climate was essentially normal, the same as the estimated 990 cooling hours (1 percent, 75°F) at the site.

Less Energy Used Than Projected

Actual consumption of energy for heating and for cooling in both homes was substantially below the projected (calculated) amount using ASHRAE modified degree-day method, see Table 12.1 below. Since this ("standard") method ignores heat gain from appliances, people, lighting and passive solar gain, it was expected that the projected energy consumption for heating would be too high. Evidently the method for determining energy consumption during summer is also too conservative (consumption estimates were higher than actual). It is probable that today's lifestyle and equipment and appliances do not result in adding a latent load to cooling equal to 30 percent of the calculated sensible heat gain, and other refinements also may be needed.

As can be seen in Table 12.1, even when adjusted for the actual local climate, the energy consumption for heating was 27 percent less than calculated in the EER and 38 percent less in the CCH. The energy required for cooling was 20 percent less in the EER than calculated and 14 percent less in the CCH. These figures include adjustments for the actual local climate, the actual air infiltration rates

TABLE 12.1 Electricity consumption—kWh, heating only and cooling only, EER vs CCH, February 1, 1978–January 31, 1979

	Heating Oct. 1–May 19		Cooling May 20–Sept 30	
	EER	CCH	EER	CCH
Projected	4,711*	18,766*	2,133	2,803
Actual	3,422	11,659	1,660	2,410
Difference	1,289	7,107	473	393
% Difference	27.4	37.9	19.5	14.0

* Adjusted for actual number of heating degree days, actual measured air infiltration and, for the EER, a heat pump SPF of 1.9. Cooling projected use adjusted, for estimated actual equipment EER based on manufacturers data.

and, for the EER, the actual heat pump SPF of 1.9. The EER home showed a significant reduction for heating compared to the CCH building. Table 12.2 summarizes the energy use for the two homes broken down by sector. For heating only, the EER home used 70.6 percent less energy, or a total of 3422 kWh for 231 days.

The large percentage reduction is even more significant when it is realized that there was nearly a 50 percent decrease in energy used for water heating (during the heating season), and therefore, the energy gain to the living space from the water heater was lower in the EER than in the CCH. Also, there was nearly 9 percent less energy used for appliances. This difference in internal use for appliances and water heating is nearly 2700 kWh for the heating season or about one half a kilowatt per hour.

However, actual savings for heating would have been a greater percentage had it not been for the considerably larger internal use of energy in the CCH home during the heating season.

Cooling Energy Use Less in EER than CCH

For cooling, the results are significant, although not quite as striking. Total cooling energy used was 31.3 percent less in the EER home, a saving of 750 kWh for the cooling season.

TABLE 12.2 Summary total energy use, CCH vs. EER, February 1978–January, 1979

	CCH kWh	EER kWh	Diff. %
Heating	11,659	3,422	70.6
Cooling	2,410	1,610	31.1
Water Heater	7,330	3,725	49.2
Range	502	917	(45.3)*
Refrigerator	1,710	1,117	31.1
Dishwasher	57	149	(61.7)
Clothes Washer	117	65	44.4
Clothes Dryer	1,035	805	22.2
Dehumidifier	—	45+	—
Lights and Misc.	1,689	1,515	10.3
Subtotal Appliances	5,110	4,673	8.6
Subtotal Appl. plus H.W.H.	12,440	8,398	32.5
Instruments	222	270	(17.8)
Total House	26,731	13,750	48.6

*( ) indicate % energy use greater in EER.

During the cooling season the internal use of energy for appliances and water heating was 34 percent lower in the EER than in the CCH, a difference of 1357 kWh or a little more than 0.4 of a kW per hour. In this case, the heat gain from this internal use works in the direction of making the cooling energy savings for the EER home appear to be better than it would have been had the internal loads been the same. As noted above, however, the effect is small since 89 percent of the difference is due to energy for water heating, only a small part of which adds to internal load.

Large Reduction of Total Energy Use in EER vs CCH

Total energy use during the heating season was 53.8 percent lower, and during the cooling season, 32.3 percent lower in the EER than in the CCH home. Total energy use in the CCH during the heating season amounted to 20255 kWh or 75.8 percent of the annual use. In the EER, total energy use during the heating season was 9358 kWh or 68.1 percent of the total annual use.

As can be seen in Table 12.2, the total difference for all energy use between the two homes was 12981 kWh, a 48.6 percent reduction. This was equal to an actual energy saving of $545 for the year at the then weighted average rate of $0.042/kWh. At the 1980 rate of about $0.05/kWh, the saving would be $649. Actual people hours of occupancy showed essentially identical internal loads due to occupancy.

Comfort

The comfort level in the CCH home was rated good by the occupants. Summer and winter temperature measurements, room-to-room, floor-to-ceiling, and mean radiant temperature (MRT) confirmed this. However, the comfort conditions in the EER were noticeably superior. Air temperature measurements in the EER showed that the abbreviated and unconventional air duct distribution system provided excellent comfort conditions. Floor-to-ceiling air temperature distribution in both homes was good. Generally, there was a difference of 2° to 3° from the floor (3 inches above) to ceiling (6 inches below) during the wintertime and somewhat smaller differences during the summer. Maximum room-to-room temperature variation at the 6 foot level above the floor was 1.9°F in the EER except on a sunny winter day when the temperature rise in the family retreat kitchen area increased that difference to about 4.8°F. In the CCH the maximum room-to-room temperature variation on a winter day with or without sunshine was about 4.6°F.

With the thermostats in both homes set at 70°F, the basement air temperature averaged 2.5° higher in the EER than in the CCH. Basement wall surface temperatures in the EER averaged about 5° higher in the EER than in the CCH.

The MRT, an important determinant of comfort, averaged over 4° higher in the EER than in the CCH. According to conventional wisdom, this means that the same family living in the EER would lower the thermostat some 4° to 7° below the temperature at which they would set the thermostat when living in the CCH. If so, that would have further reduced heating energy use by about 10 percent to 15 percent. This did not occur because we asked both families to keep the thermostat set at 70°F in the winter and 75° in the summer which they did.

The EER had higher (winter) interior surface temperatures: 4° to 6°F for walls; 5° to 13°F (except for single glazed areas, see below) for window and door surfaces; and 2° to 7°F for ceilings. Other surface temperature measurements quantified some known thermal short circuits. In the winter, the inside surface temperature of the through-the-wall brick fireplace (in the CCH) was 13.5° lower than the adjacent air temperature; the CCH attic scuttle closure (partially insulated) inside surface temperature was 10.5° below the adjacent air temperature; the single glazed picture window and lights in the entry door were 17° below the adjacent air temperature; and the range hood with metal ducts was 8°F below.

Cost Effectiveness

The exact energy saving contribution of each of the many different energy conserving techniques (ECTs) could not be determined in this experiment. However, by grouping the ECTs, it was calculated that the ECTs applied to the building envelope accounted for about 47 percent of the total saving of 12981 kWh; the water heater and the reduction of its operating temperature accounted for a little less than 28 percent; the heat pump, nearly 22 percent; the appliances (as used in these

TABLE 12.3 Added cost to homebuyer of energy efficient residence energy conserving features (1977 dollars)

Energy Feature	Cost
1. 2 x 6 wall framing with OVE details, plywood headers, and 7′-6″ ceiling	$ −75
2. Cantilever truss and overhang	176
3. Ceiling insulation (R-38)	334
4. Wall insulation (R-19)	115
5. Wall sheathing (R-5)	129
6. Basement insulation (R-19 and R-11) (includes furring)	407
7. Pipe insulation	89
8. Windows	949
9. Exterior doors	91
10. Floor plan and modifications (family retreat)	185
11. Vestibule, carport, storage and porch	1,039
12. Exterior wall outlets	82
13. HVAC system	482
14. Bathroom heaters	91
15. Fireplace	−185
16. Hot water preheater	544
17. Water heater	57
18. Range	585
19. Refrigerator	111
20. Dishwasher	141
21. Washer	35
TOTAL	$5,382

Table 12.4 Cost effectiveness of energy conserving techniques, EER vs. CCH, based on one year occupied measured performance

Item	*Added Cost*	*Savings*	*Time-to-recoup Investment*
Total—All ECTs	$5,382	$545	9.4 years
Total—All ECTs without hot water preheater and vestibule, etc.	$3,799	$545	6.7 years
Total—All ECTs without hot water preheater, vestibule, etc., and the four appliances (microwave oven, dishwasher, refrigerator and clothes washer)	$2,927	$542	5.2 years
Envelope including vestibule, storage, porch & carport modifications	$3,336	$256	12.3 years
Envelope without vestibule, etc.	$2,297	$256	8.6 years
HVAC system	$ 482	$119	4 years
Refrigerator	$ 111	$ 22	4.9 years
Total—All ECTs without hot water preheater, vestibule, etc., and without cost and savings of hot water heater and its lowered operating temperature	$3,742	$394	9.1 years

two homes) about two percent; and lights and miscellaneous a little over one percent of the total energy saving.

The total cost of the added energy conserving techniques to the buyer (1977) was $5,382. This includes $1039 for the vestibule, added outdoor storage space and modifications to the porch and carport. It also includes $544 for the desuper heater for preheating water going to the water heater. See Table 12.3 for detailed list of costs to the home buyer of the ECTs.

The researchers conclude that in a Maryland climate, the vestibule and, of course, the changes to the porch, carport and outdoor storage, contributed an insignificant amount of energy saving and were not cost effective. This is essentially because the well insulated thermal entry door also fitted very tightly and allowed very little air infiltration. Actually the two doors fitted so tightly that an air lock was produced, and the weatherstripping on the outer door had to be removed for closure and condensation control in the unheated vestibule area. Also, the inner entry door would have been protected from the prevailing winter wind if there had been no vestibule. The hot water preheater was not cost effective in this installation because this first-of-a-kind model only functioned part of the month of August and the resulting savings were negligible. Table 12.4 summarizes the cost effectiveness of the energy conservation features installed in the EER home based on one year of occupied measured performance.

This research has clearly demonstrated that energy conservation techniques actually do work. It showed that substantial amounts of energy and dollars can be saved using currently available products and techniques. It identified and highlighted some 70 techniques, most, but not all, of which can be used in most homes. Many are cost effective, some are not. It demonstrated that energy conserving homes are more comfortable, quieter, and cleaner.

In a more technical sense, this project provided the facts and data to establish a rational, practical, and realistic basis for comparisons and conclusions.

CASE STUDY 2—The Design and Construction of a Suntempered Home

Until recently, passive solar applications have been restrained by a number of barriers which have retarded their widespread acceptance and adoption by both homebuyers and homebuilders alike. These barriers have included less than acceptable architectural appearance, scant knowledge of costs and performance, unavailability of products with known performance and costs, and a general lack of trustworthy information on the marketability of homes with passive solar features. A principal objective of the project presented here has been to provide additional information to the building industry in order to overcome these real and perceived barriers to the utilization of passive solar concepts and principles such as these presented in this book. To determine the benefits and associated costs of direct gain passive solar design techniques, two homes of the same model were selected for a comparative side-by-side evaluation.

The homes discussed in this case study are part of a more extensive passive solar building system design, testing, and evaluation program conducted jointly by the National Association of Homebuilders Research Foundation, the Department of Energy, and builder firms throughout the United States. The purpose of the program has been to examine the thermal performance and cost effectiveness of a broad range of passive and active solar design strategies, systems, and products. The focus of this case study is one building which uses passive solar concepts and techniques described in detail throughout this book. They are most often referred to as suntempering or direct gain passive solar design techniques.

The home design used in this comparison study was selected because of its wide market acceptance by the home buying public and building industry. The design is commonly termed a bi-level home with a split foyer. The first home constructed was a conventional bi-level design with no provisions for passive solar gain or window management beyond standard builder practice. The south-facing glazing area is approximately 5.0 percent of the standard home's livable floor area. The second home, also a bi-level split foyer design, was modified to use the sun's energy in the most cost-effective manner. The south-facing glass area of the modified home is roughly 11 percent of the conditioned floor area. The homes are built on adjacent lots with a nearly due south orientation to allow easy comparison of their performance (Fig. 12.6). The two homes are located in Frederick, Maryland and were completed in January 1981. Since that time both homes have been thoroughly monitored to establish the thermal benefits and associated incremental costs of the passive solar design techniques and strategies that were presumed to be of a cost effective nature at the beginning of the study.

Building Description

The standard bi-level split foyer design is a 44-foot × 26-foot rectangular-shaped structure, with a contiguous living-dining-kitchen area on the upper level, and a plumbing core containing two bathrooms that divide the more public collective spaces in the home from the more private spaces comprised of

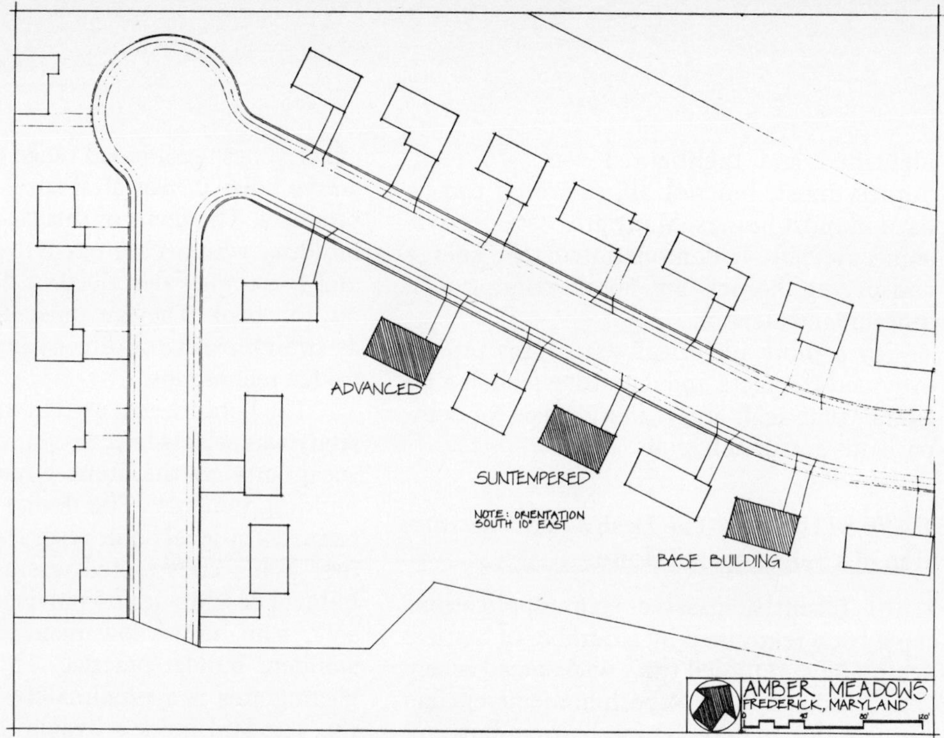

Fig. 12.6 Case study 2 site plan, Frederick, Maryland.

Fig. 12.7 Upper level floor plan of standard home.

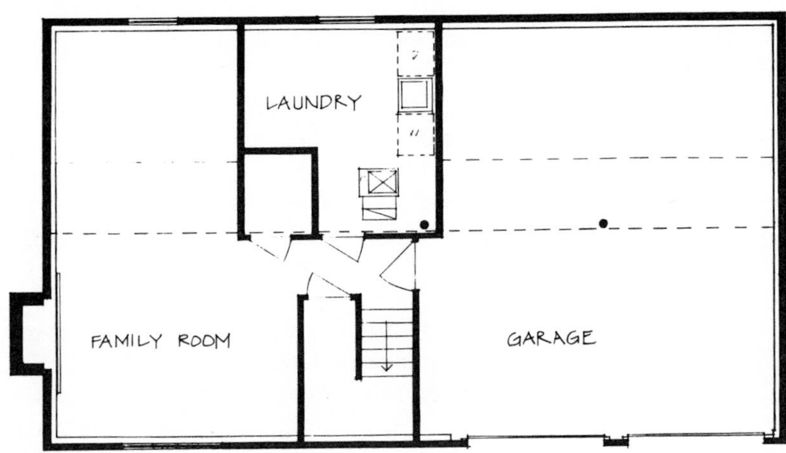

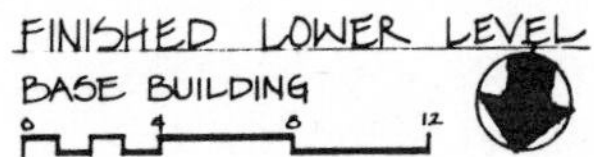

Fig. 12.8 Lower level of standard home.

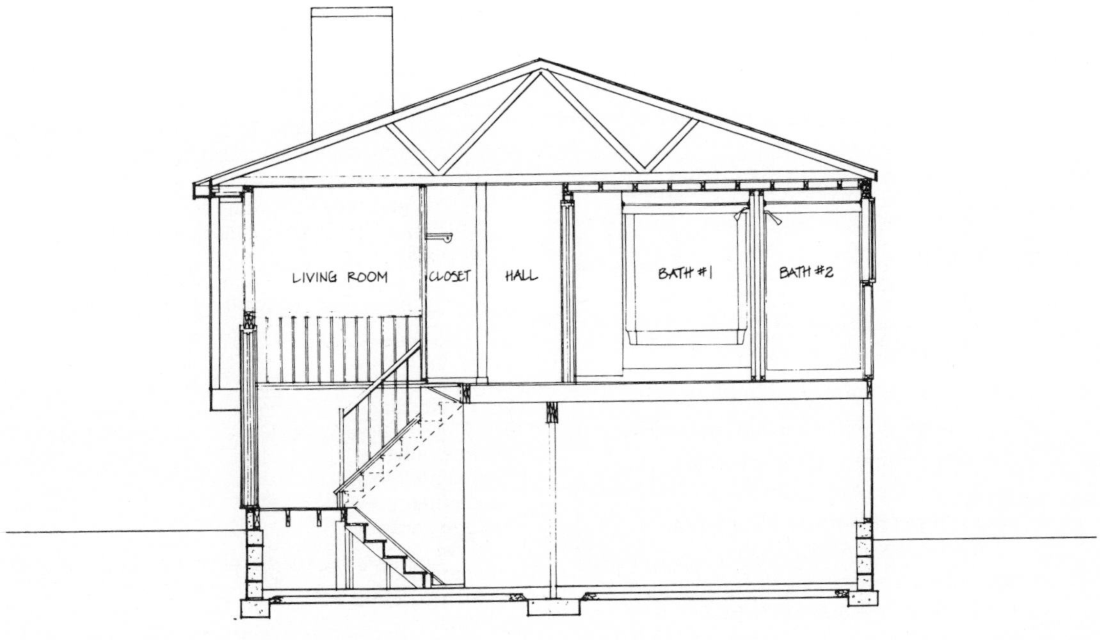

CROSS SECTION
BASE BUILDING
0 2 4 6 8

Fig. 12.9 Building section of standard home.

three bedrooms. (See Fig. 12.7.) The lower level is comprised of a family room, utility room and unconditioned double garage (Figs. 12.8 and 12.9). The standard or base house (the terminology used to describe the unmodified home) is insulated to industry standards (HUD recommended guidelines for this region). This includes R-30 ceiling, R-14 walls, double glazing on all windows, steel insulated doors, and foundation perimeter insulation. The building is equipped with a General Electric 24,000 Btu/hour heat pump with electric strip duct heaters that provides heat to the home during winter and removes heat from the conditioned space during the cooling season. During the monitoring period the heat pumps were not used, and heat was supplied by the electric strip heaters only in order to more easily quantify the auxiliary energy used in each home. The basic building characteristics are summarized in Figure 12.10.

The standard home's rear wall faces nearly due south and has 92 square feet of glass. There is no glass on the east or west walls of either the standard or suntempered home. The north-facing wall, which faces the street, of the standard home has 88 square feet of glass.

The suntempered bi-level home is essentially the same building as the standard home with some modifications for passive solar heating. The south-facing window area has been increased to approximately 150 square feet, or 61 percent over the standard home, and the north-facing glass reduced to 74 square feet or 16 percent less than the standard home. All the windows are triple glazed, and have an ASHRAE calculated U-value of 0.38. A two-foot overhang is pro-

A. *Building Characteristics of Standard and Suntempered Homes*

- 44′ × 26′ rectangular two-level home
- Bi-level with split foyer entry
- Open space plan
- Rear elevation faces south within 10°
- Ceiling insulation—R-30 (U = 0.03)
- Wall insulation—R-14 (U = 0.07)
- Basement insulation—R-14 (U = 0.07)
- Windows (ASHRAE calculated values)
  Standard home—clear insulating glass U = 0.58
  Suntempered home—clear insulating glass plus interior storm sash U = 0.38
- Auxiliary energy: Air to air heat pump with electric resistance furnace C.O.P. = 1.7

B. *Thermal Performance Summary: Normalized Performance of Standard and Suntempered Homes at 70°F Operating Temperature*
Location: Frederick, Maryland
Measurement Period: October 1, 1981–April 30, 1982

	Standard Building	Suntempered Building	Units
Gross south glass area	92	150	Sq. ft.
Load collector ratio	96	54	LCR
$Base_{70}$ degree days	5883	5883	D.D.
Internal gains	1.5	1.5	MMBtu
Transmitted solar radiation	6.65	11.29	MMBtu
Auxiliary heating energy requirement	44.81	32.35	MMBtu
Auxiliary cooling energy requirement	7.90	6.80	MMBtu
Percent solar contribution	13	26	%
System cost (1983 dollars)	–0–	950.00	$

Fig. 12.10 Building characteristic and thermal performance summary

Fig. 12.11 North elevation of standard home.

Fig. 12.12 South elevation of standard home.

Fig. 12.13 North elevation of suntempered home.

vided on the south side to shade the upper level windows during the cooling season. Seasonally installed fiberglass shade screens

Fig. 12.14 South elevation of suntempered home.

are used to shade the glass area not protected from the sun by the overhang. Figs. 12.11–12.14 provide views of the north and south elevations of each completed, occupied home.

The heat distribution system in the suntempered home is equipped with a fan-only cycle that recirculates air to minimize temperature stratification and enhances the building's effective heat storage capability. The fan-only cycle removes air from the ceiling of south-facing spaces via a return duct located high in the wall. The warm room air is circulated to the supply plenum, by-passing the heater coils, and distributed through the supply air register located at the floor level in each room. This system minimizes vertical stratification within each room and horizontal temperature stratification between north and south rooms. Minor floor plan modifications have been made in the kitchen and family room to accommodate the additional south-facing glass. These changes have resulted in a more open kitchen-dining area and a larger family room. Both changes reflect an increasing homebuyer desire for larger open, more informal spaces that can serve a multiple function. This concept is often referred to as a great room, where cooking, dining and living areas are closely linked.

Costs

The building modifications add approximately $1,250.00 to the sales price of the standard home in 1982 dollars. Triple glazing adds $225.00 or $1.00/square foot to the cost of the windows. The shade screens for the south windows add approximately $230.00 or $1.50/square foot. The increased south glass area including a credit for the decreased north glass area increases the sales price by approximately $450.00 or $10.00 per square foot of glass area. The windows have aluminum frames with a complete thermal break and are of good quality. Higher or lower quality windows could of course affect their incremental cost. The fixed overhang, minor partition changes and the high return air ducts and controls for the fan-only cycle add an additional $355.00 to the selling price. It may be observed that the fixed overhang and seasonal shade screens perform a redundant function in shading the upper level windows. Due to the limitations of fixed overhangs which have been verified in this field test, we recommend using only the exterior seasonally operated shade screen. The shade screen used for this study has a shading coefficient of 0.34 yielding a total glazing assembly shade coefficient of 0.25. The shade screen system eliminates the need for the overhang and thus could reduce the total cost of the passive solar modifications from $1250.00 to $950.00, or by $300.00, resulting in more effective annual shading, especially during the spring and fall months. The screen is usually deployed in early June and removed at the end of September.

Performance Summary

The two buildings have been extensively monitored since their completion in January 1981. During the winters of 1981 and 1982 the passive solar modifications have accounted for a 25 percent reduction in annual heating and cooling energy consumption. The standard building energy consumption is approximately 40 million Btu's while the suntempered home consumes roughly 30 million Btu's. The simple payback period for the modifications made to the reference house to increase the passive solar contribution is 6.5 years in the region that the homes are located. This is based on an electric rate of $0.05/kWh. Importantly, the annual savings generate a positive cash flow within the first two years, which means the annual savings are greater than the incremental increase in the mortgage payment attributable to the modifications after two years of operation. This is assuming a 13 percent fixed rate mortgage.

Conclusion

Modest modifications to a conventional popular style home can produce a 25 percent reduction in annual energy consumption without significant incremental costs. This savings is even greater when compared to homes with non-south orientations and little or no window management. Results from studies presented in Chapter 10 show savings as high as 40 percent in the Washington region where another comparative study was undertaken.

The purpose for reporting these two projects has been to support and validate many of the recommendations presented in earlier chapters. The case studies have been intentionally brief, including only the primary bottom line results. More extensive reports are available for the two case studies as well as the computer studies used to prepare Chapter 10 by writing the sponsors cited in the reference section.

Residence Description and Parametric Computer Study Methodology Summary—CCB/Cumali Associates

The residence used in this computer study to determine beneficial window areas and effects of window management strategies was a 1232-square-foot single-story home. For the purposes of the study, the home was divided into three thermal zones: a combined living room/bedroom zone having windows facing primarily to the south; a dining/kitchen zone to the northwest; and combined bedroom/bath zone to the northeast (Fig. A.1).

The home studied was insulated to HUD Residential U—Value Requirements. The insulation levels in the external walls, roof and floor were adjusted to yield the overall U-value required by the HUD standard in each climate region studied.

- South facing window areas were varied in the following manner: Eight areas of glazing were analyzed, ranging from a low of 15 percent of the south wall area (4.3 percent of the floor area) to a high of 50 percent of the wall area (14.3 percent of the floor area) in increments of 5 percent (1.4 percent of floor area).
- The west facing dining/kitchen window was fixed at 20 percent of the wall area and the east facing bedroom was fixed at 18 percent of the wall area. (These areas reflect the gross window size which includes framing.) The actual pane area is 0.887 times the gross area.
- Two-foot overhangs along the north and south elevations of the building were used to shade the windows from summer sun.
- An active window/shade management scheme, including the dropping of interior roller shades and the opening of windows in each of the three thermal zones, was incorporated into the analysis to reduce cooling requirements.
- The roller shades were used during sleeping hours from 11:00 PM to 6:00 AM and also during the hours the sun was down, defined by calculations performed from parameters on each climate weather tape. Likewise, windows were not opened during these times.
- In general, the management scheme was deployed based primarily on the computed zone temperature. During the winter months of January, February, March, November and December, this temperature was set to 79°F; in all other months, the value was 75°F. The management option was not implemented at zone temperatures below these values.
- For roller shades, a shading coefficient equal to 0.37 was used to adjust the transmitted solar radiation and the overall

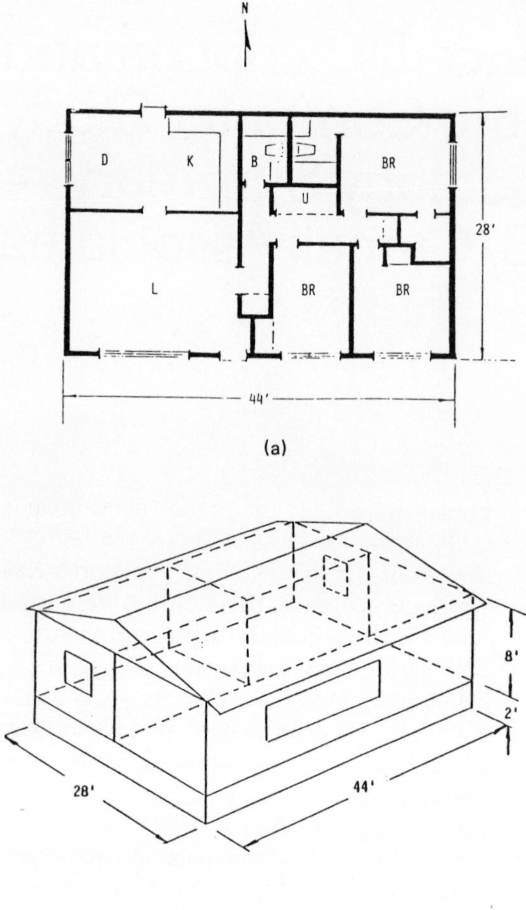

Fig. A.1 (a) Floor plan of DOE 2-A house, (b) Isometric showing thermal zones for blast simulation.

window U-value was decreased by 0.1 Btu/hr/°F.

- A constant value of 10 air changes per hour (ACH) was used to define the natural ventilation quantity obtained by opening the windows. The assumption also was made that this value occurred at a window opening equal to 50 percent of the window area.
- If the 10 air changes resulted in excessive cooling, operation of the heating unit was reduced in increments of 25 percent of the base value. The natural ventilation provided by opening the windows was reduced by 50 percent if the roller shades previously had been deployed.
- A dual set-point thermostat was used to control the heating and cooling units. The cooling set-point was defined as 80°F throughout the year and the heating unit set-point at 65°F during sleeping hours (11:00 PM through 6:00 AM) and at 68°F at all other times. In addition, the cooling unit was operated in the residence for excessive humidity/temperature conditions, defined as relative humidity levels greater than 70 percent of zone temperatures of 75°F.
- The heating unit was a gas-fired furnace with a seasonal efficiency of 60 percent. The cooling unit was defined as an air-cooled reciprocating compressor having a COP of approximately 1.8. Both of these values varied with climate and building configuration.
- Infiltration was specified as 0.6 ACH to which a wind speed correction was applied. Changing the infiltration calculation to account for temperature variations between outside air and indoor temperatures yields an increase in the heating load of 175 to 200 percent, depending on the climate analyzed. Although this procedure dramatically affects the absolute values presented graphically in Chapter 10, the slope of the curve would not be altered. Therefore, irrespective of which method is used to calculate the effect of infiltration, the effect of increased glazing areas can be assessed from the data presented.
- A total of seven cities (climates), two floor types, three to eight primary orientations and eight window areas were studied.
- A version of the DOE-2A Energy Analysis Computer Program, modified by Cumali Associates, was used to perform this study.

Residence Description and Parametric Computer Study Summaries—Lawrence Berkeley Laboratory Solar Group

Some of the results presented in the text are drawn from two computer studies conducted by the Lawrence Berkeley Laboratory's Solar Group: *Human Comfort and Control Considerations in Passive Solar Structures*, and *The Impact of Orientation on Residential Heating and Cooling* (see Bibliography). In both studies a parametric analysis was performed to compare heating and cooling loads for a residential prototype building at different orientations in 25 United States cities distributed throughout a variety of representative climate zones.

The building energy analysis computer program, known as "Building Loads Analysis and System Thermodynamics" (BLAST), was used for the simulations. BLAST was developed by the United States Department of the Army Construction Research Laboratory.

While it is not possible to define a "typical" residence in the United States, the structure analyzed in these studies is reasonably representative of a broad range of designs. The building is a rectangular (49 foot × 24 foot) single-story home having 1176 square feet of conditioned floor area. The home was divided into three thermal zones (Fig. A.2).

Constructions and details of analytical assumptions follow:

- The home's floor construction is a 4-inch concrete slab-on-grade with two inches (R-10) of foam board beneath. Half of the floor area is assumed to be covered with carpet.
- The walls are constructed of normal 2 × 6 framing lumber with half-inch gypsum board, R-19 insulation, foam insulation board sheathing and wood siding.
- Heat transfer through the stud and insulated wall cavities are analyzed separately. A 20 percent "stud" (solid lumber) fraction of each external wall is aggregated for each thermal zone and wall orientation. The average exterior wall R-value is 21.
- A nominal R-38 insulated gypsum ceiling separates the conditioned living space from the attic.
- All windows are double glazed and are considered to have an average U-value of 0.53.

South facing window areas were varied in the following manner: In the first study, four areas of glazing were analyzed ranging from a low of 11.2 percent of the south wall area (3.7 percent of the floor area) to a high of 44.8 percent of the south wall area (14.9 per-

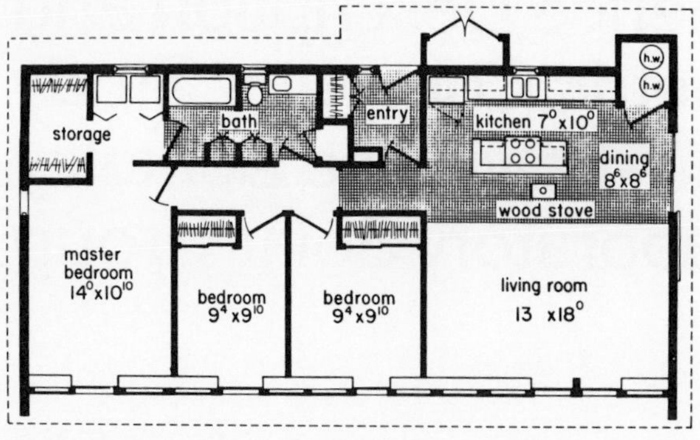

(a)

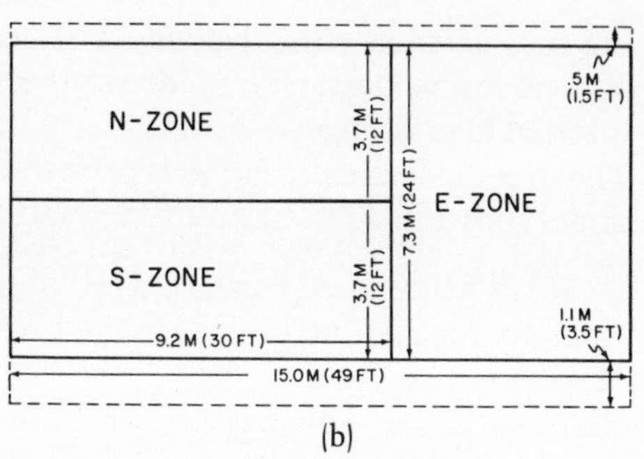

(b)

Fig. A.2 (a) Floor plan of LBL house. (b) Floor plan showing thermal zones for blast simulation.

cent of the floor area) in increments of 11 percent (3.7 percent of the floor area) for the cities of Washington, D.C., and Albuquerque, New Mexico.

In the second study, the glazing is unevenly distributed over the four exposures: 132 square feet appear on one of the long facades, while the remainder (44 square feet) is allocated to the opposite side of the structure to provide a path for ventilation air. There are no windows on the gable end walls of the home.

- A 1.5-foot overhang along the north and south elevations of the building was used to shade the windows from summer sun.
- The results do not consider any special window controls or even common window management such as drawing shades (although the ventilation simulation can be said to approximate the effect of opening windows at appropriate times).
- The building is assumed to be occupied and to have typical levels of internal equipment and lighting loads. The auxiliary heating and cooling equipment is controlled entirely by air temperature thermostats. The heating and cooling systems are assumed to have sufficient capacity to meet the loads in the structure for all hours of the year. Since the three zones in the structure are considered to be thermally coupled through conduction and not convection, the heating and cooling system is controlled separately for each zone. The cooling thermostat is set at 78°F for the entire simulation period while the heating thermostat is at 70°F during the daytime hours and has a nighttime setback to 60°F from 11:00 PM to 7:00 AM.
- Temperature Schedule—Interior temperature in the occupied space is maintained in the range of 70°F to 78°F for the entire year. Heating loads occur when the lower limit must be maintained by the auxiliary system; cooling loads occur to maintain the upper limit. The interior temperature is allowed to float between those limits without causing any load. The attic temperature is allowed to float unconstrained.
- The total daily load attributed by internal gains is 15.6 kWh (53,240 Btu). The load has been allocated between the three zones on an hourly basis. They include the effects of 2.2 occupants and of appliances and equipment typically found in homes.
- For the conditioned space, 0.6 air changes per hour (ACH) at design wind and temperature difference conditions is assumed. A design rate of 2 ACH is assumed for the attic.

TABLE A.1 Configurations analyzed

Double pane, slab on ground	
Minneapolis MN	N NE E SE S SW W NW
Chicago IL	SE E SW
St. Louis MO	SE E SW
Atlanta GA	N NE E SE S SW W NW
Dallas TX	SE E SW
Boston MA	SE E SW
Portland OR	SE E SW
Double pane, crawl space	
Minneapolis MN	SE S SW
Chicago IL	SE S SW
St. Louis MO	SE S SW
Atlanta GA	SE S SW
Dallas TX	SE S SW
Boston MA	SE S SW
Portland OR	SE S SW
Triple pane, slab on ground	
Minneapolis MN	N NE E SE S SW W NW
Chicago IL	N NE E SE S SW W NW
Atlanta GA	N NE E SE S SW W NW
Boston MA	N NE E SE S SW W NW
Portland OR	N NE E SE S SW W NW

Important Note: The data presented for the reference home should not be extrapolated to determine the actual energy consumption of other homes. Its value is to provide a sense of the relative impact of orientation, glass area and type and thermal mass on a typical home's annual energy consumption.

- Two ventilation strategies, one for the heating season and one for the cooling season, were instituted. The former consisted of ventilation of the space only during the occasional cooling load, when the outside temperature permitted immediate ventilation cooling. During the cooling season, the building was ventilated whenever it was possible to lower the inside temperature by such a strategy. If the heating set-point (70°F) was reached, the ventilation was shut off. The period in which this precooling strategy was employed was determined by heating and cooling loads from baseline simulations.
- The building energy analyses utilized in this study were a developmental version of the public domain program BLAST 3.0.

For this book several features of the program are especially important:

- Heating and cooling loads are calculated on an hourly basis.
- Analysis of solar gains through windows and opaque surfaces is performed in considerable detail using beam, diffuse and ground reflected solar radiation data, taking into account time dependent effects of conduction through outside walls and internal heat storage.
- The thermal load calculation is performed under controlled floating air temperature conditions. The control strategies are user defined and scheduled so that thermostat setbacks can be reliably simulated.
- The program utilizes an interactive thermal balance technique which allows simultaneous simulation of adjacent zones while properly accounting for the dynamic effects of thermal storage in conductive heat transfer through the constructions defining the individual zones.

The weather data used in the loads calculations was taken from TMY weather tapes derived by the National Oceanic and Atmospheric Administration (TMY tapes and documentation are available from NOAA, Asheville, NC). They are aggregates of statistically selected "typical" months from the long term SOLMET data base. TMY data provide sufficient detail and a consistent format for reliable parametric studies. Of particular importance to orientation issues is the heavy weighting given to measured solar radiation in the statistical selection of "typical" months. The hourly data were used to drive annual BLAST simulations of the prototype residence.

APPENDIX III

References

FURTHER INFORMATION ON SOLAR LAND PLANNING

American Institute of Architects Research Corporation, *Regional Guidelines for Building Passive Energy Conserving Homes*, U.S. Department of Housing and Urban Development, Washington, D.C., 1978.

American Institute of Architects Research Corporation, *Solar Dwelling Design Concepts*, U.S. Department of Housing and Urban Development, Washington, D.C., 1978.

American Planning Association, *Energy-Conserving Development Regulations: Current Practice.* Prepared for the Energy and Environmental Systems Division, Argonne National Laboratory, May, 1980. (ANL/CNSV-TM-38.)

American Society of Landscape Architects Foundation, *Landscape Planning for Energy Conservation*, Environmental Design Press, Reston, VA, 1977.

Overcoming Land Use Barriers to Solar Access: Solar Planning Recommendations for Local Communities, Central Naugatuck Valley Regional Planning Agency, Waterbury, CT, 1980.

Zanetto, J., Hammond, J. J., Adams, C.; *Planning Solar Neighborhoods*, prepared for the California Energy Commission, Sacramento, CA, April 1981. Contract #P5 00-81-018.

Erley, Duncan and Martin Jaffee: *Site Planning for Solar Access: A Guidebook for Residential Developers and Site Planners*, The American Planning Association for the U.S. Department of Housing and Urban Development and the U.S. Department of Energy, September, 1979. (HUD-PDR-481.)

Geiger, R.: *The Climate Near the Ground*, Harvard University Press, Cambridge, MA, 1975.

Givoni, B.: *Man, Climate, and Architecture*, Elsevier Publishing Company, London, England, 1976.

Jaffe, Martin and Duncan Erley: *Protecting Solar Access for Residential Development: A Guidebook for Planning Officials*, prepared by the American Planning Association for the U.S. Department of Housing and Urban Development and the U.S. Department of Energy, February, 1980. [HUD-PRD-445(2).]

Johnson, Ralph J., and Arthur W. Johnson: *Designing, Building and Selling Energy Conserving Homes*, National Association of Home Builders, Washington, D.C., 1978.

Johnson, Ralph J., and Arthur W. Johnson: *Insulation Manual-Homes/Apartments, NAHB Research Foundation, Inc., Rockville, MD 20850, 1979.*

Johnson, Ralph J., Donald F. Luebs, and Ronald K. Yingling: The Energy Efficient Residence (EER) Research Results, prepared by NAHB Research Foundation, Inc., for the U.S. Department of Housing and Urban Development, September, 1980.

Land Development 2, National Association of Home Builders, Washington, D.C., 1981.

Mazria, Edward: *The Passive Solar Energy Book*, Rodale Press, Emmaus, PA, 1970.

McClenon, Charles, ed.: *Landscape Planning for Energy Conservation*, American Society of Landscape Architects Foundation, Environmental Design Press, Reston, VA, 1977.

McHarg, Ian: *Design with Nature*, Doubleday/Natural History Press, NY. 1971 edition.

Cost Effective Site Planning: Single Family Development, National Association of Home Builders, Washington, D.C., 1976.

Planning for Housing: Development Alternatives for Better Environments, National Association of Home Builders, Washington, D.C., 1980.

Residential Site Planning Guide, National Association of Home Builders, Washington, D.C., 1975.

National Solar Heating and Cooling Information Center, *Local Solar and Conservation Legislation*, Solar Data Bank Report, Rockville, MD, revised ed. October, 1980. (CBR-120.) List is updated quarterly.

Olgyay, Aladar and Victor Olgyay: *Design with Climate*, Princeton University Press, Princeton, NJ, 1963.

Olgyay, Aldar and Victor Olygay: Solar Control and Shading Devices, Princeton University Press, Princeton, NJ, 1957.

Ridgeway, James and Carol S. Projansky: *Energy Efficient Community Planning*, J. G. Press, Emmaus, PA, 1979.

Robinette, Gary O., ed.: *Land Planning for Energy Conservation*, Environmental Design Press, Reston, VA, 1977.

Robinette, G.: *Plants/People/and Environmental Quality*, Stock No. 2905-0479, U.S. Government Printing Office, Washington, D.C., 1972.

Site and Neighborhood Design for Energy Conservation—5 Case Studies, prepared for the U.S. Department of Energy, Community Systems Program in cooperation with the Argonne National Laboratory, Energy and Environmental Systems, n.d.

Solar Envelope Zoning, Solar Energy Research Institute, Golden, CO, 1980.

Building with Passive Solar, Southern Solar Energy Center, Atlanta, GA, 1981.

Solar Site Planning, Southern Solar Energy Center, Atlanta, GA, 1981.

Spivak, Paul: *Land-Use Barriers and Incentives to the Use of Solar Energy*, Solar Energy Research Institute, Golden, CO, August, 1979. (SERI/TR-62-267.)

U.S. Department of Commerce, *Climatic Maps of the United States*, Publications Unit, National Climatic Center, Asheville, NC, 1977.

Zanetto, James: "The Location and Selection of Trees for Solar Neighborhoods," *Landscape Architecture*, vol. 68, no. 6, November, 1978.

SOLAR HOME DESIGN AND GLAZING

Anderson, Brandt, Ronald Kammerud, Wayne Place: *Human Comfort and Auxiliary Control Considerations in Passive Solar Structures*, Lawrence Berkeley Laboratory Report-10034. Prepared under contract to the U.S. Department of Energy #W-7405-Eng-48, April, 1980.

Anderson, Brandt, Ronald Kammerud, Wayne Place, Peter Scofield: *The Importance of Residential Building Orientation*, Lawrence Berkeley Laboratories. Prepared under contract to the U.S. Department of Energy #W-7405-Eng-48.

Energy Efficient Windows, Architectural Aluminum Manufacturers Association (AAMA), 35 East Wacker Drive, Chicago, IL 60601.

Builders and Remodelers Handbook 1980: A Collection of Articles, Facts and Figures on Energy Efficient Building and Rebuilding: The Profit Opportunities. Prepared by the Northeast Solar Energy Center, 470 Atlantic Avenue, Boston, MA 02210.

Builders Reference Manual—Guidelines to Affordable Housing, National Association of Home Builders, Washington, D.C. 2005, 1981.

Building with Passive Solar: An Application Guide for the Southern Builder. Prepared by the Southern Solar Energy Center, 61 Perimeter Park, Atlanta, Georgia 30341, March, 1981.

Crowley, John S.: *The Design and Construction of Three Passive Solar Homes —A Field Test.* Proceedings of the 1981 Annual American Section of the International Solar Energy Society.

Cumali Associates/CCB: *The Determination of the Maximum Beneficial Window Size for Single Family Residences—Final Report.* Available from the National Fenestration Council, National Office, White Lakes Professional Building, 3310 Harrison, Topeka, Kansas 66611.

Colins, Belinda, R. Chapman, Rosalie Ruegg, T. Kusuda: *A New Look at Windows*, Center for Building Technology, National Bureau of Standards, January, 1978.

Hannifan, Mark, C. Christensen, R. Perkins: *Comparison of Residential Window Distributions and Effects of Mass and Insulation.* Proceedings of the International Solar Energy Society, Volume 6, Passive Solar Conference 1981, page 213.

Hastings, Robert and R. Crenshaw: *Window Design Strategies to Conserve Energy*, Center for Building Technology, National Bureau of Standards, June, 1977.

Johnson, Ralph J., and Arthur W. Johnson: *Designing, Building and Selling Energy Conserving Homes*, National Association of Home Builders, Washington, D.C., 1978.

Johnson, Ralph J., and Arthur W. Johnson: *Insulation Manual-Home/Apartments*, NAHB Research Foundation, Inc., Rockville, MD 20850, 1979.

Johnson, Ralph J., Donald F. Luebs, and Ronald K. Yingling: *The Energy Efficient Residence (EER) Research Results.* Prepared by NAHB Research Foundation, Inc., for the U.S. Department of Housing and Urban Development, September, 1980.

Kohler, Joe and Dan Lewis "Passive Principles: Let the Sun Shine In," *Solar Age Magazine*, November, 1981.

Kohler, Joe and Dan Lewis "Passive Principles: Choosing Your System," *Solar Age Magazine*, December, 1981.

Kohler, Joe and Dan Lewis "Passive Principles: Seeing through Window Options," *Solar Age Magazine*, January, 1982.

Kohler, Joe and Dan Lewis: "Passive Principles: Glass and Mass," *Solar Age Magazine*, February, 1982.

Lau, Andrew and T. Hyatt: *Residential Heating and Cooling Loads and Costs for the South.* Proceedings of the American Section of the International Solar Energy Society, vol. 6, Passive Solar Conference 1981, p. 809.

Mazria, Edward: *The Passive Solar Energy Book*, Rodale Press, Emmaus, PA, 1979.

McCulley, Michael T. and M. Siminovitch: *Optimum Window Sizing for Super-insulated Passive in the Midwest Using BLAST, A*

Large Hourly Calculation Computer Program. Proceedings of the International Solar Energy Society, vol. 5.1, Passive Solar Conference 1980, p. 101.

Olgyay, Victor and A. Olgyay: *Solar Control and Shading Devices*, Princeton University Press, Princeton, NJ, paperback printing, 1976.

Olgyay, Victor: *Design with Climate—Bioclimatic Approach to Architectural Regionalism*, Princeton University Press, Princeton, NJ, 1963.

Builders Reference Manual—Guidelines to Affordable Housing, National Association of Home Builders, Washington, D.C. 20005, 1981.

Passive Solar Design Handbook Volume II: Passive Solar Design Analysis. Prepared by the Los Alamos Scientific Laboratory for the U.S. Department of Energy—NTIS #DOE/CS-0127/2, January, 1980.

Professional Builder Magazine, "Consumer Survey: What Home Buyers Will Want in 1982." December, 1981, pp. 64–81.

Regional Guidelines for Building Passive Energy Conserving Homes. Prepared by the AIA Research Foundation for the U.S. Department of Housing and Urban Development, Washington, D.C., July, 1980.

Socolow, Robert H.: *Saving Energy in the Home*, Ballinger Publishing Company, Cambridge, MA. 1978.

Solar Age Magazine "Window Insulation Directory," January, 1982.

Summer Attic and Whole-House Ventilation. Proceedings of a workshop held at the National Bureau of Standards, edited by Mary Reppert. July, 1979. GPO #003-003-02089-3.

Suntempering in the Northeast: A Selection of Builders Designs. Prepared by Steven Winter Associates for the Northeast Solar Energy Center, 470 Atlantic Avenue, Boston, MA 02210.

A Sunbuilders Primer: An Introduction to Passive Solar Design for Professional Homebuilders. JEP Graphics. Available from the Passive Solar Industries Council, 125 South Royal Street, Alexandria, VA 22314.

The Thermal Mass Pattern Book—Guidelines for Sizing Heat Storage in Solar Homes. Total Environmental Action, Inc., Harrisville, NH 03450, 1980.

Utzinger, Michael "A Simple Method for Sizing Overhangs," *Solar Age Magazine, July, 1980, p. 37.*

Wing, Charles: From the Ground Up, Atlantic Monthly Press, Little Brown Publishing Company, Boston, MA, 1976.

Wray, William: *Design and Analysis of Direct-Gain Solar Heated Buildings.* Prepared for the U.S Department of Energy under contract #LA-885-MS. Available from NTIS, 5285 Port Royal Road, Springfield, VA 22161. Issued June, 1981.

Index